Preventive Stress Management in Organizations

Preventive Stress Management in Organizations

James Campbell Quick, PhD

Jonathan D. Quick, MD, MPH

Debra L. Nelson, PhD

Joseph J. Hurrell, Jr., PhD

American Psychological Association

Washington, DC

First edition published 1984 as *Organizational Stress and Preventive Management* by McGraw-Hill. Revised edition published 1997 by the American Psychological Association.

First printing June 1997
Second printing September 1998

Published by
American Psychological Association
750 First Street, NE
Washington, DC 20002

Copies may be ordered from
APA Order Department
P.O. Box 92984
Washington, DC 20090-2984

In the United Kingdom and Europe, copies may be ordered from
American Psychological Association
3 Henrietta Street
Covent Garden, London
WC2E 8LU England

Typeset in Century Schoolbook by EPS Group Inc., Easton, MD

Printer: Data Reproductions Corporation, Auburn Hills, MI
Cover designer: Minker Design, Bethesda, MD
Technical/production editor: Edward B. Meidenbauer

Library of Congress Cataloging-in-Publication Data
Preventive stress management in organizations / edited by James Campbell
   Quick . . . [et al.].
      p.   cm.
   Includes bibliographical references and index.
   ISBN 1-55798-432-8 (acid-free paper)
   1. Stress management.   2. Job stress.   3. Organizational change.   I. Quick,
James C.
HF5548.85.P762   1997
658.3'82—dc21   97-12689
                                                                                  CIP

British Cataloguing-in-Publication Data
A CIP record is available from the British Library.

Printed in the United States of America

We dedicate this book to our father

James Francis Quick, Jr.
20 March 1911–7 November 1996

Harvard College
Class of 1933

He lived with faith, hope, and optimism . . .
He died with grace, dignity and peace!

James Campbell Quick
Jonathan D. Quick

Contents

List of Figures   ix

List of Exhibits and Tables   xi

Foreword   xiii
    Paul J. Rosch

Preface   xvii

1. Stress in Organizations   1

2. Organizational Demands and Stressors   21

3. The Stress Response and Its Modifiers   41

4. Individual Consequences of Stress   65

5. Organizational Consequences of Stress   89

6. Basic Concepts for Stress Diagnosis in Organizations   111

7. Survey of Stress Diagnostic Measures   125

8. Preventive Stress Management: Principles and Methods   149

9. Organizational Prevention: Modifying Work Demands   163

10. Organizational Prevention: Improving Relationships at Work   187

11. Primary Prevention for Individuals: Managing and Coping With Stressors   207

12. Secondary Prevention for Individuals: Modifying Responses to Inevitable Demands   231

13. Tertiary Prevention for Individuals: Healing the Wounds   257

14. Preventive Stress Management for Healthy Organizations   277

15. Preventive Stress Management: From Threat to Opportunity   301

Appendix A: Sources of Diagnostic Instruments   309

Appendix B: Resource Groups   313

References   317

Index   357

About the Authors   367

Figures

1.1. The Yerkes–Dodson Law   5
1.2. A brief history of the stress concept   7
1.3. The general adaptation syndrome   9
1.4. The preventive stress management model   16
2.1. Composition of hypothetical role set   31
3.1. The stress response and its modifiers   42
3.2. Anatomy of the stress response   44
3.3. Organization and action of the sympathetic nervous system   46
4.1. Individual distress: Behavioral, psychological, and medical   66
        consequences
5.1. The direct and indirect costs of cardiovascular disease   90
5.2. The basis for individual–organizational exchange   91
5.3. A framework for viewing organizational health   95
5.4. The economics of turnover management   99
5.5. Direct costs of distress: Accidents and grievances   102
6.1. The process of organizational stress diagnosis   114
8.1. The stages of preventive stress management   155
8.2. An expanded Yerkes–Dodson curve   156
8.3. Organizational and individual preventive stress management   157
9.1. The job characteristics model   165
9.2. The psychological demand–decision latitude model   168
9.3. The effort–reward model   170
9.4. Redesigning a physical setting   184
10.1. Formal and informal elements of organizations   189
10.2. An organization member's role set   190
10.3. A model for goal setting   194
10.4. Potential effects of social support on work stress and health   196
10.5. Social support network   198
12.1. Example of the feedback loop in biofeedback   240
13.1. Personal preventive stress management plan   273
14.1. Occupational stress in five U.S. Air Force organizations   281
14.2. The stress and performance relationship   287
14.3. Ten years of referrals within ICI-Zeneca   289
14.4. Implementation cycle for preventive stress management   294

Exhibits and Tables

Exhibit 2.1.	Organizational Demands and Stressors	22
Table 4.1.	Leading Causes of Death: United States and All Developed Countries, 1990	77
Table 4.2.	Disability-Adjusted Life Years (DALYs) Lost, by Major Illness Category, All Developed Countries, 1990	78
Table 4.3.	Relative Risk of First Myocardial Infarction, High Strain Compared with Low Strain Occupations	80
Exhibit 5.1.	Costs of Organizational Distress	96
Exhibit 7.1.	Selected Stress-Related Diagnostic Instruments	126
Exhibit 7.2.	Life Events Scale	134
Exhibit 7.3.	Physiological Parameters Use in Management	137
Table 7.1.	Selections of the Cornell Medical Index	140
Exhibit 9.1.	Organizational Prevention: Job and Physical Demands	164
Exhibit 9.2.	Possible Alterations in the Physical Setting	183
Exhibit 10.1.	Organizational Prevention: Role and Interpersonal Demands	188
Table 10.1.	Five Functions of Social Support for Executives	199
Exhibit 11.1.	Preventive Stress Management for Individuals	208
Table 11.1.	Cognitive Restructuring: Ten Styles of Distorted Thinking	211
Table 11.2.	Constructive Self-Talk Alternative to Typical Mental Monologues	213
Exhibit 11.2.	Philosophical Guidelines for Changing Type A Behavior Patterns	216
Table 11.3.	Roskies' Program Structure	217
Table 12.1.	Comparison of the Physiological Changes of the Fight-or-Flight Response and the Relaxation Response	232
Exhibit 12.1.	Sample Formula for Autogenic Training	238
Table 13.1.	Sample Hierarchy for Systematic Desensitization for Public Speaking	263
Table 14.1.	ICI-Zeneca Stress Management Strategy	288

Foreword

Time magazine's June 6, 1983, cover story suggested that stress had now reached epidemic proportions, almost as if it were some sort of new plague. The situation has progressively worsened since then. The vast majority of Americans perceive that they are under much more stress now than 5 or 10 years ago (The Dream, 1994; *The Mitchum Report*, 1990). One in three reported feeling under great stress daily or several days a week, according to a 1992 survey, up 20% from one conducted less than 10 years previously (Kerber, 1994). In a September 1996 Marketdata Enterprises Survey, almost 75% said they experienced "great stress" at least one day a week, with one third indicating this occurred more than twice a week. This was in sharp contrast to the results of a similar 1983 survey, in which only 55% reported stress on a weekly basis (Greenberg & Canzoneri, 1996). Mental stress is increasingly a reason for calling in sick, and in 1996, it accounted for 11% of workers' absences, representing a 100% increase over the previous year.

It is equally clear that the leading cause of stress for adults is occupational pressures, and a September 1983 *Nation's Business* article referred to job stress as "the Number 1 health problem in the United States today." The proportion of workers who reported "feeling highly stressed" more than doubled from 1985 to 1990, and the ratio of those complaining of "multiple stress related illnesses" similarly escalated from 13 to 25% (Northwest National Life Insurance Company, 1992). In other surveys, 78% complained that work was their biggest source of stress, only 35% felt their jobs gave them pleasure or satisfaction (D'Arcy, Masius, & Bowles, 1996), and more than half reported that their lives had become more stressful over the past 10 years (Clark, 1995). The problem is not limited to the United States. The United Nations recently referred to job stress as "The 20th Century Disease," indicating that it had permeated almost every occupation around the world, and was so severe and pervasive that it had now reached the proportions of a "global epidemic" (Jones & Bartlett, 1995).

Some inkling of the growing magnitude of the problem is afforded by the escalation of workers' compensation awards for job stress. Although they were rarely encountered two decades ago, such awards now threaten to bankrupt the system in some states. In one 6-year period, claims concerning stress jumped 531% in California, in contrast to a less than 10% overall rise in workers' compensation claims. In Los Angeles, there are lawyers who regularly solicit clients through newspaper advertisements asking "Does your job make you sick?" Job stress awards are 3 to 4 times greater than the national average for other claims, and 90% of suits are successful. In at least 1 year, California companies shelled out more in medical and legal fees alone than most states spend on total awards. Many other states also are feeling the pinch. In 1990 Connecticut premiums jumped 22%, and there was a 15% rise in Maine on top of a 54% increase in 1989. The Texas hike was 22%, representing the fifth double-digit increment in 4 years.

Repetitive stress injury (RSI) has become the malady that incurs the highest workplace health cost; it currently accounts for one third of the $60 billion in workers' compensation payments paid annually. In 1994, the National Council on Compensation Insurance reported that RSI workers' compensation claims had increased 770% since 1984, with each claim costing an average of $43,000. In December 1996, a New York jury awarded $6 million to three claimants suffering from "repetitive stess injury" as a result of their computer related duties. For the first time in any court, it also held the computer company liable, because of its faulty keyboard design. Similar suits in Minnesota and Missouri in 1995, and others in previous years, had always found for the defense. With 40 million people working at computers and legal precedents and awards rising rapidly, the financial implications are staggering. RSI, which refers to various degrees of carpal tunnel syndrome, was originally called *cumulative trauma injury*, and subsequently became known as *repetitive motion injury*. The cachet of stress may have contributed to its present designation, but this designation may be more serendipitous and accurate than is appreciated. One 3 year study of 500 computer workers in a telephone company revealed that almost 25% of workers had complaints consistent with RSI. However, the study also found that psychological factors such as job insecurity and increased job stress were significantly higher in the affected workers, which may have important implications. Although RSI is a physical injury whose incidence may be reduced by ergonomic interventions, organizations could be at increased risk if it can be shown that an affected worker was subjected to excessive job pressures that management should have corrected.

How can one determine the degree of job stress and the ratio of its relevance to emotional and physical complaints compared with other sources? The relationship between job stress and coronary heart disease is apparently so well acknowledged that in New York, Los Angeles, and many other municipalities, any police officer who suffers a heart attack on or off the job is assumed to have a work-related injury and is compensated accordingly—even if the attack occurs while the person is fishing on vacation or gambling in Las Vegas! The leading cause of mortality in the world is sudden death; stress is clearly a major contributor to this, and there have been a number of suits in which work pressures in law enforcement and other occupations have been cited. But stress has also been increasingly implicated in a host of other disorders, ranging from the common cold and herpes to cancer and AIDS, and litigation incriminating job stress is starting to surface for many of these. How can one separate the impact of job stress from that of stresses encountered outside of the workplace? More important, what can organizations do to prevent or mitigate job stress? Studies show clearly that properly designed and implemented programs can provide physical and mental health rewards for workers. In addition, such programs improve the fiscal health of organizations by reducing absenteeism, turnover, and medical and legal expenses, as well as by increasing productivity and the all-important "bottom line."

This book thoroughly addresses these and every other conceivable component of organizational stress in an unusually comprehensive and authoritative fashion. I have known the senior authors since the publication of the first edition of this work in 1984, which along with *Work Stress* in 1987, was widely acclaimed and the recipient of several awards. However, this book far surpasses its predecessors and everything else that has been written on this subject. Because I have been involved in stress research for over 45 years, I can state with some confidence that this book will quickly become the gold standard in the field. I know of few individuals who could complete the Herculean task of writing this book in such a scholarly but lucid fashion. Their labors could not have borne fruit at a more propitious time.

Paul J. Rosch, MD, FACP
President, The American Institute of Stress
Clinical Professor of Medicine and Psychiatry
New York Medical College

References

Clark, C. S. (1995, August 4). Job stress. *CQ Researcher, 5*, 681–704.

D'Arcy, Masius, & Bowles. (1996, May). *Fears and fantasies of the American consumer* [D'Arcy, Masius, & Bowles report]. New York: Authors.

The Dream in Danger. (1994, November 29). *The Wall Street Journal*, p. B1.

Greenberg, E. R., & Canzoneri, C. (1996). *Organizational staffing and disability claims* (American Management Association Research Report). New York: American Management Association.

Jones and Bartlett. (1995). *Stress management* (National Safety Council Report). Boston: Authors.

Kerber, B. (Ed.). (1994). *How employers are saving through wellness and fitness programs*. Wall Township: American Business Publishing.

The Mitchum Report on STRESS in the 90's. (1990). New York: Research & Forecasts, Inc.

Northwestern National Life Insurance Company. (1992). *Employee burnout: Causes and cures*. Milwaukee, WI: Author.

Preface

Stress and strain continue to be universal experiences in organizational life, and the word *stress* continues to be a creatively ambiguous term in scientific and secular dialogues. Even with this ambiguity, stress and strain are matters of serious concern to executives, managers, employees, psychologists, physicians, social workers, human resource personnel, and occupational health specialists. This concern is based on two considerations. The first is economic in nature; mismanaged stress and strain can cost organizations billions of dollars annually in lost productivity, health care costs, and workers' compensation payments. Stress-related disorders can be expensive. Another consideration is humanitarian in nature; it is not nice to overstress individuals in the course of their work lives. In addition, when individuals are overstressed, they become dysfunctional in any number of ways. Hence, for both economic and humanitarian reasons, stress is an important occupational health issue in organizations.

Stress is inevitable; distress is not. We contend, as we have over the last 20 years, that stress is an essential agent in an individual's and an organization's growth, development, performance, and success. The response to stress is one of humans' best God-given assets for managing legitimate emergencies (which may be why Walter B. Cannon first called it the "emergency response") and achieving peak performance in vital tasks and activities. Stress is a naturally occurring, instinctual response that contributes to health and well-being. The central principle in the philosophy of preventive stress management is: Stress is inevitable, distress is not.

Although some think that stress is a somewhat popularized topic without a strong scientific base, the field has a distinguished 80-year history of medical, physiological, psychological, managerial, and organizational research. Walter B. Cannon's physiological stress response research at the Harvard Medical School just prior to World War I led him to formulate the stress concept, which he first called the "emergency response." (We are most grateful to Bradford Cannon, MD, professor emeritus of Harvard Medical School, for improving our understanding and appreciation of his father's work.) The stress concept became popularized as the *fight-or-flight response* and is widely known because of Hans Selye's extensive medical (largely hormonal) research during the middle decades of the 20th century. In the second half of the century, a number of prominent psychologists made significant contributions that extended the understanding of the stress concept. American Psychological Association (APA) past-resident Charles D. Spielberger, a pioneer who followed in the footsteps of Cannon, tracked an exponential increase in the number of journal articles addressing work stress, job stress, and family stress over the past decade.

We began our dialogue about stress while in graduate school over 20 years ago, Jim at the College of Business Administration at the University of Houston and Jonathan at the College of Medicine and Dentistry at the University of Rochester. The idea of translating the public health notions of prevention into a stress process framework seemed powerful and led us to write *Organizational Stress and Preventive Management* in the early 1980s. That book, translated into German as *Unternehmen ohne Streß*, set forth a basic philosophy and framework of preventive stress management. The prevention framework was the basis of an international stress conference and accompanying collected volume, recognized with the 1987 Distinguished Service Award by the UTA College of Business Administration, shortly after the first book's publication; the platform for graduate courses in preventive stress management, which hundreds of graduate students at The University of Texas at Arlington and Oklahoma State University have taken; numerous invited scholarly contributions, lectures, workshops, and seminars; and textbook chapters on work stress. The preventive stress management framework was the basis for APA testimony to the National Academy of Sciences on national health objectives for the year 2000 in the area of stress and for *Stress & Well-Being at Work*, published by the APA. The most unique and useful element of this prevention framework may be the conception of primary, secondary, and tertiary levels as a basis for preventive action and treatment intervention.

Although we were flattered that our hometown newspaper, the *Brighton-Pittsford Post*, ran a story entitled "Quick Stress Solutions" shortly after the publication of *Organizational Stress and Preventive Management*, the double entendre actually miscommunicates the core of the philosophy of preventive stress management. Prevention emphasizes long-term, disciplined efforts in self-reliant and responsible behavior as opposed to the faddish quick fixes that some people appear to seek. We have found no magic for the distress of work life, although we do not rule out seemingly miraculous cures that may be difficult to explain on the basis of accepted medical and psychological evidence.

This book extends, elaborates, and refines *Organizational Stress and Preventive Management* by exploring the vast research that has been conducted since that book came out. Specifically, we have separated out new chapters to bring greater attention to the stress response and its modifiers (chapter 3) and to tertiary prevention, or therapeutic treatment (chapter 13). In addition, we have updated all sources and added substantially new discussion in chapter 1 (a panoramic view of the field since its inception), chapter 3 (on self-reliance), chapter 10 (on diversity programs), chapter 11 (on learned optimism and hardiness), chapter 12 (on confession and expressive writing), chapter 13 (on posttraumatic stress disorder and traumatic stress debriefings), and chapter 14 (on creating healthy organizations).

The core framework of prevention has been retained and embellished. We still have a stress process framework, set forth in chapter 1, which examines the sources of stress (chapter 2), the stress response and its modifiers (chapter 3), and the individual and organizational consequences of stress (chapters 4 and 5). The book then sets forth a basis for organizational stress diagnosis (chapters 6 and 7). Chapter 8, the heart of the book, elaborates on the principles and framework of preventive stress management. The methods of preventive stress management have organizational (chapters 9 and 10) and individual (chapters 11, 12, and 13) emphases. These chapters on the methods of preventive stress management are followed by one on healthy organizations (chapter 14). The conclusion (chapter 15) has a future orientation.

We have reviewed hundreds of books, journal articles, and dissertations published after 1984 to update the literature in all aspects of the framework. We have had lots of support. We first thank our new coauthors, Debra L. Nelson and Joseph J. Hurrell, Jr., who have made their own intellectual contributions to the field of stress and contributed their expertise in socialization, sex and gender issues, diversity, epidemiology, and measurement to the revision. David Mack has done most of the extensive literature reviews and has done so superbly. He also prepared Appendix B for the book and worked with Nancy Foster in managing the extensive references. Dave has come to make his own intellectual contributions to the domain of stress with crosscutting thoughts and some innovative ideas, and Nancy did an extraordinary job on a variety of aspects of the manuscript. Tom Wright was most helpful as we conceptualized the revision, providing detailed chapter comments and suggestions. Susan Fisher made important contributions to several chapters. J. Lee Whittington provided valuable feedback on the manuscript and did a meticulous review of the references throughout. Joel Quintans, Hannah Frieser, and Jack Ogle prepared the figures artistically. Most of all, we appreciate the efforts of Judy Nemes, Ed Meidenbauer, Julia Frank-McNeil, Gary VandenBos, and the members of the APA book staff who supported us throughout the developmental process.

We deeply appreciate the professional support of many colleagues who have encouraged us in our work through the years and decades, notably, Joyce Adkins, Dennis Beach, Kathy Benson, Robert L. Berg, Rabi Bhagat, Wayne D. Bodensteiner, John Howard Burris, Bradford Cannon, Benito Cardenas, Winford N. (Chuck) Carroll, E. C. Cooley, Catherine Crier, Keith Davis, Jeff Edwards, Gordon Forward, Frank Gault, Edwin A. Gerloff, Jerry Greenberg, Ricky Griffin, David Gray, Hunter P. Harris, Jr., Michael A. Hitt, John C. Holland, Jim House, John M. Ivancevich, Todd Jick, Jeffrey V. Johnson, Janice R. Joplin, Tommy B. Jordan, Robert Kahn, Bob Karasek, Joseph W. Kertesz, John Kimmel, Lennart Levi, Fred Luthans, A. David Mangelsdorff, Robert Martin, Karl O. (Skip) Moe, Walter Mullendore, Lawrence R. Murphy, Wendell Nedderman, Roy Payne, Ken Pelletier, Bob Perkins, Russell Petersen, Chaya Piotkowski, Richard Rahe, Kari Rollins, Ray Rosenman, Steven L. Sauter, L. L. Schkade, Johannes Segrist, Coleen Shannon, Arie Shirom, Charles D. Spielberger, Jim Walther, Leonard D. (Danny) Williams, Robert Witt, Jerry C. Wofford, Stewart Wolf, Dan Worrell and Sheila Zummo. A special note of thanks goes to Paul Rosch for his gracious contribution of the foreword to the book and to Cary L. Cooper, who has been an especially supportive, encouraging, and positive colleague through the years in so many thoughtful and helpful ways.

We two brothers were most fortunate in our family of origin, which provided us with the support, resources, encouragement, and high expectations to go forth into a challenging and stressful world. We are equally blessed by and deeply indebted to our families of choice, who are great sources of support, comfort, and strength for both of us as we continue our journey together. Our wives, Sheri Schember Quick and Tina Lee Quick, have eased our burdens, being good friends and sisters to each other as well as to each of us. Our daughters give us faith and hope for future generations on this earth. Jim and Sheri's daughter, Kari E. Schember, has shown a mature blend of gentleness, assertiveness, and self-reliance as she has become a fine young woman. Jono and Tina's daughters, Janneke Campbell Quick, Katrina Fuller Quick, and Kimberly Cole Quick, have lived an international lifestyle on four continents, their experiences foreshadowing developments in the changing world.

This book is designed for two audiences. One audience includes professionals in the fields of psychology, medicine, and theology who are interested in organizational stress. Their interests may be either in the design and execution of research investigations to extend the current state of knowledge about stress in organizations or in the design and implementation of prevention programs aimed at successful stress management. Another audience includes organizational leaders, managers, and employees who are interested in where stress wheels meet the organizational road. Their interests are primarily in creating healthy work environments in which people may work, produce, serve, and be valued.

James Campbell Quick
Arlington, Texas

Jonathan D. Quick
Ornex, France
Geneva, Switzerland
Boston, Massachusetts

1

Stress in Organizations

There is an emerging organizational reality, not yet fully defined, that is fundamentally changing, even transforming, how people organize to get work done (Gowing, Kraft, & Quick, in press; Lawler, 1994). This new organizational reality is characterized by competitive change; a deemphasis on jobs as a way of organizing; an emphasis on an individual's portfolio of knowledge, skills, and abilities; and an effort to leverage technology to the maximum. The underlying processes driving this new organizational reality account for the mergers and acquisitions, downsizings, restructuring, reengineering, and privatization initiatives of the past decade. These systemic processes have dramatic effects on individual lives and are among the contemporary forces causing stress for people in organizations. An example of the consequences of these changes is AT&T's January 1996 announcement that the company planned to eliminate 40,000 jobs, 60 percent of them managerial and 85 percent of them domestic, over a 3-year period.

Change and stress are not new issues, especially when seen through the lens of historical context. When we place these changes and stresses against the enormous dislocations of the American Civil War era, World War I, or the Great Depression, we might ask what is new on the face of the earth. What is new and what has exploded in the past quarter of a century is the understanding of the stress response and its role in health and disease processes.

Work-related psychological disorders and distress constitute one category of the top 10 occupational health risks in the United States (Sauter, Murphy, & Hurrell, 1990). Why is this? There is no single cause for either stress or distress; the occupational health problems related to stress at work have multiple causes. An important contributing factor to contemporary distress in the workplace is the international economic competition, which has led to corporate warfare (Nelson, Quick, & Quick, 1989). International economic competition has focused on core industries in the United States, Europe, and Japan (Thurow, 1992). Corporate warfare leads to mergers, acquisitions, downsizing, downscoping, and bankruptcies (Hoskisson & Hitt, 1994). According to Cascio (in press), downsizing in the United States has led to 10 million workers being displaced or losing their jobs between 1989 and 1992, 615,000 announced layoffs in 1993, and 565,000 announced layoffs in 1994. These figures sound daunting, and some professionals believe that this is an age of anxiety or extraordinarily stressful times. We offer a different and more optimistic view—that performance achievement and health are mutually supportive in the context

1

of work organizations. To sacrifice one for the other may lead to short-term gains at the expense of long-term outcomes.

The stress response was first described in the second decade of the 20th century by medical physiologist Walter B. Cannon and initially labeled the "emergency response" (Cannon, 1915/1929a); however, it was not until the 1960s, when several psychological theories about stress were developed, that the role of stress in health and work behavior became more fully understood. This work was followed during the 1970s, 1980s, and 1990s by a dramatic increase in research articles about occupational stress, job stress, work stress, and family stress (Spielberger & Reheiser, 1994). It was during these decades that the professional and public awareness of the role of stress in health and disease processes became more fully understood. As the war against the acute disease processes succeeded during the middle decades of the 20th century, the relative importance of the chronic diseases, and the role of stress in their causation or cure, began to rise (W. S. Cohen, 1985; Foss & Rothenberg, 1987). The past decade has offered a number of highly stressful events that have challenged, and at times killed, people at work. These events include the following:

- Citibank's 1991 financial crisis, probably its worst challenge in 200 years (Kepos, 1994)
- Frank Deus's federal lawsuit against Allstate Insurance (Frank S. Deus v. Allstate, 1990–1992)
- The Great Texas Banking Crash of the mid-1980s (Grant, 1996)
- The Oklahoma City bombing of a federal office building in 1995

Work life is stressful and, at times, risky. This book is about addressing the challenge this reality offers to enable individuals and organizations to be stronger, healthier, and more productive. This book is about achievement *and* health, not achievement *or* health.

This chapter presents an overview of stress as an important issue in organizations of the 1990s and the 21st century. The first section presents important definitions under the rubric "what is stress?" These definitions are important because there is no universal scientific definition of the word *stress* (Kahn, 1987). The second section presents a historical overview of the stress concept from its identification in 1915 through the present. The third section places stress in the context of work and organizational life. The final section presents the preventive stress management model, which has its foundation in the public health notions of prevention and epidemiology.

What Is Stress?

Stress is a creatively ambiguous word with little agreed-on scientific definition (Kahn, 1987). The concept of "stress" is a wonderful overarching rubric for the domain concerned with how individuals and organizations adjust to their environments; achieve high levels of performance and health; and become distressed in various physiological, medical, behavioral, or psychological ways. Because people use the term *stress* as a rubric, we are comfortable allowing it to maintain its creative ambiguity at that level. However, at the operational level it is important to define the scientific terms within the domain of stress to give it more precise and clearer meanings, phenomenologically and scientifically. The specific terms to be defined are *stressor*, or *demand*; *the stress response*; *eustress*; and *distress*, or *strain*.

Stressors, Demands, and the Stress Response

The stress response begins with a stressor, or demand, which serves as the trigger for a series of mind–body activities.

> The *stressor* is the physical or psychological stimulus to which an individual responds.

Demand is another term for stressor. There are differences of opinion with regard to whether stressors and demands may be universally defined or whether they must be specifically defined in the context of a particular individual's experience. We think that it is best to define stressors and demands in the context of the experience of the individual owing to the roles of appraisal, coping, and individual responsiveness in the stress process, as discussed in more detail in chapter 3. However, we understand the validity of identifying stressors or demands for specific populations; that idea is discussed further as we introduce the role of public health in preventive stress management. The second term that is important to define in the domain of stress is the stress response.

> *The stress response* is the generalized, patterned, unconscious mobilization of the body's natural energy resources when confronted with a demand, or stressor.

The mobilization occurs through the combined action of the sympathetic nervous system and the endocrine (hormonal) system. These systems are activated by the release of catecholamines, primarily adrenaline and noradrenaline, into the bloodstream. The stress response is most often manifested in an elevated heart rate (even tachycardia), increased respiration and perspiration, and a bracing response characterized by the tightening of the large muscle groups throughout the body. Although these manifest signs of the stress response are the most visible, it is the four less visible psychophysiological changes that may be more important to understand. All of these actions are designed to prepare a person to fight or to flee, hence the description of the stress response as the fight-or-flight response. In addition, there are some individuals who appear to freeze rather than engage in a fight or a flight posture in response to a stressor.

The four mind–body changes that constitute the stress response are as follows. First, there is a redirection, or shunting, of the blood to the brain and large muscle groups and away from the extremities, skin, and vegetative organs. This aspect of the stress response repositions the body's resources where they are needed for a legitimate emergency. Second, there is an enabling of the reticular activating system in the ancient brain stem, which leads to a heightened sense of alertness. This activation sharpens vision, hearing, and the other sensory processes and attunes an individual to the environment more fully. Third, there is a release of glucose and fatty acids, which are the fuels that sustain an individual during this period of emergency. Fourth, there is a shutting down of the immune system and the body's emergent and restorative processes, such as digestion. Although they are important to long-term health and well-being, the immune system functions and the emergent and restorative processes are not essential during periods of emergency. This complex of four basic mind–body changes prepares a person to do what is essential during a stressful situation. The stress response is highly functional when properly managed, leading to eustress and elevated performance. However, there is also a downside to the stress response, for individuals and for organizations, which is called *distress*. Distress occurs when the stress response is not well managed or when it goes awry. Following are the discussions of eustress and distress.

Eustress and the Yerkes–Dodson Law

Eustress is "good stress," from the Greek root *eu* for "good" (Selye, 1976b, p. 15). Hans Selye suggested thinking of eustress as *euphoria + stress*, hence *eu*-stress. Eustress refers to the medical way of identifying healthy stress, with *eu* being a prefix meaning normal or healthy. Some executives prefer a different word or term to refer to healthy stress in place of eustress. For example, *challenge* is the word preferred by Gordon Forward, President and CEO of Chaparral Steel Company (Quick, Nelson, & Quick, 1990). Regardless of the particular language or term,

> *eustress* may be defined as the healthy, positive, constructive outcome of stressful events and the stress response.

Some of the positive, healthy effects of an optimum stress load on performance have been known since 1908 and are expressed in the Yerkes–Dodson Law, shown in the graphic in Figure 1.1 (Yerkes & Dodson, 1908).

As the figure shows, performance increases with increasing stress loads up to an optimum point, and then the stress load becomes too great, resulting in depressed performance. The optimum stress load that maximizes performance varies by individual and by task, on the basis of several considerations. Individual considerations include susceptibility to stress, fatigue, psychological and cognitive skills, and physical capacity. Task considerations include complexity, difficulty, duration, and intensity. The interaction, as reflected in the person's familiarity with the task, also affects the shape and size of the particular Yerkes–Dodson curve. A situation

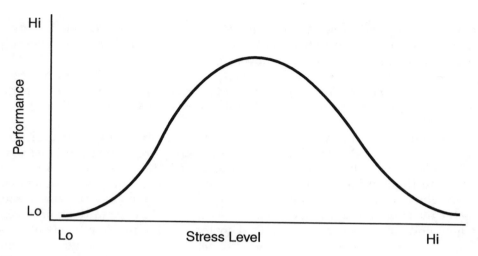

Figure 1.1. The Yerkes–Dodson Law.

with too little stress and arousal often fails to stimulate performance, just as too much stress and arousal can interfere with performance, especially on complex tasks. A key focus of this book is on strategies for enhancing eustress to create high levels of health, well-being, and performance.

Distress and Strain

The word *distress* contains the Latin prefix *dis*, meaning "bad" (Selye, 1976b, p. 15) and refers to the unhealthy, negative, destructive outcomes of stressful events or the stress response. *Strain* is another word for distress, and the two terms are used here interchangeably. Our definition of these terms at the individual level is as follows:

> *Individual distress* (*strain*) is the degree of physiological, psychological, and behavioral deviation from an individual's healthy functioning.

Individual distress and strain are expressed in commonly seen disorders such as cardiovascular disease (physiological), depression (psychological), and violence (behavioral). Stressful events and the stress response are not the sole cause of these forms of individual distress and strain, yet they are important contributing factors to the onset of the distress or the acceleration of the strain process.

Individual distress and strain have important implications for organizations because they can manifest themselves in various forms of organizational distress and strain. For example, although an accident on the job is a form of individual distress for the employee, it is also a form of organizational distress for the company in the form of medical costs, lost work time, and replacement work costs. Organizational distress or strain may be expressed in terms of direct costs, such as absenteeism and dysfunctional turnover, or indirect costs, such as low morale and poor working relationships. It is defined as follows:

> *Organizational distress (strain)* is the degree of deviation an organization experiences from a healthy, productive level of functioning.

As we discuss later, individual and organizational predispositions are important in understanding individual and organizational distress. Whereas some individuals may be predisposed to physiological distress owing to their unique vulnerability, other individuals may be predisposed to psychological distress. Likewise, some organizations have cultures that foster absenteeism in response to distressing working conditions or workloads, and others have cultures that foster apathy and low levels of productivity while individuals are on the job. Hence, the individual's and organization's unique vulnerability become important ingredients in understanding the experience of stress and expression of distress and strain. Not all stressful events turn out badly, as distress.

The Stress Concept: A Historical View

The stress concept has its foundations in medicine and physiology in the early and middle part of the 20th century. The elaboration of the stress concept was undertaken by several prominent psychologists during the middle and latter part of the 20th century. In the last few decades of the 20th century, a public health dimension has been added to the stress domain, reshaping how the stress concept is viewed and understood. This section of the chapter traces the history of the stress concept over the past 90 years, as depicted in the timeline in Figure 1.2. The figure identifies the major events and persons that have shaped the stress concept over this century.

The Medical Foundations

The conceptualization of the Yerkes–Dodson Law by psychologist Robert Yerkes and his collaborator John Dodson preceded the identification of the stress response. In about 1915, following a line of medical investigation in laboratory animals, Walter B. Cannon extrapolated from his basic findings and hypothesized that there was a complex of psychophysiological activities occurring within the body under stressful conditions, which he labeled the "emergency reaction." His later discussions of the stress response viewed it as rooted in the "fighting emotions," thus setting the stage for its identification as the fight-or-flight response. An active member of the American Psychological Association in its early decades, Cannon had a lifelong interest in the relationship between emotional or psychological states and physiological responses. This interest began during his under-

1900   1910   1920   1930   1940   1950   1960   1970   1980   1990   2000

The Public Health Dimension
Work-related psychological disorders and stress: top 10 occupational health risks
Staw—threat-rigidity thesis
Quick & Quick—prevention

Legislation to establish National Institute for Occupational Safety and Health

The Psychological Elaborations
Kahn—role stress and person-environment fit model
Lazarus—cognitive appraisal and coping model
Levinson—ego-ideal/self-image discrepancy model

1941–1945 World War II, combat stress, and battle fatigue; war traumas

The Medical Foundations
1932 Cannon—the homeostatic model and the wisdom of the body
1935 Selye—the general adaptation syndrome and the diseases of maladaptation

1920s An era of labor–management conflict and violence in the U.S. steel industry

1915–1916 Cannon—the discovery of the emergency response, rooted in the fighting emotions; the study of traumatic shock with the Harvard medical group in Europe, World War I

1908 The Yerkes–Dodson Law: stress–performance curvilinear relationship (the inverted U)

Figure 1.2 A brief history of the stress concept.

graduate years at Harvard when he took a course with William James, developing an admiration for James that endured despite his later professional difference of opinion over the James–Lange theory of emotions (Cannon, 1929).

Following these basic discoveries and working largely independently, Hans Selye became curious about the general syndrome of "being sick." Selye's systematic investigations into the effects of environmental stress on humans and other animals began in 1932; he showed that a chief effect was the release of adrenal gland hormones, normally leading to an appropriate adaptation to the stress-causing situation (Selye, 1976b). The adaptation mechanism may malfunction, leading to one or more diseases of maladaptation. Selye's (1973, 1976c) framework is summarized in the general adaptation syndrome (GAS). The GAS, depicted in Figure 1.3, has three primary stages: alarm, resistance, and exhaustion. The alarm reaction can be associated with what we have defined as the *stress response* and Cannon labeled the *emergency reaction*. The great power of Selye's contribution centers in the resistance stage of the GAS, for it is from this stage that so much distress proceeds; Selye termed the result the *diseases of adaptation*. At the resistance stage, the individual struggles with the demand, or stressor, and in many cases struggles with him- or herself. As the president of the International Institute of Stress from 1976 until his death in 1982, Selye did more than anyone in this century to raise awareness of the role of stress in health and disease processes.

Although Cannon and then Selye primarily focused on the medical and physiological dimensions of stress and the stress response, with particular attention to the sympathetic nervous system and endocrine system activities, they were mindful of the role that fear, anger, rage, and other emotions might play in the process. However, it was for the later psychologists to elaborate on the psychological dimensions of the stress concept.

The Psychological Elaborations

There have been three psychological elaborations of the stress concept during the middle and latter part of this century. First, Robert Kahn and his colleagues examined the social psychological processes of role conflict and ambiguity (i.e., role stress) in organizations (Kahn, 1964). Second, Richard Lazarus and his colleagues focused on the processes of cognitive appraisal and coping (Lazarus, 1967). Third, Harry Levinson framed a psychoanalytic view of occupational and executive stress (H. Levinson, 1975, 1978).

Role stress in organizations. Kahn, Wolfe, Quinn, Snoek, and Rosenthal (1964) extended the stress concept by incorporating a social psychological theory into the stress domain. Their focus in studying organizational stress was on the role-taking process in organizations and on the constructs of role conflict and role ambiguity, with later attention to the notion of person–environment fit within the realm of one's social role. The

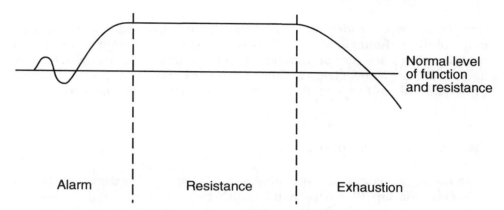

Alarm | Resistance | Exhaustion

Figure 1.3. The general adaptation syndrome.

core contribution of their research was to show how the conflict and confusion that occur in the social process of an organization can lead to individual distress and strain, with its associated organizational costs. Hence, rather than focusing on the individual, this line of elaboration focuses on the network of social relationships that compose any form of organization, from a small business to a family, a military unit, or a religious order.

Cognitive appraisal and coping. Lazarus and his associates extended the stress concept and introduced the notions of cognitive appraisal and coping (Lazarus, DeLongis, Folkman, & Gruen, 1985). Their basic line of argument was that individuals see the same demands and stressors differently on the basis of their cognitive appraisal of them; some individuals see a specific demand or stressor as a threat, whereas other individuals see the same demand or stressor as a challenge or opportunity. From this perspective, the focus shifts away from the actual demand or stressor to the individual's perception of that demand or stressor. Lazarus argued that it is not possible to separate fully the individual's perception of and response to a demand or stressor from the demand or stressor itself. This psychological elaboration of the stress concept led to an interactionist framework for understanding eustress, distress, and strain (Lazarus et al., 1985). The implications of this conceptual model are that individuals may engage in either problem-focused or emotion-focused coping strategies to manage their experience of stress (Bodensteiner, Gerloff, & Quick, 1989).

The psychoanalytic perspective. H. Levinson (1975, 1978) took still another approach to elaborating the stress concept, with particular attention to an executive's psychodynamics. He defined stress through the use of two basic concepts: the ego-ideal and the self-image. The ego-ideal is the personality element that embodies an individual's idealized self. This unconscious or semiconscious element of the personality arises out of parental models, a person's hopes and fantasies about self-perfection, and the desirable characteristics an individual sees in heroes, heroines, and mentors. This perfect or idealized self stands in contrast and tension with an individual's self-image. The self-image is composed of both positive and negative attributes that an individual understands to characterize him- or herself. For Levinson, stress is the tension or discrepancy between the ego-ideal and the self-image; the greater the discrepancy, the greater the stress.

The Public Health Dimension

With the identification of work-related psychological disorders and distress as among the top 10 occupational health risks in the United States, the stress concept moved into the public health domain (Quick, Murphy, & Hurrell, 1992; Sauter et al., 1990). Starting in the mid-1970s, Quick and Quick (1984a) translated the public health notions of prevention into a stress framework, leading to the development of the preventive stress management model. A detailed presentation of this model is found in the last section of this chapter. Although he is not explicitly oriented toward organizations, Winett (1995) proposed a framework for health promotion and disease prevention programs that is grounded in the epidemiological notions of the public health model for disease identification and management.

Stress in an Organizational Context

Stress in organizations is of concern to both managers and professionals because of the costs associated with job strain and job distress, which are the adverse consequences of job stress. Organizations pay a price for dysfunctional work behaviors, either violent or nonviolent (Griffin, O'Leary-Kelly, & Collins, in press). The price takes the form of direct and indirect costs, which are detailed in chapter 5. The direct costs include dysfunctional turnover and absenteeism, health care, and compensation awards of various categories. The indirect costs include poor morale and job dissatisfaction. However, it bears repeating that not all stress at work is bad and not all job stress is destructive. We suggest that job stress does not necessarily lead to distress or strain.

Job Stress

In addition to the terms within the domain of stress defined earlier in the chapter, there are two additional terms that should be defined. One of them is *job stress*, which is neither denotatively nor connotatively pejorative within our lexicon.

> *Job stress* is the mind–body arousal resulting from physical and/or psychological demands associated with a job (J. C. Quick & Nelson, 1997).

Job stress may lead to enhanced job performance up to an optimum level of stress (eustress); conversely, job stress may place an employee at risk of distress if it is too intense, frequent, or chronic (Selye, 1976a, 1976b). Understanding job stress is important in order to reduce the job strain (job distress) all too often associated with stress in organizations. This is often achieved through stress management programs.

> *Stress management programs* are strategies for preventing job strain and channeling *job stress* into healthy and productive outcomes (J. C. Quick & Quick, 1997).

Job stress is triggered by a wide variety of job demands, including task-specific demands, role demands, interpersonal demands, and physical demands (Quick & Quick, 1984a). These demands may or may not be inherently or necessarily harmful. In line with Lazarus's perspective, the degree of stress they elicit in a person depends in part on the individual's cognitive appraisal of that demand.

Lack of control over and uncertainty about aspects of the psychosocial and physical work environments in industrialized nations are major sources of job stress (Sutton & Kahn, 1987). Extreme working environments such as those of military fighter pilots or oil field service personnel in Arctic climates create unique physical and extreme demands (Gillingham, 1988). Whether the job stress level is healthy or unhealthy is determined in part by the prevalence of job strain within a work population. High strain jobs, characterized by high job demands and low employee control, have significantly higher rates of distress, manifested in diseases such as myocardial infarction (Karasek et al., 1988; Theorell & Karasek, 1996).

Work: Benefits and Risks

Work is an important feature of a full and healthy life. Weber (1930) believed that work was for the glory of God and the basis for the Protestant ethic. Levi (1995) referred to Freud's response to a question about the distinguishing features of a healthy life: *Lieben und arbeiten* ("to love and to work"). Vroom (1964) was among the first to specify the important features of employment work roles. He set out the following five features: (a) They provide wages for the role occupant in return for services; (b) they require from the occupant the expenditure of mental or physical energy; (c) they permit the role occupant to contribute to the production of goods or services; (d) they permit or require of the role occupant social interaction with other persons; and (e) they define, at least in part, the social status of the role occupant. From this can be drawn several benefits for individuals engaged in a work organization. Specifically, individuals realize at least three benefits from their work.

First, work for economic gain provides for the necessities of life by affording individuals income and benefits. Income and benefits are factors that enable a person to meet a range of human needs, including basic needs for food and shelter as well as higher level needs for esteem and discretionary or leisure times activities. Income is one of three components determining an individual's socioeconomic status (SES), and SES is a strong and consistent predictor of morbidity and premature mortality (Adler, Boyce, Chesney, Folkman, & Syme, 1993). This predictive power is found also for each of the key components of SES, which are income, education, and occupational status. Hence, income, education, and occupational status positively benefit the individual in terms of health.

Second, work is a defining feature of a life that affords individuals a basis for identity and human connection. Therefore, one's work and occupation are vehicles that bring meaning into one's life and give one's life value. Work is not the only basis for meaning, identification, and value in life, but it is one basis.

Third, in accordance with Freud's comment, work is one of two key elements that contribute to a person's psychological health and well-being. Just as work contributes to psychological health and well-being, the absence of work through displacement or unemployment can lead to significant adverse health consequences (Maida, Gordon, & Farberow, 1989; Westcott, Svensson, & Zollner, 1985). Hence, there is a psychological benefit for individuals in their work involvement.

In addition to the benefits, there are also health risks associated with work. The health risks vary by occupational category, organization, and specific work setting. The two major categories of health risks are physical and psychological. Although the nature of the physical risks of work changed with the industrial revolution, there are also health risks associated with agrarian work. For example, farm equipment accidents are among the leading causes of death for young people in the agricultural sector of the United States. In industrial work settings, equipment accidents and injuries are among the most serious and life-threatening events associated with work. In Germany during the 1860s, Chancellor Bismarck proposed that employees were entitled to medical care and some form of wage supplement to assist them in dealing with on-the-job injuries (G. T. Adams, 1987). Hence, physical injury was to become a work-related risk with costs for employers as well as employees.

Health risks emerge also from the psychological, social, and interpersonal dimensions of a person's work environment. Dysfunctional conflicts, psychological or interpersonal abuse, confusion and uncertainty, and other psychosocial risks may take a toll on a person at work.

Occupational Stress: A Leadership Challenge

Occupational stress, which is a broader concept than job stress, has become a leadership challenge primarily owing to the direct and indirect organizational costs associated with these risks and the distress associated with work (Adkins, 1995; Macy & Mirvis, 1976; Mirvis & Lawler, 1977; Mirvis & Macy, 1982). The challenge for leaders is to create organizational cultures and work environments in which people may produce, serve, grow, and be valued. This challenge is not, however, exclusively a leadership challenge. It is a challenge for each and every member of a work organization; it is a challenge for management and labor, men and women, leaders and followers, employers and employees alike. Leaders must take the lead in setting the tenor for healthy work environments, and followers must accept their responsibility to enhance the health of the work environment.

An increasingly important direct cost is that of the legal liability to which a company may be exposed unless it learns to monitor, diagnose, and treat a distressful situation before it goes to court (e.g., Frank S. Deus v. Allstate Insurance Company, 1990–1992). These costs and the Deus v. Allstate case are discussed in more detail in chapter 5. Ivancevich, Matteson, and Richards (1985) argued for a five-point program consisting of (a) formulation of a preventive law strategy, (b) development of a stress diagnostic system, (c) involvement of top-level management, (d) evaluation of current programs, and (e) documentation of what has been done. Responsible action cannot prevent all job distress or all litigation; however, it is an important first step in implementing a program of preventive stress management in organizations.

The Power of Prevention

It would be nice . . . if there were no risks associated with work . . . if people did not get injured on the job . . . if there were no dysfunctional conflicts among people at work . . . if cooperation, productivity, service, and health were the hallmarks of all working environments! Yes, it would be nice; unfortunately, that is not the current organizational reality. Therefore, there is a need for prevention and therapy in dealing with the health risks in work organizations. We believe the platform for action in this regard is the preventive medicine model used in public health for dealing with health risks and disease epidemics in human populations (Last & Wallace, 1992). There is great power in the public health notions of prevention for ameliorating the burden of suffering that individuals and human communities experience. We begin to set forth our prevention framework by focusing first on life expectancy as the "acid test" in stress management.

The Acid Test: Are You Dead or Alive?

Valliant (1977) did not believe that stress killed people. Rather, he argued that it was the capacity of the individual to adapt to the demands and stressors of life that enabled people to live. Hence, the acid test of one's stress management skills might well be: Are you dead or alive? A national news headline in 1988 stated the following: "Stress: The Test Americans are Failing!" We do not believe that this headline reflects the truth, especially when life expectancy at birth is taken as the yardstick for the test. During the course of the 20th century, Americans have increased their life expectancy by more than 50 percent. In the closing decade of the 19th century, life expectancy was less than 50 years for both men and women. By 1985, life expectancy at birth had topped 75 years (*Vital Statistics of the United States, 1988*).

Two important developments during the first 7 decades of the twentieth century provided the wind under the wings of this 25-year rise in life expectancy: (a) improvements in public sanitation and personal hygiene and (b) the development of the miracle drugs—antibiotics and vaccines. Both of these developments were designed to deal with the acute and infectious diseases, such as the influenza epidemic early in the century. The public sanitation and personal hygiene programs put into place just after the turn of the century in the United States were designed to address environmental health risks in the form of germs, rodents, and the like. Miracle drugs, such as vaccines were designed to strengthen the individual against health risks present in the environment. Hence, one type of preventive action targeted the environment, whereas the other targeted the individual. Both sets of preventive action are firmly rooted in public health and preventive medicine.

Public Health and Preventive Medicine

Much of what has been learned about public health and prevention has come from the study of disease epidemics over the centuries. Most major disease epidemics have been stopped by preventing the spread of the disease to the uninfected rather than by treating the infected. Preventive medicine is a relatively young branch of medicine concerned with averting a wide range of health risks to human populations. Public health and preventive medicine are highly relevant to work organizations because these organizations are composed of large human communities. Health risk assessment, public education, psychological intervention, and medical treatment are all elements of preventive medicine. Chapter 8 sets out in more detail the elements of preventive medicine and epidemiology that are relevant to the practice of preventive stress management in organizations.

Sauter et al. (1990) proposed a national strategy for the prevention of work-related psychological distress that is based on public health concepts and preventive medicine. The four major components of their strategy are (a) work and job redesign, (b) surveillance of stressors and distress in the workplace, (c) education and training programs, and (d) mental health service delivery for distressed employees. The core intent of this national strategy is to encourage the development of psychologically healthy occupational work environments. The strategy is comprehensive because it addresses aspects of the organization as well as the individual as points of intervention for change, accommodation, and development.

Occupational Health Psychology

Occupational health psychology, a term first used by Raymond, Wood, and Patrick (1990), is an emerging specialty at the crossroads of public health and health psychology. *Public health psychology* is a related psychological specialty that builds on elements within the domain of public health (Ewart, 1991). Occupational health psychology is distinguished by its focus on occupational settings and work environments; it is about healthy people in healthy work environments as well as healthy interactions between work and family–home environments. The field of occupational health psychology incorporates the preventive and therapeutic interventions designed to bring about healthy work environments. This discipline has a threefold focus on the work environment, the individual, and the work–home interface; the intent is to achieve a healthy fit of people in their work environment by modifying one, another, or a combination of these three dimensions.

The Chaparral Steel Company exemplifies an occupationally healthy work organization. Forward, Beach, Gray, and Quick (1991) described the organizational culture and values of this learning organization. One of the unique attributes of Chaparral's culture is the emphasis on its people as human resources as opposed to labor costs and on *mentofacturing*, which means made by the mind. The concept of mentofacturing emphasizes the intellectual and psychological contributions people make in the production process, as compared with the manual and physical contributions embodied in the word *manufacturing*. Hence, the company works to provide the broadest possible growth experience for every person employed, believing that the company grows in excellence in direct proportion to the growth of its people. Chaparral has found, even in a challenging industry such as steel production, that health and performance are mutually reinforcing objectives.

Preventive Stress Management in Organizations

Preventive stress management takes the public health notions of preventive medicine and translates them for application to a stress process framework in work organizations. The preventive stress management model is set forth in Figure 1.4. The definition of preventive stress management is as follows.

> *Preventive stress management* is an organizational philosophy and set of principles that employ specific methods for promoting individual and organizational health while preventing individual and organizational distress.

The major foci within preventive medicine are health risks, asymptomatic disease, and symptomatic disease. Health risks predispose one to develop disease, either with or without symptoms, such as pain or discom-

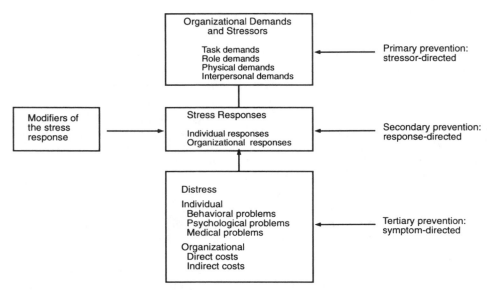

Figure 1.4.   The preventive stress management model.

fort, or recognizable clinical signs. The power of preventive medicine is found in the development of prevention strategies to address health risks (primary prevention), asymptomatic disease (secondary prevention), and symptomatic disease (tertiary prevention). When translated into a stress process framework, the major foci in preventive stress management are (a) demands, or stressors; (b) stress responses; and (c) the various forms of distress. The translation of the notions of prevention again leads to one of three foci; these are the primary, secondary, and tertiary stages of prevention. Primary prevention aims to modify the demands, or stressors, to which people are subject in the work environment. Secondary prevention aims to change how individuals and organizations respond to the necessary and inevitable demands of work and organizational life. Tertiary prevention, which is therapeutic, aims to treat the psychological, behavioral, or medical distress that individuals, groups, and organizations may encounter.

Preventive stress management is the framework we propose for designing, organizing, implementing, and evaluating stress management interventions in organizations. The stress process model shown in Figure 1.4 and the three stages of prevention are the organizing schema for the whole book. Chapters 2 through 5 address the stress process model, beginning with organizational demands and stressors, a detailed treatment of the stress response and its modifiers, and a careful examination of individual and organizational consequences of stress. Chapters 6 and 7 set out a diagnostic approach to developing knowledge about individual and organizational stress and distress in a specific organizational context. Chapter 8 sets forth the complete preventive stress management framework, including its principles and underpinnings. Chapters 9 through 13 address primary, secondary, and tertiary prevention interventions for organizations and individuals. Chapter 14 examines specific preventive stress management approaches for creating healthy organizations. Chapter 15 is the conclusion of the book.

Stress: Threat or Challenge?

Work and organizational life are undergoing dramatic changes in the 1990s, and there is reason to expect that the rate of change will continue, maybe even increase, as the 21st century approaches. Change is therefore a major source of stress for people in organizations. Is the stress induced by these environmental and industrial changes a threat, or is it a challenge and opportunity? Although the mind—body system may interpret it as a threat, we suggest that it is also a challenge and opportunity.

Staw, Sandelands, and Dutton (1981) showed us that there is a general tendency for individuals, groups, and organizations to experience environmental change as a threat. They found that the experience of threat leads to a response of rigidity, again within the individual, group, or organization. There are two key aspects of this threat—rigidity thesis that result from the experience of environmental change (a stressor) as a threat. First, the experience of threat results in the restriction of information flow. Second, the experience of threat results in constriction of control. The restriction of information flow and the constriction of control combine to lead to a rigidity of response. This rigidity is manifest in a reliance on well-learned or dominant responses. Unfortunately, well-learned or dominant responses may be the least functional ones for new and changed situations, especially radically changed situations. For situations characterized by incremental change, the reliance on well-learned or dominant responses may be functional. In these settings, individuals who are well trained for specific stressful, challenging, and threatening situations are likely to perform well by relying on their dominant and well-learned patterns of behavior; hence, the rigidity of response becomes functional for the well trained and prepared. For those who are not well trained and prepared for specific stressful, challenging, and threatening situations, the rigidity of response is likely to lead to dysfunctional outcomes.

The threat—rigidity thesis challenges people to transcend the instinctual stress response that prepares us to fight or flee changing and stressful circumstances. The thesis suggests that the actions we are most prepared to take in response to changing circumstances may well be counterproductive because they are not responsive to the new and changed reality in which we find ourselves. The challenge and opportunity in stressful and changing times is to learn more about ourselves and how we may better respond to a changed world of work and organizational life. Change and stress present the opportunity to grow, learn, accommodate, and change ourselves as we simultaneously change the world in which we live.

Summary

This chapter presents an overview of the stress concept from its earliest descriptions by Walter B. Cannon in the first decades of the 20th century through its current importance in organizations. During the intervening decades from Cannon's research to the current new reality, three significant advances have taken place that have led to a better understanding of the stress concept. First, Hans Selye made important advances through his exploration of the endocrine (hormone) system's role in the stress response and his conceptualization of the General Adaptation Syndrome (GAS). Second, psychologists Robert Kahn, Richard Lazarus, Harry Levinson, and Charles Spielberger have made distinct contributions to the understanding of the social psychological, appraisal and coping, psychoanalytic, and clinical psychology aspects of the stress response. Third, the first edition of this book brought forth the role of public health and preventive medicine for managing the occupational health risks associated with stress and psychological disorders in the workplace.

Occupational stress is now a leadership challenge for executives, psychologists, and physicians concerned with executive health and employee well-being. The personal and collective costs of excessive, prolonged, intense, or mismanaged stress in the workplace warrant attention by all to the importance of prevention. This chapter presents a comprehensive, systematic framework for preventive stress management that includes a three stage model of primary, secondary, and tertiary (therapeutic) prevention. Preventive stress management aims to channel stress induced energy along constructive and healthy avenues for eustress and to avert the costs associated with distress. Stress may be seen as a threat or a challenge! Our perspective is that stress is one of our best assets for managing legitimate emergencies and achieving high performance in the new organizational reality of international competition for business success.

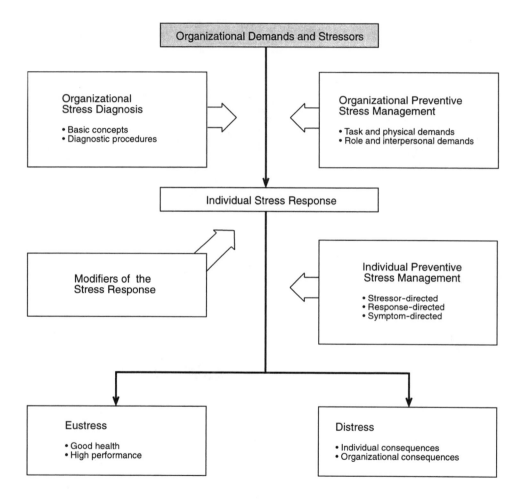

2

Organizational Demands
and Stressors

Although stress is an individualized experience, there are a variety of demands that serve as stressors for groups and individuals in organizations. Some stressors discussed in this chapter have little or no impact on some individuals, yet are major stressors for others. In addition to organizational stressors, extraorganizational stressors (e.g., marital discord) and transitional factors (e.g., preparing for retirement) can be of equal or greater importance to an understanding of an individual's stress and strain. It is essential to look at an individual's entire life experience (i.e., not just work) if one is to understand the individual's stress and strain. Extraorganizational stressors and transitional factors are discussed briefly at the end of this chapter and elsewhere in the book.

The four major categories of organizational demands and stressors that are identified and discussed in this chapter are presented in Exhibit 2.1. The first major category is physical stressors, composed of the elements in one's physical setting or environment (Gunderson, 1978; Steele, 1973). Discomforts caused by too little free space in the physical environment exemplify this category of stressor. The second category of stressors is task demands. Any job is composed of a specific set of tasks and activities that are assigned to the employee who occupies the job. The task demands discussed in this chapter are included in the exhibit. Task demands as sources of stress are distinguished from other stressors by their task-oriented origin (Beehr & Newman, 1978). Work overload, which everyone experiences at one time or another, is a task demand. All of the task stressors are based on the nature of the work itself.

The third set of stressors is composed of role demands associated with the process of making and assuming an organizational role (Kahn et al., 1964). A role is typically defined in terms of the expectations others in the work environment attribute to it. It is the dysfunctional aspects of this role-making and role-taking process that cause stress to an individual. Finally, there is a set of interpersonal demands that occur as people work together and interact on a regular basis (Blau, 1964). All four sets of demands require a response on the part of the individual, and therefore they generate stress.

Physical Demands

Some occupations, by their very nature, appear to be particularly vulnerable to stressors emanating from the physical environment in which the

Exhibit 2.1.   Organizational Demands and Stressors

Physical demands	Role demands
Indoor climate and air quality	Role conflict
Temperature	Interrole
Illumination and other rays	Intrarole
Noise and vibrations	Person–role
Office design	Role ambiguity
	Work–home demands
Task demands	
Occupational category	Interpersonal demands
Routine jobs	Status incongruity
Job future ambiguity	Social density
Interactive organizational demands	Abrasive personalities
Work overload	Leadership style
	Team pressures
	Diversity

work is performed. Work in the construction, lumber, and mining industries is physically demanding. It is a mistake to assume that only blue collar workers encounter physical demands. White collar jobs involve a different set of stressors that are also physically demanding. Working with a computer is one such stressor.

Selye (1976b) was among the most attentive to the issues of physical stressors. According to him, there are a host of physical agents that cause individuals stress. These include temperature variations; burns; sound and ultrasound (e.g., sonic booms); ionizing, light, and ultraviolet rays; vibrations; air blasts; compression and decompression; gravity, magnetism, electricity, and electroshock; as well as osmotic pressure. Although many offices are buffered against physical stressors, a manager may encounter these stressors in times of travel and during office modification or work in the field.

In a series of research studies of United States Navy surface vessels in the Atlantic and Pacific, Gunderson (1978) and his associates found various divisions of the ship to be unfavorable and hazardous work environments. These divisions included the boilers, machinery, and deck areas. The key environmental concerns of the research team were temperature, ventilation, cleanliness, odor, size, number of people, lighting, color, privacy, noise, and safety. The authors found that poor physical settings generated more stress for the crew members and resulted in a number of adverse individual and organizational outcomes.

Indoor Climate and Air Quality

People vary in terms of both their physiological and their psychological responses to temperature levels. Temperature extremes at either end of the continuum may cause a stress reaction. Individuals need both physical setting protections and garment and other safeguards as temperatures move into the freezing region (32°F) or it becomes excessively hot (over 100°F). During the energy crisis of the 1970s, the issue of temperature as a stressor even affected office workers in the Sun Belt during the summer months.

In 1982, the World Health Organization recognized sick building syndrome (SBS) as a condition wherein a cluster of work-related symptoms of unknown origin are significantly more prevalent among the occupants of certain buildings in comparison with others (Bain & Baldry, 1995). Sick building syndrome evolved from the energy crisis of the 1970s, when builders included energy-efficient features such as sealed windows and heating and cooling systems that used minimal fresh air, allowing airborne pollutants to build up (Minicucci, 1988). The symptoms of SBS include eye, nose, throat, and sensory irritations; skin irritations; neurotoxic symptoms such as headache, nausea, and fatigue; and odor and taste complaints (Hedge, Erickson, & Rubin, 1992).

Illumination and Other Rays

Lighting and illumination levels were the concern of the original Hawthorne investigators back in the 1920s (Roethlisberger, 1941). Besides discovering the Hawthorne effect, they found that workers tended to produce less work under moonlight intensity. However, beyond that fact they did not uncover the systematic relationship between illumination level and productivity that they had anticipated. It was not until later that they understood that unaccounted for variables, such as the individual attention the workers received, confounded such a relationship.

Most work environments require 20–40 foot-candles of light to be well illuminated (Ivancevich & Matteson, 1980). However, this may need to be increased markedly for especially fine or detailed work tasks. Extremes in lighting cause stress that is manifested in a variety of ways, such as headaches and nervous tension.

Rays outside of the visible spectrum also have the potential for generating stress, although their effects are subliminal and therefore further from the individual's awareness. X-rays, infrared, and ultraviolet rays are now used in a host of settings, such as dental offices, inspection stations, military operations of various sorts, and welding activities, as in shipbuilding. Precautions are increasing to protect workers from the harmful effects of overexposure to these physical stressors.

Video display terminals (VDTs) are used in most jobs, and many employees report them to be stressful. Among 500 directory assistance operators at U.S. West, 189 were diagnosed as suffering from VDT-related cumulative trauma disorder, at a cost of $5 million to the company (Fernberg, 1990). There continues to be controversy surrounding the health hazards of electromagnetic radiation exposure from VDTs. Other potential sources of such radiation include high-tension wires, cellular telephones, and other modern communication devices.

Noise and Vibrations

Exposure to excessive noise (roughly, 80 decibels) on a recurring, prolonged basis can cause stress (Ivancevich & Matteson, 1980). Anyone who has been exposed to a noisy, second-generation computer printer or to an airplane such as the Air Force's C-130 or to a naval aircraft carrier flight deck is well aware of the stress that can be caused by excessive noise levels. In extreme cases, temporary and permanent hearing losses may result from overexposure without proper protection, such as the ear protectors issued to military personnel who are exposed to such noise.

Closely associated with sound waves is vibration, which, according to Selye (1976a), is a powerful stressor. Vibrations typically occur as a result of some rotary or impacting motion or a combination of the two. Equipment such as choppers, ramming machines, pneumatic and riveting hammers, and aircraft propellers generate vibrations. Therefore, construction sites and aerospace activity centers are common locations of such stress. A central element of the stress response is elevated catecholamine levels, which have been noted in response to vibration (Selye, 1976b). In addition, there are various alterations that occur in psychological and neurological functioning as a result of exposure to this stressor.

Occasional noisy conditions at work can be a nuisance, but chronic exposure to noise and vibration can lead to irreversible hearing loss. The Occupational Safety and Health Administration (OSHA) has implemented hearing protection standards to reduce these risks. However, there is an increase in ambient noise from the use of open office systems ("cubicles") without enclosed walls and doors. Thus, office design can be a related physical stressor.

Office Design

According to Steele (1973), physical settings fulfill one or more of six basic functions, which are to (a) provide shelter and security, (b) facilitate social contact, (c) provide symbolic identification, (d) enhance task instrumentality, (e) heighten pleasure, and (f) stimulate growth. If physical settings are not designed to fulfill the function for which the space is intended, those attempting to use the space may experience stress. Therefore, if office settings do not serve their first function effectively, they expose the inhabitants to some of the environmental vagaries already discussed. But even if they are well designed for meeting this function, they may cause stress because other functions are not fulfilled by the design of the work environment.

As incidents of workplace violence have increased, the need for shelter and security has become more critical. Assaults and violent acts are the second leading cause of death in the workplace, following transportation accidents, which are the leading cause of workplace fatalities (Bureau of Labor Statistics, 1995). During the 1980s, nearly 7,600 U.S. workers were murdered on the job (Harvey & Cosier, 1995). Whereas some have argued that media attention overstates the threat of workplace violence, the very fact that these incidents do garner media attention increases the perceived threat for employees and thus the potential for stress.

The ability of offices to fulfill the need for symbolic identification has diminished as budgets have been slashed and open office systems have become a trend in workplaces. In addition, studies have indicated that clerical employees are more satisfied with traditional partitioned offices because they provide greater opportunities for focusing on the task and communicating in private (Cooper & Cartwright, 1994).

Physical settings should facilitate certain kinds of social contact associated with the work. When a large office of a state department of human resources was temporarily relocated to an unused supermarket, all the social workers were spread out in long rows and aisles with no partitions between them. An entering social welfare client was struck by the overwhelming nature of this sprawl. This was a stressful environment in which to discuss such private matters as child abuse.

Too much physical dispersion may cause stress. One example occurred in a military computer installation that had units located in four different buildings. The computer operations were all in one main building, but there were programmers spread out through three other buildings. This physical dispersion caused some disruptions in communications, contributed to distrust among the groups, and heightened the stress and tension among the workers.

The trend toward "virtual offices" includes offices at home used by entrepreneurs and telecommuting workers, as well as the temporary offices that some firms use to accommodate workers who travel most of the time. Virtual offices may create stress owing to their low potential for social contact. By the end of 1995, the number of telecommuters grew to 9.24 million workers, an increase of 10 percent over 1994 (DeMarco, 1995). At first, telecommuting arrangements were initiated by employees who wanted more flexible work hours to accommodate their family concerns. Now companies are attempting to reduce real estate costs and respond to environmental mandates by offering telecommuting. A survey conducted by the Olsten Corporation of 1,022 executives indicated that 29 percent of the companies involved encouraged telecommuting among workers (Davis, 1995).

Traditional office atmospheres provide discipline, structure, and social interaction, along with the opportunity to learn from interaction with others. The virtual office eliminates this social support system. As long as telecommuting is voluntary, it is linked to higher satisfaction and productivity among workers who choose it (Connelly, 1995). However, if cost-cutting measures force employees to telecommute, it may become stressful.

Physical settings and office space are intended to protect employees from certain demands. They can, however, cause stress for employees in a variety of ways when basic functions are not adequately fulfilled.

Task Demands

According to Drucker (1954), organizations are goal-directed entities that have an existence of their own beyond that of the individuals who compose them. An organization's basic structural building block is the job, which is typically defined in terms of various tasks and activities. There are several task characteristics of these structural units that generate stress for individuals.

Occupational Category

The occupational category that a job falls into has been found to be an important determinant of the amount as well as the type of stress an individual experiences (French, Caplan, & Harrison, 1982). On the basis of a study of 22,000 individuals in 130 occupations who either died, were admitted to a hospital, or were admitted to a mental health center owing to stress-related disease, the National Institute for Occupational Safety and Health (NIOSH) was able to distinguish high- and low-stress occupations (Smith, Colligan, & Hurrell, 1977). Office managers, administrators, first-line supervisors, and secretaries had the most stress-related disorders, whereas personnel employees, craftspersons, and university professors had the lowest incidence of stress-related disorders.

In a study of the Goddard Space Center, French, Caplan, and Harrison (1982) found that the administrators were subject to different sources of stress than were the engineers and scientists. For example, the administrators reported more stress because of too much work than did the engineers or scientists. On the other hand, the engineers and scientists reported more stress owing to the challenges and demands of the tasks than did the administrators. Therefore, there are differences not only in the total *amount* of stress that various occupations cause but also in the *nature* and *source* of the stresses across occupations. Bus drivers in the United Kingdom reported substantial stress from handling money and from the risk of assault (Duffy & McGoldrick, 1990), whereas income tax officers reported autocratic management to be their major source of stress (Cooper & Roden, 1985).

In a study of over 2,000 individuals in 23 blue and white collar occupations, Caplan, Cobb, French, Harrison, and Pinneau (1980) detailed a variety of occupational differences in terms of stress physiology (e.g., differences in blood pressure, heart rate, and cholesterol level), personality factors (e.g., Type A–Type B patterns and defense mechanisms), and psychological factors (e.g., dissatisfaction and anxiety). They were particularly interested in job stress and individual strain, either of a physiological, psychological, or behavioral nature. Their conclusions suggest that some occupations, such as supervisor, are more stressful than others, such as research scientist. A study of 244 full-time employees in health services, banking, social welfare, manufacturing, and education found that social welfare workers exhibited the highest levels of work-related stress (Matthews, 1990).

Surveillance systems that track job risk factors across occupations are insufficient in the United States. However, many European countries have initiated surveys that permit such tracking over time. The Netherlands

Central Bureau of Statistics, for example, conducted a national survey of the 20 largest professional groups and the 19 largest branches of industry in the Netherlands from 1977 to 1989 (Houtman & Kompier, 1995). The survey indicated that the psychosocial demands of work, such as work pace, increased markedly during this period, especially among health care workers.

One occupation included in the NIOSH study mentioned earlier was that of manager. Managerial jobs were listed twice among the 12 most stressful occupations. A variety of factors may be responsible, such as time deadlines and performance evaluation activities (Cooper & Marshall, 1978). However, managerial work is not easily or concisely defined. In an effort to study and define the nature of managerial work more systematically, Mintzberg (1973) found that a major component of a manager's work involves a variety of decision-making activities and role demands. Therefore, one stress-related factor appears to be the latitude the manager has in the decision-making process (Karasek, 1979).

There may be differences in stressors between status groups and subcultures within the same organization. In a study of 262 office workers from three public service organizations, two distinct clusters emerged: a high stress group and a lower stress group (Carayon, 1994). Computer users belonged to the high stress group, which was characterized by high demands and job future ambiguity and low skill utilization, support, and control. The lower stress cluster was composed of managers, supervisors, and professionals, whose jobs also included high demands but with high skill utilization, support, and control.

Routine Jobs

Jobs that demand too little in terms of demonstration of skills or use of knowledge and experience are just as stressful as those that demand too much of the person's abilities, talents, and skills. A study of 249 workers in a large university showed that having unchallenging work was more predictive of adverse strain outcomes than were role overload and responsibility (Decker & Borgen, 1993). Repetitive work is one example of a job situation that does not provide the employee with adequate physiological or psychological arousal (T. Cox, 1980). The problem with repetitive work is not in temporary exposure to it but in prolonged exposure. The result is stress attributable to low levels of both self-reported and physiological arousal, which leads to boredom, shifts in attention, and associated physiological problems.

Mass production technology frequently leads to the design of jobs that are stressful because they are understimulating (Levi, 1981; Thompson, 1967). Jobs that support this technological process are dominantly characterized by robotic activities. In an intensive study conducted in the automobile industry, Walker and Guest (1952) identified the characteristics of these assembly-line jobs that make them stressful: (a) a mechanically controlled work pace, (b) repetitiveness, (c) minimum skill demands of the worker, (d) predetermination of tools and techniques, (e) a high degree of task specialization, and (f) a requirement for only surface mental attention. One aspect of their field study involved intensive interviews with assembly-line workers, during which it was revealed that many of the workers aspired to better jobs that provided greater opportunities for interpersonal contact (arousal) to overcome the boredom associated with their current jobs.

A frequent characteristic of routine work is the piece-rate method of payment for work accomplishment. Taylor (1911) originally proposed this method to increase the employee's task motivation. Subsequent research has supported his contention (Levi, 1981). What occurs under the piece-rate system of compensation is an increased experience of physical discomfort and fatigue as well as increased adrenaline excretion into the bloodstream. These changes suggest that there may be a physiological basis for the increased motivation of individuals working under incentive compensation systems. Although this system may be positively stressful, there is also the possibility that it contributes to the distress associated with routine work. Whether such situations are distressful or not may depend on factors like the proportion of pay that is incentive pay, the minimum standards to be achieved before incentives are earned, and the magnitude of the incentive for each piece produced.

Repetitiveness in some jobs has also increased owing to the use of electronic tools such as computers and mass telecommunications. Keyboarding is just as restrictive and repetitive as working on a production line. In conjunction with such technological advances has come the prevalence of electronic monitoring of performance as a stressor. Employees who work under electronic performance monitoring systems report more anxiety, depression, anger, and tension than other employees (Aiello & Kolb, 1995). Electronic monitoring adds more stress to already stressful routine jobs.

Job Future Ambiguity

The perceived uncertainty of having one's job in the future, or job future ambiguity, is a source of stress that undoubtedly has increased in recent years. With the massive organizational restructuring of the 1990s, few employees enjoyed job security. The expectation that one would progress through a series of rewarding jobs within a single organization was replaced by a new psychological contract between individuals and organizations: To continue employment, workers must demonstrate that they can add value to the organization. Two factors that can dramatically affect career expectations are the involuntary interruption of a career when one's job is eliminated through "downsizing" and gender differentials in career experiences.

The prevalence of "rightsizing" and "reengineering" in the highly competitive global market put hundreds of thousands of employees at risk for job elimination. A pervading sense of job future ambiguity has replaced the expectation of guaranteed employment. The media coverage of massive layoffs has led many more employees to face the possibility of a layoff, not finding another equivalent job, or having to switch careers. The survivors of downsizing face not only more job future ambiguity but also survivors' guilt, loss of company loyalty, and a loss of trust in the organization (Armstrong-Stassen, 1994).

Women face job future ambiguity when they elect to interrupt their careers to bear children. With organizational restructuring as the norm, they may fear that while they are on leave, their jobs are easy targets for elimination. The "glass ceiling," or invisible barrier that prevents women from rising above a certain level in organizations, is an involuntary barrier. It shortens the career path expectations of women and diminishes their opportunities for rewards from career investment (Morrison et al., 1992). In a study comparing stressors among male and female human resource professionals, Nelson, Quick, Hitt, and Moesel (1990) found that lack of career progress had a significant negative effect on health and job satisfaction among women.

Interactive Organizational Demands

The rapid growth of the service sector of the economy, the customer service imperative, and the focus on service quality mean that vastly greater numbers of personnel are now required to interface with the "customer." The customer may be internal or external to the organization. Flatter organizations require high communication and negotiation skills outside the boundaries of the hierarchy. Most jobs now require interaction with a variety of constituencies, which we call *interactive organizational demands*.

Traditionally, these activities have been called *boundary spanning*. Because these boundaries are designed to protect the organization, boundary-spanning activities are often stressful for the individuals who engage in such work (French & Caplan, 1972; Miles, 1980). Jobs that involve boundary-spanning activities include sales, procurement, and public information. Employees who occupy boundary-spanning jobs engage in various tasks concerned with managing the "face" of the organization (how it presents itself publicly), processing various kinds of environmental information, and managing relations with organizations in the environment (Miles, 1980).

In 1991, 78 percent of all U.S. employees worked in service-oriented industries (Jackson, 1992). Service work has been called a "game between persons." To succeed at the game, employees must interact with customers by understanding their perspective, anticipating their needs, and responding sensitively to these needs.

Customer service, whether the customer is internal or external, is inherently stressful for individuals. It is a high burnout activity owing to the requirement to give high quality service to irate customers (Singh, Goolsby, & Rhoads, 1994). Key factors that contribute to the high stress associated with boundary-spanning activities include the following:

1. Having required and nonroutine activities
2. Maintaining frequent and long-term relations with individuals in other organizations
3. Relating to dynamic, complex environments
4. Dealing with diverse organizations
5. Lacking screening mechanisms, such as secretarial assistance
6. Being evaluated on the basis of precise performance standards

This description can be applied to virtually all jobs in organizations that require interaction with various customers, colleagues, and teams.

> What has been until now the reward for an exceptional few salespeople, researchers, and specialists may increasingly become the rule. Job descriptions may be intentionally vague, rewards often linked to the performance of teams, with the place where the work is to be sometimes left undefined. Some employees find that they interact more with suppliers or customers than with their fellow employees. (Davidow & Malone, 1992, p. 214).

Work Overload

Work overload is a stressor that may be manifested in two ways. The first is quantitative overload resulting from the employee being assigned too many tasks or insufficient time to accomplish the assigned tasks. This form of overload has increased exponentially for survivors of downsizing, who are expected to handle the prelayoff workload.

The second form of work overload is qualitative in nature. This occurs when employees do not feel that they possess the required skills, knowledge, abilities, or competencies to do the job. This form of overload is frequently experienced by new first-line nursing supervisors, who have been promoted on the basis of excellent clinical practice but have no knowledge of or skill training in such supervisory practices as performance appraisal or delegation. They do not have the skills and knowledge to manage because their clinical training excluded management training.

There is potential for increased qualitative overload in organizations because of technological advancements. A 1992 study revealed that 11 percent of all occupational absence claims involved "technostress," which results from the introduction of new technologies in the workplace (Brandon 1992). New technologies require workers to learn new skills and are often accompanied by expectations of increased production and speed. Trends toward "total quality management" and self-directed work teams, although positive, may increase the likelihood that employees will suffer from qualitative work overload.

Role Demands

A third major category of stressors at work is associated with the organizational role that an individual assumes. Whereas task demands are concerned with specific work activities that must be accomplished, role factors are related to the behavior others expect of employees as they fulfill their organizational functions. Roles are typically defined in terms of the behavioral expectations that various individuals and groups communicate to an individual at work. A *role set* is composed of all the various individuals, called *role senders*, who have expectations of a particular person. A typical organizational role set might look like the one shown in Figure 2.1. In this illustration, the role senders include the supervisor and supervisor once removed, the various peers and friends, the employees and the employee once removed. All these individuals together with the individual in the focal office compose the role set. Each role sender places unique demands on the focal person. For example, the supervisor may establish deadlines and assign various projects to the focal person. The employees may be concerned with performance review procedures. They may also expect a consistency in managerial style on the part of the focal person. The various behaviors that these different role senders expect of the focal person are not always consistent or compatible.

There are two broad types of dysfunctions in role-making and role-taking activities in organizations, as identified by Kahn and his associates (1964) during their extensive examination of organizational role stress.

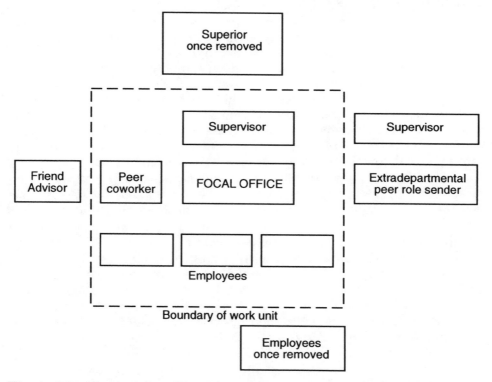

Figure 2.1. Composition of hypothetical role set. Reprinted from *Organizational Stress* (p. 41) by R. L. Kahn, R. P. Wolfe, R. P. Quinn, J. D. Snoek, and R. A. Rosenthal, 1964, New York: John Wiley & Sons, Inc. Reprinted by permission.

These are *role conflict* and *role ambiguity*. These problems may be caused in a number of ways, which we discuss separately. Both kinds of role dysfunctions cause stress and strain for the individual who is subject to them.

Role Conflict

Role conflict occurs for an individual when a person in the work environment communicates an expectation about how he or she should behave and this expectation makes it difficult or impossible to fulfill another behavioral expectation or set of expectations. Stress is caused by the inability to meet or difficulty in meeting the various expectations for behavior (Van Sell, Brief, & Schuler, 1981).

Intrasender role conflict occurs when a single person communicates conflicting or incompatible expectations. Intrasender role conflict may occur in one's relationship with the boss, although it is not limited to that relationship. For example, if a vice president expects one of the sales managers to increase sales by 10% per year while cutting costs by an equal amount, the sales manager may well experience this as a conflict.

Intersender role conflict occurs when two or more role senders communicate conflicting or incompatible expectations. Intersender role conflict is a risk in matrix organizations. When individuals report to the project managers, for example, they may be given conflicting assignments.

Person–role conflict occurs when there is a perceived incompatibility between an individual's values or beliefs and the expectations held by various role senders. This form of conflict puts an individual in direct opposition to the behaviors that others expect. This form of conflict occurs, for example, when employees are asked by organizations to act in ways that violate their ethical standards or religious beliefs.

Interrole conflict occurs when the requirements of one role are incompatible with the requirements of a second role occupied by the person. This form of conflict might arise, for example, when the duties of a director of nursing in a hospital demand her presence at the same time that her daughter's school awards program is scheduled.

Role overload is a final form of role conflict, analogous to work overload. Work overload is based on actual tasks, whereas role overload is based on the behaviors that are expected of the individual. Role overload occurs when too many behaviors are expected of an individual or the behavior expected is too complicated or difficult for the individual to execute. Engaging in too many roles at once—for example, CEO, father, president of Rotary, church elder, and little league coach—can produce overload.

These various forms of role conflict contribute to increased stress levels for people at work. However, they are not the only kinds of dysfunction that occur in the role-making and role-taking process. Role ambiguity is a second form of role stress in organizations.

Role Ambiguity

Role ambiguity results when there is inadequate, unclear, or confusing information about expected role behaviors; unclear or confusing information about what behaviors may enable the incumbent to fulfill the role expectations; or uncertainty about the consequences of certain role behaviors (Van Sell et al., 1981).

In the first case, the ambiguity arises because the role senders, especially the key ones such as the supervisor, simply do not communicate adequate information to the role incumbent about what is expected. As a result, the incumbent does not understand his role in terms of specific behaviors. An example of this occurred for a young graduate student who worked in the merchandise distribution department of a major retailer. Told by the supervisor on the first day to "do what that person does," the student was left to do the job with no further information.

In the second case, the ambiguity arises because the role senders communicate information that is unclear or confusing. This situation is prone to occur in work environments where technical terms or jargon unfamiliar to the role incumbent are prevalent. For example, administrative or non-professional staff in health care or hospital settings might initially experience role ambiguity because of the use of large amounts of medical and surgical terminology.

In the third case, ambiguity is attributable to uncertainty about what behaviors may enable the incumbent to fulfill the role expectations, which are clear in and of themselves. For example, a personnel manager for a major airline is given responsibility for improving several personnel practices for the maintenance, data processing, and finance personnel at a particular location. The assignment is to reduce the intraorganizational conflicts at that location, improve the performance appraisal processes, and reduce the number of union grievances. Although these role expectations are relatively clear, it is not clear immediately what behaviors and activities may enable the manager to fulfill these expectations.

Finally, ambiguity for the role incumbent may arise if the consequences of a specific role expectation are unclear. For example, a sales representative may be required to establish a sales goal for the territory as a result of a new corporate management by objectives (MBO) program. This task of estimating and stating such a goal may not be difficult at all. However, ambiguity intrudes into the situation because there is no clarity regarding the result of meeting the goal (a bonus?), exceeding the goal (a bigger bonus or no bonus because the goal was too low?), or failing to meet the goal (no consequence because it was a difficult goal or a commission penalty?).

As in the case of role conflict, these forms of role ambiguity generate stress for the role incumbent. For the vast majority of office employees and professionals, these role dysfunctions and the job factors previously discussed are the major sources of stress.

Work–Home Demands

By the year 2000, 75% of all families may be dual-career families (Guinn, 1989). Work–home demands put special pressures on dual-career couples; when both partners are employed, the demands of home life often conflict with those of work. The potential for both work overload owing to time pressures and role overload from multiple expectations is high. Even if the couple has no children, home maintenance must be done. Picking up the dry cleaning, shopping for groceries, mowing the lawn, and other necessities are often a challenge when both individuals work long hours.

Parenting adds another dimension to work–home demands. In one study of 2,773 employees that included married and single parents and nonparents, fathers reported greater stress than mothers from child care problems (Tetrick, Miles, Marcil, & VanDosen, 1994). Other studies have consistently shown that the presence of children in the household creates more stress for women than for men (Piltch, Walsh, Mangione, & Jennings, 1994). Parenting may have an additive effect on workplace stress regardless of the gender of the parent.

Interpersonal Demands

Interpersonal stressors at work are concerned with the demands of the normal course of social, personal, and working relationships in the organization. Individuals have various distinctive personality and behavioral characteristics that are sources of stimulation for some people (positively stressful) and aggravation or irritation for others (negatively stressful). Individuals with clear-cut, powerful personalities may be more stressful to deal with than bland, withdrawn individuals, although the reverse can also be the case. As Selye (1974) pointed out, learning to live with other people is one of the most stressful aspects of life. There are various individual characteristics that people possess as well as various aspects of informal group behavior within organizations that make this so.

The interpersonal stressors should not be confused with individual characteristics that are moderators of the stress response. Individual modifiers of the stress response such as hardiness and Type A behavior are discussed in detail in the next chapter, where the individual consequences of stress are examined. The interpersonal stressors come from the demands and pressures of social system relationships at work. The demands of these social relations are in part related to the role stressors previously discussed, but they are different in that they are not based on expected behaviors.

Five specific interpersonal stressors are examined here. They are status incongruity, social density, abrasive personalities, leadership style, team pressures, and diversity.

Status Incongruity

Each individual occupies a unique social status within a group in an organization. This social status is based on many factors, such as educational and family background, technical competence, professional accomplishment, membership in associations and clubs, income level, and formal position and responsibilities. Individuals of higher social status within an organization receive prerogatives and privileges that are not enjoyed by individuals of lower social status. Individuals of lower social status also defer more frequently to those in higher status positions. Stress is caused for individuals if their social status is not what they think it should be.

The truncated career paths that result from job displacement owing to downsizing can result in status incongruity. Middle managers are especially vulnerable when they must accept jobs with lower status and compensation than they had previously. They may be forced to swap a prestigious full-time job with a well-known corporation for several part-time jobs with no benefits.

Social Density

Individuals have varying needs for interpersonal space and distance, referred to as *social density*. When their preferred distance is violated and other people are too close, they experience stress. The effects of crowding have been studied in a variety of settings by V. C. Cox and his associates. Their findings suggest that crowding leads to significant psychological stress, which in turn contributes to increases in both contagious and noncontagious illnesses (V. C. Cox, Paulus, McCain, & Karlovac, 1982). On the other hand, lack of adequate proximity for social contact also is perceived as stressful. As in the case of all the stressors, there are individual differences in terms of the amount and intensity of stress caused by a particular social density.

As we discussed earlier, open offices (using partitions or cubicles) may be stressful. The setup decreases privacy and intensifies the perceptions of increased social density. Although most people report more stress from an open office space, extroverts report an increased capacity to be effective in the open office (Tetrick, 1992).

Abrasive Personalities

Coworkers with abrasive personalities may cause stress and strain to others (H. Levinson, 1978). These persons may unintentionally cause stress for others by ignoring the interpersonal aspects of human intercourse, the feelings and sensibilities of fellow employees, and the depth and richness of their own emotional lives. Persons with abrasive personalities are often achievement-oriented, hard driving, and intelligent. They may function well at the conceptual level but not nearly as well at the emotional level.

There are several other ways in which abrasive personalities cause stress and strain at work. First, their condescending and critical style places others in a constantly subordinate position in which they are viewed as "unimportant." Second, their need for perfection in each task they undertake often causes others to feel inadequate or "outdone." Third, their attention to self leaves little energy for thoughtful and sensitive attention to the needs of other individuals at work. Fourth, they prefer to do *their work* by themselves, leaving others out of their projects and activities. This provides a fertile ground for feelings of uselessness and inadequacy in others. Finally, their competitive nature fosters a conflicted and divisively competitive work environment as opposed to a cooperative, achievement-oriented environment.

In the past, coworkers may have found abrasiveness a barrier to social cooperation but avoided the stressor by avoiding the person. With today's emphasis on self-directed work teams, abrasiveness in a team member affects productivity and even compensation. Abrasiveness in a coworker can be just as significant as abrasiveness in one's supervisor.

Leadership Style

Managers and supervisors are in a unique position to cause stress for their employees, either wittingly or unwittingly. The interpersonal leadership style adopted by a manager, as opposed to the technical aspects of supervision, has long been seen as a potential source of tension for employees (Lewin, Lippitt, & White, 1939). For example, authoritarian behavior on the part of a leader tends to cause pressure and tension for followers because of the high number of influence attempts undertaken by the leader. Alternatively, a leader who employs a participative style asks far more of the employee and can be intimidating for certain personality types. A lack of leadership can also be frustrating because it substantially increases the ambiguity of work. What one person sees as satisfying autonomy may be perceived by another as a dissatisfying lack of role clarity (Fisher & Gitelson, 1983). The point regarding leadership style is that it may be a source of stress to the extent that it does not meet the followers' needs.

Team Pressures

Much is accomplished in organizations through teamwork. By 1990, half of the Fortune 100 firms had implemented work teams, and the other half planned to use them in the near future (Davidow & Malone, 1992). Although teams fulfill many individual needs, they can also be a source of stress.

As a team matures through its developmental stages, it establishes a variety of behavioral norms that function as standards of conduct for members of the team. These behavioral norms are frequently unwritten and operate through a process of consensual understanding. A violation of these informal codes of behavior typically results in group sanctions to realign the individual's behavior with the norms. The silencing treatment given a West Point cadet is an example of such sanctioning behavior on the part of a group. The purpose of such group sanctioning behavior is to establish control over individual group members. As such, it causes stress and tension for the individual involved.

Teams place demands on workers for much higher levels of interpersonal skills. Working in teams is not comfortable for some individuals, who prefer more independence. In addition, the team concept often results in more role ambiguity and conflict as self-directed teams take on tasks that were once the domain of managers.

Diversity

Differences between individuals exacerbate the difficulties of interpersonal relationships. Although the U.S. workforce has always been diverse, it is now more diverse than ever. Diversity encompasses all forms of differences among individuals: culture, gender, age, ability, religious affiliation, personality, economic class, social status, military attachment, and sexual orientation. The workforce is now more culturally diverse than previously owing to globalization. By the year 2000, the workforce may be balanced with respect to gender. The aging baby boomers are contributing to the "graying" of the workforce.

Employees who are members of minority groups experience stress from conflict, confusion, deprivation, and denigration. The prevalence of ethnocentric attitudes in the workplace contributes to this stress (Marsella, 1994). Because heterogeneous work teams are more productive, diversity is often intentionally designed into teams to stimulate creativity (Jackson, 1992).

Most individuals are more comfortable working with people similar to themselves because of shared understandings. Working with those who are different can be stressful.

Extraorganizational Stressors

It is difficult to understand an individual's stress and strain without examining the whole experience, at work as well as away from work. Stressful life events of a personal nature, or extraorganizational stressors, also have an effect on an individual's performance effectiveness and adjustment at work (Bhagat, 1983). For example, individuals working in heavily populated urban areas, such as Houston or New York, may experience significant extraorganizational stress from the process of commuting to and from work.

Whereas some individuals can compartmentalize the different aspects of their lives well, other individuals have difficulty in doing so. Regardless of how well one can separate the different aspects of one's life, however, one's marriage and family relationships are important extraorganizational stressors (Hall & Hall, 1980; Handy, 1978). There is a clear potential for role stress in this area owing to the conflicts inherent in assuming family roles, such as spouse, child and parent, in addition to work roles. Like any stressor, these family relationships may contribute to improved work performance and adjustment or they may detract because of the distress they cause (Bhagat, 1983).

The distinction between the demands of personal and work life is a conceptual and somewhat artificial one. Although the major focus of this book is on organizational stressors, the role of extraorganizational stressors cannot be ignored in diagnosing and preventing distress for individuals and organizations.

Transitional Factors

Individuals and organizations go through stages of growth and evolution over the course of time. The periods of transition from one life stage to the next give rise to stress and strain within either the individual or the organization (Kimberly & Miles, 1980; D. J. Levinson, 1978) and have an effect on behavior and performance. For some individuals or organizations, these transition periods may become crises that contribute to distress. One particularly important transition period is the change from active work life to retirement, which is a stressful transition for most individuals, although it need not be distressful (D. T. Hall, 1976; J. F. Quick, 1990). How individuals and their organizations manage this transitional factor influences not only the individual's stress with regard to the experience but also the stress of others in the individual's work environment.

Summary

This chapter focused on four major categories of organizational stressors: physical demands, task demands, role demands, and interpersonal demands. Which set or sets of demands create the most stress differs among individuals. However, there are some conclusions that may be drawn from the chapter. First, role demands are dominant and pervasive sources of stress for many individuals working in large or small organizations. It is inevitable that conflicts and confusion at work will cause employees stress. Second, the amount of stress attributable to task and interpersonal demands may vary markedly by job and individual. Third, although physical demands such as extreme temperature and office designs are sources of organizational stress, steps toward mastery of the physical environment over the past century have contributed to reducing the amount of stress directly attributable to the physical setting.

Finally, in developing a stress profile for an individual, it is important to consider a number of unique life demands that are beyond those originating in an organization. Of particular importance are such extraorganizational stressors as the general business climate (which may affect job security), family considerations (which may create conflicts with one's work role), commuting and travel activities (which can increase one's sense of being hassled), and social change. In addition, there may be transitional factors, such as impending retirement, that contribute to an individual's stress. Therefore, a number of sources of stressors, including the organizational ones discussed in this chapter, must be considered in accurately determining an individual's stress profile.

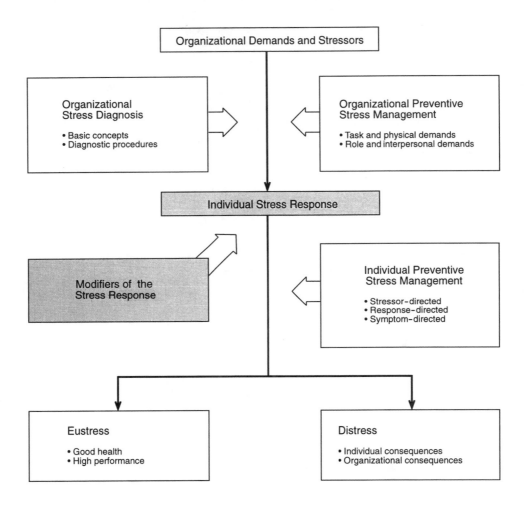

3

The Stress Response
and Its Modifiers

The diverse organizational demands and stressors described in chapter 2 lead to one common result: the triggering of a stereotypical psychophysiological reaction known as the stress response. Each individual exhibits the same basic response, although the immediate and long-term consequences of the stress response vary greatly among individuals. This variance across individuals is influenced by a number of modifiers of the stress response. These modifiers affect whether the stress response is channeled into positive and constructive outcomes (eustress) or negative and destructive outcomes (distress). The individual consequences of stress and individual distress, which may be behavioral, psychological, or medical, are discussed in chapter 4, and the organizational consequences of stress and organizational distress, which have direct and indirect costs, are discussed in chapter 5.

This chapter contains two major sections. First is a review of the psychophysiology of the stress response. Second is a discussion of individual and interpersonal modifiers of the stress response and its consequences. Figure 3.1 illustrates the pivotal role that the individual stress response plays in the organizational stressor–individual distress connection. As depicted in the figure, organizational stressors trigger the individual stress response, which may lead to one of three categories of individual distress or, alternatively, to eustress. The figure depicts 10 individual modifiers of the stress response. These modifiers influence individual vulnerability and whether the stress response leads to healthy or unhealthy consequences. The focus in this chapter is on the psychophysiology of the stress response and its modifiers.

The Psychophysiology of the Stress Response

When confronted with news reports and journal articles describing the spectrum of conditions that have been associated with stress and stressful events, it is reasonable to ask, "How can this be? How can accidents, heart attacks, and diabetes *all* be associated with something such as stress?" Inevitably, the answer is found in the biological and psychological linkages that govern humans' inner workings. Through the work of Walter B. Cannon, Stewart Wolf, Hans Selye, and other medical scientists and students of psychosomatic medicine, many of these linkages are now known.

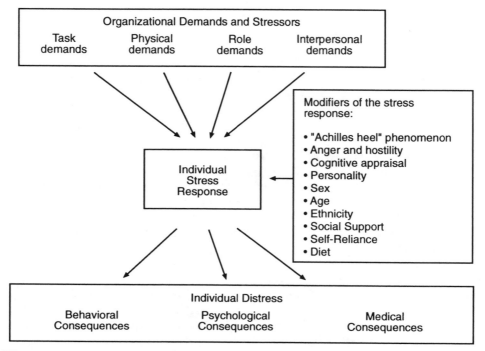

Figure 3.1. The stress response and its modifiers.

As indicated in chapter 1, the stress response consists of a generalized pattern of psychophysiological (mind–body) reactions. The response is generalized in that its pattern is not determined by the individual stressor or the individual being stressed. The individual experiences a generalized mobilization, resulting from the combined actions of the sympathetic nervous system and the endocrine (hormone) system, as a result of the response.

Many aspects of the mind–body response are familiar. Imagine, for example, that it is the early 1980s and you have just taken over Chrysler Corporation, which is having financial difficulty. You have a host of ideas on how to save the company, but you know cost cutting is important and that means releasing thousands of the more than 125,000 employees. You are confident about the future of the *new* Chrysler Corporation, but inevitably many individuals will be terminated in the process and many more will be upset; healing the wounds is not going to be an easy process (Noer, 1993). Not everyone will agree with your recommended solutions or with your plan of action to address current problems. In fact, some may be irate about certain of your ideas.

While you are looking over your notes, one of your officers is calling for order and beginning to introduce you. In about 30 seconds you will be standing in front of these employees with only your notes. If you pause and observe your body, you notice a sense of pounding in your chest: your heart is beating about 120 times a minute, rather than its usual 60 times, and each beat is more powerful as it raises your blood pressure. Your breathing is deeper yet somewhat tighter. Your stomach is a bit queasy; you are aware of a feeling of gnawing in the pit of your stomach. Despite the air conditioning, your brow and palms are sweating, moistening your scribbled notes.

As you step to the center, you realize that your mouth is dry, or cottony. You take a sip of water and raise the glass with a slightly tremulous hand. You clear your throat and begin to speak, focusing all your attention on the audience and the comments you are about to make. Your muscles are tense as you rock forward on your feet.

What you are experiencing is the normal response to an emergency or stressful situation. This response is sometimes called the *fight-or-flight response*. At this point, the flight option probably feels extremely attractive. Through biological mechanisms that developed in humans' primitive past, your body is preparing for a physical response to a challenging situation.

The stress response consists of a well-organized series of events involving the sympathetic nervous system and the endocrine (hormonal) system. The anatomy of the stress response is summarized in Figure 3.2. Our basic understanding of the role of the sympathetic nervous system and, in particular, the role of adrenaline comes from the work of the physician-researcher Walter B. Cannon and his colleagues at Harvard University (Cannon, 1994). Much of the information regarding the role of the endocrine system is provided by Selye's research (Selye, 1976b). Asterita (1985) provided a detailed and thorough treatment of the physiology of stress, with special reference to the neuroendocrine system.

The four combined effects of the sympathetic and endocrine responses to stress are as follows:

1. To redirect blood flow to the muscles and brain and away from the skin, intestines, and other vegetative organs
2. To mobilize glucose and fatty acids from storage sites and pour them into the bloodstream to provide readily available fuel for the body
3. To increase alertness through a sharpening of the sensory processes, such as vision and hearing
4. To reduce immune system functioning, restorative processes, and less emergent activities, such as digestion

These responses are highly adaptive in preparation for physical challenges, such as attack by wild animals or warring neighbors, or psychological challenges, such as legal debates in a court of law. As seen in chapter 4, however, these responses may be highly maladaptive when engaged in for too long a time, with too much intensity, or with too great a frequency. In particular, chronic stressors and psychosocial demands can affect the sympathetic nervous system and endocrine system, in turn influencing the immune system, thereby providing shared mechanisms that may affect disease susceptibility and progression across the broad spectrum of disorders identified in chapter 4 (Kiecolt-Glaser & Glaser, 1995).

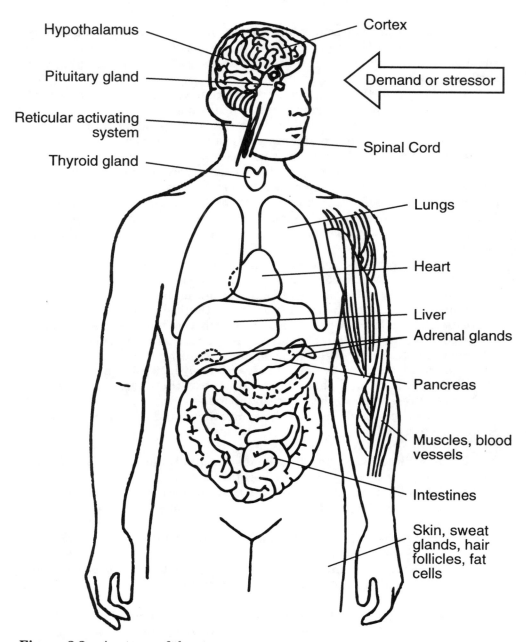

Figure 3.2. Anatomy of the stress response.

The Sympathetic Nervous System

The human nervous system has two major divisions: the somatic nervous system, which controls the skeletal muscles, and the autonomic nervous system, which controls the visceral organs. The actions of the autonomic nervous system were once thought to be entirely involuntary. It is now known that some actions of the autonomic nervous system may be voluntarily controlled. Nevertheless, basic life functions such as heartbeat, blood pressure, digestion, and breathing are maintained by the autonomic nervous system without conscious effort.

The autonomic nervous system is further divided into the sympathetic nervous system, which is responsible for activating functions such as the stress response, and the parasympathetic nervous system, which stimulates vegetative or reparative activities as well as the relaxation response, which may be thought of as a way to turn off the stress response.

Figure 3.3 summarizes the organization of the sympathetic nervous system and describes its major actions. Sympathetic activity is caused by the release of catecholamines, primarily adrenaline and noradrenaline, into the bloodstream. Catecholamine release has a direct, activating effect on the central nervous system and, in particular, the reticular activating system (RAS), or reticular formation. This structure has a deep, central location in the brain, and in terms of evolution it is one of the oldest parts of the brain. Stimulation of the RAS leads to the awake, alert state that usually occurs in stressful situations.

The Endocrine System

The second major system that is involved in the stress response is the endocrine, or hormonal, system. Hormones are, in essence, chemical messengers released by specific organs that travel in the bloodstream and stimulate specific responses by the target organs. The most important stress hormones are adrenocorticotrophic hormone (ACTH), cortisol (a form of cortisone), glucagon, adrenaline, and noradrenaline. Adrenaline and noradrenaline serve both as transmitters for the sympathetic nervous system and as hormones in their own right. Thyroid hormone, growth hormone, and aldosterone are also stimulated by stress, but their primary role is to serve other functions.

Within seconds after an individual has been presented with a condition or event that is perceived as stressful, a message is transmitted from the cortex to the hypothalamus and finally to the pituitary gland, a pea-sized organ located behind the eyes. The pituitary releases ACTH, which travels in the bloodstream to the adrenal cortex. There, ACTH stimulates the conversion of cholesterol to steroid hormones and the release of cortisol and similar steroids in the hormone group known as glucocorticoids. Figure 3.2 illustrates this sequence.

Cortisol acts on a variety of organs; its major effect is to increase the supply of glucose and fatty acids in the bloodstream. It stimulates the liver to produce and release glucose, stimulates fat cells to release fat, and causes tissues such as skin to consume less glucose. Cortisol also has several other effects on the body, some of which can be harmful. It causes the breakdown of protein for use as energy, inhibits immunity and inflammatory responses, shrinks lymphoid tissue (like the glands in the neck that swell with infection), and weakens bones. Moderate levels of cortisol

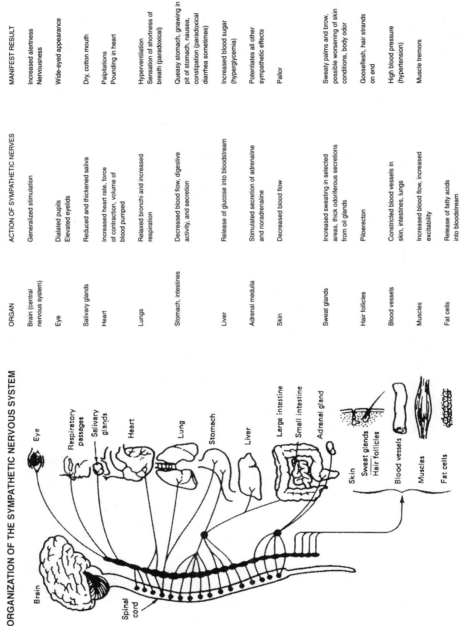

Figure 3.3.   Organization and action of the sympathetic nervous system.

can strengthen muscle contraction, but prolonged or excessively high levels can weaken muscles. Cortisol in large doses, such as those used to treat inflammatory diseases, can also cause psychosis or other mental changes.

Glucagon, like insulin, is released from the pancreas. It stimulates the release of blood glucose and fatty acids. In addition, it causes a slight increase in the rate and strength of the heartbeat.

When ACTH acts on the adrenal cortex, it also causes the release of aldosterone and related hormones known as mineralocorticoids. Mineralocorticoids help to regulate blood pressure by causing the kidney to retain salt and thereby increase blood pressure. Although ACTH is not the primary stimulant for aldosterone release, persistently high levels of ACTH can lead to increased blood pressure.

The sympathetic nervous system and the endocrine system work together to mobilize the body's various resources. With regard to the immediate behavioral and psychological consequences of stress, the heightened alertness and sense of apprehension that result from increased adrenaline are the predominant effects. However, it is the cardiovascular and metabolic effects of stress that lead to many of the adverse medical consequences.

Modifiers of the Stress Response

Figure 3.1 shows that a range of organizational demands and stressors may lead to a variety of behavioral, psychological, or medical consequences under the rubric of individual distress by way of the individual stress response. But how is it that the stress of shift work, for example, may lead to alcoholism in one individual and hypertension in another? Why do some individuals develop recurrent ulcers, whereas other individuals never develop ulcers? Why do some individuals in high stress, demanding jobs survive and thrive and others become distressed, almost from Day 1? The answers to these and related questions may lie in the modifiers of the individual's response to stress. Important individual and interpersonal differences influence individual vulnerability and help account for significant portions of the variance in these diverse results.

Selye (1976c) identified two categories of such modifiers, internal conditioning factors and external conditioning factors. Internal conditioning factors include such variables as family history and behavioral patterns, past experiences, cognitive functioning, age, sex, and personality. Selye (1976c) noted that "heredity and past experiences have some trace, some 'tissue memories,' which influence the way we react to things (p. 123)." In addition to the internal factors, there are external conditioning factors such as diet, climate, drugs, interpersonal relationships, and social support.

Social scientists and medical researchers have not sorted out all the complex relationships that determine the relative importance of the various modifiers of the response to stress. Indeed, the importance of many of these modifiers is only recently becoming recognized and understood. A better understanding of these modifiers and of individual vulnerability may help pinpoint those who are at greatest risk (Kiecolt-Glaser & Glaser, 1995). This section of the chapter discusses the 10 modifiers of the response to stress noted in Figure 3.1.

In thinking about the dynamics of the stress response, the distinction between modifiers of the stress response and coping mechanisms or intervention techniques is not always clear-cut. However, modifiers may be considered preexisting conditions or characteristics that influence the way in which a person responds in stressful conditions, and some of the modifiers are modifiable themselves by the individual. For example, although an individual may not be predisposed to hardiness or self-reliance, these attributes may be enhanced through effortful skill development. Coping mechanisms and intervention techniques are considered in chapters 11, 12, and 13.

The Achilles Heel Phenomenon

Part of the explanation for different patterns of distress lies in individual response specificity and vulnerability. The "Achilles heel," or "organ inferiority," hypothesis was developed in part through the work of Harold Wolff, a pioneer in psychosomatic medicine, in the 1950s. He and others since have suggested that there is an individual response stereotype whereby each individual reacts to stress with a particular pattern of psychophysiological responses. On the basis of his work, Wolff (1953) concluded the following:

> An individual may have been a potential "nose reactor" or "color reactor" all his life without ever actually having called upon a particular protective pattern for sustained periods because he did not need to. A given protective pattern may remain inconspicuous during long periods of relative security, and then with stress, becomes evident as a disorder involving the gut, the heart and vascular system, the vasorespiratory system, the skin or general metabolism. (p. 35)

Medical research supports this hypothesis. Studies have shown that individuals with stomach ulcers tend to respond to stress with gastric secretion (Wolff, 1953), that individuals with diabetes respond to stress with greater changes in blood glucose than do normal individuals (Hinkle & Wolf, 1952), and that individuals with cardiovascular disease show greater variability in heart rate and respiration than do other people (Masuda, Perko, & Johnston, 1972). The influence of family medical history was clearly demonstrated in a study of hypertensive and nonhypertensive people. Rise in blood pressure in response to three different stressors (a frustration task, intravenous injection of normal saline, and a cold stimulus test) was greater not only in hypertensive patients but also in normal persons with a family history of hypertension (Shapiro, 1961).

The study of family history leads to the identification of a possible

Achilles heel for a particular individual (Krause, 1994). This does not mean a person is predestined to succumb to heart disease or cancer because there is evidence of one or the other in the family history. However, the presence of these health problems establishes a risk factor to be monitored. After learning of the presence of a health risk factor in one's family history, some people wrongfully conclude, for example, that "if my father died of a heart attack at age 48, so will I." In most cases, family history represents only a *predisposing* influence—possibly a necessary but by itself not a sufficient condition for the development of an illness. Family history does not make family illness inevitable! In fact, the whole second half of this book addresses a wide range of ways that preventive stress management can help individuals and organizations reengineer their behavior so that distress is not an inevitable outcome.

Anger and Hostility

Two experienced cardiologists, Milton Friedman and Ray Rosenman, began to recognize a pattern in the behavior of the coronary patients they were treating in the late 1950s. In the years since then, the Type A behavior pattern (TABP) has been more clearly defined, and its relation to coronary artery disease has been extensively studied. Competitive overdrive, devotion to work, time urgency, anger, and hostility are the predominant features of the pattern. Friedman and Rosenman (1974) defined the Type A behavior pattern as an "action-emotion complex that can be observed in any person who is *aggressively* involved in a *chronic, incessant* struggle to achieve more and more in less and less time, and if required to do so, against the opposing efforts of other things or other persons" (p. 84; italics in original). TABP results from an interaction of specific personality characteristics and an environmental challenge or stressor. Booth-Kewley and Friedman (1987) suggested that TABP increases the risk of coronary heart disease (CHD). Suls and Wan's (1989) meta-analysis found that Type A individuals were more distressed than their Type B counterparts. In their study of workers in Israel, Kushnir and Melamed (1991) found that high strain jobs combining high workload and low perceived control were stressful for Type A but not for Type B individuals.

TABP is also a response to a challenge in the environment. In the absence of a challenging situation, Type A behavior patterns may not be manifested. As Friedman and Rosenman (1974) pointed out, an environmental challenge serves as a fuse that ignites Type A behavior patterns and causes an explosion. It is the interaction of specific personality characteristics and an environmental challenge, usually a stressor of some sort, that results in the Type A pattern.

The complement to the Type A pattern is the Type B pattern, characterized by a less harried, less competitive existence. Type B individuals are equally intelligent and may be just as ambitious as those who are Type A, but they approach their life in a more measured way.

Working independently during the same time, Stewart Wolf identified coronary-prone behavior as the Sisyphus reaction (1960). Wolf (1986) used as his interpretative model Sisyphus, king of Corinth, who was condemned to the lower world where he had to roll up hill a huge marble block that, once it reached the top, always rolled down again. This pattern of continuous, unsuccessful effortful activity well characterized the coronary-prone individual's striving against real or imagined odds coupled, irrespective of the outcome, with the inability to relax and enjoy the satisfaction of achievement. The Sisyphus reaction and TABP are closely similar descriptions of a coronary-prone person. Rosch (1983) notes that in earlier times, Von Dusch (1868) had called attention to excessive involvement in work and Osler (1910) identified time urgency as contributors to cardiovascular problems.

Early research showed a striking relationship between the Type A behavior pattern and the occurrence of heart attacks and coronary deaths. More recent studies have begun to clarify the mechanisms by which these personality traits lead to heart disease. For example, in a study of 236 managers sampled from 12 Canadian firms, Howard, Cunningham, and Rechnitzer (1976) found that Type A managers had higher blood pressure and cholesterol levels, were more frequent smokers, and had less interest in exercise than those who were Type B. Other studies have found that Type A individuals have a higher resting pulse and catecholamine excretion rate during waking hours. Therefore, these individuals incorporate previously discussed risk factors in their daily living.

Even when blood pressure, smoking, cholesterol and other known risk factors are taken into consideration, Type A individuals have 1.5–2 times the risk of heart attack in comparison with Type B individuals. The most convincing evidence comes from the Western Collaborative Group Study (WCGS), a long-term study of 3,524 men in the San Francisco Bay area. At the end of 8.5 years of study, the men judged at the outset to be Type A had twice the rate of primary coronary heart disease and an even higher rate of recurrent coronary events than did Type B individuals. These differences remained even after statistical adjustment for all other risk factors, and the relative risk was even greater for younger men.

Although Type A behavior pattern constitutes an important cardiac risk factor, more recent research has attempted to isolate the lethal component of the behavior pattern. Anger and hostility have been set against time urgency for acceptance as the explanatory, active ingredients in TABP that contribute to cardiovascular problems. Although some conceptual ambiguity exists concerning anger, hostility, and aggression (Spielberger, Krasner, & Solomon, 1988), Wright (1988) has pointed to anger and hostility, rather than time urgency, as the lethal ingredient in TABP. Barefoot, Dahlstrom, and Williams' (1983) 25-year study of hostility in 255 medical students further supports the notion that the anger and hostility component is the lethal component of TABP. Additional support comes from Spielberger (1991), who found that high levels of experienced or expressed anger interfered with interpersonal relationships, and caused psychological distress and physical disorders.

Cognitive Appraisal

R. S. Lazarus (1967; Lazarus & Folkman, 1984) drew attention to the importance of an individual's cognitive appraisal in influencing the degree to which that individual experienced a stressor as subjectively stressful, or threatening. The cognitive appraisal process is the platform on which subsequent emotion-focused and problem-focused coping may occur. R. S. Lazarus (1991) proposed that cognitions and emotions are linked in an ongoing evaluation of stressors as well as reaction to these stressors, hence forming an interactionist or transactional definition of the stress process (R. S. Lazarus et al., 1985). A cognitive–affective approach to understanding individual differences in stress propensity and strain response was formulated by Wofford and Daly (in press) within the domain of cognitions and emotions. Wofford and Daly's conceptualization views the cognitive–affective conceptualization as a mediating process in the stressor–strain linkage. From a psychological perspective, cognitive appraisal influences an individual's judgment and reactivity to stressors. However, as Wofford and Daly (in press) implied, there is not a clean separation of the psychological and physiological in the cognitive domain. In the physiological area, Schwartz, Pickering, and Landsbergis (1996) postulated that physiological susceptibility is a key variable moderating the perceived stress–blood pressure response linkage. What is unresolved is whether there is an individual difference variable that moderates or mediates the linkages between the stressor, the stress response, and strain reactions.

Personality

Rather than treating personality as a global moderating variable, as suggested in Figure 3.1, it is helpful to look at five personality variables that act as moderators of the response to stress. These variables are locus of control, hardiness, optimism–pessimism, negative affectivity, and self-esteem. Other personality traits that have been associated with individual responses to organizational stress include tolerance for ambiguity (Ivancevich & Matteson, 1980), anxiety (Chan, 1977), introversion–extraversion, flexibility–rigidity, and dogmatism (Brief, Schuler, & Van Sell, 1981). Common to all these traits is the fact that the presence or absence of the trait increases or decreases the likelihood that a particular event or condition is perceived as a stressor.

Locus of control. In their extensive review of the literature on personality as a moderator of the stress–distress relationship, Cohen and Edwards (1989) found generalized expectancies of control to be the construct with the most powerful results. Generalized expectancies of control are most often operationalized and discussed as locus of control, which refers to the extent to which individuals perceive that they have control over any situation. Internally oriented individuals believe that their decisions and their actions influence what happens to them. Externally oriented individuals, in contrast, tend to believe that rewards or positive reinforcements are beyond their control and not contingent on their actions; they are believers in luck or fate.

When the two types of individuals face a potentially stressful situation, their responses appear to be different. "Internals," perceiving themselves to have greater control, tend to be less threatened than "externals" by stressful situations and conditions and, therefore, experience fewer adverse reactions. They may, however, experience more anxiety in situations in which they, in fact, have less control.

The impact of locus of control on stressful occupational events was illustrated by C. R. Anderson's study (1977) of 102 owner-managers of small businesses in a small Pennsylvania community that was extensively damaged by a flood. Following the flood, the internally oriented managers responded in a more task-oriented way and demonstrated less stress. The externals responded with anger, greater anxiety, and hostility. Although the concept of perceived personal control does not indicate why one individual responds to stress with a headache and another with increased smoking, it provides insight into why the same events appear stressful to some individuals and not to others.

Hardiness. People who have hardy personalities resist strain reactions when subjected to stressful events more effectively than do people who are not hardy (Kobasa, 1988). Maddi and Kobasa (1984) focused their primary attention on the hardy executive in an original study of 200 Illinois Bell Telephone male middle- and upper-level executives who had experienced an unusually high number of stressful events during the AT&T divestiture period. This concept of personality hardiness was replicated in a similar study of 157 attorneys in general practice, many of whom had experienced significant work changes and, in some cases, severe home stressors. In both studies, personality hardiness was a moderator in the stress–distress linkage.

Personality hardiness is conceptualized with three components (Kobasa, 1988): commitment (versus alienation), control (versus powerlessness), and challenge (versus threat). *Commitment* is a curiosity and engagement with one's environment that leads to the experience of activities as interesting and enjoyable. *Control* is an ability to influence the process and outcomes of events, with an emphasis on one's own responsibility and personal choices. *Challenge* is the viewing of change as the normative mode of life and as a stimulus to personal development, which leads to the experience of activities with openness.

Persons with hardy personalities appear to use these three components actively to engage in transformational coping when faced with stressful events (Maddi, 1994, 1995). Transformational coping is a healthy preventive stress management skill discussed in chapter 11, whereas regressive coping is an unhealthy strategy that may lead to short-term stress reduction at the cost of long-term healthy life adjustment.

Optimism–pessimism. Optimism and pessimism are alternative styles people use to explain the good and bad events in their lives to themselves

(Seligman, 1990). These explanatory styles are habits of thinking learned over time, not inborn attributes. Pessimism was found to be a risk factor for depression, physical health problems, and low levels of achievement in a 52-year study of 30 people (Burns & Seligman, 1989). Furthermore, pessimism predicted poor health from age 45 through age 60 in a 35-year study of 99 Harvard College graduates (Peterson, Seligman, & Vaillant, 1988). Optimism is an alternative explanatory style that enhances physical health and achievement and averts susceptibility to depression. The extent to which hardiness and optimism, and possibly self-mastery (Marshall & Lang, 1990), are separable constructs is not empirically clear. For example, Kobasa, Maddi, and Courington (1981) found that the healthy group of executives in their Illinois Bell Telephone study expressed an optimistic point of view.

Optimistic people moderate distress by understanding the bad events and difficult times in their lives as temporary, limited, and caused by something other than themselves. Optimistic people face difficult times and adversity with hope. Whereas optimistic people take credit for the good events in their lives, pessimistic people take credit for the bad events. Optimists see these good events as more pervasive and generalized than do pessimists. Learned optimism is an approach to nonnegative thinking that is discussed in chapter 11.

Negative affectivity. Negative affectivity is implicated as a moderator that explains high stressor–distress correlations in cross-sectional research studies of stress. More specifically, high negative affectivity appears to inflate relationships between work-stress measures and psychological symptoms (Brief, Burke, George, Robinson, & Webster, 1988). Negative affectivity is a broad, pervasive personality variable that appears to influence significantly the psychological and emotional reactions individuals have to stress (Watson & Clark, 1984; Watson & Slack, 1993). It is a personality variable with variance such that individuals may be either low or high in negative affectivity. Although negative affectivity has not been empirically demonstrated to relate to pessimism, people high in this variable may be more pessimistic because they tend to focus on the negative aspects of the world and are predisposed to experience more distress and dissatisfaction.

Self-esteem. The most extreme demonstration of the relationship of self-esteem to individual responses to stressful situations was provided by Bettelheim's studies (1958) of individual behavior in concentration and forced-labor camps. In trying to discover why some of those who escaped death at the hands of their captors were able to maintain a degree of physical and mental health whereas others succumbed to mental and physical deterioration, Bettelheim concluded that a key factor was regaining the self-esteem initially shaken by the shock of the camps. At a less extreme level, individuals with high self-esteem are more likely to experience a decrease in psychological and somatic problems compared to individuals with low self-esteem (DeLongis, Folkman, & R. S. Lazarus, 1988).

Self-esteem also appears to be an important factor in the workplace. Research at the University of Michigan demonstrated that individuals reporting low self-esteem also perceived greater job overload (Mueller, 1965). The importance of self-esteem as a buffer against adverse stress reactions is demonstrated by several studies of occupational groups that indicate that coronary heart disease risk factors rise as self-esteem declines (J. S. House, 1972; Kasl & Cobb, 1970). There is also a caveat with regard to high self-esteem. Specifically, persons with inflated, unstable, or tentative self-esteem that is disputed by some person or circumstance may lash out with aggression or violence as a response to the threat (Baumeister, Smart, & Boden, 1996).

Sex

The role of sex in the stress process and its effect on relationships in the workplace continue to be important. A wide range of literature on women, work, and stress has emerged over the past decade (Barnett, Biener, & Baruch, 1987; Frankenhaeuser, Lundberg, & Chesney, 1991; Gearing, 1994; Long & Kahn, 1993). Earlier attention focused on the unique stressors for women in organizations, with a variety of books aimed at assisting the professional working woman (Adams & Lenz, 1979; Barnett & Baruch, 1978; Kinzer, 1979; Newton, 1979; Stewart, 1978). Despite the fact that more recent studies have focused on the relationship between gender, family roles, and occupational stressors, several basic questions remain unanswered (Keita & Hurrell, 1994). For example, do women suffer from greater occupational stress than men? Or do women cope with occupational stress differently from men?

Although these questions currently do not have clear or consistent answers, there is a set of epidemiological and social demographic data pointing to important differences between the sexes in their experience of distress (Matuszek, Nelson, & Quick, 1995). Specifically, whereas women report higher levels of distress at the less lethal end of the stress-related disorder spectrum, being male is riskier than being female on the basis of the lethal stress-related illnesses such as cardiovascular disease. Death rates at all ages are higher for men than for women, and the overall life expectancy for men is almost 8 years less than for women, even though women appear to experience significantly higher rates of nonfatal distress (Nelson, Hitt, & Quick, 1989; Verbrugge, 1989a; 1989b). Although organizational stressors, dispositional factors, and coping style differences may account for some of the distress variance between the sexes, they do not fully explain the differential death rates (Matuszek et al., 1995); genetic and hormonal differences between the sexes are important considerations in explaining the differential death rates (Ramey, 1990).

Research before 1990 found that female managers smoked more than women in other occupational groups and more than their male counterparts (B. Jacobson, 1981); that female executives took significantly more tranquilizers, antidepressants, and sleeping pills than male executives

(Cooper & Melhuish, 1980); and that the proportion of women alcoholics more than doubled between the early 1960s and late 1970s (Cooper & Davidson, 1982). Studies performed subsequent to 1990 have added to this early research base (Frankenhaeuser, 1991; Ohlott, Ruderman, & McCauley, 1994; O'Leary-Kelly, Paetzold, & Griffin, 1995). Role stress and overload, occupational stereotypes, organizational politics, and sexual harassment are important considerations related to sex and gender in the workplace.

Role stress and overload. Role conflict, especially role and work overload, presents particular difficulties for working women (Frankenhaeuser, 1991; Jick & Mitz, 1985; Nelson & Quick, 1985). The basic conflict is between the traditional role of the woman as mother, homemaker, and wife and the contemporary role of the woman as a professional. Home—job conflict has been cited as a source of stress and obstacles for women's managerial success for over 30 years (Bowman, Worthy, & Greyser, 1965), and Frankenhaeuser (1991) recently found that women's higher total workload interferes with their "winding down" ability, inhibiting physical and mental health.

Even in families and social settings where the home and work roles are viewed as compatible, the demands of both roles may create role overload. Housekeeping activities, child care, and work demands coupled with a husband's low involvement in home management may present particular difficulties. A similar problem does not exist for men, who spend about half as much time on housework and shopping as women and have a lower total workload (Matuszek et al., 1995). The overload problem appears to be worse for women who have overcome the "glass ceiling" effect and reached upper management (*Decade of the Executive Woman*, 1993).

It is not surprising that role stress appears to have important organizational and individual consequences. Bhagat and Chassie (1981), for example, found that role stress was a strong predictor of organizational commitment in working women, second only to satisfaction with promotional opportunities. There is also some evidence to suggest that working women with several children are more likely to suffer from stress-related heart disease than are single working women or housewives with children (Brief et al., 1981).

Occupational stereotypes. Terborg (1977) identified a variety of studies documenting the pressures exerted by vocational counselors and family members to discourage women from pursuing occupations other than those traditionally assigned to women, such as school teacher. Although there have been changes in the past 20 years, a number of occupations continue to be dominated by one or the other sex. For example, nursing and secretarial jobs are traditionally stereotyped as female, whereas the positions of truck driver and business executive are traditionally stereotyped as male. Men and women who cross into occupations traditionally dominated by the opposite sex may find as much career satisfaction in these occupations as those of the opposite sex do, although their reasons or motivations may be different.

The existence of occupational stereotypes can provide at least two types of stress. The first is the stress of adhering to the stereotype and taking an undesirable and unsatisfying job. For example, a capable woman may feel her talents are underused in a particular secretarial job, but her own acceptance of occupational stereotypes or her employer's adherence to such stereotypes may prevent her from transferring to a potentially more satisfying job in a traditionally male occupation, such as technical or managerial work. The second type of stress might be experienced by a woman who accepted a traditionally male job as a manager. Successful managers have traditionally been described in masculine terms by both men and women (V. E. Schein, 1975). The female manager will feel pressure to meet the male stereotype standards rather than draw on her own unique gifts and abilities. A basic problem with stereotypes and between-sex differences is that they ignore the important within-group variance that exists for each sex.

Organizational politics. One study of 2,000 human resource professionals found that women experienced significantly more stress from organizational politics than did their male counterparts (Nelson, Hitt, & Quick, 1989). One of the important issues in organizational politics is access to informal power networks through which individuals are developed, selected, and advanced within an organization or profession. Although Ohlott et al. (1994) found few indications of blatant discrimination in their study, they postulated that women may be denied access to some important developmental opportunities available to men. Organizational politics and the informal organization are important considerations in gaining access to organizational resources necessary to manage effectively the demands of the work environment. These organizational resources include information, position, influence, and power. To the extent that women are denied access to these resources because of organizational politics, they become more vulnerable in the work environment.

Sexual harassment. As early as the 1970s, unwanted, repeated, and coercive sexual advances were reported by 70–90 percent of working women (Lindsey, 1977; MacKinnon, 1979). Although sexual harassment of employees by their supervisors has been officially considered a civil rights violation since 1980 and several states are moving to make sexual harassment a criminal violation, it continues as a problem in many work environments and is an important issue for both men and women (Keita & Hurrell, 1994). There are a number of problems researchers face in investigating sexual harassment, such as response bias. In addition, the practical problems women may encounter in efforts to end harassment include jeopardizing their jobs or becoming embroiled in frustrating and time-consuming bureaucratic or legal action. At its core, sexual harassment is an aggressive form of behavior (O'Leary-Kelly et al., 1995).

Age

The impact of stress on the individual may be influenced by the person's age in at least two ways. First, age may determine in part whether a given situation or condition is perceived as a stressor by an individual. Second, the individual's biological age may determine how the stress response is manifested.

The concept of career stages was introduced in chapter 2. Although career maturity need not correspond precisely to age, individuals at the same stage tend to be roughly within the same age range. The objectives are different at each stage, and therefore the types of events and conditions that are perceived as stressful are different.

As the body ages, the overt manifestations of stress may change. For example, in a highly stressful situation, such as the presentation of a deficit financial report to the board of directors, a young executive may respond with an imperceptible rise in pulse and blood pressure, whereas an older executive, with many years of elevated cholesterol level and cigarette smoking behind him, may experience severe chest pain or even a heart attack. Conversely, some ailments become less frequent with age. For example, slipped disks and the resulting back pain are less likely to occur among older workers.

Ethnicity

The American workforce is much more culturally and ethnically diverse in the 1990s than it was in the several previous decades. However, the United States is largely a land of immigrants, and the large migrations of Europeans to the eastern United States and Asians to the western United States, dating to the late 1800s, presented challenges for these ethnic minority groups as well as the society into which they immigrated. For example, language and communication were challenges for the Scots, Irish, and Hungarians who helped to build the steel industry in western Pennsylvania during the late 1800s and early decades of the 1900s. Taylor's (1911) scientific approach to management may be seen as an effort to create a standardized way of working for peoples from a wide variety of cultures and ethnic backgrounds to overcome language and communication barriers. Cultural and ethnic group differences have a complex and constantly changing impact on relationships in the workplace. Although there is an established knowledge base about cultural and ethnic group issues (e.g., Ford, 1976; Burack, Staszak, & Pati, 1972), little is currently known about the specific impact of workforce diversity on organizations or about the stress that such diversity imposes on members of different cultural and ethnic groups (Keita & Hurrell, 1994).

Blatant prejudice, like blatant sex discrimination against women, is the most obvious source of stress for those in minority ethnic groups. Although the civil rights legislation in the United States has taken aim at such discrimination and many African Americans have experienced significant progress occupationally over the past 3 decades, the impact of racist attitudes and behavior at work can still have an adverse effect. As in the case of women, role models may be helpful in mitigating the stress and strain associated with socioeconomic advancement. For example, General Colin Powell has been an excellent role model in the military.

Although much attention has been given for decades to African Americans as an important ethnic minority group, increasing attention is being devoted to Hispanics and other ethnic minority groups (Keita & Hurrell, 1994). Early research by Triandis, Feldman, Weldon, and Harvey (1974) focused on the in-group challenges for ethnic minorities and the distrust that may develop within a minority subculture. The suggestions emerging from this line of investigation included cross-cultural training of *both* minority and majority group members. Achieving ethnocultural pluralism is a challenge for everyone, and the American workplace is increasingly so characterized.

The educational system traditionally has fueled the progress and success of immigrants to the United States. This was true for Germans, Scots, and Irish in the early decades of this century. The challenge for African American, Hispanic, and other ethnic minority groups is gaining and maintaining access to the educational systems that lead to managerial and professional success within the society. At the managerial level, persons from ethnic minority groups who are not familiar with the norms and standards of the business world experience a disadvantage.

Performance evaluations are a major source of stress for many individuals, but for ethnic minority groups, the stress of these evaluations is sometimes exacerbated by the confusion that results from basing evaluations on nonwork behaviors. One early study of 48 black supervisors by Beatty (1973) found that employers tended to evaluate performance less on task-oriented behaviors related to the training program than on other behaviors demonstrated at work. The confusion and anguish generated by inconsistency or unexplainable subjectivity in performance appraisals are vividly described in E. W. Jones's (1973) autobiographical review of life as a rising black manager; it is as poignant today as when it was written nearly a quarter of a century ago.

E. W. Jones (1973) also described the difficulties black managers have because of lack of access to the informal organization, or network of informal personal contacts at work. Current research does not give a clear picture of how much this has changed over the past quarter of a century (Keita & Hurrell, 1994). Unfortunately, racial prejudice or simply a nonjudgmental discomfort with persons from ethnic minority groups may exclude minority group members from informal networks and relationships, thus limiting their access to the organizational resources necessary to manage effectively the demands of organizational life and to achieve success. As a result, the social support needed to deal with common demands, such as boundary-spanning activities and work overload, as well as the guidance needed to recognize and resolve role conflicts or ambiguity, is lacking. As Jones pointed out, lack of acceptance tends to amplify other shortcomings or difficulties.

Ethnic minority managers and supervisors may also suffer from lack of support from the formal organization. Affirmative action efforts may result in effective procedures for locating and recruiting minority supervisors but fail to recognize their unique, ongoing training and support needs. This situation leads to stress and strain for ethnic minority managers, who are already under pressure in a new position because of the inevitable visibility of their group membership. This high visibility simply magnifies the common demands of managerial jobs.

Social Support

Social isolation is a major risk factor for morbidity and mortality, and social support is the ameliorating moderator of this process (J. S. House, Landis, & Umberson, 1988). Immunological alterations resulting from social isolation may provide one possible physiological explanation of these results (Kiecolt-Glaser, Malarkey, Cacioppo, & Glaser, 1994); the link between personal relationships and immune function is one of the most robust findings in the field of psychoneuroimmunology (Kiecolt-Glaser & Glaser, 1992). Social support is more important as a moderator now, when traditional societal structures such as the extended family and the township are being attenuated and individual mobility continues to increase. J. S. House (1981) pointed out that social support comes in four forms: emotional, instrumental, informational, and appraisal. To these, J. C. Quick, Nelson, and Quick (1990) added protection from psychological, interpersonal, and physical stressors. Social support derives from a variety of social relationships at work, at home, and in the community. For example, although one's spouse may be the key source of emotional support, it is the supervisor who provides much informational and appraisal support at work.

The buffering effect. Social support appears to be beneficial primarily through its buffering effect (J. S. House, 1981). The individual's *existing* support system at work and at home may then be viewed as a wealth of resources that the individual may draw on in managing various stressful situations. Informational or instrumental resources help the individual meet the demands causing the stress, thereby reducing the level and intensity of the stress. Although there is a large body of research demonstrating the positive effects of social support on psychological and physical health, there is some research pointing to negative effects of unhealthy social relationships (J. D. Quick, Nelson, Matuszek, Whittington, & Quick, 1996).

Hence, social support is a key moderator of the stress–distress relationship, further contributing to the understanding of individual variations in the response to organizational stressors. Unlike some of the other moderators that influence individual responses to stress, additional social support may be engendered by management, and to the extent that this is possible, it can serve as an important preventive intervention. The use of social support as an organizational method of preventive stress management is discussed in chapter 11.

Peer group. Why do some people smoke more cigarettes when they are under stress, other people drink more alcohol, and still other people increase their lunch-hour athletic activities? Part of the answer may lie in the habits of the occupational peer group. It was noted previously that persons in certain occupations are prone to alcohol abuse. Similarly, there are differences in cigarette and drug consumption among various occupations. In one study, peer pressure was hypothesized to lead to increases in smoking behavior, which outweighed the positive effects of the social support network (Romano, Bloom, & Syme, 1991). One hypothesis, therefore, is that individuals are more likely to turn to alcohol under stress if their occupational peer group has a higher baseline level of alcohol use. Unfortunately, there is little evidence to support or refute this hypothesis. Future studies of organizational stress may shed more light on this possibility.

The peer group within an organization can be instrumental in easing and enhancing the adjustment of newcomers to the organization, as was seen in a study of 91 newcomers (Nelson & Quick, 1991). Peer groups and other social supports in the workplace may serve as secure forms of attachment.

Self-Reliance

Self-reliance refers to a healthy, secure, interdependent pattern of behavior related to how people form and maintain supportive attachments with others (Bowlby, 1982; J. C. Quick, Joplin, Nelson, & Quick, 1991). It is one distinguishing characteristic of healthy executives (J. C. Quick, Nelson, & Quick, 1990). The theoretical framework for self-reliance is attachment theory, and new research suggests that behavioral attachment patterns extend into adulthood in professional as well as personal relationships (Hazan & Shaver, 1990). Self-reliant people respond to stressful, threatening situations by reaching out to others appropriately. Self-reliance is a flexible, responsive strategy of forming and maintaining multiple, diverse relationships. Self-reliant people are confident, enthusiastic, and persistent in facing challenges. Hence, high levels of self-reliance help moderate the stress–distress relationship by dampening the conversion of stressor impacts on the individual into distressful consequences.

Individuals who are not self-reliant may engage in either or both of two alternative patterns of behavior. The two unhealthy, insecure patterns of behavior are counterdependence and overdependence. *Counterdependence* is an unhealthy, insecure pattern of behavior that leads to separation in relationships with other people. Counterdependent people draw into themselves when faced with stressful and threatening situations, attempting to exhibit strength and power. Counterdependence may be characterized as a rigid, dismissive denial of the need for other people in difficult and stressful times. Such people exhibit a fearless, aggressive, and actively powerful response to challenges. Unable to ask for appropriate help as needed, officer candidates in the military who failed to complete training successfully were significantly more counterdependent than their graduating counterparts (Joplin, Quick, Nelson, & Turner, 1995). *Overdependence* is also an unhealthy, insecure pattern of behavior. Overdependent people respond to stressful and threatening situations by clinging to other people in any way possible. Overdependence may be characterized as a desperate, preoccupied attempt to achieve a sense of security through relationships. Overdependent people exhibit an active but disorganized and anxious response to challenges. Overdependence prevents a person from being able to organize and maintain healthy relationships and thus creates much distress. For example, a prospective study of basic military trainees found that those who were unsuccessful in completing training were significantly more overdependent than their graduating counterparts (J. C. Quick, Joplin, Nelson, Mangelsdorff, & Fiedler, 1996).

Diet

Diet is another moderator of the response to stress. Balance in the diet helps to prevent stressors from becoming distress, and imbalance in the diet allows stressors to be converted into distress more easily. Diet has an impact on blood chemistry, weight, and energy level and reserves (C. L. Cooper, 1982). High sugar content in the diet can stimulate the stress response, and foods high in cholesterol can adversely affect blood chemistry. Good dietary practices contribute to a person's overall health, making the person less vulnerable to distress. Ornish (1990) emphasized the role of fat in the diet as a contributor to heart disease, setting forth diet plans for both the prevention and reversal of cardiovascular disease without using surgery or drug therapy.

With or without the presence of stressors, most dietary extremes are associated with adverse health effects. Extreme weight reduction, as sometimes seen in anorexia nervosa, can be associated with specific nutritional deficiencies and, commonly, with temporary hormonal abnormalities. Overeating and the resulting obesity are, of course, associated with cardiac and respiratory ills. Moderation is clearly the healthiest route.

Diet and stress can interact in some rather striking ways. An individual predisposed to hypertension may be able to maintain normal blood pressure even under stress, but when high stress is combined with excess consumption of table salt, abnormally high blood pressure can result. Similarly, an individual predisposed to peptic ulcers may be free of symptoms until the stress of a report deadline combines with the ulcer-inducing effects of caffeinated drinks (coffee, tea, and many carbonated beverages), smoking, and alcohol, resulting in a typical ulcer or severe gastritis.

This phenomenon is illustrated by the case of Mr. A., a 58-year-old businessman who had occasional chest pain from mild heart disease but no previous stomach trouble. As the rush of Christmas orders accelerated and he became tense, he treated the resulting headaches with up to eight aspirin tablets each day. After attending several Christmas parties one weekend, at which he drank moderate amounts of Scotch, he developed some stomach discomfort and vomited up a small amount of fresh blood and clots. He was hospitalized for 2 weeks and treated for an acute bleeding ulcer, attributed by his doctors to the combination of stress, aspirin, and alcohol. During the hospitalization, he developed persistent chest pain, which was finally relieved when the anemia caused by his bleeding was treated with blood transfusions. Fortunately, he did not suffer a heart attack, and his ulcer healed. He did miss the rest of the Christmas business activity, however.

Other illnesses for which the impact of stress may be modified by dietary factors include diabetes (stress plus overeating or high consumption of sweets), the common cold (some high-risk individuals may benefit from vitamin C), and certain heartbeat irregularities (arrhythmias caused by caffeinated drinks).

Summary

The individual stress response is one of the best innate assets for dealing with legitimate emergencies and achieving peak performances in a wide variety of tasks and activities. When elicited too frequently, too intensely, or for too long a period of time, the stress response may lead to distress, which is a main concern of the next two chapters. The two main concerns of this chapter have been (a) an understanding of the stress response and its psychophysiological roots in the sympathetic nervous system and the endocrine (hormonal) system and (b) an appreciation for the range of modifiers of the response to stress that influence individual vulnerability.

Familiar signs of the stress response are pounding in the chest, palpitations, shortness of breath, gnawing feeling in the stomach, sweaty palms and brow, muscle tension, and nervousness. In addition, the blood pressure, heart rate, blood glucose, fatty acids in the blood, and stress hormones, such as cortisol, glucagon, and adrenaline, are elevated. All these signs of the stress response are normal ones to be expected in emergency and high performance situations. What is neither normal nor healthy is the individual distress that all too often results from stressful experiences. This individual distress may be manifested in the behavioral, psychological, or medical consequences discussed in chapter 4.

An apparent paradox is the observation that a wide variety of stressors can lead to a rather stereotyped psychophysiological stress response, which in turn may or may not be manifested in distressful consequences. The explanation for this paradox can be found, in part, in the modifiers of the response to stress. Among these modifiers are the Achilles heel phenomenon, anger, cognitive appraisal, coronary-prone behavior patterns, personality differences, sex, age, ethnicity, social support, self-reliance, and diet.

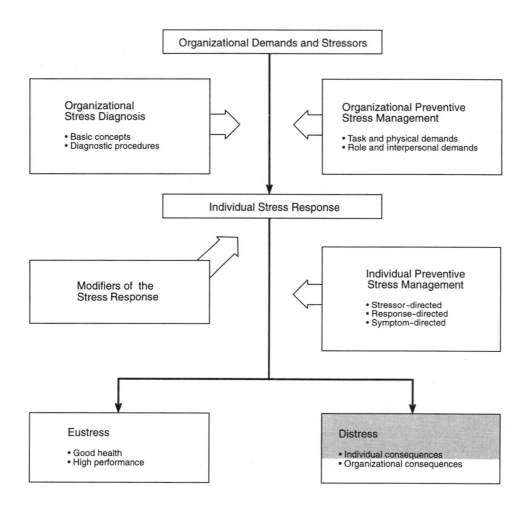

4

Individual Consequences of Stress

Properly channeled, the stress response contributes to a state of well-being by stimulating productivity and supporting optimum performance. When the stress response is elicited too intensely or too frequently and the individual is unable to find a suitable outlet, however, the result is individual *distress*. Consider, for example, the following incidents:

- Jerry R. Junkins, Chairman, CEO, and President of Texas Instruments Inc., was in the early stages of a major corporate downsizing when he suffered a heart attack on Wednesday, 29 May 1996, while riding in a car in Stuttgart, Germany. He died at age 58 with no known heart problems.
- Admiral Jeremy M. Boorda, Chief of Naval Operations, committed suicide on Thursday, 16 May 1996, apparently in response to pressures he felt related to investigative reporting of his past combat record. He was 56 years old at the time of his death.
- W. Howard Beasley III, Chairman, CEO, and President of Lone Star Technologies, Inc., was transforming the company when he took a medical leave in 1989 because of Hodgkins lymphoma. He died Thursday, 1 November 1990, of lymphoma-related pneumonia at age 44.

Are these events the consequences of organizational stress? Perhaps, at least in part. Death from suicide or a heart attack may be the extreme individual consequence of poorly managed stress. Alcohol abuse, burnout, and chronic back pain are other individual consequences.

The manifestation of distress varies with the individual and may include the behavioral, psychological, and medical consequences shown in Figure 4.1. This chapter reviews adverse individual consequences that have been associated with stressful life events and, in some cases, with organizational stress in particular.

Behavioral Consequences

The behavioral changes that can accompany rising levels of stress include increased cigarette smoking, alcohol and drug abuse, accident proneness, violent behavior, and eating disorders. Each of these behavioral changes can, in turn, have an important health impact.

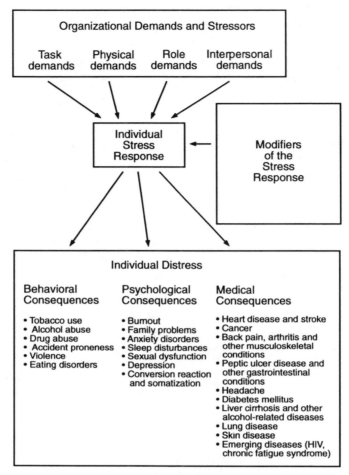

Figure 4-1. Individual distress: Behavioral, psychological, and medical consequences.

Tobacco Use

Cigarette smoking and the use of other tobacco products constitute the single most devastating preventable cause of death in the United States. One quarter to one third of all deaths from coronary heart disease (CHD) and cancer are attributable to smoking. In the United States, the annual excess mortality from cigarette smoking is estimated to be 390,000, including 138,000 deaths from cancer, 115,000 deaths from CHD, and 57,000 deaths from chronic bronchitis and emphysema (Department of Health and Human Services [DHHS], 1986). Smoking also causes immeasurable suffering and disability from chronic bronchitis and emphysema, angina pectoris, nonfatal strokes, and other tobacco-induced diseases.

During the 1980s, a considerable body of research demonstrated the adverse health consequences of "passive smoking": the involuntary exposure of nonsmokers to tobacco smoke from smokers in a closed environment (DHHS, 1986). This research has led to increased restrictions on public smoking in the United States and recently in other countries.

The total annual direct cost of smoking was estimated to be $34 billion in 1995; the indirect cost of lost productivity was estimated to be $18 billion (DHHS, 1987a). Smoking in the United States has decreased by an average of 0.5% per year since 1964. Between 1974 and 1985, the gap between smoking rates for men and women narrowed, as more women than men started smoking and fewer women quit (Fielding, 1992). In 1987, one third of adult men aged 25–64 and nearly 30% of women in this age range still smoked.

Cigarette consumption may serve as pleasure smoking, social smoking, or stress smoking. There are occupational differences in the frequency of smoking that may represent in part social influences in the work environment, but stress is also an important factor. In a survey of 12,000 professional men in 14 occupational categories, Russek (1965) found 46% of men in high stress occupations to be smokers versus 32% in low stress occupations. Both stress and cigarette consumption were related to the incidence of heart disease. Similarly, in a study of U.S. Navy petty officers, Conway, Vickers, Ward, and Rahe (1981) found a significant correlation between occupational stress and cigarette consumption. Smoking and alcohol consumption both increase with unemployment (Wilson & Walker, 1993).

Studies have not only confirmed the relationship between smoking and stress, but also shown that the tendency to increase smoking under stress appears to be proportional to the number of stressors present within a given period of time (Hillier, 1981; Lindenthal, Myers, & Pepper, 1972; Parrott, 1995).

Changing social attitudes and data on the adverse effects of passive smoking have led to a prohibition of smoking in public places and greater restrictions on smoking at the workplace. These changes, combined with more effective behavioral and clinical programs, are likely to lead to an even greater reduction in smoking.

Alcohol Abuse

Excessive alcohol consumption is a major personal and societal hazard. About 10 million Americans and up to 10% of the workforce are alcoholics. Alcohol consumption is a major factor in one half of this country's motor vehicle fatalities and homicides, one third of the reported suicides, the majority of the nation's 30,000 annual deaths from liver cirrhosis, and a substantial number of serious birth defects (Trice & Roman, 1981).

The problem of alcohol abuse is also costly in economic terms. The cost of alcohol-related problems in the United States was estimated to be nearly $120 billion in 1983, including about $90 billion in lost productivity due to disability and death (DHHS, 1987b). Alcohol abuse also contributes to occupational injuries, although the magnitude of the contribution has not been quantified (Stallones & Kraus, 1993).

Alcohol abuse varies widely from occupation to occupation. For the assembly-line worker or night guard, stressed by the boredom of the job, alcohol addiction may become part of the daily work routine. Drinking may begin before the workday even starts, with routine drinking leading to increased accident rates and decreased productivity. For the white collar worker, the impact of alcohol may be more insidious, affecting work performance and judgment. These subtler effects contribute to a downward spiral of stress, alcohol consumption, declining performance, increasing stress, increasing alcohol consumption, and so on. Without the intervention of a supervisor, coworker, or family member (who demonstrates true concern by speaking out rather than overlooking the problem), this downward spiral may continue until personal or professional self-destruction occurs.

Occupation may be one of the most influential factors in determining drinking habits and consequent alcohol-related problems (Ojesjo, 1980; Plant, 1979b). Various explanations have been given for the strong relationship between occupation and alcohol use, including differences in social pressures and social controls that allow or encourage drinking within some groups, recruitment and selection trends that attract alcoholism-prone individuals to certain careers, and variations in occupational stress (Cosper, 1979; Plant, 1979a). Several studies have linked job stress to alcohol misuse among police officers, customer-service staff, and retail workers (Jones & Boye, 1992). For police officers, alcohol consumption during working hours increased with reported measures of job stress.

Whatever other occupational factors influence drinking behavior, organizational stress must be considered a major contributor, and the individual consequences of alcohol abuse should be seen in part as stress-related illness.

Drug Abuse

Alcoholism continues to be the most devastating form of drug abuse, but abuse of illegal "recreational" drugs (cocaine, marijuana, and a variety of other natural and synthetic drugs) and prescription drugs also takes a major toll. At any one time, 1–2% of the U.S. population have a drug abuse problem that interferes with daily living, and about 6% of the population have a significant drug abuse–drug dependency problem during their lifetime. The annual cost to the United States of drug use was estimated at $75 billion in 1988, including costs owing to lost productivity, crime, treatment, and social welfare programs (Schuster & Kilbey, 1992). When drug abuse begins to affect work performance and individual relationships, it becomes part of the same downward spiral that characterizes alcohol abuse.

Family history, current family situation, economic status, age, peer drug use, and psychological factors have all been implicated in the initiation or continuation of drug abuse. Rates of drug abuse appear to be related to the number of risk factors. Employment and marriage both have been positively associated with decreased drug use in young adults (Schuster & Kilbey, 1992).

Job stress has been associated with a higher incidence of absenteeism owing to illicit drug use and greater on-the-job use of illicit drugs (Jones & Boye, 1992). Reports of the use of marijuana, cocaine, and other recreational drugs by armed services personnel underline the vulnerability to drug abuse of individuals in repetitive or monotonous jobs.

Accident Proneness

A subtle but potentially important effect of organizational stress is to predispose the individual to both industrial and nonindustrial accidents: "A person under stress is an accident about to happen" (Warshaw, 1979, p. 193). The annual cost of work accidents has been estimated at $48.5 billion (National Safety Council, 1990).

The role of stress in industrial accidents has long been noted anecdotally, but the classic studies of the accident process were conducted in the mid-1960s by two Cleveland psychiatrists who reviewed about 300 cases of industrial accidents leading to disability (Hirschfeld & Behan, 1963, 1966). Stress was found not only to contribute significantly to the occurrence of an accident but also to slow the recovery process and prolong disability. A recent study of 833 employees at an industrial work site found the frequency of injuries at work to increase with stressful life events, especially in combination with low job satisfaction (Webb et al., 1994).

Other studies have shown that work-related stressful events often may immediately precede automobile and domestic accidents as well as industrial accidents (Whitlock, Stoll, & Rekhdahl, 1977). In addition, automobile drivers who had experienced recent social stress, including job stress, were found to be 5 times more likely to cause a fatal accident than drivers without such stress (Brenner & Selzer, 1969).

The potential benefits of stress management programs in accident reduction have been explored in several studies (Murphy, DuBois, & Hurrell, 1986; Steffy, Jones, Murphy, & Kunz, 1986).

Violence

Perhaps the most extreme but fortunately less common manifestation of stress is violence on the part of the stressed individual. Although current information on workplace violence is inconclusive, the data available confirm that workplace violence is a serious matter worthy of sustained attention (VandenBos & Bulatao, 1996). Occasional news stories record the more publicly visible episodes of violence: the overworked, unassertive secretary who, asked once too often to do too much in too short a time, sends the boss to an emergency room for stitches with a well-directed throw of an ashtray; the disgruntled graduate student who wounds the professor with a shot from a small service revolver; or the distraught assembly-line supervisor who returns at night after being fired to "torch" the former employer's factory.

Violence is responsible for 12% of all deaths in the workplace, and between 1980 and 1989, it was the leading cause of occupational death among women (Pastor, 1995). Violence by disgruntled employees and former employees appears to be on the increase. Assaults, harassment, threats, sabotage, and related nonlethal acts cost U.S. employers an estimated $4.2 billion per year. Job stress has been linked to violent on-the-job behavior among police officers, customer-service staff, and retail workers. For police officers, increased job stress has been correlated with the number of times an officer used his or her gun or club (Jones & Boye, 1992).

Violence includes assault, homicide, spouse abuse, sexual assault and rape, child abuse, and elder abuse. Recent discussions have emphasized the fact that violent behavior typically results from the interaction of multiple developmental, psychological, situational, economic, and other factors (Rosenberg & Fenley, 1991). Occupational stressors can be viewed as one of several categories of precipitating factors that can lead to violence in violence-prone individuals. In examining the dynamics of violence, Newman (1979) suggested that violence grows out of frustration. The frustration of natural urges and drives leads to aggression, which may be displaced from the original source of frustration. This is illustrated by the husband who becomes violent at home as a result of critical comments by a supervisor or other stressful events at the office.

The risk of work-related violence may be reduced through measures such as stress reduction programs, better preemployment screening, enforcement of nonharassment policies, employee assistance programs, better outplacement services, and employee education (Pastor, 1995).

Eating Disorders

Individuals may respond to stress with markedly increased or decreased appetite. Loss of appetite is a common symptom of depression in older people. Extreme weight loss may also be seen in younger women who have anorexia nervosa. People may respond to stress by overeating or by consuming high-fat foods such as those commonly found at fast-food chains.

Obesity (defined as body weight more than 20% above that in standard height–weight tables) is associated with higher rates of heart disease, diabetes, back and other musculoskeletal complaints, respiratory problems, and accidents. Genetic factors are now known to be critical determinants of obesity, but other important influences include dietary patterns; physical activity; and social, psychological, and developmental factors. Stressful life events can contribute to obesity and eating disorders, perhaps more so among women (Karlsson, Sjostrom, & Sullivan, 1995; Walcott-McQuigg, Sullivan, Dan, & Logan, 1995).

Psychological Consequences

Closely related to the behavioral consequences of distress are the psychological effects. Among the problems to consider are burnout, family problems, anxiety disorders, sleep disturbances, sexual dysfunction, depression, and psychogenic disability.

Burnout

Burnout, a concept dating to the late 1970s (Maslach, 1978), is a chronic pattern of negative affective responses that can result in reduced job satisfaction, reduced productivity, increased absenteeism, or increased turnover (Peters, Youngblood, & Greer, 1997). Burnout tends to occur in individuals in professions characterized by a high degree of personal investment in work, high performance expectations, and emotionally demanding interpersonal situations (Maslach, 1982; Cordes & Dougherty, 1993). Burnout is most frequently described as found among members of the helping professions, including doctors, nurses, therapists of various disciplines, police officers, teachers, and social workers (Burke & Richardsen, 1996).

Individuals with a strong commitment to work often derive much of their self-image and sense of worth from their occupation. This limits the amount of investment in recreational and family activities. When difficulties arise at work or there are limited rewards for increasing labor, burnout-prone individuals begin to invest even more time at work and further neglect outside supports.

Maslach (1982) described burnout as a process that typically proceeds through three phases: emotional exhaustion, depersonalization, and reduced personal accomplishment. Emotional exhaustion reflects a depletion of emotional resources and inability to give psychologically. Depersonalization, probably a coping mechanism, includes negative, cynical attitudes about the recipients of one's services. Finally, reduced personal accomplishment refers to decreased job satisfaction and a reduced sense of competence.

Burke and Richardsen (1996) noted that burnout is a process and that it is possible to intervene at any of several points in the process to reduce burnout and its adverse consequences. Several of the individual and organizational stress management techniques described in chapters 8, 9, 10, and 11 can be targeted toward burnout.

Family Problems

Early work on organizational stress and family problems focused on the working husband and on the impact of work life on family life. For example, Burke, Weir, and DuWors (1980) studied 85 senior male administrators and their wives. Increased levels of various specific work stressors were associated with decreased marital satisfaction and increased psychosomatic symptoms, smoking, and alcohol use among wives. The stress of responding to change at work was a particularly strong predictor of problems at home. Burke and associates (1979) also found that the wives of men who exhibited unbalanced professional striving and competitive overdrive reported greater levels of depression; less satisfaction, fewer friends and less contact with those friends; and more feelings of tension, anxiety, isolation, worthlessness, and guilt.

Similarly, in another early study, Handy (1978) looked at the marriages of 23 successful midcareer executives training at the Sloan Programme at the London Business School. He found four principal marital patterns as defined by the attitudes and values of each spouse. One low-stress pattern involved a husband who was a high achiever and a wife who played a caring, supportive role. In this traditional marriage, there was a "hidden contract" in which the wife derived security from her husband and functioned as the "support team" so that the husband could pursue his professional aspirations. Another relatively low-stress pattern involved spouses who were both achievement and dominance oriented, but who both valued a strong, supportive relationship. The highest-stress pattern involved spouses who were both achievement and dominance oriented, but who tended to act on their own without regard for the feelings of others.

Over the last decade, studies have focused on working women and have recognized that the work–family conflict is bidirectional. Work and family roles may conflict when work demands interfere with meeting family demands or when family demands impinge on work responsibilities (Greenhaus & Beutell, 1985). Work demands may be real and unavoidable or, as in the case of the workaholic, perceived demands that may be more controllable. A marriage may serve as a source of support to sustain one spouse through stress at work, or it may serve as a further source of stress and frustration. A critical factor is the marriage pattern established by the two partners. Demographic trends that have increased the potential for work–family tension include increasing numbers of working married women with children and increases in dual-earner families, single-parent families, and families faced with the demands of elder care.

Lack of fit between work and family life, manifested as work–family conflict, has been associated with lower life satisfaction, psychological distress, heavy alcohol use, and increases in physical complaints (Frone, Russell, & Barnes, 1996; Zedeck, 1992). It is not surprising that adverse effects of work on family life are related to the levels of job stress, job involvement, work-related efficacy, and time at work. In reviewing the impact of work on family life, Fletcher (1991) identified a series of work factors that increase the impact of work stress on spouses and children. These include job mobility, job relocation, and job-related travel.

The relationship of organizational stress to family life also is influenced by the particular life stage. For example, the young manager or executive in a traditional family setting must devote a great deal of energy and time to building his career. At the same time, his wife, housebound with small children, is in need of increasing support. The executive may respond by compartmentalizing or creating distance between his wife and his organization. That this response is dysfunctional is now recognized by some companies.

The kind of support base at home in the traditional marriage is not always available in the dual-career marriage. Unless the two partners consciously work at the support functions for each other, this form of marriage is especially vulnerable to the shattering effects of work stress. A dual-career marriage is less at risk if there are others—for example, extended-family members—who play key roles in the support functions.

Early assessments suggested that working women experience greater work–family conflict than male counterparts, including greater multiple role conflict, less support at home, and greater intrusion of family into work (Davidson & Cooper, 1983; Mannheim & Schiffrin, 1984). This was especially true for women with children, in particular, those with small children at home. More recent studies, however, indicated fewer differences between men and women in their experience of work–family conflict (Frone et al., 1996).

Family businesses provide a unique setting for interactions between family pressures and work pressures. When stressful situations develop, they may be intensified in this setting as the distinction between family and business fades and both suffer (Barnes & Hershon, 1976; H. Levinson, 1971). Such a situation was reported by a nationally prominent lawyer whose wife was also his legal secretary. In assessing the end of his 28-year marriage, he attributed the decay of the relationship largely to the home–work combination.

Anxiety Disorders

The American Psychiatric Association has defined a number of specific abnormal psychological conditions that together are known as "anxiety disorders." The term *anxiety* is sometimes used to describe the stress reaction and other times to describe a general state of uneasiness, apprehension, and worry. In contrast, anxiety disorders have specific definitions that are meant to guide diagnosis and treatment. Anxiety disorders, which affect roughly 1 in 6 Americans, include acute stress disorder, posttraumatic stress disorder, panic disorder, agoraphobia (abnormal fear of being in an open space), social phobia, obsessive–compulsive disorder, and generalized anxiety disorder (American Psychiatric Association, 1994).

Acute stress disorder (ASD), a diagnosis first introduced in the 1994 *Diagnostic and Statistical Manual* (American Psychiatric Association, 1994), refers to a characteristic pattern of anxiety, dissociative, and other symptoms that occur during or immediately after a traumatic event, last for at least 2 days, and resolve within 1 month. This is in contrast to *posttraumatic stress disorder* (PTSD), which refers to a debilitating reaction lasting longer than 1 month and occurring after an overwhelming traumatic event. ASD can resolve with or without treatment, or it can evolve into depression, PTSD, or one of several other chronic conditions.

Work on PTSD has focused on combat veterans, victims of torture or other abuse, and survivors of natural disasters. Increasingly, however, attention is being directed to traumatic events in the workplace (Braverman, 1992; Marsella, Friedman, Gerrity, & Scurfield, 1996; VandenBos & Bulatao, 1996). Occupations at greater risk for workplace trauma include law enforcement, fire fighting, emergency rescue, retail banking (in which armed robbery is common), and certain types of intensive manufacturing (with specific injury risks). Traumatic workplace events may include homicide by a disgruntled employee, work-related suicide, exposure to mass killing, bank robbery, and occupational accidents that result in severe injury or death. Less violent but still traumatic events include downsizing, restructuring, and relocation.

Panic disorder is characterized by periodic panic attacks, which include palpitations, sweating, trembling, shortness of breath, and any of a number of other acute symptoms. Panic attacks may be situational or spontaneous (no identifiable stimulus). Situational attacks result from specific, usually predictable triggers such as public speaking, flying, or similar events.

People with symptoms of anxiety disorders should not simply be labeled (by themselves or others) as "stressed" and left to suffer. Previously, management of anxiety disorders was rather nonspecific, but in recent years improved diagnosis and outcome assessment have led to provision of more specific treatment. For example, panic disorders may respond best to antidepressants, obsessive–compulsive disorders to newer drugs that affect serotonin metabolism, social phobias to a combination of beta-blockers and cognitive and behavioral methods, and PTSD to group support and education programs (Baughan, 1995).

Anxiety disorders can result in lost time and productivity at work. These effects can be reduced through employee assistance programs and other workplace interventions. For example, in discussing posttraumatic crisis intervention in the workplace, Braverman (1992) observed that "stress related to traumatic crises and situations is one of the most preventable of job-related health risks" (p. 301).

Sleep Disturbances

Inability to fall asleep the night before a stressful event, such as a key briefing of the company's senior officers or a difficult performance-review session, is a common if not universal experience. However, occupational stress can lead to chronic and sometimes debilitating sleep disturbances.

Insomnia, the inability to fall asleep or to stay asleep, affects one-third of adults in the United States. Insomnia owing to stress, including the stress of acute illness, accounts for an estimated 35% of sleep disorders. Worries over promotion, conflict at work, or project deadlines frequently cause difficulty in falling asleep. As many as 1 in 5 people experience sleep disturbances caused by poor sleeping habits, shift work, caffeinated drinks, tobacco or alcohol, or irregular sleep schedules (Jamieson & Becker, 1992).

Excessive use or evening use of caffeinated liquids, such as coffee, tea, cola drinks, chocolate drinks, and many noncola drinks, can amplify the problem of stress-induced insomnia. Excess nicotine consumption from stress-induced cigarette smoking can also lead to difficulty falling asleep.

Sleep disturbances may be aggravated by the common home remedy for insomnia: alcohol. The depressant effect of beer, wine, or liquor often helps a person to fall asleep, but alcohol disrupts sleep cycles and leads to a rebound increase in adrenaline in the middle of the night. This may awaken the person, making it difficult to get back to sleep. The person is left fatigued in the morning, which sets up a self-replicating cycle of stress-alcohol-awakening-fatigue-stress.

An example of this cycle is seen in the case of Steve W., a 42-year-old director of sales whose increasing concern with the poor performance of his salespersons led to his having three to five shots of bourbon each evening. He would quickly fall asleep about midnight, but by 3 a.m. he was wide awake again, alert, and often unable to return to sleep. He was eventually hospitalized for stress-induced palpitations, and by the third night in the hospital he was sleeping soundly through the night—without alcohol.

Insomnia leads to impaired concentration, alertness, memory, and task performance. In addition, people with chronic insomnia are 2.5 times more likely to be involved in a fatigue-related motor vehicle accident (Jamieson & Becker, 1992). Because sleep deprivation has a negative impact on mood and performance, it can exacerbate the work situations that caused the sleep disturbance to begin with. It is important to recognize insomnia as a possible consequence of stress at work and to confront the problem as soon as it is recognized.

Sexual Dysfunction

Another potential consequence of mismanaged stress is the inability to function sexually and to enjoy sexual relations. Stress and stress-related anxiety disorders are common causes of inhibited sexual desire. Alcohol and drug abuse, sometimes stress-related, can also lead to inhibited sexual desire, impotence, or other forms of sexual dysfunction.

Stress can reduce sex hormones in both men and women, which in turn may reduce sexual functioning. In practice, however, it is unclear what portion of stress-related sexual dysfunction is attributable to physiological as opposed to psychological mechanisms. In women, disruption of menses and temporary infertility have also been attributed to hormonal changes associated with the stress response.

Deterioration in sexual relations is undoubtedly one of the factors contributing to marital difficulties among executives and other individuals experiencing significant stress at work. Because satisfying sexual relations are an important part of one's mental health and well-being, preventing or resolving sexual dysfunction is a necessary element of stress management.

Depression

Depression is the most common significant psychological condition seen by the family physician and by many psychiatrists and psychologists. It is often accompanied by extreme anxiety. It may be mild and self-limited, or it may be severe enough to lead to suicide. Stressful events such as business failure, termination, and even promotion have led some employees and managers into varying depths of depression and sometimes suicide (Paykel, 1976). Although family and personal events such as death of a spouse or illness in the family show the strongest relationship to the onset of depression, work-related events are also important.

The experience of a young company president is a case in point. He rose through the ranks of his company quickly and by his early 40s was president of a strong, but small, growth company that was listed on the over-the-counter exchange. His personal worth was about $8 million, largely on the basis of company-owned stock. His company got overextended, wrote orders it could not fill, and within a 1-year period had its stock trading frozen. The board of directors relieved the president, who subsequently went into a deep depression of several years' duration. His is a dramatic example of how work stresses may induce depression.

Conversion Reaction and Somatization

Psychological trauma or conflict can sometimes be expressed as a frank disability: acute laryngitis, acute blindness, paralysis of one hand, acute amnesia, and similar physical impairments. Although the disability or discomfort associated with such a psychogenic condition, or "conversion reaction," is real to the patient, no physical basis for the complaint can be found. Sudden inability to speak just prior to a major presentation is an example of such a reaction. Symptoms may be of brief duration, resolving without intervention. Often, however, conversion reactions reflect serious underlying psychological disturbances and require skilled psychiatric care.

Somatization disorder, characterized by multiple unexplained somatic symptoms, and hypochondriasis are two other conditions in which psychological distress is expressed as physical symptoms. Major stressful life events can play a role in the onset of such conditions, but generally such problems are indicative of a fundamental psychiatric disorder.

Medical Consequences

Although the behavioral and psychological effects of organizational stress are in themselves immense, they may in turn have a potentially more devastating and irreversible effect on an individual's medical health and physiological well-being. A combined set of empirical research studies and skilled clinical observations have confirmed the association between a wide range of stressors and serious physical disease (Selye, 1976b, c).

Table 4.1. Leading Causes of Death: United States and All Developed Countries, 1990

Rank and cause of death	United States Deaths (no.)	United States Deaths (%)	All developed countries Deaths (no.)	All developed countries Deaths (%)
Heart disease	690,591	32.1	2,813,700	25.9
Cancer	505,322	23.5	2,430,800	22.3
Strokes	144,088	6.7	1,447,900	13.3
Injuries	91,983	4.3	557,700	5.1
Pneumonia/influenza	79,513	3.7	330,000	3.0
Suicide & homicide	55,520	2.6	248,900	2.3
Diabetes mellitus	47,664	2.2	176,500	1.6
Infectious diseases	30,424	1.4	153,000	1.4
Chronic liver disease	25,815	1.2	146,300	1.3
Emphysema, chronic bronchitis	24,125	1.1	358,300	3.3
Total for top 10 causes	1,695,045	78.9	8,663,100	79.6

Note. United States data from *World Health Statistics Annual 1993* (pp. D114–D117) by World Health Organization, 1994, Geneva, Switzerland: Author. Data for all developed countries from "Global and Regional Cause-of-Death Patterns in 1990," by C. J. L. Murray and A. D. Lopez, 1994, in *Global Comparative Assessments in the Health Sector* (pp. 33–34). Geneva, Switzerland: World Health Organization.

Heart attack, stroke, cancer, peptic ulcer, asthma, diabetes, hypertension, headache, back pain, and arthritis are among the many diseases and symptoms that have been found to be caused or worsened by stressful events. Early studies of strictly job-related stress concentrated primarily on heart disease and peptic ulcer disease, but there is growing evidence that the same relationship exists between organizational stress and disease that exists between other life stressors and disease (e.g., Keita & Sauter, 1992).

Table 4.1 lists the leading causes of death in the United States and in all developed countries. Many of these conditions, including heart disease, hypertension, peptic ulcer disease, and certain cancers, have been referred to by Selye (1976c) as "diseases of adaptation" or "diseases of civilization."

In Table 4.2, major health problems are listed in descending order of disability-adjusted life years (DALYs) lost owing to the illness. The DALY calculation is a method for factoring into the assessment of health impact not simply the number of deaths but also the number of years of life lost (accidental death at an early age weighs more heavily than death late in life) and the number of years lived with a disability (Murray & Lopez, 1994). Using the DALY measure, such problems as mental disorders, traffic accidents, and alcohol dependence weigh more heavily than they would simply on the basis of numbers of deaths.

Organizational stress, like other sources of stress, has cumulative effects that contribute to the development of many common causes of death and disability. Genetics, biological development, and many other factors

Table 4.2. Disability-Adjusted Life Years (DALYs) Lost, by Major Illness Category, All Developed Countries, 1990

Illness	DALYs (no. in millions)	(%)
1. Cancer	18.019	19.2
2. Heart and vascular disease	17.084	18.2
3. Mental disorders	9.640	10.3
4. Traffic and other accidents	7.375	7.9
5. Strokes	4.974	5.3
6. Musculoskeletal conditions	3.896	4.1
7. Alcohol dependence	2.822	3.0
8. Suicide	1.947	2.1
9. Homicide	1.774	1.9
10. Pneumonia/influenza	1.695	1.8
11. Liver cirrhosis	1.685	1.8
12. Emphysema, chronic bronchitis	1.596	1.7
13. HIV–AIDS	1.582	1.7
14. Drug dependence	1.576	1.7
15. Diabetes mellitus	1.331	1.4
All other causes	16.923	18.0
Total	93.919	

Note. From "The Global Burden of Disease in 1990: Summary Results, Sensitivity Analysis and Future Directions," by C. J. L. Murray, A. D. Lopez, and D. T. Jamison, 1994, in C. J. L. Murray and A. D. Lopez (Eds.), *Global Comparative Assessments in the Health Sector* (pp. 112–113). Geneva, Switzerland: World Health Organization.

influence the appearance and course of these diseases, but stress can play a role in hastening the appearance of disease and in worsening its impact.

Heart Disease and Stroke

Each year over 900,000 Americans and more than 3 million people in developed countries die from heart disease and stroke. A variety of studies and anecdotal evidence suggest that both fatal and nonfatal heart attacks occur more frequently among individuals under stress. Established primary risk factors for coronary heart disease (CHD) are family history of heart disease, hypertension, smoking, blood lipids (cholesterol and triglycerides), diet, diabetes, and physical inactivity. Obesity is associated with several of these primary risk factors, but it is still unclear whether it has a direct effect on heart disease. Stressful life events, behavior patterns, or personality factors may contribute to CHD and strokes, either directly through a primary effect or indirectly through their effect on other primary cardiovascular risk factors.

The relationship between stress and smoking was noted earlier. The onset or worsening of hypertension has long been associated with psychological stress (Henry, 1976). The popular notion is that continual arousal of the stress response leads to sustained hypertension. Many anecdotal reports and some laboratory studies have supported this notion, but recent reviews of the clinical literature have concluded that a cause–effect relationship has not been proved (Goldstein & Niaura, 1992; Rosenman, 1996).

Abnormal blood lipid levels represent another cardiovascular risk factor. In one of the earliest studies of blood lipids and stress, Friedman, Rosenman, and Carroll (1958) found that cholesterol levels of tax accountants increased as the deadline for filing federal income tax returns approached.

In the late 1950s, Friedman and Rosenman, two cardiologists, developed the concept of the Type A, "coronary-prone" personality, characterized by competitive overdrive, devotion to work, and time urgency. Early studies found that Type A individuals had higher blood pressure and cholesterol levels; were more frequently smokers; were more likely to be heavy drinkers; and were less active (Dorian & Taylor, 1984). Even after adjustment for these risk factors, Type A individuals were thought to have up to twice the risk for heart attack. However, more recent, better controlled studies have found little or no relationship between Type A behavior and either cardiac risk factors or CHD (Blackburn & Leupker, 1992). It may be that only one component of the Type A behavior pattern, such as hostility, contributes to risk for heart attack. It has been suggested that it is the Sisyphean pattern of "joyless striving" that leads Type A individuals to develop CHD (Jenkins, 1982).

Two meta-analyses (Booth-Kewley & Friedman, 1987; K. A. Matthews, 1988) considered over 80 published studies and concluded that the independent effect of the Type A behavior pattern on coronary heart disease is small or nonexistent. However, measures of hostility and competitiveness/hard-driving behavior were predictors of CHD. The authors of the first study concluded that it is not the hurried, impatient workaholic who is prone to CHD but the person who is hostile, aggressively competitive, and perhaps depressed or anxious.

Since the mid-1970s, there has been growing interest in the concept of "job strain": the combination of high psychological demand at work and low decision latitude (control) in the job. Compared to stressful life events, job strain is more narrowly focused on work stress. It is also more concerned with persistent characteristics of work, rather than isolated stressful events. As such, job strain might be expected to show a stronger relationship to CHD than stressful life events.

In a recent review of job strain and cardiovascular disease, a team of researchers from Sweden and the United States reported that 16 of 22 studies found a significant association between job strain and cardiovascular morbidity or mortality (Theorell & Karasek, 1996). In some cases, job strain was associated with increases in serum cholesterol, smoking, or high blood pressure. Other studies found a direct relationship between job strain and CHD but no relationship between job strain and these known risk factors. The authors suggested that job strain may influence CHD through a direct effect on catecholamines, other neurotransmitters, or hormones.

An example of the impact of job strain on CHD comes from a Swedish

Table 4.3. Relative Risk of First Myocardial Infarction, High Strain Compared with Low Strain Occupations

Job features by age–sex categories	Relative risk	95% Confidence Interval
Men 30–64 years		
Monotony	1.2	1.1–1.4
Few possibilities to learn new things	1.3	1.2–1.5
Low influence on planning work	1.3	1.2–1.5
Low influence on work tempo	1.2	1.1–1.3
Low influence on working hours	1.3	1.2–1.5
Men 30–54 years		
Monotony	1.2	1.0–1.5
Few possibilities to learn new things	1.4	1.2–1.7
Low influence on planning work	1.6	1.2–2.0
Low influence on work tempo	1.2	1.0–1.5
Low influence on working hours	1.5	1.2–1.8
Women 30–64 years		
Monotony	1.4	1.0–1.9
Few possibilities to learn new things	1.3	1.1–1.6
Low influence on planning work	1.3	1.1–1.6
Low influence on work tempo	1.1	1.0–1.3
Low influence on working hours	1.2	1.0–1.4

Note. Low strain occupations involve less hectic work and more decision latitude; high strain occupations involve more hectic work and less decision latitude. Relative risk is adjusted for age, county, and calendar year. From "Job Characteristics and Incidence of Myocardial Infarction," by N. Hammar, L. Alfredsson, and T. Theorell, 1994, *International Journal of Epidemiology, 28*, p. 281. Adapted with permission.

study of individuals who remained in the same occupation for at least 5 years and who had a first myocardial infarction (Hammar, Alfredsson, & Theorell, 1994). Table 4.3 summarizes the relative risk of heart attack for study participants in high strain jobs compared to those in low strain jobs. High strain jobs were characterized by more hectic work with less decision latitude. Relative risks were adjusted for age, county, and calendar year but not for other CHD risk factors.

As predicted, high strain occupations were associated with a relative risk of 1.1–1.6 times that of low strain occupations. Relative risk depended on age and sex: The relative risk of myocardial infarction among those in high strain occupations was higher for younger men but lower for women. Relative risk also varied with associated job features.

Abrupt and serious cardiac rhythm disturbances can lead to "sudden cardiac death," which accounts for a portion of cardiac deaths. Such work stressors as public speaking have been found to stimulate abnormal heartbeats in one quarter of normal patients and abundant abnormal beats in nearly three quarters of patients with coronary artery disease (Taggart, Carruthers, & Somerville, 1973). Although laboratory and physiological evidence is highly suggestive, studies of the relationship between life stresses and sudden death are inconclusive (Binik, 1985).

The potential effect of positively stressful events is illustrated by the case of a recently retired 89-year-old pediatrician and child psychoanalyst who was to be honored at his ninetieth birthday by the pediatrics department he had once chaired. The night before the big event, while anxiously rehearsing his reflections on 65 years of practice, he developed severe left-sided chest pain and was hospitalized for an acute heart attack. He had no previous manifestations of heart disease and quickly recovered from this attack. Unfortunately, the carefully rehearsed recollections were never presented.

The impact of organizational stress on heart disease has been studied much more extensively than its impact on strokes. The risk factors that lead to stroke are quite similar to those for heart attack including smoking, hypertension, poor diet, and diabetes. To the extent that organizational stress influences these risk factors, it can also be expected to influence death and disability from strokes.

Finally, if work stress has an impact on cardiovascular diseases, stress reduction should reduce cardiovascular morbidity and mortality. Several studies have supported this notion. In a controlled study of 453 male patients who had heart attacks, participation in a stress reduction program was associated with fewer deaths (Frasure-Smith & Prince, 1985). In Sweden, a program of individual counseling and work reorganization aimed at stress reduction was associated with improved blood lipid profiles in the intervention group compared with the control group (Orth-Gomer, Eriksson, Moser, Theorell, & Fredlund, 1994).

Cancer

Stress does not cause cancer. Primary risk factors that account for the majority of causes—each applicable to different groups of cancers—include smoking, alcohol consumption, occupational risks (certain industrial chemicals, radiation), dietary factors (animal fat, smoked meat), infectious agents (AIDS virus, other viruses), and sexual behavior. But a large body of research data suggests that stress is a contributing factor to the appearance or progression of cancer. Stress has been linked to increases in some of the preceding primary risk factors for cancer, increases in the appearance of cancer, greater metastatic spread of cancer, and poorer response to cancer treatment.

The leading cause of cancer deaths is lung cancer, a rapidly fatal form of cancer for which early detection has proved difficult and current treatments offer little survival benefit. The major risk factor for cancer is cigarette smoking, which accounts for three-quarters of lung cancers. To the extent that organizational stress increases tobacco consumption, it also increases lung cancer. The relative increase in cigarette smoking among women is beginning to be reflected in rising rates of lung cancer among women. In addition, cigarette smoking contributes to the development of bladder cancer; stomach cancer; and cancers of the mouth, throat, and larynx.

Animal research and some studies in humans indicate that stress may have a direct effect on decreasing the immune response, which might otherwise control a small nidus of cancerous cells. Several books and articles on stress and cancer review evidence suggesting that stressful life events are associated with the appearance of a variety of cancers, including breast cancer, uterine cancer, and malignant melanoma (Cooper & Watson, 1991; Faragher, 1996; Fletcher, 1991; Taché, Selye, & Day, 1979). The strongest evidence links onset of cancer to major life change events such as death of a spouse, divorce or separation, and death of a close family member.

As early as the second century, the Greek physician Galen concluded that women with "melancholic dispositions" were more inclined to develop breast cancer. In recent years, it has been suggested that there is a "Type C," cancer-prone personality, which is described as cooperative, conforming, compliant, and unassertive, with a tendency to suppress anger (Temoshok & Dreher, 1993). Although there are numerous studies demonstrating a relationship between personality and cancer, this relationship is not universally accepted (see Eysenck, 1996).

People under stress may not respond optimally to treatment. A prospective study of 208 women with breast cancer, for example, found that higher stress levels were associated with decreased survival (Funch & Marshall, 1983).

Finally, it appears that stressful life events and coping strategies may have an interactive effect on the development of cancer. A recent large study of breast cancer used multivariate methods to distinguish the associations among patient characteristics, stressful life events, coping strategies, personality, and social support (Cooper & Faragher, 1993; Faragher, 1996). Each of these factors, including stressful life events, was significantly related to development of breast cancer.

Back Pain and Arthritis

Chronic back pain is the most common cause of chronic disabiity in people of working age, affecting 15 million Americans (Adams & Benson, 1992). An estimated 200 million work days are lost each year in the United States owing to back conditions, with annual direct and indirect costs totaling more than $60 billion (Branch, Gates, Susman, & Berg, 1994).

Back injury is more common among certain occupations, including materials movers, truck drivers, and those who work in environments with poor ergonomic designs. Back pain, back injuries, and related disability are *less* common among the physically fit, residents of rural areas, women, nonsmokers, and people living in areas in which there is less disability compensation available (Branch et al., 1994).

Work stress may contribute directly or indirectly to some acute back injuries. More important, however, is the fact that occupational stress, job dissatisfaction preceding injury, and poor work evaluations are all associated with delayed recovery and a greater likelihood of chronic disability owing to back problems (Bigos et al., 1991; Polatin, Kinney, & Gatchel, 1993).

Chronic back pain may result in part from muscle spasm induced by stress and from the lack of strength and flexibility that results from a sedentary occupational and recreational life. Stress-induced muscle spasm can also lead to chronic neck pain, jaw pain, and other musculoskeletal complaints. In addition, although stress does not appear to cause rheumatoid arthritis or osteoarthritis, stressful conditions can worsen these diseases.

Peptic Ulcer Disease and Other Gastrointestinal Conditions

The history of the association between stress and peptic ulcer disease demonstrates some of the difficulties in proving a cause–effect relationship between stress and adverse health consequences. Ulceration of the stomach and duodenum (the first part of the small intestine) has been thought of as the classic psychosomatic illness. This description is due in part to the early work of Stewart Wolf, a neurologist at Cornell University in the early 1940s, now at Trotts Gap, and pioneer in psychosomatic medicine (Wolf & Wolff, 1943). For many years Wolf studied the gastric functioning of a patient named Tom, who had a gastric fistula (an artificial opening between the stomach and the outside). Wolf noted that during times of prolonged emotional conflict, the stomach lining became engorged with blood and that its surface eventually developed minute, bleeding erosions.

Despite this persuasive case study, large-scale epidemiological studies have been less convincing. One problem with early studies of the relationship between stress and ulcer disease was the failure to control for cigarette smoking or other proven risk factors. Cigarette smoking, family history, and aspirin use have been demonstrated to be independent risk factors that increase severalfold the chance of developing peptic ulcer disease. Evidence is less consistent linking peptic ulcer disease to use of alcohol, coffee, peppers, or other dietary factors (Garland & Garland, 1986).

Peptic ulcer disease had not been thought of as an infectious disease, but over the last decade studies coming from Australia have demonstrated unequivocally that 75–95% of people with peptic ulcers have the spiral-shaped bacterium Helicobacter pylori in their gastrointestinal system. Furthermore, treatment of this bacterial infection may speed healing and dramatically reduces an otherwise high chance of recurrence (NIH Consensus Conference, 1994).

Studies from the 1950s to the 1970s have found an increased incidence of peptic ulcers in air traffic controllers, forepersons, those in middle management, and executives. However, an association between increased stressful life events and occurrence of peptic ulcer disease has not been convincingly demonstrated. Contrary to earlier views, there is no convincing evidence for an "ulcer personality" (Garland & Garland, 1986; Schindler & Ramchandani, 1991). Although psychological stress has not been shown to cause peptic ulcers, clinical experience and other evidence suggest that stress may precipitate and exacerbate ulcer disease.

In addition to ulcers, other gastrointestinal illnesses have been associated with chronic stress. Irritable bowel syndrome, one of the most common gastrointestinal conditions, is characterized by painful spasms of the large intestine. Ulcerative colitis, another problem of the large intestine, is characterized by bleeding ulcerations. In both conditions, psychological stress is associated with the onset or worsening of symptoms.

Headache

Headache is one of the most common symptoms of stress. Stressful occupations and life events typically lead to common tension headaches but can also precipitate migraine headaches, cluster headaches, and less common types of headache. Headache is one of the features of a syndrome described by Sewil (1969) as "Wall Street sickness." Investors plagued by this sickness develop headache, stomach trouble, and fatigue. One regional office of a national financial services organization found headaches to be a common symptom during a period of substantial growth during the late 1980s.

Although most headaches last only a few hours and are readily treated with simple analgesics, more severe headaches can last several days and result in lost time at work. The annual cost of migraine alone is estimated to be $5–7 billion owing to lost productivity and related indirect costs. Direct medical costs may be twice this amount. One study found that over half of migraine patients lost time at work, with the average loss being 2.2 workdays per month. Individuals who were not frequently absent reported that their productivity was affected for at least 1 week per month (Osterhaus, Gutterman, & Plachetka, 1992).

Job demands, shift work, excessive noise, unpleasant odors, and other physical stressors have all been associated with a higher incidence of work-related headaches. In one of the earliest studies in this area, Johansson, Aronsson, and Lindstrom (1978) found that sawmill employees in jobs associated with high stress experienced 36% more headaches than controls. Performance appraisals may be adversely affected in employees with frequent and more severe headaches.

Diabetes Mellitus

Diabetes is a metabolic disorder characterized by abnormally high blood glucose and a wide range of adverse effects on the vital organs. It is the seventh leading cause of death in the United States (Table 4.1) and a major contributing factor to cardiovascular, kidney, and eye disease. Risk factors include family history, obesity, physical inactivity, and residing in an area of rapid economic development.

One of the predominant effects of the stress response and stress-related hormonal changes is to increase the availability of blood glucose for fast energy. Although it is unlikely that stress can cause diabetes in a nonsusceptible individual, in someone predisposed to diabetes, stress-induced obesity and stress-related stimulation of blood sugar increases may tip the balance. Therefore, it is not surprising that stress induced by intense life changes is associated with the appearance of diabetes or other disturbances of blood glucose control (I. Grant, Kyle, Teichman, & Mendels, 1974).

Liver Cirrhosis and Other Alcohol-Related Diseases

Cirrhosis of the liver, largely caused by excessive alcohol consumption, remains a leading cause of death and disability despite widespread occupational and community efforts to help the alcoholic worker and citizen. Excessive alcohol consumption also contributes to the incidence of heart disease and diabetes.

Lung Disease

The occurrence of pneumonia, influenza, and in particular emphysema is also strongly influenced by cigarette smoking, which is in turn influenced by stress levels. In addition to this indirect effect, stress appears to have a direct effect, at least with regard to asthma. Asthma is another of the "classic" psychosomatic illnesses in that the impact of psychosocial events on asthma attacks has been frequently studied. According to the current practice of medicine with allergies, stress is an important precipitating factor for individuals prone to asthma attacks (Apaliski, 1997). Stress can also be a factor in the development of tuberculosis (Holmes, Hawkins, Bowerman, Clark, & Joffee, 1957).

Skin Disease

Perhaps the most visible medical consequences of stress are the skin diseases that appear to be precipitated or worsened by stressful events. Although the common skin disorders rarely pose a serious threat to one's health, their unsightliness can be a major source of anguish. Eczema, neurodermatitis, hives, and acne are all skin conditions that are generally felt to be associated with stress. For example, in individuals prone to eczema—a condition characterized by itching, redness, swelling, and eventually scaling and fluid discharge—emotional arousal leads to specific changes in the skin cells. Similarly, it has been shown that individuals prone to developing hives often do so under stressful conditions.

Emerging Diseases

During the 1980s and 1990s, several new diseases have come to the fore. For at least two of these diseases, acquired immunodeficiency syndrome (AIDS) and chronic fatigue syndrome, consideration has been given to the relationship between disease onset and stressful events including those occurring at work. The human immunodeficiency virus (HIV), which causes AIDS, is transmitted through sexual relations, through blood, and perinatally from mother to child. Becoming HIV-infected is in itself a stressful occurrence. But can stress contribute to transmission of the HIV virus? For example, stress may be associated with unsafe sexual practices, failure of health staff to adhere to universal precautions aimed at preventing occupational exposure to the AIDS virus, and increased abuse of intravenous drugs.

It has been suggested that adherence to universal precautions might be related to characteristics of the job and work environment. To date, it appears that failure to adhere to universal precautions is related to job factors such as the perception that job duties interfere with practicing the precautions. Standard measures of work stressors such as workload and role ambiguity do not appear to be related to poor compliance with universal precautions (Murphy, Gershon, & Dejoy, 1996).

Chronic fatigue syndrome (CFS) has been increasingly recognized over the last decade to be a condition characterized by persistent fatigue sufficient to interfere with daily activities, a variety of physical complaints, and usually low-grade fever or swollen lymph nodes. CFS has at times been attributed primarily to psychological causes. Alhough the cause remains controversial, the pattern of accurately diagnosed CFS is consistent with an organic illness, possibly an immune deficiency or viral infection. Nevertheless, a number of studies have suggested that stressful lifestyles or stressful life events may contribute to the onset of CFS, its effect on daily functioning, or the duration of illness (Lewis, 1996).

Assessing the Relationship Between Stress and Its Consequences

Among managers and academics concerned with organizational behavior, there is a tendency to infer a cause–effect relationship between stressors and related adverse behavioral, psychological, or medical outcomes. It is apparent from the preceding information, however, that the existence and strength of stress–adverse outcome relationships vary considerably.

As additional research is carried out using more reliable study designs and better measures of stress, conclusions regarding cause–effect relationships will change. It was noted previously that early research showed a positive relationship between the type A behavior pattern and heart disease whereas more recent studies have failed to confirm the relationship. Stressful life changes, as a group, have now been found to have little if any impact on heart disease. Perhaps this is because the list of stressful life events does not adequately weigh individual reactions to stressors. In contrast, recent studies with more narrowly defined measures of stress have indicated that hostility and job strain may be important factors in heart disease.

Chapters 6 and 7 provide a detailed discussion of stress diagnosis and measures. In addition to having well-defined measures of stress and strain, studies hoping to show cause–effect relationships between stress and individual outcomes must use a proper control or comparison group, avoid simple *post hoc, ergo propter hoc* reasoning, and avoid unwarranted extrapolation from basic physiological changes to inferred health consequences.

Summary

The consequences of individual distress appear to result from frequent or intense arousal of the stress response, in particular, from the mental arousal that is induced by stress. The stress response represents an inherent biological pattern of sympathetic nervous system and endocrine reactions. In response to this state of arousal, individuals may experience behavioral, psychological, or medical effects. Some of the more significant behavioral changes include increased cigarette smoking, alcohol abuse, and accident proneness. Psychological effects, which may be profound, include family problems, sleep disturbance, depression, and possibly suicide. Medical conditions that may be influenced by stress are heart disease, stroke, back pain, stomach ulcer, cancer, and diabetes.

An apparent paradox is the observation that a wide variety of stressors can lead to a rather stereotyped psychophysiological stress response, which in turn can be manifested by the range of behavioral, psychological, and medical effects just mentioned. The explanation for this paradox can be found, in part, in the individual modifiers of the stress response, discussed in chapter 3.

The individual consequences of organizational stress can be devastating. In addition, organizations may suffer significant adverse consequences as a result of workers' stress. Accident proneness increases medical claims; alcoholism increases absenteeism; exacerbation of medical conditions increases sick time; and so on. These and other organizational consequences of stress are the subject of the following chapter.

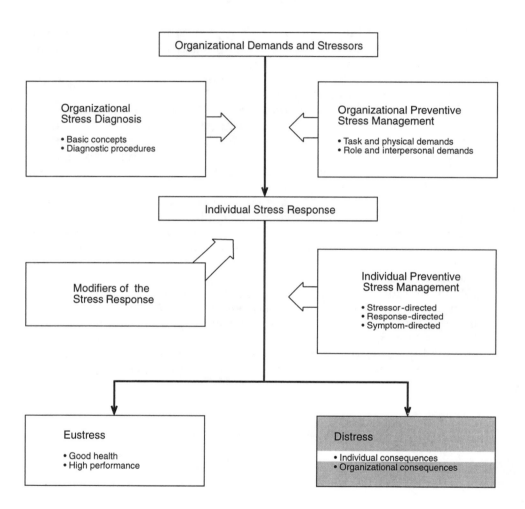

5

Organizational Consequences
of Stress

Both organizations and individuals benefit from an optimum level of stress, and both pay a price for mismanaged stress and distress. The healthy consequences of optimum stress in organizations include high performance and vitality within the organization. The unhealthy consequences of excessive, insufficient, or mismanaged stress in organizations take the form of organizational distress. Whereas chapter 4 examined the price of individual distress, this chapter discusses the cost of organizational distress. The first of the three major sections examines the nature of the relationship between the organization and the individual. The second section examines organizational health, and the third section addresses the costs of organizational distress, both direct and indirect.

Individual forms of distress can have an adverse effect on an organization, financially and in other ways. Heart disease, which, as we noted earlier, is the leading cause of death in the United States, exemplifies this process. In addition to the individual distress that cardiovascular diseases cause, there is significant organizational distress associated with them in the form of economic costs to companies. To examine the financial impact on organizations, the American Heart Association (1980) developed a relatively simple procedure for roughly calculating the number of lost personnel as well as the direct hiring and training costs associated with replacing employees lost to heart disease. For an organization of 100,000 people in 1980, the price included 150 heart deaths per year, 75 premature retirements per year, over $800,000 in annual human resource replacement costs, and an eventual death rate of 50,000 (50%) for the company's working population (i.e., 50% of the present employees would eventually die of heart disease). However, premature death and disability rates have dropped between 24 and 36% over the past 15 years. In addition, cardiovascular diseases are not simply a medical problem; there are significant psychological, behavioral, and stress components to cardiovascular disease. Although the proportion of explained variance is not clear, the risk factors for heart disease include smoking, poor diet and nutrition, anger and hostility, and lack of exercise.

In 1997, the cost of cardiovascular disease was estimated by the American Heart Association at $259.1 billion. Figure 5.1 shows the total estimated direct productivity–morbidity and indirect economic costs by type of expenditure. In addition to the $100.6 billion in lost indirect costs, which includes $76 billion in lost future earnings of persons who will die in 1997

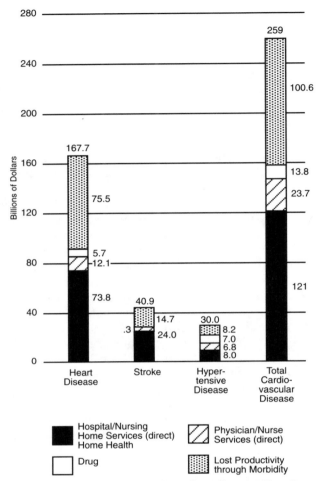

Figure 5.1. The direct and indirect costs of cardiovascular disease. From *1997 Heart and Stroke Statistical Update*, p. 28, by the American Heart Association, 1997. Dallas, TX: Author. Adapted with permission.

discounted by 6%, that organizations must bear, many of the health care costs are borne by organizations as well. Hence, cardiovascular diseases affect several of the direct costs of organizational distress, and they are only one disorder that drives these costs. Although many organizations have not historically tracked the data on cost to their human resources that are discussed in this chapter, organizations such as AT&T and Johnson & Johnson have, and more organizations are beginning to do so.

The Organization–Individual Relationship

Individuals and organizations are engaged in interdependent relationships such that the individual costs of distress inevitably translate into

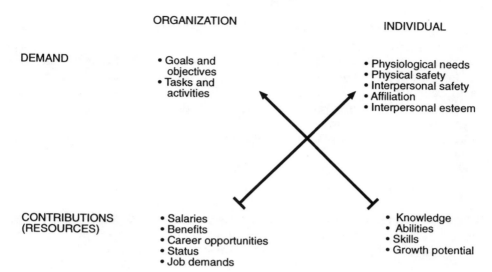

Figure 5.2. The basis for individual–organizational exchange.

various forms of organizational distress, with its associated costs. The basis for this interdependent relationship between the individual and the organization is a cooperative social exchange of contributions from each to the other. Furthermore, the individual and the organization make demands on the resources and assets of the other. The expectation is that each party to this exchange benefits from the cooperative, interdependent relationship, and there is a challenge for each party to make adjustments to ensure the success of the relationship. A framework for understanding the demands and contributions of the individual and the organization in this exchange relationship, which is based on the work of Porter, Lawler, and Hackman (1975), is depicted in Figure 5.2. Balance in the demands and contributions between individuals and organizations is important. The effort–reward imbalance model is one of the newer theoretical conceptualizations for assessing adverse health effects of stressful experiences at work (Siegrist, 1996). The focus of the model is on reciprocity of exchange in occupational life and the importance of balance for health and well-being. Siegrist (1996) showed that high-cost/low-gain conditions are considered particularly stressful. Other research has shown that worker compensation stress claims are the result of an imbalance between the needs of employees and the demands of the organization (Woodburn & Simpson, 1994).

Woodburn and Simpson (1994) set forth a topology of seven categories of employees who are at high risk for filing stress claims. These categories include (a) the Replicated Family employee, who views the workplace as an extended family; (b) the High Achiever employee, who sees work as a competency-based extension of high school or college; (c) the Assaulted Superego employee, who develops deep concerns over being asked to perform tasks he or she views as unethical; (d) the Maligned employee, who is treated by supervisors as though he or she has acted wrongly; (e) the Outcast, who does not fit into the social milieu of the job; (f) the Constant

Turmoil employee, who brings multiple preexisting conditions and conflicts to the job; and (g) the Malingerer, who feels the world owes him or her a living and files stress claims as an ongoing attempt to get something for nothing. The challenge of adjustment for individuals and organizations is to cooperate in achieving a balance in the demand–contribution exchanges in which they engage. Within Woodburn and Simpson's (1994) framework, the adjustment may occur in employee needs, in organizational demands, or in placing employees in positions that lead to a better balance.

Organizational Contributions

Organizations exist to produce products or deliver services to the society in which they operate. As a result, every organization has specified tasks and activities to accomplish in the pursuit of its goals and objectives. These tasks and activities, as well as the goals and objectives, form the core of demands that the organization places on the individual. Whether the organization offers basic products, such as steel in the case of Chaparral Steel Company, provides consumer products, such as automobiles, minivans, and trucks in the case of Chrysler Corporation, or delivers services, such as telecommunication in the case of AT&T or overnight delivery in the case of Federal Express, the survival of the organization hinges on its capacity to achieve its goals effectively and efficiently. Failure to do so may lead to organizational death, as was the case for many prominent airlines such as Eastern, Pan Am, and Braniff during the 1980s and early 1990s.

Organizations have a variety of resources and assets at their disposal to contribute to the exchange relationship with individuals. As Figure 5.2 sets forth, salary and benefits for particular tasks and jobs are among the more prominent benefits. However, financial and material contributions are not the only resources organizations offer. Career advancement and development opportunities may be equally if not more important to individuals who are making important contributions to organizational goal attainment. Note, for example, the U.S. Army's slogan, "Be all that you can be," or the U.S. Air Force's "Aim High." Status is another valued resource that many organizations attempt to capitalize on in their recruiting slogans and efforts, such as the U.S. Marine Corps' "A few good men." Most organizations differentially allocate these resources among their various members and stakeholders in exchange for their contributions to the relationship.

Individual Contributions

Individuals have a variety of resources in the form of competencies and assets to contribute to the exchange, to earn the organizational resources, and to meet the organization's goals. The concept of earning is an important underlying value in the exchange relationship because of the performance and productivity problems associated with an entitlement value

(Bardwick, 1991), as reflected in the Malingerer category mentioned previously. Most employees are selected on the basis of a variety of skills, abilities, and knowledge that they can contribute to the organization. In addition to these resources for task accomplishment, individuals have varying degrees of growth potential; that is, they have the capability of expanding their knowledge or skill base so that they can contribute more effectively to the organization, take on additional responsibilities, and add value to the organization.

Individuals are willing to contribute these resources only if their own demands in the exchange relationship are met. These demands take the form of human needs, as depicted in Figure 5.2. Whereas the classical management theorists assumed that basic human motivational needs were economic, the later behaviorists and human relationists assumed that humans were primarily social beings. Of course, both groups were in part right, but the approaches of Maslow (1943) and Alderfer (1972) are more accurate portrayals of the diversity of human needs. Meeting the diversity of human existence, relatedness, and growth needs is a central aspect of health and a key aspect of the exchange relationship with the organization. The medical profession has known for decades that various debilitating illnesses result from psychological and physiological deprivation, and management scholars (e.g., McGregor, 1957) have also identified the emotional illnesses that result from failure to meet relatedness and growth needs at work.

Need deprivation or an imbalance in the exchange may contribute to individual distress (Siegrist, 1996), raise the risks of stress claims (Woodburn & Simpson, 1994), and elicit other health risks, as noted in the discussion of individual distress in chapter 4. Individual distress is not simply an individual problem; it leads to varying degrees of difficulty or inability to use the resources at the employee's disposal for organizational goal attainment and therefore has organizational consequences. Excessively high levels of stress lead to exhaustion and burnout, whereas too little stress leads to debilitation and boredom. Both are undesirable from an organizational point of view. An optimum level of stress on the individual at work stimulates him or her to grow and develop within the organization, thus contributing to the exchange relationship.

Each organization and individual should seek a good match as well as a dynamic equilibrium in this exchange. An imbalance may have significant adverse consequences in individual health costs (Siegrist, 1996) and organizational costs (Woodburn & Simpson, 1994). A good match and balance contribute to both individual and organizational health. Individual health is one of several prerequisites for organizational health, and organizational health contributes to individual health through need gratification as well as opportunities for growth and development.

Organizational Health

Organizational health is a concept central to preventive stress management and the emerging discipline of occupational health psychology. Beer

(1980) talked about organizational health as "the capacity of an organization to engage in ongoing self-examination aimed at identifying incongruities between social systems components and developing plans for needed change" (p. 41). This process-oriented definition implies that healthy organizations do not necessarily stay that way. They must engage in a systematic process of adaptation and change to maintain healthy functioning. This process involves examining the internal functioning of the organization as well as its relationship with its task environment. Although environmental change may be experienced as a threat, at least initially, healthy organizations engage in adjustment and adaptive responses designed to enhance long-term vitality, as opposed to engaging in rigid and nonadaptive responses to environmental changes (Alderfer, 1972; Staw et al., 1981).

Mott (1972) identified three characteristics that distinguish healthy organizations from unhealthy ones and are related to the effectiveness of the organization: adaptability, flexibility, and productivity. These are consistent with the dominant characteristics identified by Steers (1975). The adaptability characteristic refers to the ability of an organization to change and to resist becoming rigid in its functioning and operating procedures, especially vis-à-vis its task environment (i.e., the part of the organization's environment related to its goal-attainment efforts). Related to this characteristic is that of flexibility. Flexibility differs from adaptability in terms of response time. Adaptability is concerned with long-term adjustment, whereas flexibility is concerned with adjusting to internal and external emergencies. The productivity characteristic is concerned with the amount of products or services provided by the organization.

Healthy organizations are self-renewing and self-examining in an effort to maintain their adaptability, flexibility, and productivity. They make planned changes in key internal dimensions to achieve (a) integration and congruity among these dimensions as well as (b) consistency and congruity with their task environments. These key internal dimensions of the organization in which planned changes may be made, identified in Figure 5.3, include people, structure, technology, and task (Leavitt, 1965). At the center of the figure is the organizational culture, which may be considered the connective tissue knitting together the people and other internal elements of the organization (Cummings, 1996; J. C. Quick, 1992; E. H. Schein, 1990).

The first aspect of organizational health refers to the internal adjustment activities aimed at having the people, structure, technology, and task of the organization work in harmony. A misfit between two or more of these dimensions may cause internal health problems for the organization. Such a problem may be illustrated by the case of a manager placed in a job for which he is not fully qualified. In this example, the organization may either change the manager through a training and development effort or change the job, reassigning job functions for which the manager is not qualified to another job. In either case, the organization achieves an improved person–job fit, with the associated improvement in health.

The second aspect of organizational health refers to the organization's

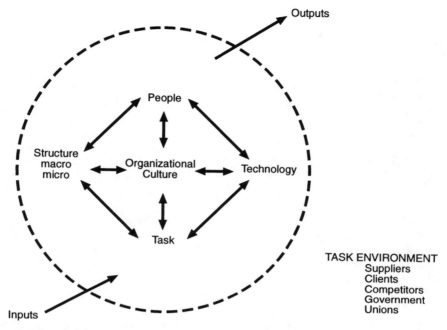

Figure 5.3. A framework for viewing organizational health.

adjustment to the demands of the task environment. Important agents in the task environment are identified in Figure 5.3. This external adjustment dimension is essential primarily because of the organization's dependence on these environmental agents in achieving its objectives. Good external adjustment is essential to organizational health and vitality and is best achieved through the reciprocal exchange of knowledge, products, and other resources between the organization and the agents in its task environment (Alderfer, 1976).

An example of the problems that may occur when there is poor external adjustment to the task environment is the following experience of a small, family-owned printing company. After nearly 75 years of successful operations, the firm bordered on bankruptcy for a year. This circumstance arose because the firm had developed too large a debt structure for the fragmented, turbulent market that it operated in. Had it been more sensitive to its task environment and therefore more conservative in its debt structure, it would not have risked bankruptcy and dissolution.

The maintenance of organizational health requires an active process of planned change and adjustment to avoid a crisis like the one illustrated in the preceding paragraph. There must be constant efforts to achieve integration and wholeness within the four internal dimensions of the organization as well as adjustment to the task environment. This ongoing process of adjustment to internal and external demands requires both resources and commitment from the organization's management as well as a long-range perspective. Short-run cost effectiveness should not be achieved at the expense of long-term health and growth. For example,

Exhibit 5.1.   Costs of Organizational Distress

Direct costs	Indirect costs
Participation and membership • Absenteeism • Tardiness • Strikes and work stoppages • Turnover Performance on the job • Quality of productivity • Quantity of productivity • Grievances • Accidents • Unscheduled machine downtime and repair • Material and supply overuse • Inventory shrinkages Health care costs Compensation awards	Loss of vitality • Low morale • Low motivation • Dissatisfaction Communication breakdowns • Decline in frequency of contact • Distortions of messages Faulty decision making Quality of work relations • Distrust • Disrespect • Animosity Aggression and violence Opportunity costs

failure to invest sufficient capital and resources for retooling and updating organizational technology on a regular basis can lead to even greater costs at a later date. This is illustrated in the American automobile and steel industries, both of which were obliged to initiate major capital investment programs.

If the organization does not maintain a state of relative health, it risks its long-range effectiveness and survival. Healthy organizations are better equipped to survive and grow, and they are also in a better position to contribute to individual health and well-being. Failures and flaws in organizational health may lead to the various direct and indirect costs identified in Exhibit 5.1, which are discussed in the next section. The thrust of preventive stress management is to minimize these costs while encouraging the maximum degree of organizational health.

Costs of Organizational Distress

Organizational distress may be divided into two major cost categories: direct costs and indirect costs, as summarized in Exhibit 5.1. *Direct costs* include the loss of an individual through absenteeism or turnover; the results of the poor performance of that individual while in the workplace (Macy & Mirvis, 1976); and the payment of worker compensation awards, health care benefits, and court-ordered awards for distress on the job. *Indirect costs* include broken and disrupted communication between people, poor morale, faulty decisions, and aggression and violence in the workplace. The direct costs of distress are discussed first.

Direct Costs

The diseases of maladaptation and individual distress discussed in chapter 4 have an organizational cost correlate. For example, as pointed out at the beginning of this chapter, the American Heart Association estimated that cardiovascular diseases—high blood pressure, hardening of the arteries, heart attack, stroke, rheumatic heart disease, congenital heart defects, and congestive heart failure—cost the United States a total of $137.7 billion in 1995. Of this amount, $20.2 billion (or about 15% of the total) was attributable to lost production. Medical care, loss of managerial skills, and retraining account for most of the remaining costs. Of course, not all the diseases of adaptation or the organizational costs of detrimental behaviors are directly attributable to mismanaged stress.

One of the difficulties in tracing cause-and-effect relationships in this area is the pervasive nature of stress. Virtually all the experiences and demands of life, including work, stimulate the stress response. The mismanagement of this response causes distress, which may be manifested in a host of ways. There is no one individual or one organizational manifestation of distress. To isolate the precursors and the consequences as well as their causal relationships is an extremely complex task, one that is only now being approached by Johnson & Johnson and other concerned organizations and researchers. However, this is an important area of investigation if organizations and individuals are to succeed in preventive stress management. Some preliminary efforts are underway in this regard.

One of the most comprehensive efforts to identify the direct economic costs of various employee attitudes and behaviors was undertaken at the Institute for Social Research by Mirvis, Macy, Lawler, and others (see Mirvis & Lawler, 1977; Mirvis & Macy, 1982). These investigators developed a detailed guide to behavioral costing that traces the variety of direct costs associated with a specific employee behavior, such as absenteeism. They developed costing procedures for behaviors related to participation and membership (e.g., turnover) and to performance on the job (e.g., poorquality work). In addition to the direct economic costs associated with specific employee behaviors, organizations are now being required by some courts to provide compensation for on-the-job distress encountered by employees. Each of these three general categories of costs is examined separately.

Participation and membership. There are numerous reasons that an individual may not be available to work in an organization. If an employee is not participating in work at the appointed time or elects to leave the organization altogether, the organization pays a price for unperformed work. *Absenteeism* and *tardiness* are two behaviors associated with nonparticipation. As short-term coping strategies for the individual, these behaviors may benefit the organization in the form of improved morale and quality of work. In the aggregate, they cost the organization in terms of both lowered morale for other workers and money for the overstaffing needed to cover the absent worker's station.

For example, an automobile assembly plant located near a major university runs approximately 10% absenteeism on the Friday and Monday shifts. The plant's response to the absenteeism is to hire a pool of local university students to serve as "fillers" for the absent workers. This response inflates the personnel payroll. When studying a similar automobile production plant in the rural South, Mirvis and Lawler (1977) calculated the cost of each absence for the plant to be $55.36. Using the same method, they determined that the absence of a bank branch manager in the Midwest cost $218.15. Clearly, each occurrence of nonparticipation has a direct cost for the organization.

Absenteeism may have an adverse effect on the quality of care in health care organizations. One study of absenteeism owing to illness in a hospital organization in the Alicante province of Spain from 1988 to 1990 found a rise in absences from 19.7 days per employee in 1988, to 24.23 days in 1989, to 26.45 days in 1990 (Mira, Vitaller, Buil, Aranaz, & Herrero, 1992). The researchers concluded that excess absenteeism may call into question quality assurance in health care for patients and clients, thus harming the overall health of the organization.

Strikes and *work stoppages* are other forms of nonparticipation that cost varying amounts to the organization. There are not only the direct costs associated with loss of production and replacement of personnel, as occurred in the 1980s in an attempted strike by air traffic controllers, but also the indirect costs of lost opportunities and disruption of relations with suppliers, clients, and others in the task environment. These indirect costs are discussed in more detail later in the chapter.

How costly a work stoppage may be is shown by an incident in an automobile assembly plant. One disgruntled employee, who was not getting adequate attention, effectively "pulled the power plug" on the entire assembly line. He idled approximately 3,000 workers at once and prevented a resumption of normal activities for several hours. By applying the pertinent costing rules from the Mirvis procedures, one can see that in addition to lost production, this incident cost the assembly plant several thousand dollars in wages, salaries, and fringe benefits.

Turnover, the final cost in this category, has functional as well as dysfunctional consequences for the organization (Dalton, Tudor, & Krackhardt, 1982). Turnover may have functional consequences in enabling the organization to maintain a state of relative health by improving the quality of its human resources. If overpriced or unproductive employees leave and make room for new, vital personnel, turnover is healthy. If individuals leave because of a change in organizational tasks and goals, the result can be positive. Although high or unstable rates of turnover are costly for the organization, it is important to note that the functional aspects of turnover have often been overlooked (Dalton, Krackhardt, & Porter, 1981).

The actual costs of turnover vary with several factors; however, they are frequently in the range of 5 times the employee's monthly salary. In empirically determining the economic costs of turnover, Mirvis and Macy (1982) established that the cost of replacing one toll operator for a Northeastern telephone company was approximately $1,900, whereas the cost of replacing a top manager for a Midwestern manufacturing company was $30,000. Even these costs may be outweighed by the benefits of terminating a nonproductive employee who is absorbing organizational resources while giving nothing substantive to the organization in return.

The organization's objective should be to achieve an optimum level of turnover, which is determined by considering both the functional and dysfunctional aspects of turnover within a group of employees. Bluedorn (1982) attempted to make this calculation in economic terms by considering both marginal usefulness and marginal costs, as opposed to considering economic costs alone. Figure 5.4 shows Bluedorn's (1982) hypothetical example in which the optimum turnover rate is about 25%. The determination of a specific optimum turnover rate for a company or for one of its employee groups is based on both functional and dysfunctional aspects of turnover. The key point to note is that an optimum turnover rate may be determined for an organization to realize maximum economic benefit.

Organizational policies may be helpful in enhancing a healthy amount of turnover, such as the up-or-out policies of the United States military services. By setting tenure limits in each enlisted and officer grade, the military services stimulate growth, development, and increased responsibility among its enlisted and officer corps. This set of policies encourages healthy turnover throughout the services. The policy is coupled with the recognition that not all turnover is desirable, and it allows for exceptions

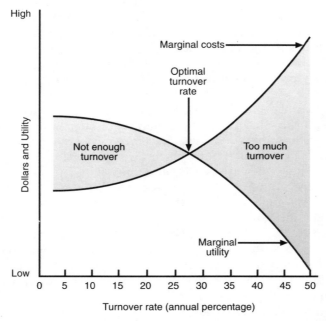

Figure 5.4.   The economics of turnover management. From "Managing Turnover Strategy," by A. C. Bluedorn, 1982, *Business Horizons, 25*(2), p. 8. Reprinted with permission.

to hold especially valuable personnel in a grade beyond the established tenure limits.

Performance on the job. Stress not only influences the various degrees of participation, or lack of it, by individuals in work organizations but also affects behavior at work. For example, whereas one individual may choose to be absent because of distress, another individual may show distress in poor-quality performance. Alternatively, distress might manifest itself in aggressive conflicts at work. Therefore, job performance is a second major realm in which there are direct consequences of organizational stress. Amount of productivity, quality of production, grievances, accidents, unscheduled machine downtime and repair, material and supply overuse, and inventory shrinkages are all aspects of job performance (Mirvis & Macy, 1982).

Performance decrements attributable to excessive levels of stress were identified by Yerkes and Dodson at the turn of the century. When stress becomes distress because the degree has passed the optimum level for the individual, both the quality and quantity of the employee's work may suffer. This result may occur routinely in repetitive work situations in which the employee starts losing concentration after approximately 30 minutes: When the employee's attention starts drifting, quality and quantity of performance can suffer. Fatigue owing to work or role overload can also contribute to poor quality or quantity of work.

Executive burnout is a form of distress at work that results in loss of enthusiasm and vitality at work; it is often accompanied by declining job performance. Burnout is a form of emotional and psychological fatigue, akin to depression, that appears to result from work or role overload. This condition appears to influence both the quality and quantity of work that an individual produces. People who work directly with employee problems are particularly prone to experience this form of distress, as discussed in chapter 4.

Grievances and *accidents* are also behaviors that reduce an employee's performance on the job. Informal complaints or suggestions that are acted on by managers or supervisors and therefore never reach the formal grievance stage are not included here. Such informal action may be extremely beneficial to organizational health and may cost the organization little beyond supervisory and employee time to resolve the issue. Here we refer to formal actions such as those that result from work overload during periods of economic difficulty or downsizing activities, a common occurrence during the 1990s (Gowing, Kraft, & Quick, in press). Some organizations respond to economic stress and industrial competition by seeking cost savings through reductions in their labor force. When commensurate reductions in work activities do not accompany the human resource reductions, some employees experience a work overload, which in turn can lead to grievance actions and accidents.

The *Wall Street Journal*'s coverage of this practice suggested the presence of two consequences. One consequence was that unions and employees were filing more grievances concerning the practice of job loading. This consequence has only organizational cost implications. The other consequence of job loading was an increased incidence of employee accidents, which has both individual and organizational cost implications. The individual cost implications were discussed in chapter 4.

The organizational costs associated with these forms of employee behavior were identified by Mirvis and Macy (1974) in their behavioral costing procedures; the applicable sections are identified in Figure 5.5. (The entire set of procedures includes about 10 pages of 30 or more costing rules, which were subsequently reported by these authors; see Macy & Mirvis, 1976, 1982.) To these direct costs for the organization, it may be necessary to add the costs associated with nonparticipation if the employee involved in the accident or grievance is absent from the work station. Still additional costs are incurred if such an employee is permanently disabled or leaves the organization.

Mirvis and Macy (1982) also delineated the direct costs associated with unscheduled machine downtime and repair, material and supply overuse, and inventory shrinkages. Not all such incidents of employee behaviors are attributable to employee distress; fatigue, poor judgment, anger, inattention, and other outcomes of distress at work are factors contributing to occurrence of these dysfunctional behaviors. In addition to the direct costs of performance decrements attributable to the previously mentioned behaviors, poor job performance may be attributable to the sublimation of negative feelings on the part of the employee. Feelings of anger, hostility, and anxiety are normal responses to stressful situations at work such as conflict with one's boss or other superior, role ambiguity about expected work performances, work overload, and other related experiences. However, many organizations do not legitimize the formal verbalization or expression of these normal feelings. The repression of these feelings may lead to some of the psychosomatic disorders discussed in chapter 4; alternatively, individuals sometimes find expression for these hostilities through subversive behaviors such as intentional machine malfunctions or poor-quality work.

Illustrations of these circumstances may be seen in the American automobile industry during the past several years. Ford Motor Company attempted to counteract this trend through a mass media campaign by pointing out that "quality is job 1." This effort was occasioned by cases in which employees sabotaged individual car quality by slipping bottles in the assembled door, dropping bolts in the engine cylinders before assembly, or placing notes saying something like "I'll be gone by the time you find this one!" in an empty soda can in a fender housing. There are numerous "humorous" stories of such subversive activities, all of which are detrimental to product quality. Employees use these means to express negative feelings that have found no more effective channels for release.

Some of these poor performance behaviors are consciously or unconsciously designed to get the individual attention at work; there is interpersonal stress associated with being ignored at work. Employees may seek dysfunctional ways of gaining attention if they cannot get adequate attention in a functional manner. For example, one frustrated automotive

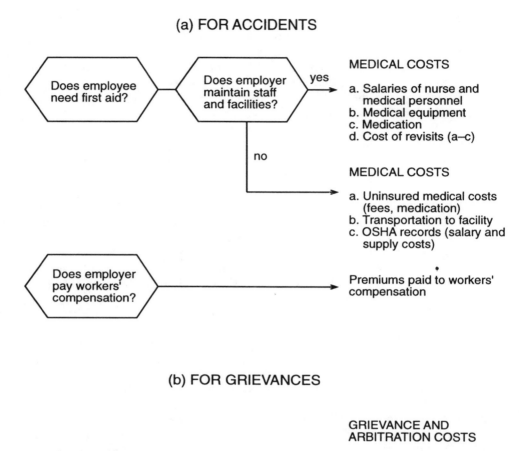

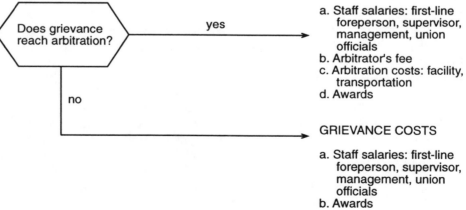

Figure 5.5. Direct costs of distress: Accidents and grievances. OSHA = Occupational Safety and Health Administration. Adapted from *Guide to Behavioral Costing* [working paper] by P. Mirvis and B. A. Macy, Institute for Social Research, University of Michigan, Ann Arbor, 1974.

assembly line worker shut down the entire line by pulling the emergency switch as a way to get attention. Alternatively, employees may change jobs as a way to seek greater self-fulfillment, appreciation, and overall satisfaction.

Health care costs. A third category of direct cost for organizational distress is health care costs. Health costs may be continuing to rise because companies are not eliminating the primary cause of health problems—stress. Organizational preventive stress management is needed to win the battle against health care costs (Wall & Nicholas, 1985). As indicated in Figure 5.1, $117.5 billion (or 85% of the costs of cardio-vascular diseases) is spent on health care: hospital and nursing home services, physician and nurse services, and drugs. If the proportion of variance from job stress as a contributing factor to cardiovascular disease were known, the proportion of the health care costs attributable to job stress could be estimated. For example, if 13% of cardiovascular disease was caused by job stress, then $15.2 billion (13% of $117.5 billion) of the health care costs in 1995 are attributable to job stress. In fact, most distress is preventable and about 50% of diseases are lifestyle-related, which means preventable through changes in lifestyle (Last & Wallace, 1992). Although health care costs have risen substantially over the past couple of decades in the United States and exceed all corporate profits, Johns Hopkins public health researchers concluded from a study of 135 health-care providers that low-cost care did not necessarily lead to low-quality care (Woolsey, 1995). Their results indicated that constant program monitoring can improve quality and reduce costs. However, many industries, such as the grocery industry, are still challenged by rising health care and health insurance costs (Schaeffer, Donegan, Garry, & Mathews, 1995).

Compensation awards. The fourth category of direct costs for organizational distress includes workers' compensation payments and court-ordered compensation awards to distressed employees. This concept originated in Germany in about 1860 under Chancellor Bismarck, who thought that employees should have medical care and some form of wage supplement to assist them in case of on-the-job injuries (G. T. Adams, 1987). Workers' compensation stress claims are extremely difficult to analyze because injuries to emotions are not objective in the manner of physical injuries and the same situation can affect two individuals in dramatically different ways (Gice, 1993). Even with these difficulties, stress claims jumped 531% in California between 1980 and 1986, and the premiums doubled, in contrast to a less than 10% rise in the overall claims over the same period (Rosch, 1991). Nine of every 10 California job stress suits were successful, with an average award of $15,000, compared to a national average of $3,420.

The success of the workers' compensation systems in each state rely on the integrity of both employees and organizations and on the management of overall costs. Nationally, costs to employers soared from $25.1 billion in 1984 to about $62 billion in 1991, an increase of well over 100%.

There have been some successful attempts to address the cost-escalation issue. For example, in 1993 Oregon successfully decreased insurance rates by 34% and increased wage-loss benefits for permanent disabilities (Kilgour, 1993). The Oregon successes were the result of three waves of reform: (a) the introduction of a competitive rate-making system in 1982; (b) the restriction of stress claims not inherent to work in 1987; and (c) more radical reforms, such as the promotion of return-to-work programs, in 1990.

An American Management Association (AMA) research report (1996) estimated that employers spent approximately $80 billion dollars on disability and workers compensation claims during 1996. Furthermore, the report indicated that 70% of the companies surveyed reported increases in disability claims, particularly in areas related to tension and stress, and companies that eliminated jobs between 1990 and 1995 were more likely to report increases in seven of eight disability categories. Although the increase in claims is more often seen among employees directly affected by the job eliminations, disability claims also rose among those who survived job cuts. The greatest increases were in the disability claim categories most directly reflecting stress: mental illness, psychiatric treatment, substance abuse; cardiovascular problems and hypertension; and back pain, strain, or injury. Employers began aggressively attacking disability costs during 1996 through modified-work and back-to-work programs (Jeffrey, 1996; see also Reed, 1994). However, the AMA (1996) found that employers were much more aggressive in their attempts to bring ill or disabled employees receiving occupational workers' compensation benefits back to work and somewhat less aggressive with employees on nonoccupational disability leave.

The organization's liability in legal cases varies substantially, as do the amount of compensation awards. For example, Burroughs Corporation had to pay one of their secretaries $7,000 for hysteria resulting from her boss's constant criticism of her restroom trips; the secretary had filed an appeal for a larger award. In another case, the Los Alamos Scientific Laboratory had to pay an employee working with radioactive materials $75,000 for anxiety that resulted from one bout with cancer. The Equal Employment Opportunity Commission sued Mitsubishi Motor Manufacturing of America for sexual harassment and physical abuse of female employees (Sharpe, 1996). With more than 500 potential plaintiffs, Mitsubishi faces a potential liability of $150 million.

In Frank Deus's federal lawsuit, mentioned in chapter 1 (Deus v. Allstate Insurance Company, 1990–1992), the jury found in favor of Mr. Deus, who had been subjected to a high strain, highly distressful job over an extended period of time. Although the jury awarded Mr. Deus $1.5 million, the presiding judge vacated the verdict, and the U.S. Fifth Circuit Court of Appeals upheld the federal judge. Hence, the unpredictability of these cases creates substantial uncertainty for both plaintiffs and defendants. In this case, Allstate was still subject to the substantial direct and indirect costs of litigation regardless of the fact that the verdict was vacated.

Organizations can follow both state and federal court rulings to determine the trends for such direct costs. For employees who become permanently disabled, an organization may face long-term financial commitments or a large, lump-sum severance payment. An emergent risk for organizations and health care providers is posttraumatic stress syndrome (McMorris, 1996). For example, a Washington, DC, prison guard was given a jury award of $300,000 in damages for her claim that her male supervisor's sexual advances caused her to be unable to work for 2 years.

In summary, the direct costs of mismanaged stress fall into three categories: participation and membership, on-the-job performance, and compensation awards. The measurement of the first two categories has been the subject of recent investigations in several diverse industries. Organizations have been aware of these costs for a long time, even though they have not always placed economic figures on them. Compensation awards for distress at work are only recently emerging as an organizational cost.

Indirect Costs

In addition to the various direct economic costs of mismanaged stress, there are a number of indirect costs that organizations incur, which also may be contributing factors to previously discussed direct costs. Whereas researchers at the University of Michigan's Institute for Social Research, studying the quality of work life, have made notable progress in developing guidelines for many of the direct costs, and the courts can help determine compensation costs, the same sorts of guidelines, procedures, and precedents are not available for indirect costing. The absence of indirect costing procedures does not make the indirect costs any less important for organizational managers and investigators. The absence of such procedures suggests that it may be difficult to trace such costs to develop accurate estimates of their magnitude.

Loss of vitality. Selye (1974) argued that all individuals have both superficial and deep adaptive energy. The superficial adaptive energy enables individuals to cope with immediate emergency or stress situations. Individuals who constantly experience too high a level of stress for their particular abilities and energy resources may not have sufficient recuperative time to replenish the superficial adaptive energy supply that gets consumed on a daily basis. Employees who are expended in this way on a regular basis may end up accruing direct performance costs for the organization in the form of lowered work quality. Even in the absence of such direct costs, there may be indirect costs associated with the inability to cope effectively with changes at work. Long-term work overload is likely to create such a condition, with its associated problems. Individuals who are chronically distressed lose their responsiveness and resiliency because they do not have the necessary superficial adaptive energy to cope with stress. Such employees are not able to contribute constructively and consistently to organizational health and functioning.

This loss of vitality may manifest itself in varying degrees of *low mo-*

rale, low motivation, and *dissatisfaction* in the workforce. These indirect costs have been shown to contribute to some of the direct costs previously discussed, such as the connection between low morale and high turnover or between dissatisfaction and low productivity. However, these manifestations of loss of vitality have implications other than their contribution to the direct costs. They are also evidence of poor-quality work life, which has humanitarian implications over and above the economic considerations discussed. The work environment need not be a dissatisfying place. On the contrary, there are long-term benefits available to organizations that are concerned with humanitarian and morale considerations, such as the goodwill that leads individuals to seek employment with the organization.

Communication breakdowns. Distress at work also has adverse effects on communication patterns of employees. Kahn and his associates (1964) found that as role conflicts and role ambiguity intensified, there was a decline in the frequency of communication between the individual and others in the working environment. The *decline in communication frequency* was much more notable in the case of role conflict, when the individual experiencing the conflict attempts to reduce it by withdrawing from conflicted relationships. This reduction in the frequency of interactions may lead to disruption and to misunderstanding in the accomplishment of interdependent tasks and activities.

Especially at the managerial level, much of the work in an organization gets accomplished through verbal and written instructions, directions, information sharing, and clarification of objectives and activities. An example of how miscommunication can disrupt work activities occurred at a large photochemical company one summer. When told to paint the windows in one building, the crew never asked for clarification and simply painted the windowpanes in the entire building, rather than the frames as had been intended!

In addition to the reduced frequency of communication that may occur owing to stress, there is a clear potential for *distortions* to occur in communication linkages. One of the associated events of a stressful situation is the arousal of defense mechanisms. Although the psychological defense mechanisms individuals use to protect ego integrity have some functional value, they may also distort both the messages sent and the interpretation of messages received. Either is dysfunctional for effective working relationships.

Faulty decision making. Effective managerial decision making requires information about the decision situation and about judgmental processes (MacCrimmon & Taylor, 1976). The communication breakdowns discussed earlier not only are an organizational cost of distress but also may contribute to faulty decision-making processes in the organization. That is, as communication flows and patterns are disrupted, information may be either lost or not transmitted within the organization. The loss of this information can have a detrimental effect on decisions.

A second way that distress at work can lead to faulty decision making is by impairing the judgment of the manager. When a manager is distressed, his or her physiological and psychological processes may be adversely affected. Specifically, a manager who is bored because of too little stress may be inattentive and lack alertness in making a decision, whereas a manager who is overloaded with demands may not carefully weigh and evaluate the decision alternatives and the information relevant to these alternatives. Both poor judgment and lost information owing to communication breakdowns can contribute to costly bad decisions for the organization.

Two examples of faulty decision making occurred at Eastman Kodak Company and on a U.S. Navy warship in the Persian Gulf (Nelson, Quick, & Quick, 1989). In the former case, a Kodak executive experienced intense pressure from a minority-group coalition, resulting in his decision to commit the company to a course of action prematurely, failing to take into consideration decision factors that eventually would lead to the reversal of his decision. In the latter case, the captain of the warship launched a missile and downed an Iranian airliner on the basis of faulty information processing that suggested that the target was an Iranian warplane.

Quality of work relations. The communication problems that result from distress are one aspect of the overall quality of working relationships in an organization. In addition to reduced communications, Kahn and his associates (1964) found a marked increase in *distrust, disrespect,* and *animosity* occurring under conditions of stress. Individuals experiencing role distress tended to have markedly less trust in, respect for, and liking for those with whom they were working.

A deterioration in the quality of work relations in the organization can have at least two dysfunctional side effects. First, distrust and dislike may both contribute to destructive conflict and animosity in the relationship. The more energy that is consumed in this manner, the less constructive energy there is available for people to use in their work. This form of conflict is different from constructive conflict, which when managed in a confrontational manner can lead to change and growth. Second, poor working relationships have the effect of reducing employee satisfaction and, in turn, employee attendance (Steers & Rhodes, 1978). The reduced quality of relationships within the organization may contribute to the direct costs of absenteeism and to reduced organizational health in the long term.

Aggression and violence. Workplace aggression and violence appear to be growing forms of organizational distress of concern to employees and employers alike (O'Leary-Kelly, Griffin, & Glew, 1996). Organizationally motivated aggression is instigated by some factor in the organizational context and may lead to organizationally motivated violence. There are examples of aggression and violence in American industry throughout its history, such as the conflict and violence that periodically erupted in the U.S. steel industry in and around Pittsburgh during the 1920s. Aggression and violence need not be physical, however. Verbal, interpersonal, and psychological abuse can be nearly as destructive as physical aggression and violence. Furthermore, conflict originating at home can spill into the workplace when family members attack each other at work. One of the high risk target groups in this emergent problem area is composed of the medical and health care professionals who are exposed to or the subject of workplace violence. One study of 598 employees found that a work schedule that included nighttime hours was the one characteristic consistently associated with a higher risk of physical attack or threat in the workplace (Budd, Arvey, & Lawless, 1996).

Opportunity costs. Healthy organizations respond and adapt to their task environments, as do healthy individuals, to minimize the impact of threats and take advantage of opportunities. The threat–rigidity thesis discussed in chapter 1 highlights the difficulty in maintaining flexibility and adaptability during changing, stressful, or challenging times (Staw et al., 1981). Distressed employees and organizations are at a disadvantage in this regard because they may develop tunnel vision, devoting more energy to defensive, maintenance responses than to adaptive, positive ones. Distressed individuals and organizations may use most of their available energy for coping or survival. Under such conditions, the longer time perspective needed for examining future opportunities gets lost, and the possibilities for action in the task environment are simply not seen.

Summary

Organizations and individuals engage in exchange relations for mutual benefit, health, and growth. The health of one member in the exchange affects the health of the other member. Organizational health is an ideal state of flexibility, adaptability, and productivity toward which an organization may work, although the goal is never fully achieved. Optimum levels of stress within an organization enhance this process and contribute to organizational health, whereas excessive levels lead to the various sorts of dysfunctions and organizational costs discussed in this chapter.

The direct costs of distress are those related to nonparticipation and nonmembership, nonperformance, and court-ordered compensation awards. Of the three categories of direct costs, more is currently known about the first two than about compensation awards. Additional information about compensation award costs awaits the establishment of court precedents and case law development in the states as well as in the federal sector.

The indirect costs of distress are much less easily quantified but may be no less destructive for organizational health. Some of these indirect costs, such as poor quality in work relations, may be connected to the more measurable direct costs, such as absenteeism and tardiness. Both sets of costs are detrimental and should be managed in a proactive, preventive manner so that an optimum level of stress is established for organizational health. The preventive management of organizational stress must be based on an understanding of the stresses operating in a particular organization. This understanding may be arrived at through the diagnostic process discussed in the next chapter.

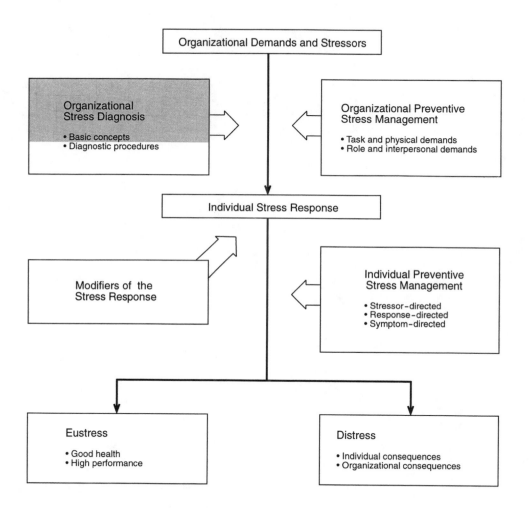

6

Basic Concepts for Stress Diagnosis in Organizations

The purpose of this chapter is to examine several relevant aspects of the process of organizational stress diagnosis. The word *diagnosis* comes from *dia*, meaning "through," and *gnosis*, meaning "knowledge of." In this case, organizational stress diagnosis is concerned with knowledge of the causes and consequences of the stress that specific organizations and individuals encounter. The role of diagnosis in organizational stress and preventive stress management was suggested in chapter 1. One of the aims of preventive management is to enhance individual and organizational health. However, to undertake activities toward that end without proper diagnosis would be ill-advised under most circumstances. Furthermore, the diagnostic process is not a one-time activity but an ongoing component of effective preventive management. The relevant aspects of the diagnostic process discussed in this chapter are the philosophy of stress diagnosis, the different types of diagnostic procedures available, the criteria for evaluating diagnostic procedures, and the characteristics of the diagnostician. Specific procedures and instruments are reviewed in chapter 7.

There are several purposes for conducting stress diagnostic activities. One purpose is to determine the cause of a current dysfunction, such as cardiovascular disease or high turnover rates. The focus here is on determining the major stressors that the individual or the organization are encountering, with the intent of altering them. A second purpose for diagnosing organizational stress is to develop an individual or organizational stress profile. The stress profile would allow the diagnostician to determine whether the individual or organization is functioning at an optimum level or might be at risk for stress-related organizational or individual distress. A third purpose for a stress diagnosis is to provide a basis for recommending and evaluating preventive stress management interventions to enhance individual and organizational health. There are no universally appropriate ways of managing stress, but there are techniques that may be applied once one has a thorough knowledge of the current organizational setting. Once these techniques are applied, their effectiveness in reducing stress must be systematically evaluated. A final purpose for a stress diagnosis is related to research regarding organizational stress. Although organizational stress has been studied for years, additional systematic studies of the causes of stress and evaluations of the methods for preventing distress at work would be beneficial to the field.

Stress Diagnosis: An Interdisciplinary Process

Diagnostic activities are appropriate for a variety of settings, including medical, social, and organizational. According to Laing (1971), diagnosis in social settings involves identifying the underlying causes of individual behavior and interpersonal dynamics within the setting. Laing indicated that the causes of behaviors and interactions may not be what the individuals in the setting say they are. The process of diagnosis does not assume that there is a problem, although most diagnostic activities are undertaken on the basis of some symptom or anticipated problem. To provide a responsible basis for preventive management activities, including treatment actions, the organizational stress diagnostician needs an understanding of both individual and organizational functioning; since both the organizational unit of analysis and the individual unit of analysis are important in the diagnostic process.

The objective of stress diagnosis is to identify the underlying causes of the stress rather than the manifestations of that stress. It is altogether too easy to deal with visible symptoms of stress and not properly diagnose the underlying causes of a problem or the preconditions that led to the occurrence of the symptom.

Interdisciplinary Nature

In dealing with a multifaceted problem such as organizational stress, it is valuable to incorporate the perspectives of several disciplines in developing an accurate diagnosis. Three key disciplines relevant to stress diagnosis are organizational science, psychology, and medicine. Most organizations, especially large ones like IBM and Mobil Oil Corporation, have individuals on staff who specialize in each of these three areas. Although they may be employed in personnel management, organizational development, or medical departments, these specialists are often available somewhere within the organization. What is important in stress diagnosis is the integration of the diverse professional expertise of these various groups. Each discipline's relevance to the diagnostic process is examined separately.

The first key discipline is *organizational science*. The discipline of organizational science takes the organization as its primary unit of analysis, although the individual and the group are of importance also. Organizational science starts with an understanding of organizational design, job design, and technology and of their impact on individuals and groups at work. People who study organizational behavior have learned over the years that it is not possible to understand an individual's behavior in organizations on the basis of psychological principles alone. An understanding of administrative and organizational principles is also needed before one can fully explain and predict organizational behavior. Without an open-system framework of organization, as presented in chapter 5, and a mastery of the fundamental concepts of organizational science, it is not easy to identify or recognize stress-related dysfunctions. Individuals who are trained in organizational science have special skills and knowledge in this area, but many managers and executives also have intuitive ability or explicit knowledge in this area.

The second key discipline is *psychology*, including the related medical discipline of psychiatry. Whereas organizational science takes the organization as its primary unit of analysis, psychology and psychiatry take the individual as their primary unit of analysis. These disciplines are important in diagnosing stress because of the role of emotions, ideas, and cognitive processes in influencing or altering individual physiological processes. If the diagnostician does not have an adequate understanding of psychology, it may not be possible to go beyond the medical symptoms to possible underlying psychological causes. Certainly not all distress comes from underlying psychological issues, but psychological processes play an instrumental role in diagnosing organizational stress.

The third key discipline is *medicine*, which is concerned traditionally with the biological and physiological functioning of the individual. An adequate understanding of physiological processes is important to identifying when an individual is encountering distress. Medicine is of primary importance because it is within the human body that the symptoms of distress are most commonly revealed. An individual's psychological distress frequently leads at some point to a physiological disorder. Therefore, it is important to recognize the symptoms of strain within the physiology of the individual.

These three key disciplines are essential underpinnings to the stress diagnostic process in organizations. In addition, there are several related disciplines, such as industrial sociology and occupational medicine, that play a role in understanding stress. Because these disciplines make contributions to the diagnostic process through their own unique perspectives and blend of experiences, thus rounding out the core of knowledge and skills contained in the pure disciplines, they should when possible be incorporated in the diagnostic process. Again, it should be noted that most large organizations have professionals employed on either a full-time or a consulting basis in each of these disciplines.

Basic Philosophy

There are several fundamental notions about organizational stress that shape the underlying diagnostic philosophy of this chapter. One notion is that stress is not necessarily bad. That is, it may be either functional or dysfunctional depending on its intensity, its source, and the individual's psychophysiological response to it. Therefore, some forms of stress in organizations require no preventive or remedial managerial response.

A second notion is that distress may manifest itself in any one of a host of individual or organizational problems. The "Achilles heel" phenomenon discussed in chapter 3 refers to the manifestation of distress at the individual's or organization's weakest point. For example, one individual

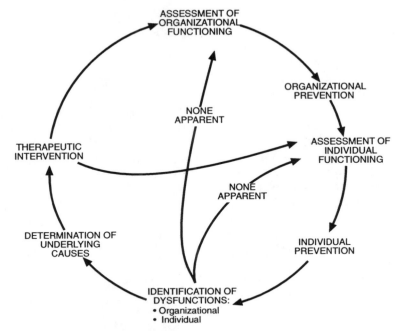

Figure 6.1.   The process of organizational stress diagnosis.

may suffer gastrointestinal disorders as a result of distress, whereas another individual may manifest cardiovascular disease. At the organizational level, one organization may experience high levels of turnover in response to distress, whereas another organization may experience a crippling labor strike. As a result, the diagnostician who attends only to the presenting disorders is not always able to identify underlying causes or may miss symptoms and causes by having too narrow a diagnostic focus. The key point here is that there are substantial and significant differences across individuals and organizations, and it is the *differences*, not the similarities, that are of particular importance to the skilled diagnostician.

The third notion is that effective stress diagnosis, at both the individual and organizational levels, is never complete. Although an individual or an organization may not encounter notable distress at one point in time, the same individual or organization may experience distress at another time. The ongoing diagnostic activities ensure the maintenance of optimum individual and organizational health.

The Process of Organizational Stress Diagnosis

The overall process for organizational stress diagnosis is presented in Figure 6.1. This model presents assessments of health and functioning at both the organizational and individual levels. On the basis of diagnostic assessments, the diagnostician must (a) propose individual and organizational activities to be used to prevent distress and (b) list the points of dysfunction at the organizational and individual levels. The points of dysfunction are identified by the problems or inconsistencies in the individual's or organization's functioning. To identify these dysfunctions requires both skill and sensitivity on the part of the diagnostician. As H. Levinson (1972) put it, "Any fool can tell that a river flows. Only he who understands its cross-currents, its eddies, the variations in the speed, the hidden rocks, its action in drought and flood, is the master of its functioning" (p. 7). So it is with individuals and organizations. Until the diagnostician has become fully familiar with the subject of the diagnosis, it is not possible to delineate the points of dysfunction.

Preventive activities should be tailored to the specific individual or organization on the basis of the diagnostic findings, taking into consideration the individual differences previously discussed. A diagnosis may reveal no notable, current dysfunctions. Even if no distress is revealed, it is necessary to continue the organizational and individual assessment activities at specified intervals. Failure to do so invites the potential problem of dealing with a crisis in its full-blown form. Periodic assessments, such as on an annual basis, provide a more fertile ground for effective implementation of preventive management.

Therapeutic interventions, also a part of preventive management, are identified in Figure 6.1. Any therapeutic interventions must be based on a determination of the underlying causes of stress, not the surface symptoms. The therapeutic activities must also be tailored to the specific individual and organization. The purpose of the therapeutic interventions is to prevent further deterioration in functioning or to rectify problems that were not precluded by other preventive activities introduced on the basis of the diagnostician's assessment activities. For example, health maintenance programs, such as exercise and fitness activities, cannot prevent all cardiovascular disease. It may be necessary in individual cases to intervene therapeutically with surgery, drugs, or both.

Types of Diagnostic Procedures

In conducting the diagnostic assessments of individual and organizational functioning, a wide variety of procedures may be used. In this chapter, the general procedures for making diagnostic assessments are considered, and in chapter 7, specific instruments are examined. Because of the nature of stress and the dual levels of assessment (organizational and individual), it is appropriate for the diagnostician to draw on more than one type of diagnostic procedure in conducting a thorough assessment at either level.

Discussions and Interviews

Simply talking to employees about their work life and concerns about their jobs and work tasks can produce invaluable information and facilitate the diagnostic process. This is especially true for small organizations or for those with little experience in the diagnosis of organizational stress. Opening a channel of communication with employees produces a rich source of information regarding stress and its perceived sources and often generates useful ideas concerning organizational stress reduction. Perhaps more important, it also "legitimizes" stress as an appropriate topic of discussion at the workplace.

Group discussions represent a slightly more formal level of diagnosis than informal discussions with employees about work. Group discussions provide an opportunity to achieve consensus regarding the most important sources of organizational stress. In addition, group discussions provide a useful vehicle for brainstorming stress interventions with the employees, who are most closely affected by the stressors and most intimately involved in any intervention efforts.

Individual interviews may be used to diagnose either organizational or individual stress, depending on the structure and focus of the interview. The loosely structured interview gives the interviewee an opportunity to depict in more detail both perceptions and feelings about stressful events. It may be used without constraining the interviewee too narrowly in terms of what he or she reports. The difficulty with this procedure is related to its user rather than its nature. That is, the success of using interviews hinges on the skills and characteristics of the interviewer as much as on the structure and design of the interview protocol. Although the protocol should have some structure, it is important that it be sufficiently open-ended to allow for unsolicited input from the interviewee.

Athos and Gabarro (1978) discussed the use of a reflective technique with its attendant reflective responses as a way of enhancing interpersonal communication. This technique is based on the listening skills of the interviewer, whose purpose is to understand the interviewee's experience in detail and depth. However, the effective use of this technique requires skill and sensitivity. Some characteristics of the interviewer inhibit an effective process, whereas others enhance that process. For example, in conservative settings such as many oil companies and military units, an interviewer decked out in jeans and a T-shirt may erect barriers to effective communication that would not be present in another setting, such as a loading dock. The importance of these reactive effects has been discussed by Laing (1971), who pointed out that a situation immediately changes as soon as a diagnostician enters it.

A key advantage of the interview is the detail and depth of perspective it can afford the diagnostician. The interview combines a procedure for self-report data collection with some observation on the part of the interviewer. The limitation of the interview is its time-consuming nature and the potential difficulties in summarizing a number of interview results. There is much room for both faulty interpretation and unconscious bias in the analysis of interview data. Feeding back the results of interviews to management also becomes more complicated and cumbersome if the open-ended interview procedure is employed.

Questionnaires

Structured questionnaires are an alternative method for conducting diagnostic activities. Questionnaires are suitable for either individual or organizational use. In addition, they enable the diagnostician to develop data from large groups of people much more easily than would be possible through interviews. Because of the quantifiable responses that result from most social science questionnaires, this type of diagnostic procedure allows for more measurable intersubject comparisons. Even with semistructured interview protocols, it is often difficult to do more than make qualitative comparisons regarding the data.

Questionnaires can be useful in developing perceptual data and some feeling-state data. However, it is more difficult for the diagnostician to develop a sense of these feeling states through questionnaires than through interviews. The most that can be hoped for when using this procedure is a rough approximation of those feeling states. What is lost in detail in using questionnaires may be gained in the volume of data that can effectively be collected.

Questionnaire results are often more easily communicated to management. Such results do not require as much interpretation as is needed when reviewing interview data, although there is some need for explanation and clarification. Although questionnaire results may look objective because of their quantitative nature, one must keep in mind the subjective viewpoint of the individuals completing the instrument. Some of the individual biases that distort interview results still operate, but they are compensated for when larger samples are included for questionnaire surveys.

There are several other limitations to cross-sectional surveys that are of concern in the diagnostic process. One limitation, response bias, can take many forms, reflecting misrepresentation of work factors (intentional and unintentional), poor memory recall, and nonresponse bias. Nonresponse bias can be particularly troublesome; some workers may be unable to read or understand the questionnaire items, whereas others may be highly motivated to complete and return the survey (or parts of the survey). It is not uncommon in job stress surveys to achieve less than a 50% response rate, and the important question becomes whether nonrespondents differ from respondents along sociodemographic or stress variables. The extent to which these groups differ determines the representativeness of the respondent sample or the work population of interest and, consequently, the generalizability of the results.

Self-administered questionnaires also lack flexibility. With no interviewer present, variations in questions posed to the worker and probing for greater insight are not possible. This can result in misleading conclusions. For example, interview studies of police officers (e.g., Kroes, Margolis, & Hurrell, 1974) have found role conflict and role ambiguity to be major job stressors for the officers, yet questionnaire surveys using traditional measures failed to replicate these findings (Caplan, Cobb, French, Harrison, & Pinneau, 1975). On closer examination, it is evident that questionnaire items typically used in organizational stress surveys assess conflict and ambiguity within the organization; however, for police officers, conflict and ambiguity involve not only organizational but also community and societal expectations, the latter of which is missed in most questionnaire assessments. Finally, cross-sectional questionnaire surveys provide only a "snapshot" view of stress, with no information on dynamic aspects like worker adaptational strategies.

Observational Techniques

There are two categories of observational techniques that lend themselves to use in stress diagnosis. The first of these is *behavioral* observation, and the second is *medical* observation. Both must be employed by a trained observer who is skilled at selecting and evaluating aspects of the field to observe. Either category of observation may be of a quantitative or qualitative nature (Van Maanen, 1979). Qualitative and quantitative observation are both important and may be used to complement and supplement each other. Neither is necessarily better than the other.

Behavioral observations can be useful in individual stress diagnosis. They are difficult to use alone, without alternative types of diagnostic procedures, but they can be helpful as supplemental sources of data. Their use requires familiarity on the part of the diagnostician with the particular individual and with the culturally acceptable patterns of behavior that specific individuals exhibit in varying degrees. Behavior that varies substantially from the norms should be more closely monitored to determine its origin; stress is only one of a number of possible causes for such deviant behavior. Within the culturally accepted norms, there are individual variations that may be considered normal; therefore, it is important to understand an individual's normal patterns of behavior before ascertaining the degree of deviance. When deviant behavior is observed, it may be attributable to stress-related causes and thus used as supplemental diagnostic data.

Behavioral observations may also be made at the organizational level in diagnosing stress. Observations at this level are frequently but not always collected in the form of institutional records or archival data. The relevant behavioral observations are associated with organizational health, as discussed in chapter 5. These behaviors, detailed in chapter 7, include (a) absenteeism and tardiness rates, (b) turnover rates, and (c) strikes and other forms of work stoppages. Some occurrences of these behaviors should be anticipated in any organization. Judgment is required in the diagnostic process to determine what are "normal" or "healthy" occurrences of these behaviors and what rates suggest organizational distress.

Medical observations make up the second category of observational data. These consist of a set of possible observations made by a clinician or a laboratory technician using urine or blood analyses. These observations are used in individual stress diagnosis and may supplement organizational stress diagnosis. Several key medical observations that may be made, detailed in chapter 7, include (a) heart rate as measured by pulse, (b) blood pressure as measured using a sphygmomanometer, and (c) high-density lipoprotein (HDL) and low-density lipoprotein (LDL) cholesterol levels as measured in blood analyses. There are normal ranges for all of these observations, and observations outside of the normal ranges suggest that the individual may be experiencing distress.

Both categories of observational data should be used in conjunction with other types of diagnostic procedures. They are limited primarily to the diagnosis of individual stress, which is not the case with interviews and questionnaires. Interviews and questionnaires should be used as primary methods, therefore, supplemented at the individual level by medical observation and at the organizational level by selected behavioral observations.

Criteria for a Diagnostic Procedure

There are several criteria that should be considered in determining the relative merit or value of any stress diagnostic procedure. A diagnostic instrument or method should meet certain minimum standards, or selected criteria. It may be improved by additional characteristics that, if absent, do not necessarily make it a poor instrument or method. There are three necessary and three additional criteria for an effective diagnostic procedure.

Necessary Criteria

Validity is probably the most important characteristic of a diagnostic instrument and the most difficult criterion to meet. It is concerned with whether the methods and procedures used measure what they are designed to measure, in this case, organizational stress. The psychometrically different procedures that may be used in evaluating validity depend, finally, on the judgment of an investigator. Of the various forms of validity, several are relevant to this discussion. *Construct validity* is concerned with the extent to which the diagnostic procedure measures the theoretical construct "stress." What makes addressing construct validity difficult in the context of stress is the current theoretical difficulty in defining the term. There is no unified, agreed-on construct called "stress."

Of more current relevance is the issue of *discriminant validity*. In the context of stress, this form of validity is concerned with the distinction between organizational stress and related constructs such as anxiety, job tension, frustration, anger, and hostility. An effective diagnostic procedure would separate organizational stress symptoms from some of these other experiences.

A final form of validity that is of concern here encompasses *concurrent* and *predictive validity*. If the procedure used yields a stress diagnosis, one would expect also to observe various indicators of the consequences of stress either concurrently or at some point in the future. These consequences most commonly take the form of the various individual and organizational distress previously discussed in chapters 4 and 5. If the diagnostic procedure cannot predict these consequences of stress, it has little value in preventive or therapeutic intervention.

Reliability is the second central criterion for an effective diagnostic procedure. Concerned with the accuracy of the diagnostic measures, reliability is sometimes determined by taking measures at two time points (test–retest reliability) and examining their degree of relationship. In the case of organizational stress, however, the stress levels vary over time, making it difficult to establish test–retest reliability. Therefore, of more concern are the issues of interrater reliability and internal consistency. *Interrater reliability* reflects the degree that the procedure yields the same result regardless of the diagnostician who uses it, and *internal consistency* refers to the degree that the questions related to a particular source of stress elicit a common response from the same individual. Reliability is particularly important as a criterion for a diagnostic procedure because it limits the validity criterion; that is, regardless of how valid the diagnosis is, its usefulness depends on the reliability of the diagnosis.

An unreliable procedure can yield one of two errors. Either the diagnosis identifies stress where none exists or it fails to identify stress where it does exist. The latter error is potentially harmful, whereas the former may simply lead to wasted time and energy in preventive or remedial treatment. Failing to diagnose existing stress may allow serious disease to evolve beyond the point of primary or secondary preventive action, leaving remedial or therapeutic (tertiary prevention) action as the only alternatives. For these reasons, the reliability of the diagnostic procedure is particularly important.

Feasibility is the third key criterion for a diagnostic procedure. The method must not be too complex either for the diagnostician to use or, in the case of questionnaires, for an employee with minimal formal education to use. Unless the procedure is feasible for a variety of organizational settings, it will not yield the needed results even if it meets the validity and reliability criteria. The procedure must be valid and reliable, but it must also be sufficiently simple and economical to use.

Additional Criteria

In addition to the aforementioned criteria for selecting a diagnostic procedure, one may want to consider comprehensiveness, depth, and degree of instrumentation. The *comprehensiveness* of the procedure is relevant when there are few apparent indications or symptoms. Because distress may be manifested in a variety of ways, it is important to ask whether the diagnostic procedure considers all the possible symptoms and causes.

Greater comprehensiveness in the diagnostic process can be achieved by using multiple types of procedures as previously discussed. The limiting consideration is whether the use of multiple procedures becomes so complex that it violates the simplicity criterion. Sequential use of multiple procedures when indicated may yield the necessary comprehensiveness without too much complexity.

Related to the comprehensiveness criterion but distinct from it is the criterion of *depth*. Whereas comprehensiveness is concerned with how well the procedure identifies all forms of stress, the depth criterion is concerned with how well the procedure details the relative importance or magnitude of any particular stressor. For example, a questionnaire procedure may identify one's marital relationship as a source of stress without providing detailed information on the nature of that stress. In this case, an interview procedure would afford the opportunity for exploring the nature of the stress in more detail. An open-ended rather than structured questionnaire would provide a similar opportunity.

Another criterion to consider is the *degree of instrumentation* in the procedure. That is, to what degree is the procedure quantitative versus qualitative? A quantified procedure allows for greater cross-subject (either individual or organization) comparison, which is of some concern when concurrent and predictive validity are considered. The alternative to a highly quantified procedure is a highly qualitative one, which may leave more discretion and judgment in the hands of the diagnostician but provide richer detail in the diagnosis. Whereas more instrumented procedures may be more useful to managers, they are not necessarily better than qualitative procedures and even have disadvantages, such as lack of contextual detail, that handicap the diagnosis (Payne, 1978).

Any diagnostic procedure should be evaluated using the key criteria as well as the additional criteria. In chapter 7, selected procedures, methods, and instruments are examined in light of the criteria established here.

The Diagnostician

Although the specific procedure used is important to the diagnostic process, the characteristics of the diagnostician are also an integral part of the process of a formal diagnosis of organizational stress. It is debatable who the diagnostician should be. There are two considerations here: the organizational affiliation and the professional grounding of the individual. Regarding the former, the individual may be an academician with a primary commitment to the university, an internal consultant whose primary commitment is to the organization, or a professional consultant who must earn a living. The nature of the diagnostician's primary affiliation colors the person's perceptions and should be considered when a diagnostician is selected.

As a rule, the cost of the diagnosis is lower when internal diagnosticians and resources are used, although the quality of such internal diagnosis is not necessarily inferior to that of a diagnosis completed by an external professional. Considerations such as the internal diagnostician's independence and freedom from political reprisals influence the quality of the diagnostic findings. The professional consultant may be similarly subject to pressures internal to the organization, depending on how the initial relationship is structured.

A second consideration is the professional grounding of the diagnostician. This grounding shapes the individual's worldview and interpretation of the observations and information uncovered during the diagnostic process. The primary disciplines that have been discussed as being involved in the diagnostic process are organizational science, psychology and psychiatry, and medicine. Each of the disciplines has its own norms and values, preferred orientations, and limitations. It is important that the diagnostic process not be prejudiced by any set of predispositions in this regard.

This professional diversity necessitates an interdisciplinary dialogue. No professional can entirely overcome the perspectives of a particular profession, but he or she can be open to interdisciplinary efforts. An open dialogue involves individuals from other professions in the diagnostic process and may use referrals to the appropriate professional group. Without this sort of exchange, the diagnostic process may be prejudiced in the examination of such a multifaceted issue as stress.

One critical requirement of a diagnostician, regardless of affiliation or profession, is respect for confidentiality. Without confidentiality, individuals and organizations may not talk freely about their stresses and strains. It is inevitable for the diagnostic process to leave individuals or groups vulnerable and exposed with regard to their inner selves. It is critical that the diagnostician and the organization be sensitive to this point so that individuals are not hurt while in this vulnerable position.

Summary

This chapter has examined the process of diagnosing organizational stress. There are various purposes for engaging in formal stress diagnostic procedures, including (a) determining the causes of various individual and organizational dysfunctions, (b) developing stress profiles for individuals and groups at risk, (c) recommending and evaluating preventive managerial interventions, and (d) providing a basis for research regarding organizational stress. The diagnosis should be an interdisciplinary one that considers organizational science, psychology, and medicine in the process. The diagnosis may be achieved by means of interviews, questionnaires, or behavioral and medical observations. Whatever procedure is chosen for the diagnosis, it should be valid, reliable, and feasible. In addition to the methods and procedures, the characteristics of the diagnostician should be considered when using a formal procedure.

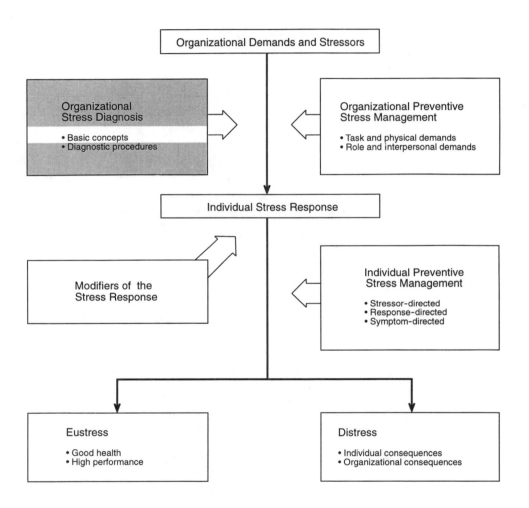

7

Survey of Stress
Diagnostic Measures

There is an ever-growing variety of questionnaires, interview procedures, and other measurement devices that may be used in the stress diagnostic process. For investigators and students of organizational stress, as well as managers interested in the health and performance of their organization, choosing a diagnostic procedure (as discussed in chapter 6) and specific diagnostic measurement tools can pose a bewildering challenge. In general, stress diagnostic measures fall into three basic categories, depending on their primary focus: (a) measures of organizational stressors, (b) measures of individual distress, and (c) measures of individual modifiers of the stress response. This chapter discusses selected instruments in each of these three areas and considers some advantages and disadvantages of individualized or customized measurement devices. Exhibit 7.1 lists the major stress-related diagnostic measures that are reviewed.

Measures of Organizational Stressors

When a specific organizational stress causes a major disruption, the source of the stress is usually apparent. In most instances, however, the impact of stressors is less obvious. There is a need, therefore, to diagnose systematically the sources and impacts of organizational stress. There are objective measures that can be used, but these tend to be rather nonspecific in identifying organizational stressors. Questionnaires and interviews provide more specific information about the sources of stress. Some of the objective measures of stress and a number of commonly used stress questionnaires and structured interview formats are reviewed in the following pages.

Although it is possible to examine work-related and non-work-related stress separately, it is not possible to understand fully an individual's overall stress level or experience without considering the two in combination. Therefore, this section also includes a consideration of relevant instruments that incorporate both aspects of an individual's life. It would be a mistake to ignore either work-related or nonwork-related factors in diagnosing an individual's stress level.

Exhibit 7.1.   Selected Stress-Related Diagnostic Instruments

---

Organizational stressors
  Objective organizational measures of stress
  Michigan Stress Assessment
  Quality of Employment Survey
  Occupational Stress Indicator
  Occupational Stress Inventory
  Job Stress Survey
  Job Content Questionnaire
  NIOSH General Job Stress Questionnaire
  Stress Audit
  Stress Diagnostic Survey
  Stressor Checklist
  Organizational Diagnosis
  Management Audit
  Life Events Scale
  Hassles and Uplifts Scale
  Work Environment Scale
  Other measures related to organizational stress
Individual distress
  Physiological measures
  Behavioral measures
  Cornell Medical Index
  Daily Log of Stress-Related Symptoms
  SCL-90-R
  Maslach Burnout Inventory
  Profile of Mood States
  Other measures related to individual distress
Modifiers of the response to stress
  Hardiness
  Type A behavior pattern
  Social support
  Coping mechanism
  Locus of control
  Other measures

Note. NIOSH = National Institute for Occupational Safety and Health.

Objective Measures of Organizational Stress

The objective measures that are available to evaluate organizational stress are, to a large extent, the measures used to assess organizational health and effectiveness. Such measures include the following:

- Tardiness rate
- Absenteeism rate
- Grievances filed
- Clinic and employee assistance program use rates
- Rate and severity of work-related accidents
- Interdepartmental employee transfer rate
- Employee turnover rate

- Performance of specific cost–profit centers in standard terms (time per unit of service, unit produced per time period, percentage of raw materials used, and so on)
- Sales volume and revenue; change in volume and revenue
- Return on equity

These and similar measures are appealing because they are objective and quantifiable. Unfortunately, they are rather nonspecific with regard to organizational stress. Each of the measures can be influenced by many factors other than stress. Even when a high absentee rate is attributable to organizational stress, knowing the absentee rate does not in itself indicate the source of the stress.

Objective measures can be useful in several specific instances. Comparison of tardiness, absenteeism, or turnover rates among subgroups within the organization may serve to identify high-risk groups worthy of further scrutiny. After these groups are identified, more specific stress questionnaires or interviews can be used to determine the reasons for poor performance. Comparing performance measures over time may help to alert management to potential difficulties. A fall in productivity or a rise in tardiness, absenteeism, clinic visits, or turnover may be an indicator of growing stress levels. What is important to note in this regard is the degree of *change* that occurs.

When preventive stress management procedures or other stress reduction activities are undertaken, the impact of the interventions can be followed by some of the objective measures. If such measures are used to assess the impact of management interventions, it is important to select carefully the measures that are likely to be affected by the intervention. For example, an organization evaluating a return-to-work program for employee disabilities might select absenteeism or tardiness but not turnover as objective measures to track because the last would not be expected to be affected.

Although the objective organizational measures of stress may indicate the existence of organizational stress, they do not provide much data or detail about the specific source of the stress. However, they provide an independent means for comparing groups within the organization and for assessing the impact of management interventions.

Michigan Stress Assessment

One of the earliest approaches to measuring organizational stress is found in the work of French and Kahn (1962). The work arose out of an interest in identifying the factors in the industrial environment that play a role in coronary artery disease. Self-report questionnaires were used to provide a subjective index of environmental stress. The principal variables were role ambiguity (unclear expectations), workload, role conflict (conflicting expectations), responsibility for persons, responsibility for things, participation, and relations with work group. Respondents rated each item on the questionnaire on a 5-point scale according to the sress it caused, ranging from *very little* to *very great* amounts of stress. The construct validity for each of the scales in the questionnaire was determined by factor analysis and judged to be acceptable. Likewise, internal consistency reliability coefficients (Cronbach's αs) for the scales were quite acceptable. The scales contained within the questionnaire have been used extensively by stress researchers over the past 35 years.

In addition to the self-report questionnaires, French and Kahn included a tally sheet for obtaining objective workload data. The tally sheet is filled out by another individual, for example, the respondent's secretary, and covers such items as phone calls, office visits, meetings, and other daily activities.

Quality of Employment Survey

Researchers from the Institute for Social Research at the University of Michigan and the National Institute for Occupational Safety and Health (NIOSH) developed and tested a series of questions that they have used to assess job-related stress in personal interviews, called the Quality of Employment Survey (Margolis, Kroes, & Quinn, 1974; Quinn & Shepard, 1974). Separate scores are obtained for six individual indices of job stress, and an overall job-stress score is obtained from these scales. The six indices are role ambiguity, underutilization, overload, resource inadequacy, insecurity, and nonparticipation.

Underutilization questions assess whether individual capabilities are untapped because there is too little to do or the work tasks are too easy. The *overload* index is just the reverse, a measure of the extent to which there is too much work or work tasks that are too difficult. *Resource inadequacy* questions determine whether there are adequate resources and information to do the job. *Insecurity* refers to job uncertainty (i.e., will there be continued employment?). Finally, the *nonparticipation* index considers whether the employee has a lack of "say" in the organization's decisions, particularly decisions that affect one's job.

The stress-related portion of the Quality of Employment Survey is somewhat inconvenient to use because it is in an interview format. Nevertheless, the Quality of Employment Survey provides a reliable overall measure of organizational stress as perceived by the individual. The indices developed for this survey have also been widely used in self-administered questionnaire formats.

Occupational Stress Indicator

The Occupational Stress Indicator, a questionnaire developed by C. L. Cooper, Sloan, and Williams (1988), is based on the C. L. Cooper and Marshall (1976) stress model and has been increasingly used as a diagnostic instrument in Europe. Like a number of other questionnaires that we describe later, this questionnaire was developed to provide a comprehensive view of occupational stress. It consists of six scales (plus a number of subscales) that measure sources of stress at work, coupled with scales measuring modifier variables (Type A behavior, locus of control, and coping strategies) as well as job satisfaction and mental and physical health. A number of studies have established the reliability of the Occupational Stress Indicator and have shown evidence for its predictive and criterion-related validity (Cooper et al., 1988).

Occupational Stress Inventory

Developed by Osipow and Davis (1988), this copyrighted instrument provides measures of three domains of occupational adjustment: occupational stress, personal strain, and coping resources. The occupational stress domain is assessed by a set of 60 items (six scales) measuring stressors related to role overload, role insufficiency, role ambiguity, role boundary, responsibility, and the physical environment. Personal strain is assessed by measures of vocational strain (problems in work quality or output), psychological or emotional problems, interpersonal problems, and physical illnesses. Coping resources are evaluated in four scales measuring recreational activities, self-care, social support, and rational–cognitive coping. Responses to the instrument's 140 items are made on a 5-point scale that gauges the frequency with which an item applies. The various subscales have demonstrated high test–retest reliability, and occupational norms are available. Plotting standardized scores on each subscale produces a "stress profile" for workers.

Job Stress Survey (JSS)

This 30-item instrument was designed to assess the perceived intensity (severity) and frequency of occurrence of working conditions that may adversely affect the psychological well-being of workers who are exposed to them (Spielberger, 1994). Questions describing stressors commonly experienced by managerial, professional, and clerical employees were selected for inclusion in this generic job stress measure.

Respondents are asked first to rate, on a 9-point scale, the relative amount (severity) of stress that they perceive to be associated with each of the 30 JSS job stressors (e.g., excessive paperwork, poorly motivated coworkers) compared to a standard stressor event, assignment of disagreeable duties, which is assigned a value of 5. To assess the "state–trait" qualities of the stressors, respondents indicate on a scale ranging from 0 to 9+ days the number of days on which each stressor was experienced during the previous 6 months. Summing the ratings for each individual JSS item yields an overall severity (JSS-S) and frequency (JSS-F) score and overall job stress index (JSS-X), which is based on the sum of the cross-products of the severity and frequency scores. Severity and frequency scores are also computed for 10-item job pressure and organizational support subscales, which were derived by factor analysis from the 30 JSS items. The frequency, severity, and index subscales show considerable internal consistency (Spielberger, 1994).

Job Content Questionnaire

The Job Content Questionnaire (JCQ; Karasek, 1985) in its original form (Framingham version) was developed to measure the risk of job-related coronary heart disease in a large-scale study. The short (original) version of the questionnaire contains 27 questions based largely on items and scales from the U.S. Quality of Employment Surveys (QES) conducted in the late 1960s and early 1970s. A longer, 49-item version of the questionnaire is recommended by the author. Scales include psychological job demands, skill utilization, job decision authority, job decision latitude, coworker support, supervisor support, job dissatisfaction, depression, and sleeping problems. A still longer version of the instrument (112 items) includes scales in the areas of customer contact, social identity, and the human–computer interface. Item scales are largely in the agree–disagree format. The scales have been demonstrated to be reliable, and the instrument has gained acceptance among those who subscribe to Karasek's (1979) "demands–control" stress model. Scores obtained through its use can be compared to national average scores from QES. The questionnaire has been translated into a number of languages, and users have formed a network to circulate their findings.

NIOSH Generic Job Stress Questionnaire

The Generic Job Stress Questionnaire (Hurrell & McLaney, 1988) was developed by the National Institute for Occupational Safety and Health (NIOSH) and contains measures of 13 job stressors as well as a host of measures of individual distress and of modifiers of the stress response. The questionnaire assesses constructs within domains contained in the NIOSH job stress model (Hurrell & Murphy, 1992). Specific stressor, distress, and modifier variable constructs were selected for inclusion in the instrument on the basis of a content analysis of the job stress literature, and the scales selected to measure these constructs were adapted from scales with known reliability and validity. The instrument was designed to be modular in form, so that the diagnostician or stress researcher can select individual scales or use the entire instrument. The questionnaire has been translated into a variety of languages (including Japanese and Finnish), and normative data on the questionnaire are currently being gathered.

Stress Audit

Developed by Miller and Smith (1987), the Stress Audit is a 238-item instrument that samples the magnitude and type of stress experienced by the respondent and assesses individuals' relative vulnerability to stress and the development of symptoms. Domains or sources of stress assessed by the questionnaire include family, individual roles, social interactions, environment, financial, and work–school (41 items). Seven different types of distress are also measured; they are labeled muscular, parasympathetic nervous system, sympathetic nervous system, emotional, cognitive, endocrine, and immune system. This instrument is available in paper-and-pencil and computer formats. Machine scoring yields computerized personal and professional individual reports as well as group reports and item analyses.

Stress Diagnostic Survey

The Stress Diagnostic Survey (SDS) was developed by Ivancevich and Matteson (1980) at the University of Houston. The questionnaire is designed to help individual employees identify specific areas of high stress at work. In addition to the work version of the SDS, there is a nonwork version that profiles individuals' personal stressors. It has also been used to profile worker subgroups and as a research tool to assess the impact of specific management interventions on individual perceptions of stress.

The work version of the SDS consists of 80 brief statements of conditions, each of which the respondent rates on a 7-point scale according to whether the condition is never, sometimes, or always a source of stress. The responses to these questions are totaled to yield separate scores for 15 categories of work stressors, and these scores are plotted to yield a stress profile. The scales in the work version of the SDS were determined by factor analysis with data from over 2,000 business executives, hospital nursing personnel, graduate management and engineering students, and medical technologists, and they generally show high internal consistency.

Stressors Checklist

Yet another questionnaire measure of organizational stress is McLean's (1979) Stressors Checklist. The checklist consists of 12 items representing common situations or problems that the respondent rates on a 5-point scale according to whether they are *never, seldom, sometimes, usually,* or *always* a concern or obstacle to doing one's job.

The results of the questionnaire provide scores for four stress-related areas: conflict and uncertainty, job pressure, job scope, and rapport with management. The scores in each area can range between 3 and 15; the author suggested that scores of 9 or above indicate that the area may be presenting a problem warranting attention. The total score can range from 12 to 60, and a score of 36 or more is felt to suggest an excess amount of stress in the work environment.

The checklist is easily administered and includes several areas of general relevance. Lack of published data on the reliability and validity of the list makes any objective interpretation difficult. Therefore, it should be considered a tool for raising employee awareness of stress, rather than a diagnostic instrument for identifying areas requiring intervention.

Organizational Diagnosis

There are many objective measures of organizational effectiveness, such as profit margins and productivity indices, and there are several stress questionnaires such as those listed previously. However, methods for conducting a comprehensive assessment of organizational effectiveness are limited. In his 1972 publication, *Organizational Diagnosis*, Harry Levinson and his coauthors (Levinson, Molinari, & Spohn, 1972) provided a systematic approach to the study and assessment of organizational performance. Drawing on psychoanalytic theory, sociology, and systems theory, they described an orderly diagnostic method aimed at understanding the operation of an organization and ascertaining areas of dysfunction. The data obtained through the diagnostic process serve as the basis for intervention and organizational change efforts. *Organizational Diagnosis* is aimed primarily at individuals involved in organizational consultation and executives interested in assessing their own managerial efforts.

The four major areas in the diagnostic process and their subheadings are as follows:

1. Generic data
   a. Identifying information (e.g., organization name, location)
   b. Historical data (e.g., reason for the study, organizational problems, circumstances of the study)
2. Description and analysis of current organization as a whole
   a. Structural data (e.g., table of organization, personnel)
   b. Process data (e.g., communication systems, previous reports)
3. Interpretive data
   a. Current organizational functioning (organizational knowledge, emotional atmosphere, organizational action)
   b. Attitudes and relationships (attachments, relations to things and ideas, authority)
4. Analysis and conclusions
   a. Organizational integrative patterns (appraisal of the organization in terms of assets and impairments, relationship of the organization with the environment)
   b. Summary and recommendations (present status, prognostic conclusions, recommendations)

Organizational Diagnosis uses a wide range of case studies and published accounts to illustrate the approach to gathering and using the information listed in each of these sections. In addition, the book includes a detailed survey, the Organization and Job Attitude Inventory. Although "stress diagnosis" is not specifically identified as an area of investigation, numerous stress-related items are included in the questionnaire. Rather than providing a quantitative measure of organizational well-being and organizational stress, *Organizational Diagnosis* provides a method for assessing these items in the context of a comprehensive study of the organization.

Management Audit

Cooper and Marshall (1978) proposed a general framework within which to diagnose the stress of managerial work. Although they did not develop or propose quantitative or qualitative instrumentation to accompany their audit, their conceptual framework is useful. They suggested that there are seven relevant aspects of managers and their work that contribute to stress and strain. (The seventh aspect is Type A behavior pattern, which they treated as a moderator of the stress–strain relationship, just as this book does. The Type A behavior pattern is not relevant to this section of the chapter.)

The six sources of managerial stress that Cooper and Marshall (1978) proposed be examined are (a) the job of management, (b) interpersonal relations at work, (c) role in the organization, (d) organizational structure and climate, (e) career prospects, and (f) home and work interface. Although the authors did not propose specific measurement devices for conducting a diagnosis, this conceptual framework lends itself to the design of interview protocols that investigate each of these six sources of stress.

The audit has primarily two limitations. Because no specific measurement device is proposed by the authors, diagnosticians are left even more on their own than in the case of Levinson's organizational-diagnosis approach. Also, this diagnostic approach is limited to managerial work and as such has limited applicability in other occupational areas.

Life Events Scale

Probably the most widely used research instrument for studying the long-term effects of stress is the Life Events Scale (LES), also known as the Social Readjustment Rating Scale (SRRS), the Schedule of Recent Experiences (SRE), the Social Readjustment Rating Questionnaire (SRRQ), and the Schedule of Recent Life Events (SRLE). The earliest version of the scale was developed at the University of Washington in the late 1950s (Hawkins, Davis, & Holmes, 1957). For several years, the degree of life change inherent in the various life events was not taken into consideration, but in 1964 scaling studies were carried out to establish a method for weighing the different life changes (Holmes & Rahe, 1967). The numbers in parentheses after each of the scale items in Exhibit 7.2 represent the number of life change units (LCU) for each item. These units were established by assigning an arbitrary value to marriage and asking individuals to rate the other 42 items in comparison to marriage.

The LES has been tested in a wide variety of settings and has been shown to have a high degree of reliability and validity. LCU ratings of the

Exhibit 7.2. Life Events Scale.

Below is a list of events that you may have experienced during the past year. In the left-hand column, please check off those events that did occur. In the right-hand column, please rate how stressful you perceived each event to have been, on a scale of 1 to 5. (Scale values: 1—not at all stressful; 2—slightly stressful; 3—moderately stressful; 4—somewhat stressful; 5—extremely stressful)

Personal

_____ Personal injury or illness (53)
_____ Outstanding personal achievement (28)
_____ Revision of personal habits (24)
_____ Change in recreation (19)
_____ Change in church activities (19)
_____ Change in sleeping habits (15)
_____ Change in eating habits (15)
_____ Vacation (13)
_____ Christmas (12)

Family

_____ Death of a spouse (100)
_____ Divorce (73)
_____ Marital separation (65)
_____ Death of a close family member (63)
_____ Marriage (50)
_____ Marital reconciliation (45)
_____ Change in health of a family member (44)
_____ Pregnancy (40)
_____ Gain of a new family member (39)
_____ Change in number of arguments with spouse (35)
_____ Son or daughter leaving home (29)
_____ Trouble with in-laws (29)
_____ Wife begins or stops work (26)
_____ Change in number of family get-togethers (15)

Financial

_____ Change in financial state (38)
_____ Mortgage over $10,000 (31)
_____ Foreclosure of mortgage or loan (30)
_____ Mortgage or loan of less than $10,000 (17)

Social

_____ Jail term (63)
_____ Sexual difficulties (39)
_____ Death of a close friend (37)
_____ Begin or end school (26)
_____ Change in living conditions (25)
_____ Change in schools (20)
_____ Change in residence (20)
_____ Change in social activities (18)
_____ Minor violations of the law (11)

Work

_____ Fired at work (47)
_____ Retirement (45)
_____ Business readjustments (39)
_____ Change to a different line of work (36)
_____ Change in responsibilities at work (29)
_____ Trouble with boss (23)
_____ Changes in work hours or conditions (20)

Note. From "The Social Adjustment Rating Scale," by T. H. Holmes and R. H. Rahe, 1967, *Journal of Psychosomatic Research, 11,* p. 218. Copyright 1967 by Pergamon Press, Ltd. Adapted with permission.

different life events have been found to follow the same basic pattern among individuals of different ages and different ethnic backgrounds (Coleman, 1973; Rahe, 1972).

Much of the research relating life stresses to illness has used the LES as the primary measure of stress. Early research with the scale demonstrated that 80% of people with scores over 300 and 53% of people with scores between 150 and 300 suffered a significant health impairment during the period following the stressful events. People with scores under 150 had a low incidence of major health problems. Significant medical problems whose onset has been associated with significant increases in LES scores include sudden death, myocardial infarction, acute respiratory illnesses, and a variety of musculoskeletal problems (Rahe, 1972).

Although the LES is the most widely tested and perhaps the most extensively used stress scale, some investigators have criticized it on the grounds that it may involve considerable measurement error; they have proposed alternative approaches to measuring life events (see Dohrenwend, Raphael, Schwartz, Stueve, & Skodol, 1993). Moreover, its application to the assessment of organizational stress is limited by the fact that only 7 of the 43 items are work-related. In the work area, as in other areas of the LES, a wide range of events that may be significant stressors to many individuals are omitted. The LES may be a useful tool to assess the general level of stress among a group of individuals and to predict the likelihood of future illness; however, it does not provide specific diagnostic information to guide organizational or individual interventions.

Hassles and Uplifts Scales

Kanner, Coyne, Schaefer, and Lazarus (1981) reported an alternative method for measuring stressful life events. As in standard life events methods, the concern is with the prediction of psychological symptoms. Both scales developed by Kanner et al. (1981) identify work and nonwork sources of stress in an interspersed format. The Hassles Scale contains 117 items identified as possible irritants for an individual, ranging from minor annoyances to major pressures, problems, or difficulties. The Uplifts Scale contains 136 items identified as sources of good feelings, such as peace, satisfaction, or joy. Each scale contains the option for adding hassles or uplifts experienced by the individual that were not covered in the scale. The items in the Hassles Scale are rated on a 3-point severity scale, and those in the Uplifts Scale are rated on a 3-point frequency scale.

In a 10-month study, Kanner et al. (1981) found the Hassles Scale to predict concurrent and subsequent psychological symptoms such as anxiety, depression, and psychoticism better than the LES. They also found the Uplifts Scale to be positively related to symptoms for women but not for men. The test–retest reliabilities were .79 for frequency and .60 for intensity of the Uplifts Scale. Like the LES, the Hassles and Uplifts Scales may be useful tools to assess the general level of stress, but they provide little diagnostic information to guide preventive interventions.

Work Environment Scale

The Work Environment Scale (WES; Moos, 1981) was not developed to assess job stress; rather, it was designed to assess the general work climate of all types of work units. It has nonetheless gained considerable popularity among stress researchers. It focuses on the measurement and description of the interpersonal relationships among employees and between managers and employees; the directions of personal growth and development that are emphasized in the work unit; and the basic organizational structure of the unit. The scale contains 90 items that are divided into 10 subscales (e.g., work pressure, control, task orientation, supervisory support, peer cohesion, physical comfort) and uses a true–false format. The subscales have demonstrated acceptable reliability and validity and have been widely used over the past 15 years. Norms are available for a limited number of occupations, and users may develop work unit profiles to compare work units and to assess work group changes over time. A 40-item short form (Form S) is also available.

Other Measures Related to Organizational Stress

In addition to the diagnostic procedures already mentioned, there are numerous other questionnaires, structured interview formats, and measures of organizational stress reported by various authors, such as Albrecht (1979). Job satisfaction surveys can be a useful adjunct measure in analyzing organizational stress and its impact. Such measures include the Job Description Index (Smith, Kendall, & Hulin, 1969), the Context Survey (McLean, 1979), the Minnesota Satisfaction Questionnaire (Weiss, Davis, & England, 1967), and other scales reviewed by Dunham and Smith (1979).

Measures of Individual Distress

Individual distress, like organizational stressors, can be measured with objective or subjective techniques. The discussion of individual consequences in chapter 4 provides a good indication of the range of behavioral, psychological, and medical factors that might be evaluated in the measurement of individual distress. This chapter focuses on some of the standardized measures of individual distress. Unfortunately, these measures do not have the specificity and comprehensiveness that individual psychological testing or a complete medical examination offers. They are, however, more feasible measures in the context of most organizations.

Physiological Measures

There are literally dozens of physiological parameters that have been used in the study of stress. These range from obvious and easily obtained mea-

Exhibit 7.3. Physiological Parameters Used in Stress Assessment

Physical measures
- Pulse
- Blood pressure
- Body weight
- Respiratory rate

Measures that use specialized electronic equipment
- Muscle tension (facial muscles, neck muscles, and others)
- Galvanic skin response (GSR; sweating or cutaneous conduction)
- Blood flow (measured by plethysmography)
- Electrocardiogram
- Electroencephalogram (brain waves)

Hormone levels[a]
- Catecholamines (adrenaline, noradrenaline, and metabolites)
- Cortisol, related hormones, and metabolites
- Adrenocorticotrophic hormone (ACTH)
- Glucagon
- Other hormones (e.g., thyroid, angiotensin, growth hormone, renin)

Glucose, lipids, and related metabolites
- Glucose
- Cholesterol
- Triglycerides
- Lipoproteins
- Free fatty acids

[a]May be measured in blood or urine, depending on the hormone and assay involved.

sures such as heart rate to obscure and poorly understood parameters such as newly discovered hormones and hormonelike substances. Exhibit 7.3 lists some of the frequently used physiological measures. These measures raise several issues for the executive, manager, or organizational consultant that are different from the issues faced with questionnaire or interview material.

First, there is the question of interpretation of physiological data. Under standard conditions, the parameters in Exhibit 7.3 can be reliably measured, but assessing their validity as stress measures is more difficult. The validity of medical tests is determined by both the *sensitivity* and the *specificity* of the test. Sensitivity and specificity are complementary measures that indicate how well a test identifies people with a given condition (sensitivity) and separates those people from people without the condition (specificity).

As tests of organizational stress, physiological measures have potential problems with both specificity and sensitivity. For example, specificity of blood or urinary measures of catecholamines is limited by the fact that there are many factors other than stress that influence catecholamine assays. These factors include severe illness; use of one or more of a wide variety of prescription and nonprescription drugs; and ingestion of tea, coffee, or any of several other drinks or foods. Similarly, heart rate can be influenced by a wide range of factors in addition to stress. Other measures are limited as objective indicators of stress by their lack of sensitivity.

Cholesterol levels, for example, tend to change slowly; they might remain relatively constant despite the occurrence of highly stressful events.

A second factor to consider in the use of physiological measures is feasibility, in terms of both cost and convenience. Pulse and blood pressure are easily determined. Company nurses can teach others to take pulses and blood pressures in a matter of minutes, and a minimum of equipment is required. Measurement of muscle tension or galvanic skin response (GSR) is also quite easy to teach nonmedical personnel, but both require special, somewhat costly equipment. Serum hormonal measures not only require someone skilled at blood drawing but can also be quite costly to process. Finally, in an era of heightened awareness regarding such issues as employee drug testing and the confidentiality of medical information (e.g., HIV status), employees may be less than eager to participate in certain stress diagnostic procedures.

The third issue of importance in evaluating physiological measures of stress is applicability. How will the results be used? For instance, demonstrating that cholesterol levels increase in accountants near tax time does not help determine what it is about tax time that is stressful or what can be done about it. Similarly, demonstrating that urinary catecholamines rise during public speaking does not provide much information about the reasons for the rise or the impact of public speaking on the individual who is speaking.

Some physiological measures, however, do have direct application to stress management. Blood pressure control, for example, is a valid objective of stress management as well as a measure of stress. Equipment used to assess muscle tension can also be used in the biofeedback techniques discussed in chapter 12.

In summary, the major advantage of physiological measures is their objectivity. Disadvantages include the lack of sensitivity and specificity of many of the measures, the inconvenience of some measures, employee concerns regarding the nature of the test and the confidentiality of the results, and the high individual cost that is sometimes involved. Physiological measures can be useful when objective measures are needed for preintervention and postintervention assessments to evaluate a stress reduction program or for comparing different occupational groups or corporate divisions. Finally, some physiological parameters represent therapeutic targets in themselves. Blood pressure and muscle tension are two such measures. Further information on the measures listed in Exhibit 7.3 is provided by Hurrell, Murphy, Sauter, and Cooper (1988).

Behavioral Measures

The behavioral and psychological consequences of individual distress that were discussed in chapter 3 suggest several possible measures of individual stress. Such measures might include the number of cigarettes smoked (possibly divided between on-the-job and at-home smoking), self-report of alcohol consumption and other drug use, recent weight change, sleeping pattern, and number and severity of accidents, both work-related and non-work-related. Some specific measures that have been used in general studies of health status include the following:

- Number of days per year lost from work
- Number of days per year of illness-related restricted activity
- Number of days per year of bed-bound disability

Although there are no standard values for absenteeism and disability, the National Center for Health Statistics provides useful comparative disability information, presented by occupational category (See U.S. Department of Health and Human Services source in Appendix B, Resource Groups).

Cornell Medical Index

The Cornell Medical Index (CMI; Brodman, Erdmann, Lorge, & Wolff, 1949) is one of the oldest and most widely used standard questionnaires for medical symptoms. It was developed in the 1940s to provide a rapid, reliable means of obtaining a patient's medical history without expending the physician's time. It consists of 195 *yes* and *no* questions that take 10–30 minutes to answer as a self-administered questionnaire. It can also be administered by an interviewer. There are four types of items (symptomatology, past history, family history, and behavior), which fall into the 18 categories listed in Table 7.1.

The questionnaire was validated by comparison of hospital case records with the CMI responses (Brodman, Erdmann, Lorge, & Wolff, 1951); 95% agreement was found. Furthermore, physicians were able to infer the specific medical condition from the CMI answers in 87% of cases. As a general screening tool, however, the CMI has been found to be most predictive of impaired emotional health and general physical health. For example, affirmative response to 30 or more items, in particular to the "psychiatric subsections" (M-R), is highly correlated with emotional disturbances of various sorts.

The CMI is easy to administer and readily scored. Specific symptom areas believed to be related to particular occupational risks can be scored and reported separately. There are no "standard values" for the total affirmative scores on the CMI, but there are comparative data regarding total scores for specific subgroups (Abramson, 1966).

Self-report questionnaires should always be viewed with caution when one is trying to assess the incidence of specific medical conditions. However, the CMI is a reliable and comprehensive measure of assessing *perceived* impairment and for this reason may be a useful tool in assessing the impact of job stress. An alternative to the CMI is the General Health Questionnaire (GHQ), which is often used as a psychiatric screening instrument. It is a 30-item, self-administered questionnaire whose results have been significantly correlated with independent clinical assessments

Table 7.1. Sections of the Cornell Medical Index

Section	Number of questions
A. Eyes and ears	9
B. Respiratory system	18
C. Cardiovascular system	13
D. Digestive system	23
E. Musculoskeletal system	8
F. Skin	7
G. Nervous system	18
H. Genitourinary system	11
I. Fatigability	7
J. Illness frequency	9
K. Miscellaneous disease	15
L. Habits	6
M. Inadequacy	12
N. Depression	6
O. Anxiety	9
P. Sensibility	6
Q. Anger	9
R. Tension	9

Note. From "The Cornell Medical Index," by K. Brodman, A. J. Erdmann, I. Lorge, and H. G. Wolff, 1949, *Journal of the American Medical Association, 140,* p. 531. Copyright 1949 by the American Medical Association. Adapted with permission.

(Goldberg, Rickels, Downing, & Hesbacher, 1976). The results of the GHQ have also been found to be highly correlated with symptoms of anxiety and depression.

Daily Log of Stress-Related Symptoms

One of the most detailed and individualized instruments for assessing individual distress is the Daily Log of Stress-Related Symptoms (Manuso, 1980). The log is intended as a self-assessment tool for use in a comprehensive stress management workshop. It is designed to help participants identify symptoms that have causes other than stress, to discover their own unique patterns of stress response, and to establish goals for stress management.

Using a symptom checklist, participants record the development of any symptoms by putting a dot on the log over the time of day when the symptom began. The symptom is rated by its intensity (vertical axis of the log) and by the extent to which it interferes with ongoing activities (number in parentheses next to each dot). Interference with ongoing activities is rated from 1 (*no interference*) to 100 (*total incapacity*). The log also has space to record number of hours at work, percentage of time interacting with others, use of medications, daily accomplishments, avoidance strategies, use of alcoholic beverages, use of relaxation and other stress-control techniques, and cigarette consumption. The daily log can be scored to establish one's relative stress level.

The amount of detail limits the use of the log as a screening or group assessment instrument. However, the amount of detail and individualization inherent in the daily log makes it a valuable tool in intensive stress management workshops.

Symptom Check List-90-R (SCL-90-R)

Derogatis (1981) developed a 90-item, multidimensional self-report symptom inventory that measures symptomatic psychological distress. The SCL-90-R results in three global measures of distress as well as nine primary symptom dimensions. The primary symptom dimensions are (a) somatization, (b) obsessive–compulsive behavior, (c) interpersonal sensitivity, (d) depression, (e) anxiety, (f) hostility, (g) phobic anxiety, (h) paranoid ideation, and (i) psychoticism. Each item is rated on a 5-point scale for the degree of distress that it causes. The internal consistency of the nine symptom dimensions ranges from .77 to .90, and the test–retest reliability of the dimensions ranges from .78 to .90. Derogatis established normative data for psychiatric outpatients, psychiatric inpatients, and nonpatient populations.

The SCL-90-R has been used as an evaluation tool in examining the effects of meditation and other relaxation techniques for the purpose of stress reduction. It has also been used with cancer patients to establish clinical levels of psychological symptoms.

Maslach Burnout Inventory

Maslach developed a 22-item measure of burnout that assesses three aspects of the experience (Maslach & Jackson, 1981a). The three aspects of burnout are incorporated in three subscales: emotional exhaustion, depersonalization, and lack of personal accomplishment. Although burnout is a stress-related experience most commonly found in human-service professions, anyone experiencing stress, including business executives, may be subject to it (H. Levinson, 1981a). The Maslach measure of this syndrome normally takes less than 30 minutes to complete and is easily scored using the key. It has been administered to a variety of occupational groups, including police officers, nurses, agency administrators, teachers, counselors, social workers, probation officers, mental health workers, physicians, psychologists, and psychiatrists (Maslach & Jackson, 1981a, 1981b). This instrument has high reliability, stability, and validity (Corcoran, 1995; Maslach & Jackson, 1981a).

State–Trait Anxiety Inventory

We pointed out in chapter 1 that stress and anxiety are not the same. Stress is often accompanied by the experience of tension and anxiety, however, and it may be useful and appropriate to develop measures of anxiety in conducting a stress diagnosis individually or organizationally. Spielberger, Gorsuch, and Lushene (1970) developed a self-administered questionnaire for this purpose. Although it was developed for normal individuals, it has also been used in clinical settings and with emotionally disturbed individuals. It may be completed in less than 10 minutes by normal individuals but may take up to 20 minutes for emotionally disturbed persons.

The instrument assesses both state (i.e., transitory) and trait (i.e., stable individual tendency) anxiety. The reliability and validity data available on the State–Trait Anxiety Inventory suggest that it is a psychometrically sound measure. In addition, norms are established for some groups, such as students.

Profile of Mood States

The Profile of Mood States (POMS) is a 65-item adjective checklist that reflects measures of six primary mood states (McNair, Lorr, & Droppleman, 1971). The mood dimensions (derived through factor analysis) are labeled tension–anxiety, depression–dejection, confusion, anger–hostility, vigor, and fatigue. Each item of the POMS is rated on a 5-point scale ranging from *not at all* to *extremely*; the measurement context is "the past week including today." The scale takes approximately 10–15 minutes to complete, is psychometrically well constructed, and has repeatedly proved itself to be sensitive to both work-related and nonwork-related stressors.

Other Measures Related to Individual Distress

In addition to the aforementioned diagnostic and assessment instruments, there are many psychological test batteries and published questionnaires covering a wide range of topics, including anxiety, depression, sleeping habits, sexual satisfaction or dysfunction, specific psychiatric conditions, and symptoms of specific diseases. In general, such techniques should be used under special circumstances and with the guidance of a physician, psychologist, or other professional familiar with the use and interpretation of the tests. These tests often provide an indication that an individual consequence of stress is impending or already operating. What is important is the rather early identification of the symptom before severe damage occurs. Sensitivity to employee privacy and confidentiality becomes increasingly important with some of the more personal, potentially threatening areas of inquiry. This factor must be considered in any significant stress diagnostic effort based on individual responses to questionnaires or interviews.

Measures of Modifiers of the Response to Stress

As we pointed out in chapter 3, several factors determine the manner in which the generalized stress response is manifested in a particular individual. In the case of the Achilles heel phenomenon, there are few accurate measures or indicators of individuals' differential responsiveness, or Achilles heel weakness. In the case of other characteristics, such as hardiness and the Type A behavior pattern, there are measures available. This section reviews a small number of the better-known or more directly applicable measurement techniques. Possible uses for these devices in the diagnosis of organizational stress are considered in the final section of this chapter.

Hardiness

Hardiness is a personality construct that reflects an optimistic orientation composed of commitment, challenge, and control. The five-scale composite described in the original prospective test of hardiness (Kobasa, Maddi, & Kahn, 1982) and the 36-item and 26-item abridged versions (Allred & Smith, 1989; Rhodewalt & Zone, 1989) are the instruments used most frequently to assess the construct. However, there are a number of concerns about the psychometric properties of these scales, and as a result there have been various attempts at developing improved measures. The 50-item Personal Views Survey (Maddi, 1990) and a 45-item version of the measure (Baratone, Ursano, Wright, & Ingraham, 1989) seem to represent improvements over the original assessment approaches.

Type A Behavior Pattern

The original research on the Type A behavior pattern is based on assessment using a *structured interview* (SI) developed by Rosenman et al. (1964). Audiovisual recordings of the interviews are rated by judges; despite the apparent subjectivity of the assessment, the interrater reliability ranges from .64 to .84. In an attempt to reduce the subjectivity and avoid the cost of the SI, self-report questionnaires have been developed for making the Type A or Type B classification. The Jenkins Activity Survey (JAS), developed by Jenkins, Rosenman, and Friedman (1967), has been the subject of the greatest amount of research and the most careful validation. Sample items from the JAS (Jenkins, Zyzanski; & Rosenmann, 1979, p. 19) are as follows:

- Frequently hurries speaker to the point
- Tends to get irritated easily
- Frequently brings work home at night
- Gives much more effort than the average worker[1]

---

[1]C. D. Jenkins, S. J. Zyzanski, and R. H. Rosenman, *Jenkins Activity Survey (Form C)*, p. 19. Used by permission from the Jenkins Activity Survey Manual. Copyright 1979 by The Psychological Corporation. All rights reserved.

Attempts to develop alternative, usually briefer, Type A scales include the 10-item Framingham Type A Scale (FTAS; Haynes, Levine, & Scotch, 1978) and the 14-item Bortner Scale (Bortner, 1969).

Evidence for all types of validity seems to be greatest for the SI. Comparisons across the JAS, FTAS, and Bortner Scale reveal relative strengths and weaknesses in particular areas, but none of these measures clearly dominates the others (Edwards, 1991).

Social Support

Another indicator of individuals' vulnerability is found in examining or profiling their social support network. House conducted several studies in this area using a brief questionnaire as the primary measure of social support. The three central questions asked were as follows (House & Wells, 1978):

1. How much can each of the following people be relied on when *things get tough at work*? (immediate supervisor or boss; other people at work; spouse; friends and relatives)
2. How much is each of the following people *willing to listen to your work-related problems*? (immediate supervisor or boss; other people at work; spouse; friends and relatives)
3. How much is each of the following people *helpful to you in getting your job done*? (immediate supervisor; other people at work)

For each potential support person mentioned, respondents were asked to indicate whether the individual was a source of support by answering, *not at all, a little, somewhat,* or *very much*. In addition, respondents were asked about their supervisors' competence, concern, and tendency to give praise.

This questionnaire and minor modifications of it have been used in numerous studies of organizational stress and social support. It has clear face validity and is easy to administer. A copy of the questionnaire appears in the monograph *Work Stress and Social Support* (House, 1981, p. 71).

Coping Mechanisms Assessment

A number of questionnaires have been developed to assess stress coping styles and strategies. The most widely used description of coping is offered by Lazarus and Folkman (1984), who distinguished between problem- and emotion-focused options and strategies. The former are concerned with directly attacking the problem, whereas the latter attack the emotional response to it. The authors developed a questionnaire to assess such strategies, called the Ways of Coping Questionnaire (Folkman & Lazarus, 1988), which has become widely used by stress researchers. This questionnaire asks respondents to identify a specific stressful situation and rate on 4-point scales their reliance on 66 specific coping responses. The questionnaire contains eight subscales measuring various types of problem- and emotion-focused coping. This instrument has been shown repeatedly to be reliable.

The Coping Responses Inventory (CRI; Moos, 1992) is composed of eight subscales that assess four types of coping processes: cognitive approach coping, behavioral approach coping, cognitive avoidance coping, and behavioral avoidance coping. This questionnaire contains 48 items with 4-point response scales. Moos and his colleagues have also developed a version of the CRI that focuses on how health care staff cope with work-related stressors (Schaefer & Moos, 1991).

Locus of Control

Locus of control is a personality characteristic that may modify an individual's experience of occupational stress as well as response to it (Hurrell & Murphy, 1991). This characteristic is concerned with the degree to which individuals perceive that they have control over events occurring in their lives. An individual with an *external* locus of control perceives that circumstances—bad or good luck, other people, or events—are responsible for what occurs in life. An individual with an *internal* locus of control perceives that people are the masters of their own destinies and responsible for their own fortunes or misfortunes.

Rotter (1966, reprinted in Rotter, Chance, & Phares, 1972) developed a 29-item, forced-choice measure of the tendency toward an internal or external locus of control. The scale includes 6 filler items intended to disguise the aim of the test and 23 items to determine an individual's locus of control. His measure has demonstrated internal consistency, test–retest reliability, and discriminant validity. Spector (1988) also developed a 16-item measure of generalized control beliefs in the work setting that shows high reliability.

Other Measures

Several other individual characteristics may influence the response to stress. For some of these characteristics, there are readily available and easily administered assessment scales. Among these characteristics are personal rigidity (Wesley, 1953), tolerance for ambiguity (Lyons, 1971), self-esteem (e.g., J. S. House, 1972; Kasl & Cobb, 1970), need for achievement (McClelland, 1961), self-efficacy (Bandura, 1986), sense of coherence (Antonovsky, 1987), and self-reliance (J. C. Quick, Nelson, & Quick, 1991). The Minnesota Multiphasic Personality Inventory (MMPI) is the broadest, most widely used, and best validated assessment of psychological parameters. It has been used in a variety of stress-related studies, but its breadth limits its routine use in the stress diagnostic process.

Summary

There has been too little practical application of many of the stress assessment measures to provide definitive recommendations regarding the selection of specific diagnostic instruments. It is possible, however, to offer a logical approach to using these instruments that is based on the purpose of the inquiry.

Chapter 6 mentioned several purposes that might be served by efforts to diagnose organizational stress. One purpose is to determine the cause of current organizational or individual dysfunction. For this purpose a fairly specific and sensitive approach is needed, and a number of measures described under the rubric of assessment of organizational stressors may prove useful. In addition, the more individualized approach described in H. Levinson and colleagues' *Organizational Diagnosis* (1972) could be fruitful. Less specific measures such as productivity rates or global stress ratings would serve only to confirm the existence of a problem and would probably not contribute substantively to determining the cause of the problem.

Stress diagnostic procedures can also be used to develop an individual or organizational stress profile, which can be useful in assessing whether an individual or organization is operating at an optimum level and whether there is a risk of stress-induced dysfunction. For this purpose, any of the general organizational stress measures discussed earlier and the Cornell Medical Index at the individual level may prove useful. For individuals interested in their own risk factors, an assessment of hardiness, the Type A–B behavior patterns, coping mechanisms, and social supports can be helpful.

Objective measures such as productivity, absenteeism rates, turnover, and possibly some of the individual physiological and behavioral measures may be most useful in assessing the impact of preventive interventions. Although these measures are not specific to stress effects, the impact of an intervention can be inferred from changes in these measures that are not explained by other changes in the organization.

With regard to organizational stress research, any of the diagnostic instruments discussed in this chapter may be of interest, depending on the research question. The field of organizational stress research has roots that go back for many decades, but the last few years have seen a rapid expansion of interest in the area. Efforts to validate existing measures and to develop new, reliable measures in specific areas of need have been and will continue to be important in the development of this field.

In considering the use of any of the measures described in this chapter, executives, managers, and organizational consultants should bear in mind that experience with some of these techniques in organizational stress diagnosis is limited. Many of these instruments, which have been developed by medical, organizational, and psychological professionals, should be used or applied with caution. Some of the scales are restricted to use by qualified professionals, whereas others have fewer restrictions on their use. Therefore, the interpretation and extrapolation of the findings from these stress instruments should be tempered by these comments. Nevertheless, if used properly, the techniques described here can serve the purpose of stimulating both management and employees to reflect systematically on their own stress and their positive and negative responses to it.

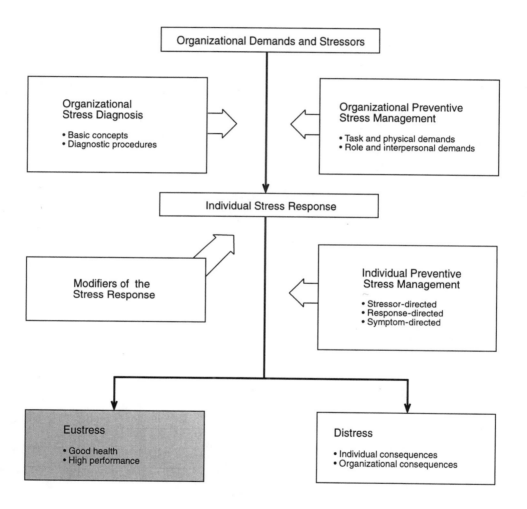

Preventive Stress Management: Principles and Methods

Chapters 1 through 7 discussed sources of stress in organizations, the stress response, individual and organizational consequences of stress, and methods of organizational stress diagnosis and measuring the stress response. Chapters 9 through 13 consider specific methods and implementation strategies for minimizing distress and promoting health and well-being in both the individual and the organization. This chapter introduces the principles and methods of preventive stress management that serve as the basis for the subsequent chapters.

Preventive Stress Management Defined

In chapter 1, preventive stress management was defined in the following way:

> *Preventive stress management* is an organizational philosophy and set of principles that employs specific methods for promoting individual and organizational health while preventing individual and organizational distress.

Preventive stress management, therefore, refers to a set of basic ideas about how an organization should operate and what approach managers should take toward the demands of organizational life. These notions may be implemented by managers and executives in any organization. Although the implementation strategy and specific techniques should be suited to a particular organization, the basic thrust is the same for all organizations.

The specific implementation strategy must consider both organizational and individual methods of preventive stress management. Organizational methods aim at altering the task, role, and physical and interpersonal stressors described in chapter 2. Individual methods aim at altering the individual's ability to manage various demands and the individual's response to these demands. Preventive stress management follows a proactive model of organizational change, as was noted in chapter 1. Under this model, an organization anticipates and averts most crises by shaping events rather than reacting to them.

The preceding definition of preventive stress management captures its two major aims. The first aim is to promote individual and organizational health. Achieving this objective requires efforts directed toward increasing productivity, adaptability, and flexibility. The second aim of preventive stress management is to minimize and, when possible, avert individual and organizational distress. The three stages of prevention involving organizational or individual interventions directed at the stressor, the stress response, or the resulting symptoms of stress are described later in this chapter.

Before defining the stages of prevention and outlining specific prevention methods, we consider some of the basic principles that guide current thinking about preventive stress management. These guiding principles form the central elements of our philosophy of preventive stress management and the basis of preventive action taken by management.

Guiding Principles of Preventive Stress Management

Preventive stress management is a conceptual framework for organizing and describing existing organizational and individual stress management methods. However, our use of the term also reflects our philosophy about the way in which an organization should operate, a philosophy based on five fundamental principles that motivate and guide the practice of preventive stress management. These principles are offered as guidelines for managers and executives who are interested in designing and implementing their own preventive stress management programs as well as for investigators interested in developing and evaluating stress management techniques.

The five principles constitute the central elements of the preventive stress management philosophy. Their application requires a knowledge of the three stages of prevention as well as the methods of individual and organizational preventive stress management. Using these principles and methods, management may formulate a specific preventive stress management plan for the organization.

Principle 1: Individual and Organizational Health Are Interdependent

The major conclusions that can be drawn from the information presented in chapters 2 through 5 are that organizational stressors can create substantial ill health among employees and that distressed employees can create considerable organizational dysfunction. This seemingly obvious but too often overlooked interdependency is the essence of Principle 1.

In addition to its financial assets, an organization has human assets that can be liquidated as surely as its capital assets can be. The well-being or ill health of human assets does not have an immediate effect on organizational health. It takes time—sometimes as much as a 1 or 2 or even 5 years—for the benefits of human resource development to have an effect on the health of an organization. It may take an equivalent time period for the detrimental effects of the liquidation of human assets to be felt in the declining health of the organization.

Organizations cannot achieve a high level of productivity, adaptability, and flexibility without vital, healthy individuals. By the same token, individuals may have a great deal of difficulty maintaining their psychological and physical health in unproductive, rigid, unchanging organizations. This interdependency is expressed more formally in the concept of the *person–organization fit*. As Harrison (1978) pointed out, this fit occurs in two ways. First, there is the degree to which *individual resources meet organizational goals and requirements*; individual health and vitality contribute to organizational health. Second, there is the degree to which *organizational resources meet individual needs*; organizational health and vitality contribute, in turn, to individual health. The person–organization fit represents an exchange relationship, in which both aspects of the exchange are important.

Principle 2: Leaders Have a Responsibility for Individual and Organizational Health

The responsibility for the active pursuit of the development of an organization lies with its leadership. Apathetic or passive leadership on the part of management is an irresponsible posture that leads to organizational decay and decline. However, the corollary to the interdependency described in Principle 1 is that leaders also have a responsibility for individual health and well-being. Although this interest can be based partly on altruism, it is rooted in enlightened self-interest: Individuals who are highly distressed are not as effective as those who are not. Leaders' responsibilities include diagnosing organizational stress, selecting appropriate organizational and individual methods of preventive stress management, and implementing programs tailored to the particular needs of the organization.

Although leaders have a key role in pursuing individual and organizational well-being, they do not have exclusive responsibility for either individual or organizational health. Employees are also responsible for their health as individuals and for the health of the organization. This too is a corollary of the person–organization interdependency described in Principle 1. An individual who accepts employment has a responsibility to contribute to the organization and to participate in efforts to combat organizational distress. To surrender that responsibility is both immature and hazardous. Principle 2 does not in any way attempt to relieve individuals of responsibility for their own health and well-being.

Principle 3: Individual and Organizational Distress Are Not Inevitable

Task, role, and physical and interpersonal demands are inescapable parts of participating in any organization. Unfortunately, too many of these demands and too much of the resulting distress are accepted as "the price of success," "part of the industrial revolution," or "a necessary evil of work." These cruel myths are used to rationalize inaction and neglect by both managers and employees. In fact, many stressors can be reduced or eliminated; the impact of other stressors can be softened; and the resulting distress can be greatly reduced. Although the stress and demands of work life are inevitable, distress resulting from stress and demands is *not* inevitable.

From the assertion that leaders have a responsibility for individual and organizational health (Principle 2), it follows that leaders have the responsibility to identify and remedy preventable sources of organizational and individual distress. The organizational and individual weapons for this assault are the subject of chapters 9 through 13. Distress is averted through preventive managerial action using these methods.

Principle 3 is based on the use of a proactive model of organizational change. It is difficult to avert distress when its consequences are already being experienced at the individual or organizational level. Therefore, it is necessary to anticipate and influence the demands that are the source of stressful events as well as to employ methods for shielding the individual or organization from their harmful effects. Leaders may be able to prevent distress through taking such a proactive posture.

Principle 4: Each Individual and Organization Reacts Uniquely to Stress

There are considerable individual differences in the demands that are perceived as stressful, in the response to these demands, in the recognition and toleration of distress, and in response to stress management interventions. These differences have important implications for diagnosing organizational stress and for designing effective preventive stress management programs.

For example, routine, monotonous work may be quite distressing for one person but reassuring and secure for another; social isolation at the job may be extremely upsetting for one person but a virtual employment requirement for another. An effective preventive stress management program must address itself to the stressors that are relevant to the individuals concerned. This observation highlights the importance of the diagnostic process described earlier.

There are also variations in the response to stress, as we noted previously. For example, some individuals might respond to a surprise short deadline with increased cigarette consumption, others with a headache, and still others with nothing but quiet, efficient productivity. Signs of distress may also be perceived differently by different organizations. For instance, a company dependent on large numbers of unskilled laborers who require minimal training may have little interest in reducing a stress-related high turnover rate. In contrast, a firm that uses internally trained technicians might be alarmed by stressors that cause even a modest increase in turnover.

Finally, the feasibility, acceptability, and effectiveness of preventive stress management interventions vary among organizations and individuals. A small firm often cannot afford on-site counselors, fitness trainers, or special health facilities. An effective system for identifying and referring individuals who have particular difficulties might suffice. At the individual level, techniques that are attractive to one individual may be entirely unacceptable to another.

It is important to recognize from the outset that the discussion of preventive stress management methods that comes later is not meant to provide a "cook book" for organizational stress management. Distress prevention methods are presented, and guidelines for designing stress management programs are considered. Nevertheless, the uniqueness of individuals and organizations requires that interventions be chosen and implemented in light of the particular characteristics and needs of the individual or organization being served.

Principle 5: Organizations Are Ever-Changing, Dynamic Entities

Organizations, like individuals, are open systems that have a life cycle of growth, maturation, and death as well as varying degrees of health and vitality (Miller & Friesen, 1984). They are at any given point in time a blend of health, vitality, and decay. They may face different developmental issues at various stages in their growth, just as individuals face different developmental issues at various stages of their lives. The nature of the stressors faced by an organization as well as the nature of the demands generated within it may change over the course of its life cycle. The strategies and techniques that are effective in managing stress at one stage may be ineffective at a later stage.

Essentially, preventive stress management is concerned with enhancing organizational health, vitality, and functioning while minimizing the amount of decay and illness within the organization. This can only be accomplished by attending to the ever-changing, dynamic nature of the organization. It requires the active involvement and participation of all organizational members in the process of organizational growth and change.

Stages of Prevention

Chronic diseases do not arise suddenly; instead, they develop gradually through a progression of disease stages, or a "natural life history." The natural history of most diseases is one of evolution from a stage of susceptibility, to a stage of early disease, to a stage of advanced or disabling disease. At the stage of susceptibility, the individual is healthy but is exposed to risk factors or disease precursors. For example, individuals who choose a sedentary life or who choose to smoke cigarettes are at the stage of susceptibility for coronary artery disease as well as several other diseases. When these and other risk factors lead to the development of arteriosclerotic plaques, or "hardening of the arteries" to the heart, the individual is at the stage of early, or "preclinical," disease. The person's body has responded to the disease precursors, but there are few, if any, symptoms. As the disease advances further, it becomes symptomatic, or clinical, disease. Angina pectoris ("heart pains") and heart attacks are advanced manifestations of coronary artery disease.

Preventive stress management is rooted in the public health notions of prevention, which were first used in the field of preventive medicine. The term *public health* encompasses a broad array of health protection activities inspired by the practice of viewing illnesses within a social context (Ewart, 1991). The dominant diagnostic model in public health involves the interaction among a host (the individual), an agent (health-damaging organism or substance), and the environment. One of the fundamental concepts of preventive medicine is that there is an opportunity for preventive intervention at each stage in the life history of a disease. These interventions are aimed at slowing, stopping, or reversing the progression of disease. *Primary prevention* is the protection of health directed at the stage of susceptibility and aims to eliminate or reduce the impact of risk factors; it is intervention before the onset of disease or disorder (Winett, 1995). *Secondary prevention* aims at the early detection of disease and involves prompt, early interventions to correct departures from health (Last, 1988). *Tertiary prevention* is therapeutic in nature and is directed at expediting or improving treatment for symptomatic, possibly advanced disease and aims to alleviate discomfort and restore effective functioning.

The impact of organizational stress also proceeds through several stages; therefore, there are several possible points for preventive stress management intervention. Figure 8.1 presents the three stages of prevention in a preventive medicine context, along with the stages in an organizational context. *Primary prevention* is aimed at modifying the organizational stressors that may eventually lead to distress. *Secondary prevention* aims at changing individual stress responses to necessary demands. *Tertiary prevention* attempts to minimize the amount of individual and organizational distress that results when organizational stressors and resulting stress responses have not been adequately controlled.

For example, multiple-reporting relationships (a stressor) might lead to chronic anxiety (a stress response) and, in turn, to absenteeism (an organizational consequence of distress). Primary prevention would attempt to simplify the reporting relationships. Secondary prevention might address the problem by providing a program of relaxation training to help alleviate signs of tension among affected subordinates. Tertiary prevention might include an employee counseling program designed to help employees cope with conflicting expectations.

What is preventable depends on the nature of the demands, the characteristics of the individual, and the resources available in the situation. The appropriate stage of prevention for precluding or arresting distress,

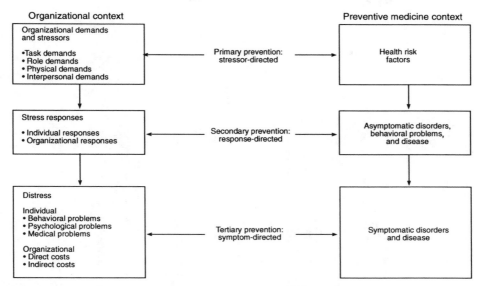

Figure 8.1. The stages of preventive stress management.

therefore, is often situationally determined. Sometimes it is not possible to change a demand or reduce one's vulnerability to the demand, which then indicates that tertiary prevention is most appropriate. What is realistically preventable at each stage may be as much a function of circumstances as of rational choice. There are available at each stage of prevention individual and organizational interventions.

At the organizational level, primary prevention is aimed at controlling the number of stressors and their intensity. At the individual level, primary prevention is intended to help individuals control the frequency and intensity of the stressors to which they are subjected. The goal is not to eliminate stressors but to optimize the frequency and intensity of stressors. When the stress response is elicited too frequently or too strongly at work, organizational and individual strain and disease become inevitable. This leads to the exhaustion stage of Selye's general adaptation syndrome (see chapter 1, Figure 1.3). When the stress response is not elicited frequently enough, lethargy as well as lack of growth and adaptation occur. Either extreme is to be avoided, and an optimum level is to be sought. This optimum level varies substantially among individuals and different groups of individuals. This point is an underlying theme in many of Selye's (1976a, b) writings on stress.

Secondary prevention is directed at controlling the stress response itself and includes efforts to optimize the intensity of each stress response an individual experiences. Whereas low-intensity stress responses may provide insufficient impetus for adaptability and growth, high-intensity responses may lead to sudden death or other serious individual consequences. Because of individual differences, the optimum intensity for one individual may not be optimum for another. The importance of optimizing both the frequency and the intensity of the stress response is reflected in the expanded Yerkes–Dodson curve shown in Figure 8.2.

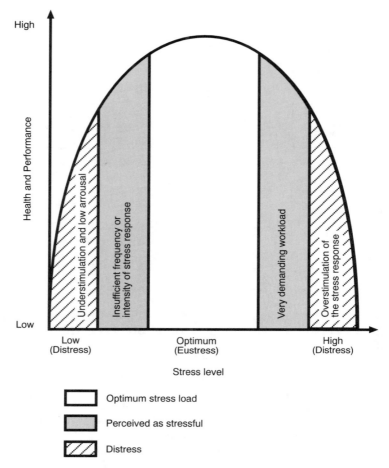

Figure 8.2. An expanded Yerkes–Dodson curve.

Tertiary prevention is concerned with minimizing the organizational costs and the individual discomfort, disability, and death resulting from frank manifestations of too much stress. At the organizational level this usually takes the form of crisis intervention, whereas at the individual level it often consists of traditional medical and psychiatric care.

Folkman, Schaefer, and Lazarus (1979); Folkman and Lazarus (1980); and Herold and Conlon (1982) have discussed coping strategies for alleviating distress that parallel the notions of primary and secondary prevention presented here. Coping is a cognitive and behavioral process of mastering, tolerating, or reducing internal and external demands (Folkman & Lazarus 1980; Lazarus, 1981). The problem-focused function of coping is concerned with managing or altering the source of stress in the person–environment relationship and parallels primary prevention. The emotion-focused function of coping is concerned with regulating stressful emotions and parallels secondary prevention. The coping scheme of Folkman and Lazarus does not incorporate a notion that parallels tertiary prevention.

Preventive Stress Management Method

The three stages of prevention provide a useful means to understand the process of preventive stress management. However, the specific methods are described more readily as organizational preventive stress management and individual preventive stress management. The distinction be-

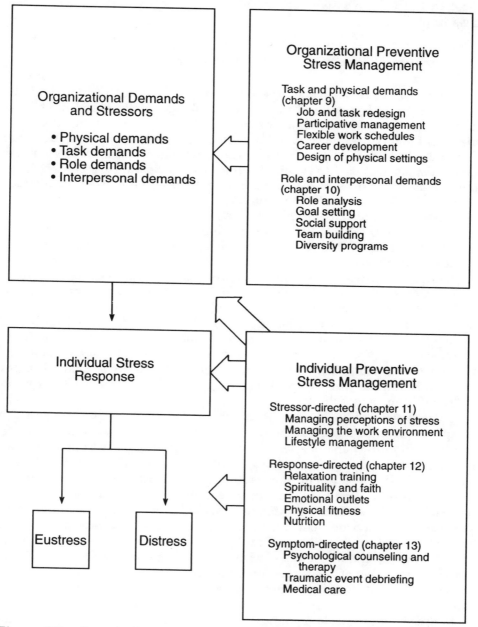

Figure 8.3. Organizational and individual preventive stress management.

tween these two levels of intervention serves to organize the following four chapters. Figure 8.3 identifies these two levels of preventive action and identifies the methods at each level that are discussed in the following chapters. It is not our intention to provide a cursory review of all possible interventions. Instead, we selectively review in detail those methods that are feasible for implementation in a variety of organizations and that, in most instances, have some empirical evidence to support their effectiveness in prevention.

Organizational Preventive Stress Management

Organizational preventive stress management is aimed primarily at the task, role, and physical and interpersonal demands discussed in chapter 2. Many of the organizational methods are aimed at changing the organization's structure and practices by altering the nature of these different demands. This means that organizational methods of preventive stress management are used to eliminate unnecessary demands while sharpening the focus of necessary demands and helping employees to manage them in healthy ways. Ten organizational methods of preventive stress management are discussed in chapters 9 and 10.

As shown in Figure 8.3, five prevention methods are examined in chapter 9. Of these five methods, three are concerned with the task demands of work: job redesign, flexible work schedules, and career development. Each of these methods is concerned with the design, structure, and sequence of an individual's work. Job redesign is explicitly concerned with the core characteristics of an individual's job and the processes whereby person–job fit may be improved. Flexible work scheduling is concerned with a specific dimension of one's job and affords the individual increased discretion in managing both professional and personal demands. Career development focuses on the sequence of jobs an individual might hold over time as well as the knowledge and skills required to grow in these different jobs.

Also discussed in chapter 9 are participative management and the design of physical settings. Participative management is concerned with the task and interpersonal demands of work. Its thrust is to increase job-decision latitude, improve organizational decision making, and increase the individual's investment in as well as adjustment to organizational life. The design of physical settings is concerned with the physical and task demands of work. Through this method of prevention, an individual's physical work environment is designed to facilitate task accomplishment as well as to stimulate pleasure and growth on the job.

Chapter 10 examines five methods of organizational preventive stress management. Two of these methods, the role-analysis technique and goal-setting programs, focus on the demands of the individual's work role. The role-analysis technique is designed to clarify, focus, and minimize the conflicts present in the role demands of work. Goal-setting programs, on the other hand, are concerned with task demands as well as role demands.

The emphasis in goal-setting programs is on explicitly identifying the manager's task-related role demands of his employees through a participative process.

Social support, team building, and diversity programs are also explored in chapter 10. These related methods of preventive stress management focus not on changing or restructuring the different demands at work but rather on providing groups of employees with support and resources in managing the necessary yet stressful demands of work. These methods complement the other techniques of organizational preventive stress management listed in Figure 8.3 aimed at changing the organizational stressors.

The emphasis in organizational preventive stress management is at the primary stage of prevention, as depicted in Figure 8.1. Although the secondary and tertiary stages of prevention are not ignored at the organizational level, a greater number of individual methods of preventive stress management are available for these stages of prevention. It is to this individual level that we now turn.

Individual Preventive Stress Management

Individual preventive stress management provides an effective complement for dealing with organizational stress. As shown in Figure 8.3, the major individual methods of preventive stress management fall under the three stages of prevention.

Chapter 11 describes some of the primary or stressor-directed techniques that are essential to a personal stress management plan. Managing personal response patterns includes changing Type A behavior patterns, talking constructively to oneself, and exhibiting uninhibited emotional expression. Management of the personal work environment includes managing time, learning how to obligate and "deobligate," and planning work activities systematically. Achieving a healthful balance between work, home, and other activities; using leisure time effectively for relaxation; and finding satisfying artistic outlets are all part of lifestyle management.

Although stressor-directed techniques may form the basis for a comprehensive individual stress management plan, it is important to recognize that these techniques have not been as widely accepted or as systematically studied as the secondary and tertiary individual preventive techniques described in chapters 12 and 13. Secondary, or response-directed, techniques include relaxation training, activities involving spirituality and faith, emotional outlets, physical exercise, and improvements in nutrition. Tertiary, or symptom-directed, techniques include counseling, psychotherapy, and medical care.

The types of relaxation training described in chapter 12 are the relaxation response, progressive relaxation, clinically standardized meditation, transcendental meditation, Zen and other Eastern meditative systems, hypnosis, autogenic training, biofeedback, momentary relaxation, and traditional forms of relaxation. Spirituality and faith provide support for transcending one's limitations. Emotional outlets constitute a form of catharsis for individuals. Physical exercise can be beneficial in any of several ways, depending in part on whether it is aerobic exercise, recreational sports, flexibility and relaxation exercises, or muscle strength and endurance building. Proper nutrition can provide the energy necessary for responding appropriately in stressful situations.

The tertiary prevention measures considered in chapter 13 include symptom-directed programs such as those for alcoholics, individual counseling, behavioral therapy, group therapy, and career counseling, as well as standard medical care using medications, physical therapy, and surgery.

Chapter 13 concludes with a brief discussion of the process for creating a personal stress management plan. The plan may vary considerably among individuals, but the process for developing such a plan is fairly standard.

Implementing Preventive Stress Management

Implementing the principles of preventive stress management and applying the organizational and individual methods takes an organizationally specific strategy. Chapter 14 contains descriptions of what several organizations are doing to combat the effects of distress. Johnson & Johnson's Live for Life program is a model emulated by many other companies. Southwest Airlines relies heavily on humor and making work enjoyable as strategies for managing stress. The chapter also contains a model for implementing and evaluating preventive stress management, along with several key questions to consider in the implementation process.

Summary

This chapter contains a discussion of the principles and methods of preventive stress management. The guiding principles, which constitute the central element in the philosophy of preventive stress management, are as follows:

1. Individual and organizational health are interdependent.
2. Leaders have a responsibility for individual and organizational health.
3. Individual and organizational distress are not inevitable.
4. Each individual and organization reacts uniquely to stress.
5. Organizations are ever-changing, dynamic entities.

These principles underlie the concept of preventive stress management that was defined at the beginning of this book. The two aims of preventive stress management are (a) to promote individual and organizational health and (b) to minimize individual and organizational distress, as manifested in a variety of asymptomatic and symptomatic diseases.

The principles of preventive stress management and the organization-ally specific strategy for implementing these principles guide both the selection and the use of specific preventive stress management methods. These methods were briefly discussed in the last section of the chapter and are listed in Figure 8.3. They are considered in detail in the following chapters, which deal first with organizational preventive stress management, second with individual preventive stress management, and finally with sample organizational programs that use a selection of these methods.

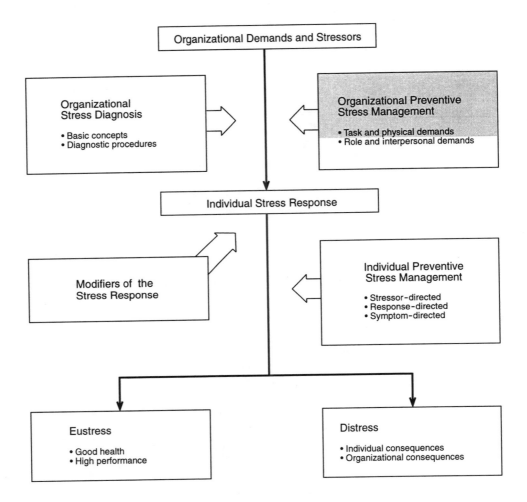

9

Organizational Demands and Stressors

Organizational
Stress Diagnosis

• Basic concepts
• Diagnostic procedures

Organizational Preventive
Stress Management

• Task and physical demands
• Role and interpersonal demands

Individual Stress Response

Modifiers of the
Stress Response

Individual Preventive
Stress Management

• Stressor-directed
• Response-directed
• Symptom-directed

Eustress

• Good health
• High performance

Distress

• Individual consequences
• Organizational consequences

Organizational Prevention: Modifying Work Demands

This is the first of two chapters dealing with preventive stress management at the organizational level. The aim of these organizational strategies is to modify and shape the organization, altering the demands placed on the individual. The intention is *not* to minimize the stress individuals experience at work but to optimize it to enhance eustress and reduce distress. To achieve this objective, organizational prevention methods attempt to buffer the effects of organizational stressors on individuals by increasing stress where too little exists and reducing stress where it becomes overwhelming. This should be done through an organizationally specific implementation strategy that incorporates individual and organizational methods of preventive stress management.

This chapter presents five prevention methods aimed specifically at one or another category of demands that individuals face at work. These methods, summarized in Exhibit 9.1, are primarily concerned with modifying the formal organization to alter the demands that it places on individuals.

Principle 2 of preventive stress management states that *management leaders have a responsibility for individual and organizational health*. Organizational prevention is concerned with the implementation of this principle in specific settings. The methods of preventive stress management discussed in this chapter are designed to maintain organizational health by preventing the occurrence of structural conditions, such as insufficient job control, that may lead to individual and organizational distress. These methods focus on the primary stage of prevention; they are directed at organizational stressors. However, they function at the secondary stage of prevention when they are directed at how groups respond to organizational demands.

Organizational prevention methods are aimed at improving organizational health through some form of internal adjustment. The process of making an organizational change and internal adjustment creates uncertainty and stress for some individuals. There is a risk of increasing rather than reducing stress within the organization if the prevention method is poorly implemented or mismanaged. The risk of problems with any of the following methods may be greatly reduced through careful planning and active collaboration with the groups and individuals affected by the change. Therefore, thoughtful and cautious use of the methods of preventive stress management is recommended.

Exhibit 9.1.   Organizational Prevention: Job and Physical Demands

---

Job redesign

This method is aimed at changing the task demands that jobs place on individuals. This is accomplished by restructuring one or more core job dimensions. The result of task redesign efforts is to improve person–job fit and to increase the job occupant's level of motivation, thus reducing distress on the job.

Participative management

This method increases the amount of discretion and autonomy that individuals have at work by decentralizing decision making and increasing participation in decision-making processes as much as possible. The individual is able to exert greater control at work and to channel stress-induced energy, while minimizing the frustration of working under authoritarian management. The result of practicing participative management is to reduce conflict and tension while increasing productivity.

Flexible work schedules

This method enhances the individual's control and discretion in the work environment. It makes possible greater flexibility for integrating and managing organizational and personal demands. The increased discretion over one's work time leads to a reduction in unresolved strain.

Career development

Through the structuring of career paths, this method encourages eustressful individual growth and development. This is accomplished by a process of self-assessment as well as an analysis of opportunities within the organization through individual initiative and in conjunction with counselors in the organization. The result is reduced individual frustration and distress.

Design of physical settings

This method minimizes the distressful effects of the physical work environment, for example, noise and excessive heat. The use of pleasant or growth-oriented settings (e.g., a fitness center) promotes eustress. If the work environment is properly designed, it will also facilitate task accomplishment.

Job Redesign

In any organization there are many points at which stress management interventions can be made. Because a job has a direct and immediate impact on the individual, the job is one critical intervention point. Four approaches to job redesign are discussed here, although other alternatives exist, such as those discussed by Lindstrom (1995) from Finland. The four discussed in detail here are the job characteristics model, the demand–control model, the effort–reward model, and job enrichment. The purposes for undertaking job redesign for organizational prevention are (a) to increase eustress by enhancing challenge and motivation within the job, (b) to increase control within the job to reduce job strain and distress, and (c) to reduce high levels of uncertainty within the job (Landy, Quick, & Kasl, 1994).

Job Characteristics Model

The job characteristics model proposes that there are five core job dimensions that interact with three critical psychological states to produce the personal and work outcomes shown in Figure 9.1 (Hackman, 1977). These relationships are moderated by employee growth need strength, as also shown in the figure, such that high growth needs interact with the core job dimensions, activating the critical psychological states and producing the personal and work outcomes listed in the figure. The relationships shown in the figure are not expected to hold true for individuals who are low in employee growth need strength. Hence, as a job redesign method, the job characteristics model is especially appropriate for employees with a high growth need strength who are in jobs that are low on one or more of the five core job dimensions.

A primary focus in this job redesign approach is the motivating potential score (MPS) for a given job. The MPS is a measure of a job's potential for motivating the individual to work. When a job achieves a minimum yet unspecified MPS, it can create the optimum amount of stress, or eustress, for the incumbent. The stress in a job is expected to increase linearly with the job's MPS (J. C. Quick & Griffin, 1980), thus suggesting that a job could have an MPS that is too high. The MPS of a particular job is determined through an additive and multiplicative combination of the five core job dimensions. The MPS ranges from 1 (*a job extremely low in all core*

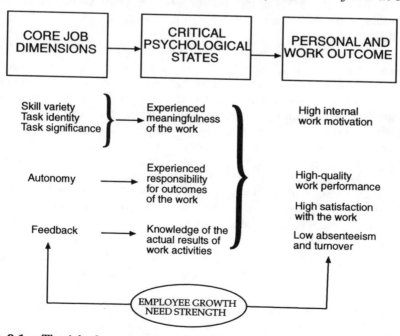

Figure 9.1. The job characteristics model. From *The Job Diagnostic Survey* (p. 3), by J. R. Hackman and G. R. Oldham, 1974, New Haven, CT: Yale University. Reprinted with permission.

dimensions) to 343 (*a job extremely high in the core job dimensions*). The average MPS is about 125 (Hackman, 1977).

The first question to ask is whether to change individual jobs or to create self-managing groups out of existing work teams (Griffin, 1982; Hackman & Oldham, 1980). There is not always a choice, because one alternative is sometimes not feasible. When choice exists, the selection of the appropriate strategy should be based on preliminary diagnostic data. Griffin (1982) suggested two additional questions: (a) Is there a need for redesign? (b) Is redesign feasible? The first question, in particular, is answerable through organizational diagnostic activities undertaken by management. Hackman (1977) also proposed a diagnostic approach to job redesign in a work setting.

Diagnose the work setting. Poor job design is not the only cause of problems in the work setting, manifested in symptoms such as absenteeism and poor-quality performance. Symptoms may result from alternative causes such as authoritarian supervision or interpersonal conflicts with peers. The diagnosis should identify the underlying causes of the symptoms. It is only when the diagnosis suggests that poor job design is the root problem that job redesign is an appropriate prevention method. One aspect of the diagnostic procedure in this case is the determination of the MPS for the group of jobs being examined. Hackman and Oldham (1976) developed normative data regarding the MPS for various categories of jobs. Comparing the MPS of the target job to normative scores for similar jobs provides a basis for comparison and may suggest whether the problem lies in design of the job.

Examine the job and each of the core job dimensions. If job design is the problem, each of the core job dimensions should be examined. Again, normative data for each of the five dimensions (skill variety, task identity, task significance, autonomy, and feedback from the work) are available. The modification of one core dimension alone may resolve the problem. For example, a low score on *feedback* or *autonomy* may result in a low MPS for a job, even if other dimensions of the core job are well designed. Individual perceptions of the core job dimensions are shaped to some degree by such social influences as supervisor and coworker behaviors and communications. These social and perceptual influences should be separated from the structural aspects of the job.

Five principles for job redesign. One or more of five redesign principles might be employed to effect the job redesign (Hackman, 1977).

1. *Form natural work units.* This involves organizing people whose work is interrelated into work groups, or teams. Task identity and task significance are the core job dimensions enhanced by this principle.
2. *Combine tasks.* This is done by despecializing a job and allowing

individuals to do several different activities. Skill variety and task identity are the core job dimensions enhanced by this principle.

3. *Establish client relationships.* This enables the worker to interact directly with people who use or are affected by the work. Skill variety, autonomy, and feedback are the core job dimensions enhanced by this principle.

4. *Use vertical loading.* This allows the worker more responsibility and discretion over the work and decisions affecting the work. Autonomy is the core job dimension enhanced by this principle.

5. *Open feedback channels.* This involves increasing the ways in which feedback from the work process itself may be made available to the worker. Feedback is the core job dimension enhanced by this principle.

Unique risks and opportunities. Each work setting is unique, complete with risks and opportunities for redesign and change. Job redesign may stir feelings of anxiety, insecurity, and resistance on the part of those affected by the redesign effort. For example, during one successful redesign effort we undertook, the computer operations manager was so insecure about the changes in his job that he appeared temporarily to be paranoid, believing that we, as change agents, were "out to get him." This reaction was due to his emotional insecurity. Once the change was finalized, his emotional upset dissipated. Although unique risks go along with change, so may unique opportunities. For example, if the life expectancy of the equipment of an organization has been reached and it is time to make capital investments for new technology, the redesign efforts can be actively integrated with the technology decisions; people may become energized and enthusiastic about the redesign and change effort.

Evaluate the job redesign. When a job redesign is undertaken, a systematic evaluation should follow to assess the effectiveness of the effort. A procedure similar to the one used in diagnosis may be followed to compare the results of the redesign with the diagnostic base data established before the change. Without such comparability, the evaluation loses its usefulness. When action is based on such symptoms as excessive absenteeism or poor-quality performance, the evaluator should look for the elimination of such symptoms. In a well-designed field experiment, Orpen (1979) used Hackman's theory to increase the MPS for 36 randomly assigned clerical employees. He did not alter the MPS or task scope for an additional 36 clerical employees. His evaluation focused on changes in individual motivation, satisfaction, and performance. Data collected 6 months after the redesign effort was completed indicated a significant improvement in both motivation and satisfaction, consistent with J. C. Quick and Griffin's (1980) predictions in such a case. Orpen did not find a similar increase in performance among these clerical employees.

Demand–Control Model

The demand–control model developed by Karasek (1979; see also Theorell & Karasek, 1996) offers an alternative basis for job redesign. Identified as either the job strain model or the psychological demand–decision latitude model, it has two core dimensions (psychological demands and decision latitude, or control) that frame it and two axes (active learning and residual strain) that run through it (see Figure 9.2). The two core dimensions of demands and control lead to four job categories: high strain, active, low strain, and passive. High strain jobs are characterized by high demands coupled with low control, whereas active jobs are characterized by high demands coupled with high control. Low strain jobs are characterized by low demands coupled with high control, whereas passive jobs are characterized by low demands coupled with low control.

High strain job risks. Because high strain jobs are at the upper end of the residual (unresolved) strain axis, they are the most distressful and risky jobs for employees. Jobs characterized by heavy responsibilities without commensurate authority and autonomy are high strain jobs, with the accompanying symptoms of exhaustion, depression, job and life dissatisfaction, elevated consumption of tranquilizers and sleeping pills, and increased illness days (Karasek, 1979). Subsequent research has shown that high strain jobs increase the cardiovascular risk for incumbents as well (Karasek et al., 1988; Theorell & Karasek, 1996). Reducing these risks associated with high strain jobs involves redesign efforts targeted at increasing employee control, reducing psychological demands, or a combi-

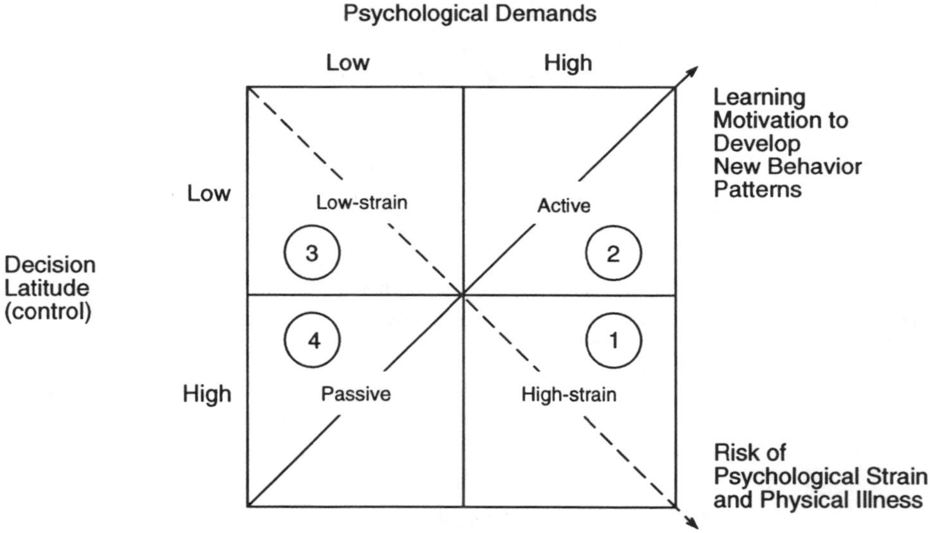

Figure 9.2. The psychological demand–decision latitude model. From "Current issues relating to psychosocial job strain and cardiovascular disease research" by T. Theorell and R. A. Karasek, *Journal of Occupational Health Psychology, 1* (p. 11), 1996. Reprinted with permission.

nation of the two. The most attention has been given to efforts at redesigning jobs to increase worker control (Landy et al., 1994; Sauter, Hurrell, & Cooper, 1989).

Redesigning high strain jobs: increasing control on the job. It is consistent with preventive stress management's explicit emphasis on enhancing health and implicit emphasis on enhancing performance that job design and redesign can increase both health and productivity (Karasek & Theorell, 1990). These are not mutually exclusive goals. The most common redesign strategy for high strain jobs is to increase control for employees. There are at least three ways in which this can be accomplished. First, employees might be given the opportunity to control various aspects of their work and the workplace. This includes work pace, task assignments, methods of payment, task content, and goal selection. The caveat associated with this first redesign strategy is that employees are interdependent, not independent, participants in the organization and that their redesign efforts need to be undertaken within the constraints of their larger work area. The process for implementing increased control then becomes an iterative, participative decision-making process in which employees and managers dialogue about the degrees of freedom and flexibility achievable within a particular work environment. (The next main section of the chapter discusses in detail participative management as a method for achieving organizational prevention through the modification of work demands.)

Second, control can be increased by designing systems with optimum response times or response ranges. Informational, mechanical, financial, performance, or other organizational systems whose response time is too fast or too slow pose problems for employees. When the response times are too fast, employees may feel pushed by the system without sufficient recovery or response time of their own. This is akin to being on a fast-moving treadmill that accelerates the employee's activity level above that which is effective or comfortable for that employee. When the response times are too slow, employees may experience frustration and inefficiency, having to wait for the machine or system to take further action. In both cases, the response times may be measured in terms of seconds for information or computerized systems, in terms of hours or days for financial status systems, or in terms of weeks or months for performance systems.

Third, performance monitoring should be appropriately introduced and implemented as a source of relevant feedback to individuals for improving the quality and quantity of performance. Performance monitoring and feedback systems, whether mechanized or interpersonal in nature, are a critical dimension of an employee's task environment and constitute a key system through which employees are influenced at work. By introducing and implementing these systems to allow for employee input and accommodation, one can enhance employees' experience of control. One key aspect of the implementation is being clear and explicit about the use and consequences of the monitoring and feedback information. It is one thing to use the information for performance adjustment or improvement, and it is quite another to use it strictly as a basis for evaluation or employee payments.

Contextual considerations. In implementing job redesign strategies to enhance control, one should consider other internal organizational variables as noted in Figure 5.2, such as the organizational culture and technology. These are context variables for the job redesign (Karasek & Theorell, 1990). Organizational culture is a key context variable to address in this regard. Learning organizations with an open, flexible, and decentralized culture may be more natural contexts for redesign efforts to increase employee control, whereas more rigid, centralized, and inflexible organizations may be less fertile grounds for such efforts (Forward et al., 1991). Furthermore, organizational cultures that place a high value on human nature and on trust in working relationships are more likely to see these efforts flourish (Hosmer, 1995; Schein, 1985). In addition to the organizational culture, technology must be considered. Although technological advances, as represented by computers and information systems, may be sources of job insecurity for some when viewed pessimistically, they are a great lever for increasing employee skill acquisition when viewed optimistically. Therefore, as job redesign is undertaken to enhance employee control, it cannot and should not be done without consideration for internal organizational context variables.

Effort–Reward Model

Siegrist's (1996) effort–reward model, mentioned in chapter 5, is a third basis for undertaking job redesign efforts in organizations. In this balancing model for job design, the core argument is that distress arises from the imbalance of effort and reward, especially high effort–low reward. The key effort and reward variables of concern to Siegrist (1996) are shown in Figure 9.3. The underlying framework for this model is the same as shown in Figure 5.2. Specifically, the exchanges in organizational life between the individual and the organization should be balanced and reciprocal in nature.

Siegrist (1996) suggested that occupational groups who experience the

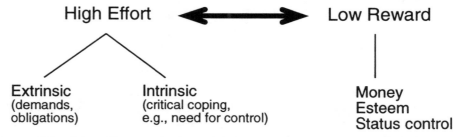

Figure 9.3. The effort–reward model. From "Adverse health effects of high-effort/low-strain reward conditions," *Journal of Occupational Health Psychology, 1* (p. 30), 1996. Reprinted with permission.

lower levels of status control are more likely to have a high incidence of high effort—low reward imbalance. This idea is consistent with the socio-economic status data of Adler et al. (1993), showing that those at the bottom of the socioeconomic status ladder have the highest incidence of morbidity and mortality. Hence, in this context of medical sociology, the approach to job redesign is not as specifically targeted at the individual job as is the job characteristics model. However, organizations and individuals may use the components of Figure 9.3 for purposes of redesign.

Job redesign in the context of the effort—reward model requires primary consideration of the three key reward variables shown in Figure 9.3. What is not clear or specified is how the three variables interplay or counterbalance each other. For example, in some organizational contexts, given the financial constraints of the organization and industry, the option of enhancing money via salary increases or bonuses may come quickly into conflict with the availability of money. Although it is not a fixed reward resource, money is more constrained than either esteem or status control. If either or both of those are able to be enhanced substantially, changes in money may be a less critical consideration.

Job Enrichment

Job enrichment can be a practical approach for enhancing employee stress and motivation. As a theory of job redesign, it increases challenge in a job by designing in motivational factors. The job's motivational factors (e.g., recognition, responsibility, and the opportunity for achievement) serve to stimulate motivation. In contrast, the hygienic factors (e.g., lighting levels, company regulations, and employee benefit programs) create dissatisfaction when poorly conceived or implemented. Some reviews of job enrichment suggest that it has not enjoyed a particularly long or happy history (Buchanan, 1987), but this might be due to implementation problems rather than the theory behind job enrichment. As a job redesign strategy, job enrichment may be useful for organizational prevention in two ways. First, it can increase functional stress in the workplace by building mildly stressful motivational factors into specific jobs. This provides for the constructive stress associated with movement up the Yerkes—Dodson curve to the optimum region. These additional motivational factors should provide regular, mildly intense stress for the job's incumbent, rather than severe, irregular stress. Second, attention to the hygienic factors in the workplace can alleviate some of the distress associated with physically or psychologically poor working conditions. The relevant physical hygienic factors are discussed in the analysis of physical settings later in the chapter. Other hygienic factors, such as company benefit programs, tuition reimbursement, or sabbatical leaves, may cause distress when absent.

The bulk of the job enrichment research and practice has been flawed, leaving this technique open to criticism. In contrast, there is more extensive experience with and research on task redesign. Proponents of task redesign have developed more psychometrically sound and advanced diagnostic tools. In addition, normative data on motivating potential scores are available for a variety of jobs. Theoretically, empirically, and practically, therefore, task redesign is a more acceptable technique than job enrichment.

Participative Management

Participative management is one strategy for implementing enhanced control in the workplace. As a method for organizational prevention in its own right, participative management is championed by major corporations and their leaders, such as General Electric's Jack Welch (Tichy & Charan, 1989). Participative management incorporates the ideas and thoughts of individuals and groups into the decision-making processes of the organization. Its intellectual roots lie in the early leadership research of Lewin and colleagues (1939). Changing organizational realities call for adjustments in leadership style to be effective in the new organizational environments. The flexibility, sensitivity, and psychologically minded nature of participative management allows leaders to understand and work better with their employees (H. Levinson, 1981a).

For General Electric's Welch, participative management is founded on an open and candid dialogue between managers and employees (Tichy & Charan, 1989). Welch expects managers to level with employees, telling them the truth about the realities of the business. Welch argues against rosily optimistic forecasts, suggesting that unrealistic optimism can be hazardous for the business and its employees. At least as important, Welch believes that employees need to challenge their bosses about wasteful activities that do not contribute to the business. This suggests that times of organizational change and downturn are rich opportunities for everyone in the organization to revisit their jobs and work demands, looking for ways to add value and dispose of wasted effort. This approach to participative management is compatible with the model of leader–follower dynamics set forth by Hirschhorn (1990). Hirschhorn's model suggests that healthy participation is achieved when (a) leaders express their vulnerability and dependence on their followers at the same time that they express their competence and authority and (b) followers are empowered to challenge their leaders' ideas and thinking while respecting and deferring to their authority. Participative management is a complex and dynamic method of leadership.

Participative leaders are less tense, engage in less destructive conflict, and are less rigid in their work groups than either autocratic or laissez-faire leaders (Lewin et al., 1939). Likert (1961) found that participative managers focused on the human aspects of the work environment and on teamwork. Followers in such an environment had considerably more freedom. The work groups under participative managers tended to be more productive than those working under authoritarian leadership. In addition to finding improved productivity, Tannenbaum and Massarik (1950) identified five other benefits of participative management: (a) a reduction in turnover, absenteeism, and tardiness; (b) a reduction in grievances and an improvement in management–labor relations; (c) a greater readiness to accept change; (d) a greater ease in managing followers; and (e) an improvement in the quality of managerial decisions. Several of these benefits directly address the various organizational consequences of stress discussed in chapter 5.

Participative management is compatible with the high levels of autonomy within the job characteristics model and the high levels of decision latitude within the demand–control model. Demanding jobs and demanding bosses who allow employees commensurate decision latitude and autonomy lead the way to higher levels of performance and achievement while lowering distress and strain at work. Demanding bosses who are also dictatorial and restrict an individual's opportunities for participation and autonomy contribute to distress, depression, exhaustion, increased illness rates, and pill consumption at work. Increasing participation and autonomy leads to greater freedom of action, still within defined limits, which enables individuals to channel and release stress-induced energy more naturally.

Decentralization

Organizational culture plays an important contextual role in job redesign as well as a central role in participative management (Schein, 1985). The process of decentralizing organizational decision making has a direct effect on the degree of job autonomy throughout the organizational hierarchy. It is a process that increases the decision latitude of individual managers in that hierarchy. Japanese researchers have taken the American notions of participative management, including decentralization of decision making, and implemented them through the mechanism of quality circles (Ouchi, 1981). Quality circles allow organizational problems to be solved at the lowest practical organizational level by having a peer group identify problem areas as well as potential solutions to the problem. The Department of Defense undertook a quality circle program in the early 1980s. The results of the program were mixed; some quality circles worked well, and others were disbanded by higher level managers.

The benefits of decentralization in terms of reduced distress and strain are illustrated in the experience of an officer of a hospital equipment corporation. Over a 10-year period, this officer worked for two different corporations. One company was extremely centralized, and the other used a decentralized decision-making approach. During his years in the centralized corporation, the officer had insomnia, depression, and nightmares about going to jail and about running afoul of corporate policies and procedures. His family reported that he was increasingly difficult to live with. After a year of this distress, he left the centralized corporation and subsequently joined the decentralized corporation. Following this move, his insomnia and depression cleared, and his nightmares about legal and procedural problems became less frequent and then stopped. His family reported that he was much easier to be around.

Although this executive's experiences may be more extreme than those of the average individual subject to centralized decision making, his story illustrates how centralized decision making and lack of decision latitude can create distress and unresolved strain, with the attendant psychological and physiological consequences.

Empowerment

Another positive vehicle for participative management is the empowerment of employees. Empowerment is about sharing power within an organization, not about redistributing power. Conger and Kanungo (1988) wrote of their view of empowerment as the basis for creating heightened motivation through the development of a strong sense of self-efficacy. Personal beliefs about competence, performance effectiveness, and responsibility are key hallmarks of empowerment. Empowered employees may have more stress from the demands for responsibility and self-management that accompany the empowerment process, but they have less distress associated with a restrictive and narrowly defined work environment. An empowered employee is not free of the boss; rather, the boss allows the empowered employee to work within a wider set of parameters with more autonomy for working independently more of the time. A caveat in this regard is that employees who have not developed a sufficiently strong endoskeleton and depend heavily on a supervisor's guidance are likely to be distressed by the responsibility and autonomy that accompany empowerment (H. Levinson, 1981a; J. C. Quick et al., 1996).

Implementing Participative Management

For participative management as advocated by General Electric's Welch to be effective, there are two requirements. Employees must meet a set of psychological requirements, and organizations must meet a different set of work-related requirements. When this approach to management is responsibly executed, it is effective in achieving benefits for employees, managers, and organizations.

   Psychological requirements. If participative management is to be effective, the individual participants must meet the following psychological preconditions: They must demonstrate the ability to become psychologically involved in participative decision making, an interest in participating in decision making, the ability to express their thoughts about decisions under consideration, and the perception that participation has personal relevance to their own future. Unless individuals meet these preconditions, participative management may not be highly effective. Even if individuals do meet these preconditions, the effectiveness of participation may be hampered unless the following organizational conditions are met.

Organizational requirements. The organizational conditions for effective participation are availability of time for individuals to participate in a decision (e.g., crisis decisions in military combat or in hospital emergency room settings should not be made participatively), existence of benefits that outweigh the costs of time and effort in the process, relative stability of working relationships between managers and subordinates, absence of decision-making situations in which the participants have a conflict of interest, shared goals and values, presence of channels whereby individuals may effectively contribute to decisions, and sufficient training and education about participation.

If the psychological and organizational requirements for participative decision making are met, an organization will benefit. As a strategy of preventive management, participation allows individuals to contribute their resources to improved organizational functioning and health. It also enables individuals to improve the degree of personal fit with the organization, which in turn provides a vested interest in organizational performance.

The Strategic Air Command and Program Buck Stop

Although the stereotype of military organizations, as exemplified by the U.S. Marine Corps, is one of nonparticipative management, this is not always the case. Even military organizations can benefit from participative management and decentralized decision making. For example, the United States Air Force's former Strategic Air Command (SAC) implemented a program called Buck Stop, which illustrates the practice of participative management. Buck Stop was designed to allow all operational and staff decisions to be made at the lowest practical level within the command. Implemented by the SAC commander through his wing commanders, its reach went down to the level of sergeant and airman. No formalized training was associated with the implementation process, but a formal monitoring procedure was established through the command's inspector general. Each team of inspectors was instructed to query junior noncommissioned officers during unit inspection tours regarding their understanding and use of Buck Stop. Experience with Buck Stop, although limited, suggested that commanders and senior supervisors were less burdened with decisions that could be made at a lower level. Commanders were freed to spend more time managing the combat wings and subordinate organizations by focusing more attention on managerial planning and action.

Flexible Work Schedules

The flexible work schedule constitutes a broad category of organizational prevention aimed at allowing employees to accommodate the total set of demands in their professional and personal lives (Nelson & Hitt, 1992). In addition to flextime and flexible working hours (Ronen, 1981), flexible work schedules encompass telecommuting (Caudron, 1990) and the 4-day workweek. For example, the United Services Automobile Association (USAA) in San Antonio, Texas, has had a 4-day, 10-hour a day workweek for at least a decade for employees who want a 3-day weekend to achieve a work–home balance that is not available through traditional work schedules. In preventive stress management, work scheduling is an important dimension of job design. Flexible work schedules have been a part of organizational life at least since the Hawthorne studies in the 1920s and 1930s (Roethlisberger & Dickson, 1939). During one of these series of studies, the researchers experimented with allowing the women to follow alternative work schedules that might better suit them. As with other aspects of redesigning work demands, flexible work schedules cannot be undertaken independently of other design considerations.

Task Interdependence

When the work is accomplished independently and task identity is high, there is more potential for success in the use of flexible work schedules. For example, within Pacific Bell, telecommuting has worked on a large scale; of 3,000 managers responding to a mail survey, 87% said telecommuting reduced employee stress, 70% said it reduced absenteeism and increased job satisfaction, and 64% said it increased productivity (Bailey & Foley, 1990). The difficulty in using flexible work schedules is introduced with interdependent tasks. The scheduling of shifts and workers becomes more difficult and restrictive under such conditions. Unless the nature of the tasks can be redesigned in content to enhance the use of flexible work schedules, the dictates of the task outweigh the issues of scheduling.

Managerial work lends itself to flexible work scheduling because of the reduced interdependence of detailed tasks and the greater responsibility associated with these positions. The manager's role is increasingly one of establishing a productive and healthy emotional work environment, which is not necessarily contingent on the manager's presence. This does not mean that the manager's presence in the workplace is not important. What it does mean is that the manager often has more discretion and latitude about working hours than may exist for individuals whose specific tasks are highly interdependent.

Flextime and Telecommuting

Flextime became a popular approach in the oil industry at a time of rapid urban growth and traffic congestion in Houston during the 1970s. Gulf Oil Corporation and Tenneco implemented flextime programs in downtown Houston and in some of their suburban locations. Gulf Oil offered their program to selected departments, whereas Tenneco allowed their personnel to volunteer for the program. Each program aided individuals in managing the stress of commuting in the congested urban location and allowed the company to remain competitive with other oil companies in the area who were doing the same thing.

Pacific Bell instituted telecommuting for 1,500 of its managers in 1990. For example, a Pacific Bell information systems designer might work 4 days at home and 1 day at the main office in 1 week. The day at the office would be packed with formal and informal meetings and work exchanges as well as coordination activities with peers, superiors, and employees. In this flexible program, a designer or manager with a heavy demand for interaction and meetings in 1 week might schedule 3 workdays at home and 2 in the main office.

Professional–Personal Balance

Because of the spillover effects of work-related stress into the home and home-related stress into the workplace, there is a need to attend to total life stress (Bhagat, McQuaid, Lindholm, & Segovis, 1985). Flexible work schedules afford employees the discretionary control to balance professional and personal demands according to their specific circumstances, thus improving the integration of individual and organizational needs. If flexible work schedules are to benefit both the individual and the organization, there must be a high level of maturity and responsibility on the part of the individual. When that is present, flexible work schedules can improve the individual–organizational exchange, increase the individual's discretion in managing personal stress demands, and dissipate some of the cumulative effects of stress while improving performance at work.

Career Development

A career is traditionally thought of as the sequence of vocational activities an individual engages in over the course of time. Career development is important in that context to maximize the employee's potential over time. Mobil Oil Corporation was among the major companies concerned with this concept of career development. Mobil used structured instruments and workshops for self-assessment and career planning aimed at benefiting both Mobil and the employee. Through this process, the company pushed its managers to plan for their futures with the help of the corporation. The two keys in Mobil's framework, as in many such programs, were self-assessment (assets, liabilities, and interests) and opportunity analysis (preferred jobs and people to work for).

Career stress in these changing times still requires looking at the career in one's life context (Quick, Hess, Hermalin, & Quick, 1990). Current work realities are revising the psychological contracts between individuals and organizations as organizations shift away from organizing by jobs to organizing by individual competencies (Lawler, 1994). The new psychological contracts are different from those of a decade or two ago, especially for newly hired employees (Rousseau, 1990). Psychological contracts are critical for an employee's socialization and adjustment in the organization (Nelson, Quick, & Joplin, 1991). Although organizational and career realities have changed, there is still a need for career planning and counseling, maybe even more so, as is discussed in chapter 13.

Career Planning and Decision Making

Career planning and decision making depend on accurate self-assessment and opportunity analyses. Because of the dynamic nature of careers in the 1990s and the demands of developing a portfolio of skills, both self-assessment and opportunity analysis are ongoing processes (Lawler, 1994).

Self-assessment. A thorough assessment of individuals' needs, interests, skills, abilities, and knowledge is the basis for effective career planning and decision making. Two key self-assessment questions are as follows: (a) What do I want and like to do? (b) What are my present strengths, abilities, and talents?

INDIVIDUAL INTERESTS. Individuals differ in their preferences and interests, and there may be varying degrees of distress associated with engaging in activities that the individual does not like. Some such activities may be present in any job or occupation; however, these points of disinterest can be minimized through effective self-assessment. Two of the most widely used measures of individual interests are the Strong Interest Inventory (Hansen & Campbell, 1985) and the Kuder Occupational Interest Survey (Kuder & Diamond, 1979). These inventories assess an individual's preferences for various courses of study, activities, kinds of people, amusements, and occupations. Although these two interest inventories are the most widely used and best researched, additional interest inventories may be chosen (see Buros, 1995). Regardless of the measurement tool employed, it is essential to the self-assessment process that individuals have a basis for understanding their interests and preferences.

INDIVIDUAL ABILITIES. In addition to interest assessment, it is essential for individuals to have a realistic and objective understanding of their abilities. This aspect of the self-assessment process concerns the special knowledge and intellectual capability that the individual has as well as the unique physical skills and talents. Both areas of ability are important. Each ability area can be developed with sufficient drive and interest, but there are upper limits to the development that may occur. Although one can overcome apparent limitations or lack of ability to some extent, it is important to assess the individual's ability base.

No one or two standardized tests provide the diverse information base needed in this area of self-assessment. The Educational Testing Service and the Psychological Corporation provide a diversity of aptitude tests that may be useful in assessing intellectual functioning. Probably the best resource to use in selecting an aptitude test is the *Mental Measurements Yearbook* (Buros, 1995). Its two volumes include a wide range of mental and aptitude tests along with an assessment of the quality of each on the basis of validity and reliability studies.

Individuals and organizations should undertake formal individual ability and talent assessments. Even informal assessments by alert, experienced professionals can be useful. From the individual's perspective, self-assessment is a necessary first step before turning to opportunity analysis. The organization can play a vital role in structuring opportunities for career development that minimize the dysfunctions of frustrated ambitions and wasted talents.

Opportunity analysis. Opportunity analysis is the process of identifying the range of organizational and occupational roles that are available for an individual. As organizations and societies change, the available roles may also change. Each role requires the incumbent to exhibit various behaviors and talents, and it is essential to develop information about these role requirements.

A key part of the opportunity analysis from the individual's standpoint is to determine the educational and physical requirements for the occupations or specific jobs under consideration. The requirements of various job levels in one industry or organization may differ markedly. For example, lower level managerial positions require substantially greater technical knowledge than top-level managerial positions, which require greater conceptual skills and knowledge (Bracey, Sanford, & Quick, 1981). In some cases there is flexibility in requirements; for example, the administrators in a hospital corporation may possess either the MBA degree, the MPH degree, or the MHA degree. In other cases there is virtually no flexibility in a requirement; for example, a lawyer must possess a J.D. degree and pass the state bar to practice.

Socialization to Careers and Organizations

Organizational socialization is a key entry point to a career and profession, and it is a stressful process, although not necessarily distressful (Nelson, 1985). The process has three phases: (a) anticipatory socialization, (b) encounter, and (c) change and acquisition. Newcomers experience different stressors, demands, and challenges as they work through each of the three phases of socialization to become established insiders within their career and organization. Reality shock in the encounter phase may be a spike point for a newcomer's stress level. However, the intensity and duration of reality shock are shaped by the extent and degree of information gathering undertaken in the anticipatory socialization phase of the process. Organizations and occupations that define career paths for employees and create opportunities for them can ease the way for a successful and profitable career.

Defining career paths. Some organizations and occupations have defined career paths for employees, whereas other organizations, such as those in extremely dynamic and growing industries, may not. The blockage of such growth and development may have detrimental effects on organizational health. Organizations and professions differ in what they believe constitutes individual growth and development. Some organizations, like private-sector corporations and military services, lend themselves to upward mobility as a characteristic of career development. Others, like professional organizations and universities, lend themselves to the horizontal cultivation of professional skills and talents as the key characteristic of career development.

The profession of nursing has experienced some career development turmoil over the years, with some nurses feeling frustrated and distressed about the lack of available opportunities for advancement and development. The avenue into hospital administration traditionally has not been open to nursing directors, although that is changing. Professional ladders are another approach in nursing to allow nurses to pursue professional development as opposed to administrative development.

Creating opportunities. Transition of one person within an organization creates opportunity for other people. A key question for Southwest Airlines is, What happens when Herb's gone? In an effort to minimize the disruption associated with the replacement of key executives, Tenneco and Ken Davis Industries, among other corporations, have required key executives to designate an heir apparent who is able and prepared to step into the key position. This form of career development and planning has advantages for both the individual and the organization in coping with the stressful aspects of career development and turnover. For the individual, it affords time to develop the necessary skills and information required in the new position. For the organization, it minimizes the disruption of a change in leadership, which can have adverse effects on performance and productivity.

The United States military services have a structured approach to careers that is established by law. Officers and enlisted service members move through sequences of assignments designed to develop their abilities and use their talents. This approach requires members to achieve promotions to the next higher pay and responsibility grade or be terminated by the service. This up-or-out policy of promotion or termination ensures the availability of opportunities for younger military members. A possible drawback is the loss of an able, effective performer who lacks the upward drive for promotion and achievement.

In summary, career development is eustressful to the extent that it requires the individual to learn new skills, acquire new knowledge, and overcome previous limitations to his or her full development. The lack of career development opportunities for an individual may lead to frustration, distress, and other negative outcomes. Therefore, career development opportunities are an integral aspect of preventive management and organizational health.

Design of Physical Settings

The first four preventive management methods discussed in this chapter were primarily concerned with the task, role, and interpersonal demands of work. The last primary prevention method is concerned with the physical factors that cause individuals stress in organizations. Despite humans' established mastery over many aspects of the physical environment, there are still work settings that are especially demanding physically, for example, the various divisions of oceangoing freighters and naval ships. Mastery over such naturally powerful forces as hurricanes and tornadoes has not been established. Nevertheless, the vast majority of white collar office workers and blue collar factory workers spend their days in physical settings that are far more controlled than they were 100 years ago.

For a manager or consultant to undertake the design of physical settings as a preventive management intervention or for a researcher to study the role of the physical setting in creating or alleviating organizational stress entails a thorough understanding of the six functions of physical settings (Steele, 1973). To reiterate what was stated in chapter 2, these functions are (a) shelter and security, (b) social contact, (c) symbolic identification, (d) task instrumentality, (e) pleasure, and (f) growth.

All these functions are of importance in stress management and in the design of physical settings, although their relative importance varies according to department, managerial preference, organizational level and function, and other formal and informal organizational considerations. Not everyone using a physical setting may agree on the priority of these various functions, however. For example, various trainees in one organization had some markedly different perceptions regarding the key functions of the training space. Some considered its most important function to be task instrumentality, whereas others considered it to be growth. Before they could effectively and successfully use the space, these differences had to be addressed.

Many aspects of a physical setting fall in the category of what Herzberg, Mausner, and Snyderman (1959) called hygienic factors, and these are typically what people think about when examining their physical environment. Steele suggested that this may be a convenient place to start people thinking; however, the examination of the physical setting must eventually turn to viewing the organization as an entire ecological system. In this case, the ecological concerns are with how individuals relate to and interact with their organizational environments. Although individuals often attend to the aesthetic and hygienic aspects of their work environment, they less frequently attend to the natural fit between themselves and their surroundings. It is the interdependence of individuals and their work environments that is the key concern of this ecological perspective in the analysis of physical settings.

Redesign

The design or redesign of a physical setting involves creativity and an understanding of the functions of space as well as some careful forethought and planning. Each physical setting should be approached without preconceptions about its limitation, because such preconceptions may limit one's imagination in redesigning the space. Once one's imagination is fully opened to the redesign opportunities, it may be possible to use the following sequences of activities for effectively designing or redesigning the space.

Ecological analysis of the physical setting. Identifying the functions of any physical setting requires input from the various individuals and groups who use the setting. Questionnaires or interviews can be used for this purpose. Questionnaires are most efficient when there are a large number of individuals whose opinions and perceptions are needed. This step is critical because a misidentification might result in an extremely dysfunctional setting. For example, if there is a need for privacy and restricted contact in a set of counseling offices but the setting was inadvertently designed to enhance social contact, individuals using the counseling services may be distressed.

The functional identification is only part of the overall ecological analysis. It is also necessary to consider how the space and people in it interact. Such an examination may result in a dynamic analysis that complements the analysis of the functions. The dynamic analysis requires that one examine how the setting places demands and stresses on individuals who are moving within it and through it. This dynamic examination is an equally important aspect of the overall ecological analysis.

Examination of the present setting. Once the purposes of the physical setting have been identified, the space must be carefully examined for several reasons. First, it is necessary to determine which aspects of the setting are fixed and which are not. Few aspects of a physical setting are fixed in a strict sense, although they may be perceived that way. The use of movable partitions and half walls is a good example of how a fixed aspect of a physical setting may be converted into an easily changed one.

Second, the setting needs to be examined for natural advantages and disadvantages. For example, a university classroom building designed with two large 250-person lecture halls, fifteen 70-person lecture halls, twenty 40-person classrooms, and four 15-person classrooms is well suited for large undergraduate classes but ill-suited for most graduate seminars.

Changes in the physical setting. Once the functions of the setting and the space itself have been carefully examined, the changes to be made should be identified and carried out. This may include bringing in furniture, removing or adding walls, lowering or raising ceilings, raising the floor, or removing unnecessary furniture. Such identified changes should be made only after a consideration of other aspects of the work environment, budgetary constraints, and the effects of these changes on the individuals in related areas of the organization. Some possible alterations in the physical setting are listed in Exhibit 9.2. The result of the entire

Exhibit 9.2.   Possible Alterations in the
Physical Setting

Structural changes
  • Points of entry and exit
  • Wall placement and height
  • Ceiling height and angle
  • Openings for vistas and lighting
  • Floor angles and elevations
  • Furniture, fixtures, and placements
Acoustical changes
  • Wall coverings, finishing, and insulation
  • Cushions and draperies
  • Floor coverings and finishing
  • Ceiling coverings and finishing
  • Plants and natural additions
Lighting changes
  • Natural openings
  • Placement of artificial lights
  • Intensity of lighting
  • Color of interior furnishings
  • Plants and natural additions

---

redesign effort should be a natural fitting and flowing together of people
and their environment in a smooth ecological system.

Impact of the analysis. The final aspect in the design or redesign of a
physical setting is to evaluate the effect of any changes that were made.
This may be done by examining accident rates and performance and productivity data or by the use of questionnaires and interviews. The analysis
of the impact of the changes should be done some months after the changes
are made to avoid or minimize any temporary effects of the change.

A Computer Operations Redesign Effort

The redesign of a physical setting is illustrated in the changes made at a
computer facility. The mainframe computer, tape drives, and tape file storage facilities were installed in an area of a building not originally designed
for a computer operations branch. This area of the building is shown in
Figure 9.4A. The operations personnel experienced some inefficiency in
their work flow and task accomplishment because of the location of the
door between the tape file storage area and the mainframe computer
system.
    The branch chief realized that the department might function more
effectively if the tape file storage cabinets and the computer system were
more directly connected. He was able to accomplish this by creating a new
entryway in the interior wall between the two operations areas. In conjunction with the new entryway, he redesigned the layout of the computer
system and tape file cabinets, as shown in Figure 9.4B. This redesign effort

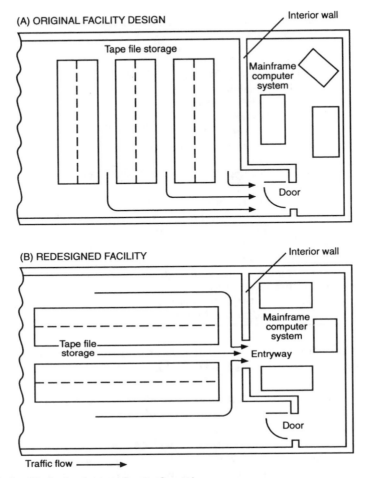

Figure 9.4.   Redesigning a physical setting.

created a more efficient and natural ecological flow so that the operations personnel and the setting worked more harmoniously in accomplishing the task for which the setting was intended. The two areas in operations were still somewhat distinct yet more easily and efficiently connected.

Cockpit Design: Solving the Problem of G-LOC

To solve the problem of gravitationally induced loss of consciousness (G-LOC) experienced by U.S. Air Force and U.S. Navy pilots undergoing sustained high linear accelerations in high performance aircraft, Gillingham (1988) and the Brooks Aerospace Medicine Center engaged in a series of physical cockpit redesign efforts, along with education and training initiatives for pilots. The three physical design changes made were (a) seat reconfiguration, specifically, use of a reclined seatback; (b) an improved anti-G suit; and (c) an assisted positive-pressure breathing device. The aircrew education and training initiatives included (a) exposure to the high-G environment frequently and regularly, (b) strength and weight training, (c) endurance training, (d) learning a straining maneuver, and (e) centrifuge training. Finally, by recommending the setting of G-tolerance standards for aircrew training and selection, Gillingham (1988) worked to achieve an improved fit between pilots and their physical work environment: the cockpit.

Summary

This chapter presents five organizational prevention methods aimed at moderating the effects of organizational stressors on individuals at work. These five methods are job redesign, participative management, flexible work schedules, career development, and the design of physical settings. A brief description of each appears in Exhibit 9.1. The methods are fundamentally concerned with the formal organization and the effects of the formal organization on the individual. The distinctions between the formal and informal organizations are clarified at the outset of chapter 10.

These five methods are not the only ways to prevent organizational distress within formal systems. They were chosen on the basis of the documented evidence of their applicability in organizations. Less extensive and elaborate methods aimed at specific sources of distress include efforts to change pay and benefit systems, formal company policies and procedures, performance appraisal systems, various aspects of the quality of work life, and equal opportunity programs. There are a wide variety of ways to change or modify the formal organization to minimize the distressful and maximize the eustressful effects that it has on the individual.

The next chapter addresses five methods of preventive management that are aimed at the informal, interpersonal, and role-related sources of stress in organizations. These aspects of organizational life generate as many demands as does the formal organizational system. Altering these demands requires different techniques from those required to redesign the formal and physical organization.

10

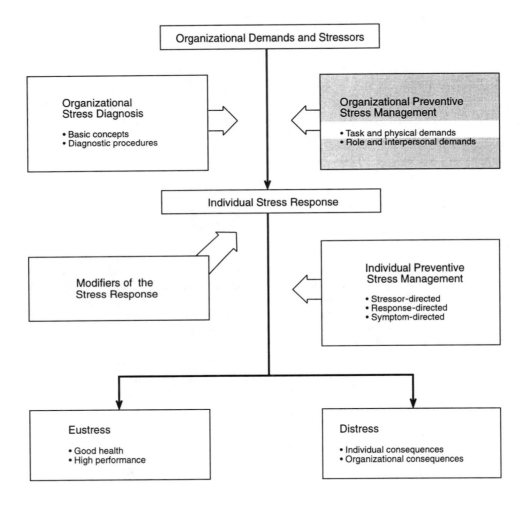

Organizational Prevention: Improving Relationships at Work

The organizational prevention methods discussed in chapter 9 focused on reshaping the formal organization to prevent excessive or insufficient work demands. Our focus in this chapter is on methods for preventing distress caused by informal and interpersonal demands placed on individuals in organizations. This may be accomplished through several prevention methods directed at role and interpersonal stressors. The five methods to be covered in this chapter are identified and briefly discussed in Exhibit 10.1. The empirical evidence regarding these methods is modest, as it is for so many intervention methods in organizations, which points out the need for more rigorous studies of interventions (Ganster, 1995).

The specific concerns of the formal organization, discussed in the preceding chapter, are the tasks that individuals perform and the physical settings in which they work. Any organization is, however, a blend of formal and informal elements. The prevention methods discussed in this chapter deal with the integration of the informal and the formal organization. Two of these methods, role analysis and goal setting, are primary prevention methods aimed at changing the demands placed on the individual at work. The other three methods, social support, team building, and diversity programs, are a mixture of primary and secondary prevention methods. They are intended to assist individuals in managing the various demands of work. The ability to understand individual and organizational functioning is hinged in part on grasping the distinction between the formal and the informal, the overt and the covert, or the conscious and the unconscious. This distinction is depicted in Figure 10.1.

One of the underlying assumptions of organizational-level preventive management is that the informal, covert, and unconscious elements of organizations and individuals are important to health (French & Bell, 1990). Some organizations and individuals attempt either to ignore the informal level or to repress its contents. Although such a strategy may be successful in the short term, it is rarely successful for long periods of time. Organizational and psychiatric literature document numerous cases of organizational and individual health problems arising from lack of integration of the informal and unconscious with the formal and conscious. For example, if management ignores the feelings and needs of employees, the employees may retaliate by using work slowdowns or other disruptive activities to frustrate management. A health problem at the individual level might involve a manager who becomes angry with his boss but represses the feeling at work, only to have a headache or upset stomach later.

Exhibit 10.1. Organizational Prevention: Role and Interpersonal Demands

---

Role analysis

This method is aimed at clarifying an individual's work role to reduce distressful confusion and conflict. A role profile is developed on the basis of expectations of superiors, peers, employees, and other key people with whom the individual must work. This *expected role* is then clarified by eliminating conflicts and confusion in the expectations. It is also integrated with the *enacted role*, resulting in reduced role stress for the individual.

Goal setting

This method focuses on the primary relationship between an individual and his immediate superior. The aim is to clarify the individual's work role by specifying major areas of responsibility and performance goals in each responsibility area. This should result in increased motivation and reduced role stress.

Social support

This is a method for ameliorating many of the effects of work stresses on the individual. The idea is to buffer the impact of stressors on the individual's psychological and physiological functioning by providing the necessary emotional, informational, appraisal, and instrumental support.

Team building

This is a method for intervening in the interpersonal processes of an intact work group. The aim is to confront, work through, and resolve interpersonal conflicts that naturally evolve within work groups. The process of resolution is thought to be better than repression for the management of these interpersonal stresses.

Diversity programs

This intervention ensures that the diversity of talents and perspectives within the organization are valued and used. The process may involve debunking stereotypes, with the emphasis on valuing all people.

The formal and informal aspects of organizational life are important when dealing with role and interpersonal demands because there are formal and informal requirements in all working relationships. For example, Payne (1980) pointed out that people receive social support from both the formal organization, as in the case of rules about work behavior, and the informal organization, as in the case of a supervisor covering a friend's shift for a few hours. Recognizing the formal and informal components of organizations and individuals may lead to alternative and complementary ways of managing the demands of organizational life.

Organizational-level preventive management requires attention to both formal and informal aspects when dealing with the relationships that influence an individual's behavior and stress level at work. In one way or another, each of the prevention methods discussed in this chapter is concerned with the individual's working relationships. The formal aspects of these relationships may cause distress or eustress. The same is true of the informal aspects of these relationships. Which of the two outcomes

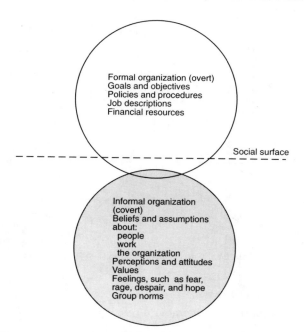

Figure 10.1. Formal and informal elements of organizations. From *Organizational Behavior: Foundations, Realities, and Challenges* (2nd ed., p. 12), by D. L. Nelson and J. C. Quick, 1997, Cincinnati, OH: South-Western College Publishing, a division of International Thomson Publishing, Inc. Reprinted with permission.

occurs—distress or eustress—is partially dependent on the application of one or more of the following preventive measures.

Role Analysis

Role analysis is designed to answer such questions as "Is my job role clear? Are the expectations placed on me consistent? Are there too many expectations placed on me?" Role analysis is a method of clarifying and defining an individual's work role to reduce distressful confusion and conflict. An individual begins a role analysis by asking people at work what they expect of him or her. By identifying the points of confusion or inconsistency in these expectations, the individual may then take action to resolve the confusion and eliminate the inconsistencies. In some cases, the role analysis may reveal that changes are necessary in job descriptions, reporting relationships, or organizational structure (Matteson, 1987). The result of role analysis is a clearer, more consistent work role for the individual. The result for the organization is an improvement in the quality of existing relationships and a reduction in the amount of dysfunctional role stress.

Organizational Roles

Organizational roles may be defined in two ways: in terms of what other people at work expect of the individual, which is the *expected role* and the

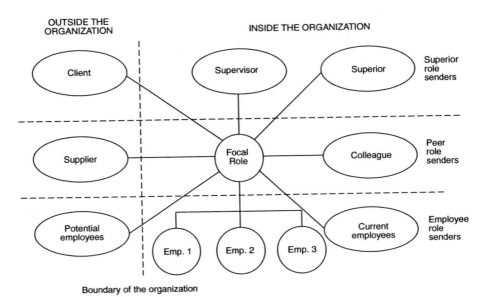

Figure 10.2.   An organization member's role set.

most common way of defining an organizational role, and in terms of how the individual in the role behaves, which is the *enacted role*. An individual's actions and behaviors "in role" define the enacted role. The expected role and the enacted role are not necessarily the same. The whole process of assuming an organizational role causes individuals stress at work (Kahn et al., 1964).

Organizational roles are more easily understood in a role-set framework. In this framework, the individual is viewed from the position of a focal role. Figure 10.2 depicts this focal role with its various role senders. People both inside and outside the organization are important in the individual's role set, each being a source of behavioral expectations.

Role senders are individuals who expect the focal person to behave in certain ways and meet certain obligations at work. As shown in the figure, there are three general categories of role senders: superior, peer, and employee role senders. Some are inside the organization, and others are outside. Every organizational member may have formal as well as informal relationships with various role senders, and behavioral expectations are generated in all these relationships. Therefore, each role sender may have both formal and informal expectations of the focal person.

Role analysis may be more important now than ever before, given the changing nature of organizations. Roles change quickly with organizational restructuring, and employees are expected to flex with the changes. When organizations were structured as rigid hierarchies, roles were easier to define. Because contemporary organizations are matrix- or network-oriented, dynamic, and flatter than in the past, roles are more dynamic and therefore less clear.

Preventive management of role stress is an active process that requires clarification and integration of the various expectations that role senders communicate to the focal role as well as alteration of the behaviors exhibited by the focal person. Any activity or method of role-stress management must focus on these essential processes of clarification and integration. For these two essential processes to occur, both role expectations and behaviors must be observed and analyzed.

The Procedure

Dayal and Thomas (1968) were the first to discuss the use of role analysis. There are a number of different ways to conduct a role analysis, some more regimented than others. These are discussed by Dayal and Thomas (1968), French and Bell (1990), and Huse (1980). Regardless of which specific approach is taken, the key elements of a role analysis are the same. The following paragraphs, based on the work of French and Bell (1990), outline how to conduct a role analysis. The procedure involves identifying key role senders and their behavioral expectations of the focal person and developing the focal person's role profile.

Role-set identification. Focal persons must identify their role set, making sure to include all relevant role senders who may have legitimate expectations of them. Classification and categorization of the various role senders is necessary to avoid ignoring any relevant role senders.

Role definition. Once the role set has been identified, it is necessary to define the focal role in terms of its place in the organization. The rationale for the focal role and the contributions of the incumbent to overall organizational functioning and goal attainment are developed by the focal person. This rationale is a broad justification of the role's necessity to the organization. The responsibilities and authorities of the focal person are identified here.

Focal person's expectations. None of us functions entirely independently in any organization. We have certain expectations regarding what other organizational members do for us in our role performance. In this step, the focal person identifies what is expected of each member of the role set, discussing these expectations with the various role senders.

Role-sender expectations. The next step requires the focal person to identify all the specific expectations that each member of the role set has of him or her. In identifying each role sender's expectations, the focal person should be particularly mindful of expectations that are ambiguous. In addition, the focal person should be aware of points of inconsistency or incompatibility between the expectations of one or more role senders.

In using this approach, the focal person should attend to any informal expectations the various role senders may place on the role. These often are not made explicit until the focal person probes for them. However, these informal expectations may play an important part in the dynamics of the relationship between the focal person and the role sender and should therefore be explored. For example, a supervisor who likes to be left alone in the morning until after her first cup of coffee may be upset with anyone who bothers her before that time.

Role profile. The final step in the role-analysis technique is the development of a written role profile that delineates the expected role of the focal person. This profile should consist of a set of clear, specific, and internally consistent expectations of the focal person. Any inconsistencies in the profile or any expectations that are not clear or explicit should be examined by the focal person in conjunction with the affected role senders. These inconsistencies and ambiguities should be eliminated from the profile as much as possible. For those that cannot be eliminated, the focal person must devise alternative ways to manage the role stress, such as drawing on social support contacts. Stress is reduced for the individual as the inconsistencies and confusion are eliminated from the role profile through discussion and negotiation with the involved role senders. Stress may be inevitable when one assumes an organizational role; the distressful elements of role stress need to be eliminated through role analysis.

Practical Difficulties

Contemporary forms of organization pose some challenges for the use of role analysis. These include matrix, project, and network organizations. All three forms of organization have become more prevalent as a result of an increasingly complex and changing business environment. The virtual organization, in which no concrete structure exists, is another organizational form that presents challenges. Although these structures make role analysis more complex, they do not negate the need for it; rather, they increase the need for role clarification. All of these organizational forms involve expectations placed on individuals. The role-analysis technique deals with the expectations of all members of a person's role set.

Role analysis is aimed at reducing the various forms of role stress that were presented in chapter 2. Evidence bears out the success of this technique. Studies have indicated that role analysis is effective in terms of reducing burnout (Burke, 1987); decreasing role stress, role strain, and absenteeism (J. C. Quick, 1979a); and reducing perceptions of role ambiguity (Schaubroeck, Ganster, Sime, & Ditman, 1993).

Goal Setting

Goal setting is a method of establishing specific objectives for an individual's job. These objectives direct and motivate the individual's behavior and actions. Goal setting is often done in collaboration with the individual's supervisor and, when done correctly, leads to a clearer understanding of the job and work environment. It may also lead to a better mutual understanding between a manager and employee.

Goal setting helps eliminate anticipatory stressors by focusing attention on goal accomplishment instead of an uncertain future. There is a large body of research on goal setting, including laboratory studies, field research experiments, and comparative investigations, much of it focusing on the factors that make goals effective.

Characteristics of Effective Goals

Effective goals are specific, challenging, measurable, time-bound, and prioritized. Specific, challenging goals lead to peak performance. People with such goals consistently outperform those with goals that are easy or non-specific (Locke & Latham, 1990). Measurable goals form the basis for feedback about goal progress. Feedback helps alleviate uncertainty and increases an individual's self-efficacy, which can in turn reduce distress. Time-bound goals enhance measurability and provide good targets for goal accomplishment. Prioritizing goals helps direct the individual's efforts and behavior.

Although goals with these characteristics help increase motivation and performance, there are other functions of goal setting. Goal setting plays a major role in reducing stress that is associated with conflicting or confusing expectations. This is done by communicating task–role expectations to employees. Supervisors, coworkers, and employees are all important sources of task-related information. The improved role clarity from goal setting is due to improved communication between managers and employees. Organizations like Ford Motor Company and Federal Express include communication-related targets in their goal-setting processes.

Organizational Goal-Setting Programs

Management by objectives (MBO) programs couple goal setting and performance evaluation that are based on a negotiated agreement between employees and managers. MBO is a participative, interactive process involving both planning and evaluation. Goal-setting programs operate under a variety of names in a variety of organizations. At Purex, the program is called "goals and controls"; at Black & Decker, it is named "work planning and review"; and at Tenneco and IBM, it is "performance planning and review"—all refer to goal-setting activities (Pritchard, Roth, Jones, Galgay, & Watson, 1988).

The planning component consists of both organizational and individual goal setting. Organizational goal setting is a prerequisite to individual goal setting, and the two must be closely linked for MBO to be successful. Discretionary control is given to individuals and departments to develop goals that support organizational objectives. This control helps reduce stress. The emphasis is on formulating not only the goal (*what*) but also the pathways to achieving that goal (*how*; Tubbs & Ekeberg, 1991).

The evaluation component consists of periodic reviews by managers and employees of goal progress, along with formal performance evalua-

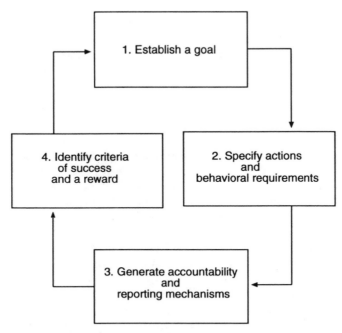

Figure 10.3. A model for goal setting. From *Developing Management Skills: Managing Stress* (3rd Ed., p. 135), by D. A. Whetton and K. S. Cameron, 1995, New York: HarperCollins. Reprinted with permission.

tions. MBO thus removes some of the anxiety and ambiguity from the appraisal process.

Merely setting goals may not lead to goal achievement or stress reduction. The dyadic activity that takes place between managers and employees must be more comprehensive, as shown in Figure 10.3.

The second step is to identify specific behaviors that lead toward accomplishment of the goal. The more difficult the goal, the more rigorous and specific these behaviors should be. The third step involves establishing accountability. The final step is to identify the criteria for goal accomplishment and a reward for success. The whole point of the goal-setting model is to eliminate distress by providing focus and direction for activity. The anxiety associated with uncertainty can be dissipated when mental and physical efforts are focused on goal-directed activity (Whetton & Cameron, 1993).

Increasing Motivation and Performance and Reducing Distress

Three important behavioral aspects of goal setting facilitate motivation, performance, and reduction of distress. These aspects are employee participation, management commitment, and performance feedback. Employee participation leads to goal commitment and goal accomplishment. Management commitment reflects the organization's commitment to the goal-setting program. Feedback on goal progress that is timely and useful provides knowledge of results that can help employees redirect their efforts and provides encouragement for further efforts.

The stress-reducing aspects of goal-setting programs revolve around task goals and manager–employee interactions. Goal setting facilitates open, supportive communication in the relationship. Because goal setting reduces ambiguity, provides support, and allows a sense of control, it is reasonable to expect an overall reduction in an employee's distress at work.

Effectiveness of Goal-Setting Programs

Significant declines in both role conflict and role ambiguity were found during one 14-month study of a goal-setting program in an insurance company (J. C. Quick, 1979a). This finding suggests that the individual's work role can be clarified through the goal-setting process, thus reducing the amount of stress it generates. A later review suggested that this result may be dependent on the existence of a participatory, interactive process between the individual and his supervisor (Tolchinsky & King, 1980). In a second study, conducted over a 2-year period in a large Western bank, similar reductions in role stress owing to the presence of a goal-setting program were not found (J. C. Quick, Kulisch, Jones, O'Connor, & Peters, 1981). This result may have been due in part to the much lower levels of employee participation found in the bank.

The insurance company study also found a significant decline in illness-related absenteeism at 5 months following the implementation of the goal-setting program. This decline was not maintained 8 months after implementation. The reduction in absenteeism is consistent with improved role clarity because individuals with clear goals feel less confused at work and therefore less prone to avoid work. Also, absenteeism was found to be significantly related to conflicting expectations from supervisors. It is not surprising that absenteeism declined as these conflicting expectations were reduced. Again, the results in the bank were not consistent with these findings. The individuals using the goal-setting program were absent more because of personal illness and took fewer holidays than those who were not involved in the goal-setting program. This result suggests that the bank's program had the reverse effect on its employees, in fact *increasing* their stress level. These studies suggest that a participatory approach to the goal-setting process is an essential prerequisite to achieving the intended stress reduction.

Social Support

Social support is a means of augmenting each individual's natural physiological and psychological resources for managing the demands at work that cause stress. Many definitions of social support have been advanced, and these concepts are complementary. Cobb (1976) defined social support

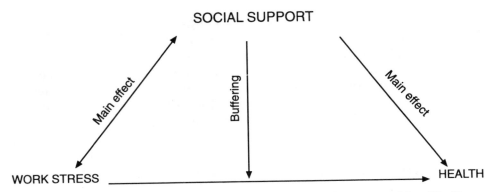

Figure 10.4. Potential effects of social support on work stress and health. From *Work Stress and Social Support* (p. 31), by J. S. House, 1981, Reading, MA: Addison-Wesley. Reprinted with permission.

as the individual perception that one is cared for and loved, is esteemed and valued, and belongs to a network of communication and mutual obligation. Shumaker and Brownell (1994) defined social support in more transactional terms as an exchange of resources between at least two individuals perceived by the provider or the recipient to be intended to enhance the well-being of the recipient. A reasonable definition of social support, based on the various definitions of the experts, is *the assistance one receives through his or her interpersonal relationships*.

Social Support and Health

The general relationship between social support and health is supported in a broad array of studies indicating that a host of diseases and causes of death are associated with social support (Bruhn, 1996). J. S. House et al. (1988) reviewed the evidence on social support and health, emphasizing that socially isolated individuals are less healthy in both psychological and physical terms and that they are more likely to die. Their extensive meta-analysis indicated that positive health outcomes, particularly a longer life span, are associated with social support. Social isolation is a risk factor for both mortality and morbidity.

Five prospective studies examined the age-adjusted mortality rate for men and women linked with their levels of social integration (for details, see J. D. Quick et al., 1996). In each study, an increased risk of mortality for both sexes was associated with lower levels of social integration. To illustrate the nature of these studies, consider the monumental research study conducted by Berkman and Syme (1979) in Alameda County, California. The researchers tracked the health histories of 7,000 non-Japanese residents for 9 years. Information was gathered on marital status, organizational memberships, and religious service attendance. Berkman and Syme found that individuals with fewer social relationships had higher mortality rates from all causes—3 times higher than those who had more social relationships. These results held even when factors such as age, race, and smoking behavior were controlled for.

We conclude that there is a strong connection between social relationships and health. What is less clear, however, is the exact mechanism whereby social relationships and social support affect health. Evidence suggests that the connection may operate in three ways. First, social support may have a direct effect on work stress by altering a work demand or modifying one's response to the demand (J. S. House, 1981). Second, social support may have a direct effect on health by improving one's physical or psychological well-being. Third, social support can buffer the adverse effects work stress may have on one's health. In the stress-buffering model, support may influence the stressor–strain connection by altering the cognitive appraisal of the stressor or by dampening health-damaging psychological processes (S. Cohen, 1992; Schwarzer, Hahn, & Fuchs, 1994). Figure 10.4 illustrates these three ways that social support may affect work stress and health.

The evidence regarding the effects of these three mechanisms on work stress is best described as mixed. Although some studies have found evidence for a buffering effect (cf. Astrand, Hanson, & Isacson, 1989; Johnson, Hall, & Theorell, 1989), other studies have found none (Ganster, 1995). The precise mechanism is not well understood, but an impressive amount of evidence from epidemiological studies shows that social support plays a clear role in enhancing individual health.

Forms of Social Support

Operationally, social support comes in four forms: emotional, appraisal, informational, and instrumental support (J. S. House, 1981). Emotional support involves empathy, emotional caring, and love, such as quietly listening to the lament of an individual who has just lost a job. Appraisal support involves transmitting information to an individual about role performance and behavior. An example would be the performance appraisal interview. Informational support entails providing information needed to manage demands or problems, for example, the specifications for a new computer software system. Instrumental support involves behaviors that directly assist another individual in need, such as taking on part of a colleague's work after one's own has been completed.

Translating J. S. House's (1981) forms of social support into the domain of work, five forms of support were identified (Nelson et al., 1991). These included protective, informational, evaluative, modeling, and emotional support.

Sources of Social Support

Every individual has a social support network that varies in both size and composition. This network consists of all the relationships in which the individual is involved. These relationships may be classified into major categories, or arenas, as depicted in Figure 10.5. Although the relationships in this social support network provide assistance in managing de-

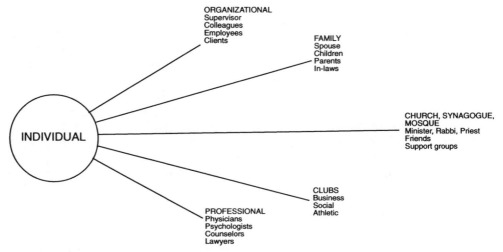

Figure 10.5. Social support network.

mands and problems, it should also be noted that these relationships may at times be a *source of demands*. This notion of social exchange is at the foundation of all human relationships. It is important to keep in mind that even the most supportive relationships place demands at times.

Familial support systems can be especially important as a source of guidance, renewal, and emotional support (Bhagat, 1983). In the childhood years, the family plays a vital role in an individual's socialization and adjustment to the broader society. In the adult years, the family is an important source of identification and strength. The family's value as a support system depends in part on its acceptance of an individual's whole personality, including the flaws and inconsistencies in that personality. It also depends on the recognition and meeting of the individual's more fundamental needs. In addition, families evaluate and regulate the behavior of their members. Therefore, the family is a vital social support system that combats loneliness and alienation and provides a source of identity and guidance.

As indicated in Figure 10.5, not all social support systems come from personal and family relationships. Effective support systems are also needed within work organizations. There are several reasons for this. First, the demands of work require responses using various resources available to the individual. Appraisal and informational forms of social support enhance employees' knowledge and use of skills in meeting these diverse demands. Without the supplemental outside resources to assist in managing demands at work, the stress response caused by specific demands may be more intense and sustained than otherwise. Second, the instrumental form of social support provides the additional resources and assistance needed to manage specific demands. Third, when emotional needs are not met, people become preoccupied with the particular need deprivation they are experiencing. If we get the emotional support we need at work, such need deprivation may not be a driving force for our behavior.

Table 10.1.   Five Functions of Social Support for Executives

Type of social support	Function
Protection from stress predators	Direct assistance in terms of resources, time, labor, or environmental modification
Informational	Provision of information necessary for managing demands
Evaluative	Feedback on both personal and professional role performances
Modeling	Evidence of behavioral standards provided through modeled behavior
Emotional	Empathy, esteem, caring, love

Note. From *Stress and Challenge at the Top: The Paradox of the Successful Executive* (p. 171), by J. C. Quick, D. L. Nelson, & J. D. Quick, 1990, Chichester, England: Wiley. Reprinted with permission.

Although social support systems may not alter the nature of a role or of an interpersonal stressor, they can be instrumental in various coping strategies that the individual attempts. For example, a role conflict may develop if two superiors expect different types of work from an employee. Even if the conflict cannot be structurally resolved, it is possible for the individual either to learn how to meet both sets of conflicting expectations with social support from a peer group *or* to feel less upset and troubled by the inability to meet both sets of demands. The sense of mastery and interpersonal competence one experiences in a situation may contribute to lowered levels of experienced stress. This is attributable to the lower levels of experienced threat and demand posed by the situation.

Social Support at Work

Effectiveness in work settings is facilitated by social support from others. On the basis of idiographic studies, we have concluded that executives have unique talents for forming relationships with others that are strong, reciprocal, and supportive (J. C. Quick, Nelson, & Quick, 1990). In other words, they are self-reliant, as we discussed in chapter 3. They have a well-developed network of individuals on whom they can rely for many different kinds of support. The forms of support are summarized in Table 10.1.

Supportive relationships at work can serve as a form of protection or as a shield from stressors. Employees often perform this defender function for their supervisors by providing an impermeable boundary around the supervisor. Protective support may be simply having someone to turn to for resources such as lunch money. Informational support is critical in work settings. Given the emphasis on organizational restructuring, information is needed to help eliminate the ambiguity and hence the anxiety that exists in the workplace. This may come from either the formal or the informal organization.

Evaluative support is of critical importance. Employees need consistent and timely feedback on performance. It should be noted that those at the upper levels of the organization need this evaluative support as well. Upward feedback should be solicited, and employees should be able to provide the feedback without fear of rejection or reprisals. Modeling support is the way individuals learn appropriate behavior. People in organizations look to those at the top to model behavioral standards that are to be emulated. Finally, emotional support at work is essential for effective functioning. An empathic listener may not be able to resolve an issue, but the concern and time spent processing the issue constitute an outlet that helps the individual manage the response to stress.

Studies have consistently demonstrated the efficacy of social support at work. The presence of support from the supervisor alters the impact of otherwise strain-producing events so that they have a weaker association with strain (Greller, Parsons, & Mitchell, 1992). The supervisor is a powerful source of support because he or she is able to provide three key factors that contribute to buffering: information, support, and esteem (Cohen & Wills, 1985). Positive feedback from one's supervisor provides evaluation and esteem. Consideration from the supervisor involves emotional support.

Support from colleagues is important as well (Quick & Quick, 1984b). Individuals who receive strong support from fellow workers also cope better with conflicts with the supervisor. In addition, a sense of support from one's fellow workers is important for job satisfaction (Gardell, 1987). Employees and customers provide several sources of support as well. The positive effects of social support on health and well-being require that organizations take steps to implement support systems in the workplace.

Building Support Systems

Building effective social support systems at work starts at the top of the organization. Management must be prepared to provide the individuals in an organization with social support, not all of which can be of a formal nature. The formal organization can be designed to provide social support of various kinds. For example, rewards and recognition ceremonies provide emotional support by way of esteem and status gratification. Evaluative support may be provided through the performance evaluation and reward allocation processes. Informational support may be provided through policy directives and written procedures. Protective support may be provided by way of capital, material, and human resources given to the manager.

The support systems of the formal organization may not be completely adequate by themselves. There is a need for informal support systems as well. These support systems should be complementary and supplemental to the support systems contained in the formal organization. The support systems of the informal organization at times may be more effective in shaping behavior and avoiding distress.

Mentoring is one avenue through which organizations can encourage and reward interdependence and social support. Some companies, like Bell Labs, have formal mentoring programs, but in many organizations mentoring relationships develop informally. Mentors can provide many valuable sources of support, including information on the political climate of the organization and modeling of appropriate behavior. Mentoring should be rewarded by the organization, and experienced employees should be encouraged to serve as mentors.

Newcomer socialization efforts provide another way for organizations to encourage social support. Newcomers should be introduced to reliable support figures early in their socialization, and they should be encouraged to develop mutually supportive relationships with other newcomers (Nelson & Quick, 1997). Providing opportunities for newcomers to socialize informally with other organization members encourages valuable networking.

Organizations can and should strive to encourage self-reliance among individuals. Employees can be trained to assess work situations, rely on their own resources when appropriate, and ask for support from others when it is needed. Some organizations emphasize independence to the extent that individuals are reluctant to seek support. To counter this tendency, leaders can send a message that seeking assistance and developing supportive relationships at work are valued activities. Employees should also be educated about the health risks of social isolation and the health benefits of social support.

There are several focal groups for workplace interventions that emphasize social support. Newcomers constitute one group. Another targeted group includes organizational members who are involved in change. Mergers and acquisitions, downsizing, and restructuring can drastically alter relationships within the organization and disrupt social support networks. Layoff survivors, for example, may retreat into counterdependent or overdependent behavior patterns because of the loss of important relationships. These individuals need organizational help in rebuilding support networks.

Some jobs by their nature put employees at risk for the development of counterdependent behaviors. Physically or geographically isolated employees need help in developing secure, interdependent relationships. Employees who travel extensively, telecommuters, and expatriate workers are especially vulnerable to social isolation.

Team Building

Team building is a prevention method aimed at improving performance effectiveness through cooperative, supportive relationships within a work group. It is also concerned with the effectiveness of the work group in accomplishing the tasks set out for it. The outcome of effective team building should be a cohesive, well-integrated work group within which individuals give and receive needed support while being highly productive as a group.

The more cohesive the group, the more support it provides to team members. Members of cohesive groups communicated more frequently and more accurately and reported higher satisfaction, lower stress, and higher performance than those who did not work in cohesive groups (Whetton & Cameron, 1995). Each of the organizations (e.g., Motorola, Xerox, Westinghouse) that has won the coveted Malcolm Baldrige national quality award has attributed the improvements in morale, productivity, and quality to the use of teams.

Teams, by their very nature, provide two important social benefits for members (Shaver & Buhrmester, 1985). Psychological intimacy, or closeness to other team members, results in feelings of unconditional positive regard and the opportunity for emotional expression and support. The other social benefit, integrated involvement, is closeness achieved through tasks and activities. It results in enjoyable and involving work, social identity, and being valued for one's skills and abilities. Both psychological intimacy and integrated involvement contribute to health and well-being. Team-building interventions that focus on increasing these benefits of teamwork may contribute to health as well.

The Team-Building Process

Team building involves three essential steps. First, the group needs to diagnose internal problems, stresses, and barriers to the group's effectiveness. Second, the group needs to establish an agenda for working through the issues identified within the diagnostic work. The group should be careful to work on underlying or basic problems, rather than the symptoms of those problems. Third, the group should reassess its performance and interpersonal relations at some time, such as 3 months, after the group's work is completed.

Four areas in team building are critical to the success of the intervention:

1. Development of communication that encourages respect for others' input and a desire to work for the good of the team.
2. Emphasis of team goals. Members should learn one another's responsibilities to help the team deal with crises.
3. Encouragement of member interaction and mutual interdependence.
4. Exemplification of effective and ineffective teamwork, with emphasis on flexibility (Swezey & Salas, 1991).

There are several approaches to team-building interventions. One approach combines the retreat format with ongoing meetings and has the advantage of being integrated into the normal operations of the team (Numerof, 1987). The retreat phase is held off-site and serves as an unfreezing mechanism. It includes an introduction to team-building concepts, a diagnosis of impediments to effective team performance, and the development of an agenda for addressing team problems. Ongoing meetings are used to implement the agenda and monitor progress.

One popular retreat format is the use of outdoor challenges. Participants go through a series of outdoor feats, such as climbing a 14-foot wall. The physical challenge requires participants to work as a team and focus on trust, communication, decision making, and leadership. Team members then apply what they have learned to the work setting.

Cautionary Notes

The effective use of team building requires an organizational culture and emphasizes trust. Three other necessary conditions are (a) participation in decision making relative to the work being performed, (b) excellent communications, and (c) commitment to collaboration. To reap the benefits of team building, employees must be actively involved in all aspects of the process. Team building may require a redistribution of power, taking it out of the hands of the manager and placing it in the hands of team members. The threat to some managers is obvious.

In addition, employees who are not accustomed to making decisions may balk at the opportunity to do so. Existing reward structures in the organization are usually directed at individual performance. Rethinking the organizational reward system and incorporating rewards that are based on team performance may be a precondition for team-building efforts.

Because team building involves change, it is essential that resistance be anticipated and that employees be involved in the process. Team building can be seen as a reframing of what is happening in the organization. When managed properly, team building can diminish the frequency and intensity of work-related stressors and pave the way for increased productivity.

Outcomes of Team Building

Team-building efforts are optimum opportunities for improving the quality of working life within organizations. Programs permit the team to confront such issues as leadership style, control, work processes, structure, and individual roles. Successful management of these issues results in responsive, goal-directed teams that are able to manage conflict well and encourage intermember support. These qualities are buffers against organizational stress. They suggest the absence of stressors such as dysfunctional conflict, role ambiguity, and lack of cohesion (Numerof, 1987).

The use of self-managed teams is a particularly effective means of improving worker health, motivation, and productivity. Self-managed teams perform tasks once reserved for managers, such as hiring, appraising performance, determining schedules, and the like. The resulting increase in control over work has been linked to decreased illness rates and lower absenteeism (Terra, 1995).

Diversity Programs

Recent years have seen an increased focus on the diversity of the work-force. Workforce 2000, a widely read report from the Hudson Institute, strongly made the point that the workforce is more diverse than ever (Johnston & Packer, 1987). Managers in organizations reacted by insti-tuting diversity programs, which are organizational interventions de-signed to ensure that the talents and perspectives that already exist within the organization are valued and used (Jackson, 1992).

Diversity encompasses all forms of differences among individuals. Some sources of diversity are culture, gender, age, ability, religious affili-ation, personality, economic class, social status, military attachment, and sexual orientation. Organizations became concerned about managing di-versity for several reasons. First, there was a fear that managers lacked the knowledge of how to motivate diverse groups. Second, managers were unsure of how to communicate effectively with those who have different values and language skills. Working with others who are different from oneself can be a source of stress. Although diversity programs do not focus directly on work stress, it is reasonable to expect a reduction in interper-sonal stressors from these interventions.

Many diversity programs are intended to improve interpersonal re-lations between different groups. Workshop activities such as frank and open discussions are used to pinpoint issues, present different points of view, and devise solutions to diversity-related problems. Such activities may involve uncovering hidden assumptions held by employees. Biases and prejudices about differences are brought out and dealt with so that differences are seen as assets and all people are valued.

Younger workers, for example, often hold false impressions of older workers, seeing them as more resistant to change, less able to learn, less physically capable, and less creative than younger employees. They fail to recognize that older employees can make valuable contributions because of their experience and that they are often more motivated and committed to the organization than their younger coworkers. Diversity initiatives em-phasize debunking stereotypes and helping employees overcome interper-sonal obstacles to working together productively.

Diversity programs take a number of forms. Levi Strauss, for example, holds a diversity council that meets regularly to work on communication issues that arise between diverse groups of employees. Xerox uses caucus groups that are communication links between upper management and other employees. African-American caucuses, women's caucuses, and many other caucus groups provide networking and support for their mem-bers. Digital Equipment Corporation's "Valuing Differences" program op-erates on the assumption that people work best when they are valued and that when they are valued they build relationships and teamwork.

Diversity programs are relatively recent interventions, and there is little research evidence that evaluates their efficacy as stress management techniques. Because they seek to improve interpersonal relationships, they hold potential for reducing sources of interpersonal stress in the workplace.

Summary

This chapter, the second one to discuss organizational-level preventive management, has presented five methods of prevention aimed at the role and interpersonal demands of organizational life. *Role analysis* and *goal setting* are methods for clarifying the individual's organizational role. Whereas it may not be possible to prevent such stressors as dual-reporting relationships, it is possible to minimize the ensuing ambiguity and conflict through the use of these prevention techniques. Not only is the emotional distress caused by these circumstances minimized, but the performance level of individuals is enhanced, especially when goal-setting programs are used.

These methods may not eliminate all role conflict and ambiguity, and they will not eliminate the interpersonal demands of work life. *Social support, team building*, and *diversity programs* can be helpful primary and secondary prevention methods for managing the distressful demands that are not eliminated by the other organizational-level methods of preventive management. These methods may not necessarily change the demands of the work settings, but they can be instrumental in assisting people to use and develop their capacities to manage their demands.

The organizational methods for preventive stress management discussed in these two chapters are ones that management can employ for groups of individuals to buffer the impact of the various job, physical, role, and interpersonal stressors. However, these methods may not eliminate all distress. It is important to combine these methods with the individual-level preventive management techniques described in the next two chapters.

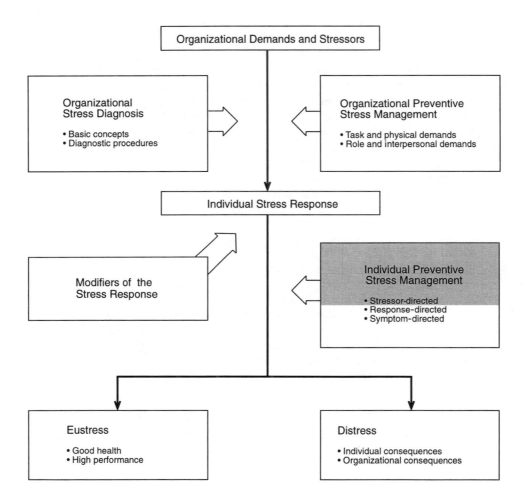

11

Primary Prevention for Individuals: Managing and Coping With Stressors

The concept of person–environment fit in the field of organizational stress suggests that the least stressful circumstances are ones in which a good fit exists between the person and the organizational environment (Edwards, 1996; Edwards & Cooper, 1990). Chapters 9 and 10 addressed strategies for changing and modifying organizations and work environments to enhance their health-creating potential. Chapters 11, 12, and 13 address strategies for changing and modifying individual perceptions, attitudes, and behaviors to enhance individual health and well-being. This set of three chapters is about individual preventive stress management and concerns the following question: What can individuals do to manage their stress responsibly? Each chapter has a specific focus within the stress process framework used throughout the book. This chapter addresses primary prevention for individuals and focuses on the demands and stressors that trigger the stress response by considering stressor-directed strategies. Chapter 12 addresses secondary prevention for individuals and focuses on the individual's stress response by considering response-directed strategies. Chapter 13 addresses tertiary prevention for individuals and focuses on distress and strain by considering symptom-directed strategies for healing.

Exhibit 11.1 presents an overview of the individual preventive stress management strategies that are discussed in each of the three chapters. Chapter 13 includes a section that discusses creating a personal preventive stress management plan, giving consideration to primary, secondary, and tertiary prevention strategies. Individuals differ in the strategies that they prefer, that are most useful for them, and that are most effective in achieving the results they seek. Therefore, a person may design a plan based on chapters 11, 12, and 13 that includes a set of psychological and behavioral strategies for his or her personal preventive stress management.

As noted in Exhibit 11.1, the primary prevention strategies considered in the chapter fall into three groups: (a) managing personal perceptions of stress, (b) managing the personal work environment, and (c) managing one's lifestyle. Within these three groups, a total of nine more specific primary prevention strategies are discussed. These are also noted in the exhibit. The strategies discussed in the chapter are ones for which there is a conceptual or evaluative research basis, or both, for their use and

Exhibit 11.1. Preventive Stress Management for Individuals

Primary prevention: Stressor-directed	
Managing personal perceptions of stress • Learned optimism • Constructive self-talk • Transformational coping • Changing Type A behavior patterns Managing the personal work environment • Planning and time management • Overload avoidance • Social support	Managing one's lifestyle • Maintaining a balance • Leisure time • Sabbaticals

Secondary prevention: Response-directed	
Relaxation training • The relaxation response • Progressive relaxation • Meditation • Medical hypnosis and autogenic training • Biofeedback training • Momentary relaxation Spirituality and faith	Emotional outlets • Talking with others • Writing it out • Acting it out Physical fitness • Aerobic fitness • Muscular flexibility • Muscle strength training Nutrition

Tertiary prevention: Symptom-directed	
Psychological counseling and therapy • Symptom-specific programs • Individual psychotherapy • Behavior therapy • Group therapy • Career counseling	Traumatic event debriefing Medical care • Medications • Surgery • Physical therapy

effectiveness. There may be other strategies not included in this set that may be useful and effective in individual cases.

Managing Personal Perceptions of Stress

A key to the definition of *stressor* (see chapter 1) is the notion that a person or event must be *perceived* as demanding or stressful by an individual if the condition is to be a source of stress. For example, selecting a $500,000 piece of hospital equipment may be quite stressful to a new health care administrator whose largest past purchase was the $25,000 family car. Alternatively, for a health care administrator of a large chain of hospitals who has occasionally bought equipment costing over $10,000,000 and often contracts for several hundred thousand dollars worth of new equipment, a decision about $500,000 may be made with relative equanimity. Hence, personal perceptions of persons and events are central to the propensity for experiencing the stress response.

Efforts to alter personal perceptions of stress are directed at changing one's cognitive–psychological evaluation of potential stressors or reducing one's affective–emotional arousal, or stress response. Some individuals are "adrenaline junkies," such as those with extreme Type A behavior pattern, who are constantly creating their own stressors and thus evoking their own stress response. Other individuals engage in destructive internal dialogues of negative self-talk, which may have distressing effects on those around them as well as themselves. The essence of managing personal perceptions of stress is embodied in the 2,000-year-old words of the Greek philosopher Epictetus: "Men are disturbed not by things but by the views they take of them." Managing personal perceptions of stress requires changing how one thinks and how one behaves. This may be done through a hopeful cognitive style of learned optimism, constructive self-talk, a transformational style of coping with demands and stressors, or changing Type A behavior pattern.

Learned Optimism

Individuals differ in how they explain the events of life—the good, the bad and the stressful—to themselves. Individuals who have an optimistic cognitive style are more hopeful and less distressed than those who have a pessimistic cognitive style (Seligman, 1990). Although optimism alters the view one has of life's stressful events, the denial of legitimate risks or real threats would be hazardous to one's well-being. Hence, optimism must be tempered by the reality of life's challenges and problems.

Optimism and pessimism. Seligman (1990) described optimism as a style of nonnegative thinking that enhances well-being and enables people to live with hope and without depression. The alternative to optimism is pessimism, which is a style of negative thinking. These are two alternative styles for explaining the good and bad events that occur in life. As such, they are cognitive lenses through which a person views life's events. Whereas an optimistic style helps people avoid distress through a view of stressful events as temporary occurrences with limited effects for which they are not personally responsible, a pessimistic style leads people toward distress and depression through a view of stressful events as permanent problems with pervasive effects for which they have some personal responsibility. Individuals whose cognitive style is optimistic face stressful and adverse events with hope; they perceive that the good events in life outnumber the bad events. In addition, an optimistic style enables persons to view success in both the personal and career realms of life as the result of their own efforts and abilities.

Although Seligman (1990) is an advocate of learned optimism, he has recognized that there is a place for cautious, even pessimistic, thinking when it comes to stressful events with a high risk of adverse consequences. For example, undue optimism on the part of a pilot attempting to land an airliner in the midst of an ice storm may lead to unreasonable risks given the circumstances. A dose of pessimism in such stressful circumstances may be healthier for both pilot and passengers, leading to a request that the control tower divert the flight to an alternative destination within fuel range of the plane.

Not withstanding this caveat concerning high-risk or dangerously stressful situations, there is a variety of evidence related to the benefits of optimism. In one study, patients were interviewed following a heart attack, and their health was assessed for 8 years. Videotaped interviews were analyzed to determine optimistic versus pessimistic explanatory style. Fifteen out of 16 of the pessimists died within the 8 years (Seligman, 1975). Another study indicated that insurance agents who were optimistic performed better at work and were less likely to quit than agents who were pessimistic (Seligman & Schulman, 1986). In addition, in a longitudinal study of senior citizens, pessimism was related to lowered immune system activity, unmediated by health or depression (Seligman, 1990).

Cognitive distortion. Cognitive distortion is a self-defeating, anxiety-causing, frequently irrational pattern of negative thinking (Beech, Burns, & Sheffield, 1982). Cognitive distortion may stress a person through a self-perpetuating series of negative beliefs, much like the pessimistic style of thinking. Unfortunately, cognitive distortions may manifest themselves as conscious, persistent beliefs. Ellis (1955) proposed a systematic approach to modifying cognitive distortion with rational emotive therapy (RET), a form of cognitive restructuring through a process of logical questioning aimed at disputing and modifying the irrational beliefs. According to RET, cognitive distortions can be disputed by detecting the irrationalities, debating them, discriminating between rational and irrational thinking, redefining circumstances to prevent cognitive distortion, and maintaining closer contact with reality. Another approach to cognitive restructuring involves thought stopping, with substitution of a key thought that cycles into a more positive and healthy way of thinking. Table 11.1 illustrates several typical cognitive distortions and key phrases that can be used to combat the distortion through cognitive restructuring. One common cognitive distortion is mind reading. Individuals often think they can read another person's mind by his or her facial expressions, imagining the worst. When giving an important speech, an individual may be confronted with puzzled expressions in the audience. The individual may react by thinking, "Oh no, they think I'm an idiot." The key phrase to use with this distortion is "check it out." Rather than guess at the source of the problem, the individual is better off simply posing a question—"Am I confusing you? Tell me what you think"—rather than imagining the worst.

Learning to be optimistic and hopeful. Learning to be optimistic is another form of cognitive restructuring. It requires changing one's style of thinking about the good, the bad, and the stressful events in life (Seligman, 1990). Learning to change to a nonnegative cognitive style begins with identifying one's negative thinking about the stressful and adverse events in life. For each stressful or adverse event, one should look at one's

Table 11.1. Cognitive Restructuring: Ten Styles of Distorted Thinking

Distortion	Mental key
1. Filtering: You take the negative details and magnify them while filtering out all positive aspects of a situation.	Don't magnify.
2. Polarized thinking: Things are black or white, good or bad. You have to be perfect or you're a failure. There is no middle ground.	Think in percentages.
3. Mind reading: Without their saying so, you think you know what people are feeling and why they act the way they do. In particular, you are able to divine how people are feeling toward you.	Check it out.
4. Catastrophizing: You expect disaster. You notice or hear about a problem and start "what if's": "What if tragedy strikes? What if it happens to me?"	Calculate realistic odds.
5. Control fallacies: If you feel externally controlled, you see yourself as helpless and a victim of fate. The fallacy of internal control has you responsible for the pain and happiness of everyone around you.	Discriminate between *I* make it happen and *they* make it happen.
6. Fallacy of fairness: You feel resentful because you think you know what's fair, but other people don't agree with you.	Think of preference, not fairness.
7. Shoulds: You have a list of ironclad rules about how you and other people should act. People who break the rules anger you, and you feel guilty if you violate the rules.	Develop flexible rules.
8. Fallacy of change: You expect that other people will change to suit you if you pressure or cajole them enough. You need to change people because your hopes for happiness seem to depend entirely on them.	Assert, my happiness depends on *me*.
9. Being right: You are continually on trial to prove that your opinions and actions are correct. Being wrong is unthinkable, and you will go to any length to demonstrate your rightness. You don't listen well.	Employ active listening.
10. Heaven's reward fallacy: You expect all your sacrifice and self-denial to pay off, as if there were someone keeping score. You feel bitter when the reward doesn't come.	Recognize that the reward is *now*.

Note. From *Stress Management for Wellness* (pp. 225–227), by W. Schafer, 1987, New York: Holt, Rinehart & Winston. Adapted with permission.

beliefs about the event and the negative consequences of those beliefs. Change occurs when one learns to argue with oneself about the underlying beliefs, disputing the negative beliefs with evidence or seeking alternative explanations. In addition, one may reevaluate the implications of a belief or even its usefulness. If the process of disputing the beliefs that underlie one's negative thinking does not seem to work, distraction from the event is another change strategy that may be employed. Whether done through distraction or disputation, once the negative pattern is interrupted one should seek to energize oneself in a new and positive direction.

Constructive Self-Talk

Constructive self-talk is a conscious effort to replace negative, self-defeating, self-effacing, often irrational narrative with positive, reinforcing, and more rational self-talk (Eliot, 1995). During their daily activities, most people conduct an intermittent mental monologue or narrative about the events they are experiencing and their reactions to the events. This monologue, or self-talk, can be positive in tone—"Gee that really was a witty remark"—or it can be negative or self-effacing—"Boy, are you dumb; why not just keep your mouth shut?" Self-talk may be conscious or unconscious, although it is often conscious and people frequently find themselves saying part of it aloud. Negative self-talk can waste emotional energy by setting up a tension-sustaining mental short circuit.

Table 11.2 lists examples of several common situations, the typical mental monologues that a person might go through, and constructive self-talk alternatives. The potential benefit of constructive self-talk can be appreciated by imagining oneself in any of the situations listed in the table and noting how one would feel after 5 or 10 minutes of the typical monologue.

An important part of constructive self-talk is *rethinking*, that is, recognizing when one has latched onto dead-end or downhill thoughts and consciously beginning to substitute constructive, forward-looking thinking. There are several other, related concepts. *Quick recovery*, for example, refers to the ability to rebound in a short period of time from a strong emotional experience (Albrecht, 1979). One person might ruminate for several days over a missed promotion or bad grade, whereas another person may brood about it for a few hours and then bounce back, determined to work even harder to earn the promotion or better grade.

Another concept is *thought stopping*. This mechanism also involves recognizing dead-end or downhill thoughts, but instead of staying on the same subject and changing the tenor of the thinking, one mentally—or verbally—says "stop" and changes the subject. The technique of *mental diversion* is also useful in reducing the extent to which one experiences anxiety or distress over daily events. For example, the morning before a test or presentation for which a student has studied thoroughly or a manager has prepared completely, the student or manager may allow him- or herself to worry obsessively. This can continue until the test or presenta-

Table 11.2. Constructive Self-Talk Alternatives to Typical Mental Monologues

Situation	Typical mental monologue	Constructive self-talk alternative
Driving to work on a day that will be full of appointments and potentially stressful meetings	"Oh brother, what a day this will be!" "It's gonna be hell." "I'll never get it all done." "It'll be exhausting."	"This looks like a busy day." "The day should be very productive." "I'll get a lot accomplished today." "I'll earn a good night's rest today."
Anticipation of a seminar presentation or public address	"What if I blow it?" "Nobody will laugh at that opening joke." "What if they ask about . . . ?" "I hate talking to groups."	"This ought to be a challenge." "I'll take a deep breath and relax." "They'll enjoy it." "Each presentation goes a bit better."
Recovering from a heart attack	"I almost died. I'll die soon." "I'll never be able to work again." "I'll never be able to play sports again."	"I didn't die. I made it through." "The doctor says I'll be able to get back to work soon." "I can keep active and gradually get back to most of my old sports."
Difficulty with a superior at work	"I hate that person." "He makes me feel stupid." "We'll never get along."	"I don't feel comfortable with him." "I let myself get on edge when he's around." "It will take some effort to get along."
Flat tire on a business trip	"Damn this old car" (pacing around car, looking at flat tire). "I'll miss all my meetings." "It's hopeless."	"Bad time for a flat" (beginning to get tools out and start working). "I'll call and cancel Jenckins at the next phone. I should make the rest of the appointments."

tion begins and may prove to be a significant mental drain. Alternatively, after completing preparations the night before, the individuals can choose to occupy their mind with other mental activities of a positive nature. Mental diversion requires that one have a few positive topics on hand to substitute.

Constructive self-talk is a primary prevention strategy that enables people to alter their view of the stressful events in life, thus reducing the adverse impact of a stressor. Acquiring the cognitive skills of learned optimism and constructive self-talk enables one to take full advantage of the power of positive thinking (Peale, 1952). As with any new behavior, practice and repetition are essential if these cognitive strategies for changing the way one thinks are to become useful, integrated skills. For those whose predisposition is pessimistic and negative, patience is another essential ingredient for realizing the benefits of these cognitive skills.

Transformational Coping

A key component of workplace hardiness is *transformational coping* (Maddi, 1995), a process of gaining perspective and understanding for the purpose of taking decisive action in managing stressful events. Transformational coping involves actively changing a stressful event by viewing it in a broader life perspective, thus reducing the emotional power and impact of the event. It also involves achieving a greater understanding of the process of the event, which enables one to alter the course and outcome of the event through appropriate action. The hardy personality (see chapter 3) uses commitment, challenge, and control to engage in transformational coping (Kobasa, 1988). Hardy individuals are committed to their work, families, and beliefs; interpret change as a challenge; and feel in control of events and their responses to events. In one study of 160 employees in a community mental health facility, persons who felt in control were less likely to respond to organizational frustration with counterproductive behavior than persons who did not feel in control (Storms & Spector, 1987). Hardy people use transformational coping to manage stress and frustration in productive, healthy ways.

Although some persons and events legitimately cause stress owing to their threatening nature, other stressors may be unrealistically interpreted as threatening and therefore cause one to experience unnecessary distress. Individuals who engage in transformational coping are more likely to interpret stressors as challenges rather than threats and to perceive themselves as able to control stressful situations. Taking an examination, for example, is stressful for many people. Students engaged in transformational coping, however, might interpret the test as an opportunity to show their knowledge, thus exerting control through preparation and study.

The alternative to transformational coping is regressive coping, a passive avoidance of events by decreasing interaction with the environment. Regressive coping may lead to short-term stress reduction but at the cost of long-term healthy life adjustment. A student who is stressed about a forthcoming examination might cope in a passive way by avoiding studying, reasoning that no amount of studying will help him pass the test. Although regressive coping is a less functional coping strategy, there are situations in which psychological withdrawal can be used judiciously as a short-term coping strategy.

Psychological withdrawal. In their study of three research and development organizations undergoing considerable stress owing to funding cutbacks, Hall and Mansfield (1971) found that the researchers in these organizations showed a remarkable resistance to the distress. Their attitudes about themselves and their work remained positive, but their identification and investment in the organization decreased significantly. The investigators suggested that this decreased investment, a form of psychological withdrawal, helped the researchers to handle the stress of cutbacks and uncertainty.

Psychological withdrawal is a form of affective isolation and distress avoidance through emotional detachment from a source of stress. Psychological withdrawal is not surrender. Developing emotional detachment does not preclude continued active involvement in the tasks from which one has withdrawn. In fact, a degree of psychological withdrawal may be essential in some jobs. Medical students, for example, learn during their training to develop an attitude of "detached concern" for their patients. The distress generated by working intensely with sick and dying patients uld be intolerable without some withdrawal of natural emotional responses.

Selective ignoring. Selective ignoring is a variation of psychological withdrawal, a process by which a person looks for the positive aspects of a troublesome situation and anchors his or her attention to these, to the exclusion of the noxious aspects of the situation (Pearlin & Schooler, 1978). This process is facilitated by magnification of the importance of the positive aspects and viewing the noxious aspects as trivial.

Psychological withdrawal and selective ignoring may be counterproductive to transformational coping if they are used too frequently, too pervasively, or for extended periods of time. Furthermore, although the feeling of control is central to the process of transformational coping, there are limits to a person's capacity for control. Dietrich Bonhoeffer's petition "God grant me serenity to accept the things I cannot change, courage to change the things I can, and wisdom to know the difference" recognizes this fact. In any organization there are circumstances, persons, and events that one may not be able to alter. Learning to accept what is inevitable helps avert some of the stress and distress that might otherwise be felt. However, if one accepts too much as inevitable, one risks greater distress in the future in the development of a sense of helplessness or impotency in the organization (Seligman, 1975). Active passivity is different from learned helplessness.

Changing Type A Behavior Pattern

In their early work, Friedman and Rosenman (1974) presented a lengthy discussion of philosophical guidelines, "reengineering" procedures, and drills aimed at undoing the Type A behavior pattern. The philosophical guidelines on which the reengineering procedures and drills are based appear with brief elaborations in Exhibit 11.2. Friedman and Rosenman (1974) asserted that everyone can alter their behavior pattern and that this can be done without any deterioration in financial status, social status, or other measures of "success." An honest, in-depth self-appraisal is the first step in the process. This includes exploring some of the philosophical issues related to life goals, means–ends questions, and so on. The next step is contracting with oneself to replace old behavior patterns with new ones, using the reengineering procedures and drills outlined in the book.

Evidence provided by Friedman (1984) has supported the efficacy of

Exhibit 11.2. Philosophical Guidelines for Changing Type A Behavior Patterns

- You must try to retrieve your total personality.
  Return to or develop interests in art, music, drama, nature, or spiritual matters outside your normal vocation. Spend time communicating with people on these and other subjects.
- You must establish life goals.
  Life goals should include an economic or professional set and a set for private life. They should help prevent sheer hyperactivity from replacing purposeful progress.
- Make some gestures toward myth, ritual, and tradition.
  Recognize existing and add new rituals and traditions that provide uniquely pleasant experiences; build and maintain social relationships and maintain your humanity.
- Stop using your right hand to do the work your left hand should be doing.
  Many daily demands are of a trivial or ephemeral nature. They are the "left-handed" activities, which should require less vigilance and should be delegated or handled with minimal effort.
- Let your means justify your ends.
  Stop trying to excuse daily "errors of living" by looking toward some great end. Each day and each activity should be valued for its own sake.
- A successful life is always unfinished.
  Life is an "unfinishedness." Life is structured on and consists primarily of uncompleted processes, tasks, and events. Only a corpse is completely finished!

Note. From *Type A Behavior and Your Heart* (pp. 214–233), by M. Friedman and R. H. Rosenman, 1974, New York: Knopf. Adapted with permission.

their approach. Of some 1,000 patients who had a heart attack and attended monthly behavioral change sessions over a 3-year period, 80% showed reductions in Type A behavior. In addition, the participants experienced significantly fewer repeat heart attacks than those in control groups (Friedman, 1984). A study of career officers in the military corroborated these findings. Officers who attended behavioral change classes over 9 months significantly reduced their Type A behavior and reported no adverse effects on work performance (Gill, 1985). There is some debate concerning the appropriateness of this approach to the Type A behavior pattern (Roskies, 1978). Friedman and Rosenman (1974) held that insight into behavior patterns and a major philosophical reorientation are essential for Type A individuals to change their behavior.

The opposing view is that the Type A behavior pattern is similar to a chronic illness: It cannot be cured, but it can be treated to decrease the harmful effects of the condition. Some people have compared Type A behavior to an addiction in that immediate gratification (success at work) is preferred to long-term harm (early heart attacks) and withdrawal symptoms in the form of anxiety with decreased activity are observed (Roskies, 1978; Suinn, Brock, & Edie, 1975). With the chronic disease or addiction model, treatment is aimed at providing a means to release the tension and hostility inherent in Type A behavior without altering the individual's basic psychodynamics. The goal of change strategies is not to convert Type

Table 11.3. Roskies's Program Structure

Modules	Skills taught
1. Introduction to the program	General overview
2. Relax: Learning to control physical stress responses	Self-monitoring of physical and emotional tension signs, progressive muscle relaxation
3. Control yourself: Learning to control behavioral stress responses	Self-monitoring of behavioral signs of tension such as incompatible behaviors, delay, and poor communication skills
4. Think productively: Learning to control cognitive stress responses	Self-monitoring of self-talk; cognitive restructuring
5. Be prepared: Learning to anticipate and plan for predictable stress situations	Identification of recurrent stress triggers; stress inoculation training
6. Cool it: Learning emergency braking for unpredictable stress situations	Identification of signs of heightened tension; application of physical, behavioral, and cognitive controls; anger control
7. Building stress resistance: Learning to plan for rest and recuperation	Identification of pleasurable activities; problem solving
8. Protect your investment: Stress management as a lifelong investment	Relapse prevention

Note. From *Stress Management for the Healthy Type A* (p. 51) by E. Roskies, 1987, New York: Guilford.

A into Type B individuals but to reduce the psychophysiological impact of Type A behavior.

Finally, some authors have questioned whether any form of individual intervention can succeed without changing the cultural, familial, and work environments that appear to generate or at least foster Type A behavior. Suinn et al. (1975) argued that because Type A behavior is learned and internalized, Type A risks can be altered through vasomotor behavior rehearsal and anxiety management. These interventions have been associated with reductions in anxiety and in specific Type A behaviors.

In addition to providing substantial clinical evidence, Roskies (1987) reported research that compared various interventions for healthy Type A individuals. Roskies's program, which includes the eight modules shown in Table 11.3, was compared to aerobic exercise and weight training in modifying the mechanisms for coronary heart disease in a sample of healthy Type A male managers. One hundred seven men, randomly assigned to the three treatment groups, completed the interventions plus pre- and posttesting in behavioral and physiological reactivity. Behavioral evidence indicated that participants in Roskies's program showed reductions of 13–23% in Type A behavior (global Type A, voice loudness and explosiveness, potential for hostility, and competitiveness) compared to no change in the aerobics group and small, inconsistent changes in the weight-training group. Participants corroborated the evidence with self-reports of behavioral change. No significant changes in physiological reactivity (blood pressure, heart rate) were observed in any of the three treatment groups.

Group counseling has been shown to be an effective method for dealing with patients who have had a heart attack. Evidence of the effectiveness of the group process approach includes reductions in Type A behavior, occurrence and severity of angina pectoris, and serum cholesterol levels (Bruhn, 1996). There is also evidence that beta-blockers, a category of drugs used to treat high blood pressure by inhibiting sympathetic nervous system activity, may reduce the amount of Type A behavior that is observed. Similarly, initiation of a program of regular exercise has been associated with decreases in Type A behavior along with a reduction of physiological risk factors.

As indicated in chapter 3, researchers are beginning to identify the noxious component of Type A behavior pattern as anger and hostility. Williams (1993) argued that physically destructive anger associated with strokes and coronary artery disease is anger turned inward. Interventions that focus specifically on reducing anger and hostility may be of particular efficacy in modifying the behavior pattern. One study of 44 unmedicated, mildly hypertensive Type A men, aged 32–64 years, randomly assigned the men to one of three conditions: stress management training, Type A management, and delayed Type A management (Bennett, Wallace, Carroll, & Smith, 1991). The results indicated that Type A management was the most successful in changing key Type A behaviors, such as anger and hostility.

Although these studies have provided some data to assess the comparative efficacy of different treatments, they are insufficient to justify recommending a single treatment over others. It is encouraging, however, to note that Type A behavior patterns—at least the physiological and psychological consequences of these patterns—are amenable to change. The variety of approaches that have favorable effects on Type A behavior suggests that any comprehensive stress management program may have an impact on individuals whose experience of organizational stress is influenced by Type A behavior.

Individuals can work to modify their own Type A patterns. The first step is recognizing the pattern. Another step is to spend time with Type B individuals, who can help Type A people take hassles less seriously and see the humor in life. Other steps for Type A individuals include pacing themselves, managing time better, and focusing on one thing at a time.

Managing the Personal Work Environment

At any level in an organization, there are aspects of the daily work routine that are in the individual's control and parts that are totally out of his or her control. It is sometimes surprising for managers and supervisors to discover that they can control their working life to a greater extent than they had originally thought.

Several techniques are available to managers, supervisors, and employees for reducing work stressors through improved management of their personal work environment. Some techniques are more applicable at certain levels in the organization than at others. Similarly, some techniques are more applicable in certain types of organization than in others. Like the techniques for managing personal response patterns, the techniques for managing the work environment are reported largely on the basis of the experience of management consultants and others who have observed their use.

Planning and Time Management

Planning and time management are central skills for managing the stress of one's personal work environment (Whetton & Cameron, 1995). Planning should not be confused or equated with time management, which we shall discuss next. Planning involves a more conceptual and comprehensive review of one's goals and activities. It also tends to be more future-oriented. Time management, on the other hand, involves prioritizing, scheduling, and delegating specific activities. Fayol (1929) was one of the first management scholars to recognize the importance of planning as a key to managerial success. Planning and time management go together for someone who aspires to be an effective "macro time manager," which may be contrasted with the distressed "crisis time manager" (Brooks & Mullins, 1989). "Macro time managers" live with a sense of purpose and know the activities that contribute the most to their long-term life development. Therefore, a "macro time manager" begins by setting life goals and works to achieve these goals through a systematic process of (a) prioritizing the goals, (b) planning goal attainment through scheduling and delegation, and (c) praising oneself for small achievements along the way (Brooks & Mullins, 1989; Weick, 1984).

In the work setting, personal planning involves looking into the future, identifying goals and possible job stressors, and developing a strategy to achieve goals, while avoiding the negative impact of anticipated stressors. The process of personal planning parallels that of organizational planning. In our study of healthy executives, we found planning to be one of the key preventive stress management strategies used (J. C. Quick, Nelson, & Quick, 1990). Planning allows executives to minimize or eliminate surprises and focus their energies, thereby helping them manage stress.

Personal planning is applicable throughout one's career. Job applicants should plan ahead to avoid distressful mismatches between job demands and personal skills and interests and between their values and those of the organization (Nelson, 1990). Applicants should learn as much as they can about the job for which they are applying. At the same time, they should make a candid assessment of their own abilities, career goals, and tolerance for stress.

Midlife changes are a frequent source of preventable distress. Planning may ensure that a midlife *transition*, rather than a midlife *crisis*, occurs. Hall (1976) suggested that individuals expose themselves to new options, exploring various alternatives and developing an attitude of flexibility. Thinking realistically about potential midcareer stressors should help the individual prepare for them. Planning to withdraw from one's career is also important. Retirement is stressful for some people yet not for others. A key component of a successful retirement is planning for the transition and identifying the activities one may be involved in once the transition is made. The best advice may be simply to plan one's retirement (J. F. Quick, 1990).

Howard, Rechnitzer, and Cunningham (1975), in a review of coping mechanisms for job tension, suggested that task planning may help an employee "work smarter, not harder." The planning process thus serves as the mechanism by which some of the other techniques such as time management and overload management are brought into play.

One of the central issues in the planning process is time management. Deadlines, productivity objectives, and project timetables bring the manager and employee face to face with time and, in doing so, create significant distress. The concept of time management represents a set of skills and attitudes that can be highly effective in reducing time stress and improving productivity. Increased job satisfaction and peace of mind are important consequences of wise time management. Davis, Eshelman, and McKay (1995) identified the following seven symptoms of poor time management:

1. Rushing
2. Chronic vacillation between unpleasant alternatives
3. Fatigue or listlessness with many hours of nonproductive activity
4. Constantly missed deadlines
5. Insufficient time for rest or personal relationships
6. The sense of being overwhelmed by demands and details
7. Having to do what one does not want to do much of the time

Lakein (1973) was a pioneer in the field of time management who outlined a systematic approach to the effective use of time. Three concepts that are fundamental to his method are (a) the goals statement, (b) the "To Do" list with priorities, and (c) a schedule. One recent study of 353 employees in a variety of jobs found that some time management behaviors may have beneficial effects on job tension, stress, and satisfaction but not on job performance as evaluated by supervisors (Macan, 1994).

One major reason for poor use of time is the lack of a clear sense of purpose. For the individual it is necessary to consider carefully what one wants out of life, to formulate a lifetime goals statement, to review it regularly, and to revise it periodically. (Lakein suggested revising the list each birthday.) A major stumbling block to effective use of time in organizations is lack of awareness or agreement about the duties, authority, and responsibilities associated with each individual job.

The central concept in time management is that of the written *To Do list*. The list should include all significant time demands and things that need to be accomplished. Some people try to keep their To Do list in their head, but this is less reliable and it makes setting priorities more difficult. The list should be expanded each time new items arise, and tasks should be deleted as soon as they are completed. A stack or pocketful of slips of paper with various undone tasks scribbled on them does not constitute a To Do list.

Whenever a list is made, each item should be given a priority. Lakein (1973) suggested an ABC priority system, with A corresponding to high priority items and B and C corresponding to medium and low priority items, respectively. The A items can be further classified as A-1, A-2, A-3, and so on. All A items should be completed before going on to B and C items. This is difficult at times, because the B and C items are more numerous and often easier to finish. This reflects a phenomenon referred to as the 80/20 rule: "If all items are arranged in order of value, 80 percent of the value would come from only 20 percent of the items, while the remaining 20 percent of value would come from 80 percent of the items" (Lakein, 1973, p. 71). This means that in a list of 10 items, 2 of them will account for 80% of the productivity or value. These 2 items should be identified, labeled A for high priority, and completed as soon as possible.

The purpose of setting priorities is simply to ensure that the important items are identified and receive enough time. Most B and C items can wait, and often they can be ignored entirely. Completing the A items requires a schedule or time plan. In preparing the plan, one should take advantage of *internal prime time* and *external prime time* by scheduling *quiet time* and *availability time*. Internal prime time is the time when one concentrates the best and works the most productively; for some people this is before sunrise, whereas for others it is late afternoon. External prime time represents the best opportunity to deal with other people, including coworkers, business associates, and social contacts. To accomplish the most within limited time, it is useful to set aside portions of one's internal prime time as quiet time. To do this it is necessary to use whatever measures are available to minimize interruptions. Limiting phone calls, educating fellow workers about time preferences, and closing an office door can help reduce interruptions.

A "macro time manager" is not a machine, and planning and time management should not become a source of distress. To the contrary, putting important items first ensures that the high-value items are completed; this contributes to a greater sense of accomplishment. In addition, an important aspect of time management is putting time aside to relax. Effective use of time also permits one to "slow down" the process of making final decisions and reduces some of the pressure inherent in making major decisions at the last minute. The best time managers are not necessarily the ones who get the most things done.

Overload Avoidance

Time management may reduce some of the stress from a demanding job, but there is a limit to what it can achieve if the demands on an individual are excessive. If preventive efforts at the organizational level have been effective, overload should be minimized. Nevertheless, there are several avenues open to the individual who is faced with excessive work obligations. Recent research found that total workload varies by gender, age, occupational level, and number of children (Lundberg, Mardberg, & Frankenhaeuser, 1994). Specifically, women were found to have heavier total workloads than men; work stress peaked in the age range of 35–39; upper managers had more control than others over their total workload; and total workload increased with an increase in number of children.

Because work overload triggers neuroendocrine and cardiovascular reactions, which may have adverse health effects (Frankenhaeuser, 1991), managing one's total workload to avoid overload is desirable. This may be accomplished in a variety of ways, such as identifying and eliminating busywork and learning to delegate tasks. Eliot (1995) proposed the following checklist for reducing or eliminating frustrating tasks:

1.   Is it necessary to do this at all?
2.   Is it necessary to do this task so frequently?
3.   What would happen if this task simply were not done?
4.   Is there an alternative?
5.   Could someone else do it?

The checklist could also be applied to household chores. Balancing work and home demands can be a challenge, and using the checklist both at work and at home can help in avoiding overload.

Equally important is learning how to avoid excessive obligations in the first place. Albrecht (1979) pointed out that employees are often unwilling to negotiate a reasonable deadline or to redefine the scope of a task assigned to them by the boss. Management frequently has only a vague idea of the resources required to complete a specific project and a limited knowledge of the employee's workload. If the individual to whom the job is assigned does not negotiate a reasonable timetable at the outset or renegotiate the timetable when it appears unrealistic, she falls victim to her own obligations.

Overload avoidance involves declining, whenever possible, requests that are unreasonable or overwhelming and renegotiating obligations that are no longer feasible. Although these sound like easy steps to take, experience has demonstrated that considerable skill may be required to control one's obligations in a demanding or insensitive environment.

Social Support

Work overload and high work demands are common characteristics of many organizational environments during the 1990s. Social support, first discussed in chapter 10 as an organizational issue, may be especially beneficial in the context of demanding and stressful jobs (Parkes, Mendham, & von Rabenau, 1994). Social support was found to have a direct, positive effect on job stressors and strains in a study of 110 AT&T employees undergoing a major organizational restructuring (Shaw, Fields, Thacker, & Fisher, 1993). Furthermore, low social support was associated with more symptoms in a study of 297 healthy men, aged 30–60 years, at various work sites (Landsbergis, Schnall, Deitz, & Friedman, 1992).

Active social support from coworkers, family, and friends is a characteristic of personality hardiness (Maddi, 1995). Active social support may help a person in managing the personal work environment in at least two ways. First, colleagues and coworkers may help a person develop perspective and an understanding of persons or events that are experienced as stressful. Through dialogue with others, the person is able to reframe how the stressor is experienced. Second, colleagues and coworkers may provide instrumental support by sharing demands, which helps ease the stress load on the person. In one study of 101 Israeli male career military officers, work sources of social support were found to alleviate job stress (Etzion & Westman, 1994). In this study, family sources of stress were not found to have a beneficial effect on the job stress of the military officers; however, the generalizability of this finding is questionable. Given the spillover effects that work stress can have on home and family environments, social support from family and friends may incrementally aid in managing workplace demands, and this may relate to the process of managing one's overall lifestyle.

Managing One's Lifestyle

Even when work demands do not take time away from family activities, work stress frequently spills over into the home when the working spouse brings the day's tensions into family interactions. Conversely, marital and other forms of family discord can readily lead to distraction or a quick temper at work. At the same time, the family can serve an important role in countering and attenuating distress at work. Therefore, the family may be a help or a hindrance in confronting stress at work, depending on the nature of the marriage, the underlying personal priorities of the individuals, and the demands of the job.

The value of helping individuals build and maintain strong family relationships is recognized by some businesses and organizations. For example, one hospital management corporation commissioned a series of workshops for hospital administrators and their spouses, as well as hospital financial officers and their spouses, as an educational device to help the marital partners develop a deeper appreciation for the demands of the work environment. The workshops helped identify sources of stress and strain for the administrators, financial officers, and spouses while providing a forum for discussing ways of managing the stress and alleviating distress.

Building family relationships is neither an individual nor an organizational intervention but an extraorganizational intervention. Although we do not consider family relationships under a separate heading, attention to family support systems and efforts at strengthening these systems should be considered a vital and valid part of any stress management effort. The emphasis throughout this book has been on preventive stress management in the workplace, yet there is an undeniably large interaction between work life and home life. The manner in which this interaction is handled may have an important bearing on an individual's overall well-being, influencing both health and work performance. There are two important aspects of the work–home interaction over which management may have some influence: the ongoing balance between work and home and the use of leisure time. A third area of lifestyle management is that of sabbaticals, or career breaks.

Maintaining a Balance

Some organizations reward employees for losing themselves in their work, which explains why it is not hard for some executives to lose their balance (Kofodimos, 1990). People who work long hours, put in extra time on weekends, and take work home may advance rapidly and appear to be succeeding marvelously. However, *workaholic* behavior eventually takes its toll (Porter, 1996). The workaholic behavior pattern is typical of the Type A individual, who as we have already noted, experiences a much higher risk of heart attack. The workaholic remains chronically in a state of distress. Often the person is unaware of his own signs of distress and may manifest the distress only through increased cigarette or alcohol consumption. This excessive involvement in work is really a form of addiction, an addiction with potentially serious consequences. One approach to establishing a healthy balance between one's career and personal life involves moderating the drive for mastery while encouraging an executive's capacity for intimacy (Kofodimos, 1990).

Workaholics perceive that they have more control over their lives when they are working (Eliot, 1995). Spending long hours at work may be an escape from responsibilities in the personal arena and from relationships. The danger of allowing one's life to be dependent on one's career is that there are no other resources for satisfaction when the career is in trouble. In contrast to the distress of the workaholic lifestyle is the eustress that is usually achieved by maintaining *balance* between work life and home life. Overinvestment in work activities frequently reflects an effort to gain rewards and a sense of value from work that are not coming from outside activities. Rather than working to make the outside activities more satisfying, workaholics submerge themselves in their job, creating extreme imbalance in life.

Home life, social life, artistic and cultural activities, and, sometimes, spiritual and religious life are all potential sources of satisfaction and significant rewards. Investing oneself in these activities in addition to work life provides a more diverse network of social and emotional supports. Individuals with a strong support network are generally better able to weather difficulties. Although work stressors may remain the same, the ability to cope with the stressors with minimal distress is enhanced by maintaining a balance.

In an intensive idiographic study of chief executives who remain healthy under high stress, maintaining a balance was found to be a key preventive stress management technique (J. C. Quick, Nelson, & Quick, 1990). A common denominator among the executives was that work, although central to their lives, was not the most important part of their lives. Family, religious commitments, community involvements, friends, and personal enjoyment of life were all mentioned as more important than work.

Leisure Time

One can assume and easily defend the notion that one virtue of leisure is stress reduction (Baum, 1991). A study of 1,929 informal caregivers found that reducing leisure led to emotional and physical stress and less life satisfaction (White-Means & Chang, 1994), yet little attention has been paid to the wise and creative use of leisure time as a stress management tool. Vacations are accepted as one of the rewards for working, and people often express the need for a vacation. Although vacations may be stress reducing for people in some circumstances, they are stress provoking in others. For example, a longitudinal study of 29 workers found that strain was as high during vacations as during pre- and postwork periods in which acutely stressful job events occurred (Eden, 1990).

Whereas 1- or 2-week block vacations represent one use of paid time off, 3-day weekends and scattered "mental health" days constitute an alternative use of vacation and leisure time. One cardiologist who deals extensively with the stress-related aspects of heart disease urges his patients to make frequent use of 3-day weekends as stress reducers (Eliot, 1984), although the meaning of a 3-day weekend clearly is different for those who work 4-day weeks of 10-hour days. A comparative study of the effects of vacation time versus 3-day weekends in the traditional 5-day workweek versus 3-day weekends in the 4-day workweek might yield interesting results. A well-planned 3-day weekend can be extremely refreshing, particularly during or following a period of extreme stress. Five 3-day weekends may be more valuable and refreshing than 1 week of vacation.

Leisure activities are best interpreted in the context of specific cultures and personal preferences. A study of 123 British and 132 German managerial and executive personnel found the work–leisure balance moderated by culture (Kirkcaldy & Cooper, 1993). Specifically, the British tended to exhibit more negative job carryover into the nonwork, leisure domains of their lives than did their German counterparts, who demonstrated compensation and achieved better work–leisure balance. In addition to cultural differences in leisure activities, personal preferences are important. *Leisure congruence* is the correspondence between personality type and selected leisure activities. A study of 160 professionals, aged 22–62 years, found that work satisfaction was higher and burnout, somatic complaints, and anxiety lower for those with greater leisure congruence.

Counselors at some psychiatric facilities are allowed to take periodic "mental health" days, or 1-day absences that can usually be taken without advance request. They are meant to be used whenever the demands of caring for severely troubled individuals become too great. Although unplanned mental health days can be disruptive in some businesses and industries, their use should be considered when feasible. The cost of burnout is much higher than the cost of a brief respite. Taking time off during the week may also be a way to rejuvenate. Lunch breaks with friends and even 5-minute getaways during a stressful day can refresh and renew one's energy. Simply getting up and walking around for a few minutes may be enough to renew one's resources.

The impact of vacations and leisure time on individual health and well-being has received little systematic study. There is some evidence that individuals have a greater tolerance for adversity and decreased nervous system responsiveness following vacations. There is also some evidence that creative use of leisure time and attention to lifestyle can be as important as diet and exercise in preventing heart attacks (Mayer, 1975). Therefore, vacation planning should be considered part of any personal stress management plan. However, it is important to recognize that vacations are not necessarily relaxing. The Type A individual who tries to squeeze as much sightseeing or golf as possible into a week's vacation may return as stressed and as tired as he was when he left. Vacations may be physically tiring, but they should be planned in a way that makes them mentally relaxing.

The use of leisure time is important. Leisure means freedom from work and the demands and control of others (Eliot, 1984). It is not the particular activity that is important but the individual's attitude toward that activity. True leisure means doing something fulfilling without having to reach a goal. Some people know how to work but not how to play. One woman, when asked what she did in her leisure time, said she cleaned house. When asked if housework was fulfilling and relaxing, she reflected and said that it added to her stress.

Some people spend leisure time with pets. The companionship of pets has been shown to contribute to health by lowering blood pressure and heart rates, and providing a sense of optimism and feelings of control (Lynch, 1977; Pelletier, 1984). Human–animal bonds have been shown to alleviate a variety of illnesses and increase life expectancy. Playing Frisbee with a dog or simply watching a cat relax may provide a different perspective on life. The unconditional positive regard provided by pets can serve as social support.

Sabbaticals

Sabbaticals, or career breaks, have been a long-standing part of university and religious life aimed at providing a period of rest, reflection, and revitalization. The term is based on the Old Testament biblical precedent of declaring a 1-year "Sabbath of solemn rest for the land" every seventh year (Leviticus 25:1–7). Industry explored the use of sabbaticals during the 1970s and early 1980s, and some companies have continued to use them.

Sabbaticals may be structured as educational programs or social service leaves or they may be unstructured (Rountree, 1979). Educational programs are the most common type of structured sabbatical. University-based programs such as Harvard's Public Health Systems Management Course and the Sloan Programs at MIT are popular examples. Structured sabbaticals are generally funded by the company. Unstructured, or free-lance, sabbaticals are often taken at the expense of the participant. They include such activities as reading and independent research, domestic or foreign travel, or simply rejuvenation through sports and recreation.

Workplace stress is the most frequently mentioned reason for companies to adopt sabbaticals. Tandem Computers offers sabbaticals to employees after 4 years of continuous service. Their program provides employees 6 weeks of leave with full pay and benefits. At Tandem, employees use these sabbaticals to pursue personal growth. Employees have spent sabbaticals climbing the mountains of Nepal and studying at a world-renowned cooking school. Wells Fargo offers two types of sabbaticals: personal growth leave and social service leave. The purpose of personal growth leave is for employees with long periods of service to take up to 3 months with full pay and benefits to pursue personal interests. Social service leave, in contrast, allows employees with a commitment to community service to work for a nonprofit agency for up to 6 months with full pay and benefits (Bachler, 1995).

Summary

This chapter has described a wide range of primary or stressor-directed methods for individual-level preventive stress management. Personal response patterns can be influenced by techniques such as learned optimism, constructive self-talk, transformational coping, recognizing the inevitable, disputing cognitive distortions, and changing Type A behavior patterns. Individuals can also influence the stressors in their work environment through methods such as planning, time management, and overload avoidance. Finally, work demands can be controlled if employees maintain a balance between work and other activities and make effective use of leisure time.

All the methods described in this chapter are concerned with helping individuals to alter the frequency, intensity, or duration of the demands and stressors they face. Chapter 12 describes methods intended to dampen the arousal or dissipate the effects of the stress response once it has been stimulated, and chapter 13 discusses methods and professional resources available to treat overt symptoms of distress. Once one has completed a reading of chapters 11 through 13, one will be prepared to develop a personal preventive stress management plan. The discussion of personal stress management plans and the choice of personal and professional prevention methods are presented at the end of chapter 13.

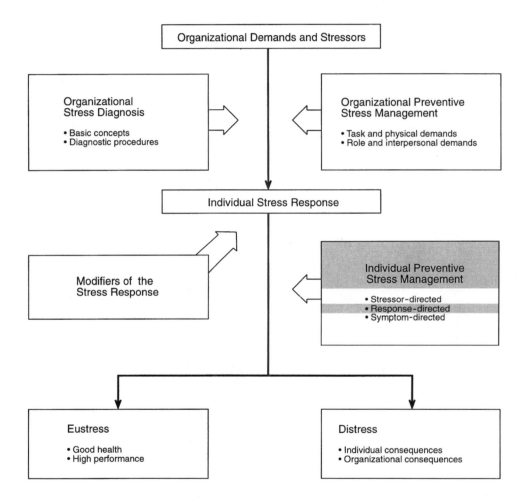

12

Secondary Prevention for Individuals: Modifying Responses to Inevitable Demands

Chapter 11 described three categories of primary prevention methods aimed at helping individuals reduce, modify, and manage the demands on their work lives, including restructuring of their perceptions of these demands as stressors. This chapter considers secondary (i.e., response-directed) prevention methods aimed at dissipating the physical and psychological energy of the stress response once it has been evoked. The methods described in this chapter are among the most widely used methods of stress management, and they may be the best-researched methods. Several of these strategies (relaxation training, use of emotional outlets, and exercise), along with the cognitive–behavioral interventions discussed in chapter 11, have generally produced positive changes in immune function (Kiecolt-Glaser & Glaser, 1992), thus suggesting their preventive role in inoculating individuals against distress and strain. The chapter is organized around the five categories of secondary prevention noted in Exhibit 11.1, relaxation training, spirituality and faith, emotional outlets, physical fitness, and nutrition.

Relaxation Training

Relaxation training encompasses a variety of methods for achieving muscular and psychological relaxation or deactivation, six of which are listed in Exhibit 11.1 and discussed here. Selection of a specific method is largely an individual matter, based on one's motivation, personal beliefs, need for a mental versus a physical emphasis, availability of instructors, and price. Selection is also partly a matter of trial and error. If one method does not seem to work well, one should remain open to trying another approach. Relaxation methods also differ in the extent to which they emphasize mental or physical relaxation. Transcendental Meditation, for example, focuses primarily on mental relaxation, whereas progressive relaxation is based on a systematic relaxation of the skeletal muscles. In practice, most methods that have been studied result in both mental and physical relaxation, even if one aspect is emphasized over the other. Finally, some relaxation methods are rooted in religious or spiritual beliefs; spirituality and faith are addressed in the next section of the chapter.

The generalized relaxation response is virtually the reverse of the

Table 12.1. Comparison of the Physiologic Changes of the Fight-or-Flight Response and the Relaxation Response

Physiologic State	Fight-or-Flight Response	Relaxation Response
Metabolism	Increases	Decreases
Blood pressure	Increases	Decreases
Heart rate	Increases	Decreases
Rate of breathing	Increases	Decreases
Blood flowing to the muscles of the arms and legs	Increases	Stable
Muscle tension	Increases	Decreases
Slow brain waves	Decrease	Increase

Note. From *Timeless Healing: The Power and Biology of Belief* (p.131) by H. Benson with M. Stark, 1996, New York: Scribner. Copyright ©1996 by Herbert Benson, MD. Reprinted with permission.

stress response. A comparison of the actions of the fight-or-flight (stress) response and the relaxation response is presented in Table 12.1 (Benson & Stark, 1996). Benson and his associates at the Harvard Medical School were the first to recognize that a wide variety of religious and secular practices appeared to achieve relaxation through a common physiological mechanism (Benson, Beary, & Carol, 1974); they termed that mechanism the *relaxation response*. The relaxation response is the patterned response leading to a generalized decrease in sympathetic nervous system activity sometimes accompanied by an increase in parasympathetic activity.

The Relaxation Response

Benson and Stark (1996) said that there are only two basic steps needed to elicit the relaxation response. *First, repeat a word, sound, prayer, phrase, or muscular activity*. The choice of a focused repetition is up to the individual. It may be a word such as *one* or *peace*, a prayer, any sound that seems appropriate for remembered wellness. or rhythmic breathing. *Second, passively disregard everyday thoughts that come to mind and return to the repetition*. Thoughts might be dismissed with a phrase such as "oh, well." There is no single method for eliciting the relaxation response, but the technique works best when individuals develop a disciplined routine that meets their needs. One example of such a discipline is as follows:

> Pick a focus word or mantra that is rooted in your belief system.
> Sit quietly in a comfortable position.
> Close your eyes.
> Relax your muscles.
> Breathe slowly and naturally, and repeat your focus word silently as you exhale.
> Assume a passive attitude, dismissing random thoughts that come to mind.

Continue for 10–20 minutes.
Do not stand immediately. Open your eyes and sit for another minute
   before rising.
Practice this technique once or twice daily.

The relaxation response can be elicited using alternative methods or
disciplines provided the two basic steps noted previously are observed. One
primary benefit of the relaxation response is in the clinical treatment of
disorders of arousal (Everly & Benson, 1989). Another primary benefit is
its ability to combat what Eastern philosophers have called "monkey
mind," the mind that leaps from thought to thought just as monkeys leap
from tree limb to tree limb. Monkey mind, from the term *papanca* used
by Buddhists, prevents the individual from concentrating, learning, or falling asleep. Excessive brain activity that overloads the system can be
calmed with the relaxation response.

Considerable evidence exists regarding the efficacy of the relaxation
response in terms of physiological and psychological benefits. For example,
individuals who frequently visited health maintenance organizations with
psychosomatic complaints reduced their number of visits by 50% by using
the response (Hellman, Budd, Borysenko, McClelland, & Benson, 1990).
Workers experienced lower levels of depression, anxiety, and hostility;
fewer sick days; improved performance; and lower blood pressure by employing the relaxation response (Carrington et al., 1980; Peters, Benson,
& Porter, 1977). Individuals with hypertension showed significant decreases in blood pressure and needed fewer or no medications after practicing the response over a 3-year period (Benson & Stark, 1996).

In a study of female bank employees and hospital cleaners in Finland,
participants were arranged in age-matched pairs and randomly assigned
to intervention and control groups (Toivanen, Lansimies, Jokela, & Hanninen, 1993). The intervention group received relaxation training and
practiced deep relaxation over a 6-month period. Heart rate variability in
the cardiac autonomic nervous system function test indicated that regular
relaxation normalized the function and that people who relaxed had an
enhanced ability to cope with stress. Eliciting the relaxation response
through any of several methods leads to a response pattern that includes
decreases in metabolic rate, heart rate, and respiratory rate. Initially,
blood pressure may remain the same, but regularly eliciting the relaxation
response often lowers that function, too. The electroencephalogram (brain
wave recording) taken during the relaxation response shows an increase
in the intensity of the slow alpha waves that are usually associated with
feelings of well-being.

There are several caveats to note with regard to the relaxation response. First, its beneficial effects may not be immediately apparent. That
is, one should expect to practice the relaxation response on a daily basis
for several weeks to over a month before experiencing notable change.
Second, one should limit the practice to once or twice a day for about 15
or 20 minutes. Extended or highly frequent periods of relaxation may have
unintended side effects, such as lethargy and even some reality dis-
orientation.

Progressive Relaxation

The earliest structured relaxation technique to appear in the medical and psychological literature was progressive relaxation, a technique developed by the physician–physiologist Jacobson in the late 1920s and 1930s for use in the treatment of anxiety. Jacobson (1929) emphasized *physical* relaxation and relied on profound relaxation of all major skeletal muscle groups as the means to prevent as well as treat anxiety. A recent review of the efficacy of abbreviated progressive muscle relaxation training across 29 experiments found moderate effects, with treatment duration and number of sessions positively influencing the strength of the effects (Carlson & Hoyle, 1993). A study of 8 patients in a cardiac rehabilitation program found that progressive muscle relaxation training (PMRT) reduced cardiovascular reactivity (Cole, Pomerleau, & Harris, 1992).

Progressive relaxation consists of sequential tensing and releasing of each of the 16 skeletal muscle groups into which Jacobson divided the body. A quiet environment with soft lights and a comfortable seated or reclining position is recommended. The muscles are tensed for 5–7 seconds and then relaxed for about 30 seconds. This process begins with the arms; progresses to the face, neck, and throat; and continues through the chest, abdomen, legs, and feet. The process, which last 30–60 minutes, provides a systematic comparison of the amount of tension in each muscle group and a comparison of the tensed and relaxed state for each group. Such comparisons train the person to become aware of even the slightest degree of muscle tension. With experience, the person learns to combine muscle groups into first seven and then four groups. It may take 30 hours or more to master the skill.

Jacobson (1978) continued to refine the technique, incorporating electromyography (EMG) to help people assess muscle tension and applying the technique to a wide range of conditions. Progressive relaxation has not achieved general acceptance as the primary mode of therapy for anxious patients; however, it was used with flight cadets in pilot training during World War II as a method of tension and stress management, and it is frequently used in conjunction with behavior therapy, psychotherapy, and drug treatment. In addition, it has served as the basis for the development of a variety of other relaxation techniques and methods of stress control.

The comparative effectiveness of progressive relaxation may be helpful for a variety of problems, including insomnia and test anxiety among college students. For individuals in whom stress is manifested primarily by muscle tension, progressive relaxation during workday, evening, or weekend relaxation breaks might prove to be the most effective means of countering the stress response.

Meditation

To a certain extent, relaxation training is a distillation of a variety of practices that induce relaxation. Benson's (1974) study of Transcendental

Meditation popularized the concept of the relaxation response. However, many other forms of meditation, including clinically standardized meditation (see the following paragraph), Zen, and yoga, can achieve similar relaxation effects. One study of the efficacy of meditation and relaxation training for 62 university students found significant benefits from both mantra meditation and yogic relaxation, with larger gains realized by those practicing meditation (Janowiak & Hackman, 1994).

A technique that falls somewhere between Benson's basic relaxation response training and the more intense classical meditation of Eastern origin is called *clinically standardized meditation* (CSM). The technique was developed over a period of several years by Princeton psychologist Patricia Carrington. Carrington (1978) made an extensive study of classical meditation and synthesized a system of mantra meditation free from a religious or mystical basis and more appropriate for Western use. Carrington emphasized preparation, attitude, and use of the mantra.

CSM is intended to be taught by a qualified instructor, who observes to ensure its proper use and helps sustain the individual's motivation until it becomes a regular practice. Some people experience considerable psychological and physical distress during the early stages of learning meditation, much of this distress stemming from misunderstanding or misuse; therefore, Carrington (1978) placed a strong emphasis on the instruction process.

The effectiveness of CSM in preventive stress management has been demonstrated in a long-term study of employees of the New York Telephone Company who had reported high levels of job stress. The employees were assigned to a relaxation group, one of two meditation groups, or a control group. Participants' learning occurred through audiotapes, and they practiced the techniques twice daily. Eighteen months after CSM training began, individuals who meditated or relaxed showed a marked decrease in depression, anxiety, and hostility and improvements in several physiological measures. CSM has subsequently been adopted for use in company-wide stress-reduction programs (Carrington et al., 1980).

Transcendental Meditation (TM) is a well-known meditation method of Eastern origin. Based primarily on Hindu practices, the method was introduced into the Western world in the late 1950s by Maharishi Mahesh Yogi. Meditators are taught to spend two 20-minute periods daily in a quiet place in a comfortable position while silently repeating their mantra, the sound or word given to the trainee by the instructor. The aim is to develop a passive attitude and a peaceful worldview. TM seemed revolutionary when it was introduced into the United States, and its aura of mysticism and secretism added to its appeal for many people.

Promoters of TM have emphasized the beneficial effects of TM in increasing the ability to cope with stress reactions and in improving physiological measures of stress, such as high blood pressure. In a retrospective study of businessmen who practiced TM, Frew (1974) concluded that regular meditators showed more job satisfaction, more stability in their jobs, better interpersonal relationships with supervisors and coworkers, less anxiety about promotion combined with a record of moving ahead quickly, and improved job performance. Furthermore, the greater the authority and responsibility the meditator held in the organization, the greater seemed to be the gain in productivity, satisfaction, and work relations. Because this was a restrospective study, however, it is difficult to determine which effects were due to the meditation itself and which effects were due to differences in the individuals who chose to meditate.

In a prospective study in two occupational settings, researchers compared two experimental groups of 45 employees trained to practice TM twice daily for 3 months to two control groups of 41 employees (Alexander, Swanson, Rainforth, & Carlisle, 1993). Employees who practiced TM were found to have greater improvements in job satisfaction, general health, employee effectiveness and working relationships and a greater decrease in sleep–fatigue, job worry and tension than those who did not.

In addition to secular forms of meditation, such as the relaxation response and clinically standardized meditation, and TM, there are numerous other meditation practices of Eastern origin including Chakra yoga, Rinzai Zen, Soto Zen, Zazen, Ananda Marga yoga, Mudra yoga, Tantra yoga, Sufism, Kundalini yoga, and Shavasana. Descriptions and comparisons can be found in a book by Pelletier (1992; see also Pelletier, 1995). In practice, the choice of a specific form of meditation depends largely on the individual appeal of a particular method. A variety of meditation centers (see, for example, the Yellow Pages of phone books) exist in cities throughout the United States, and the availability of a skilled teacher is a reasonable method for selecting one.

Medical Hypnosis and Autogenic Training

For over a century, hypnosis was defined as a state that is different from normal waking consciousness, characterized by extreme relaxation and a heightened susceptibility to suggestion (Sachs, 1982). However, the question of whether hypnosis is an altered state of consciousness has become a subject of intense controversy (Rhue, Lynn, & Kirsch, 1993). In discussing the definition of hypnosis, Rhue et al. (1993) reported that some responsive subjects believe hypnotic inductions produce an altered state that is much different from normal waking consciousness, but that most describe it as a normal state of focused attention. A hypnotic trance can be induced by focusing the subject's attention on a mental, visual, or other sensory image and suggesting an increase in relaxation and well-being. Although the popular image of hypnosis portrays the person as falling into a "sleep," the brain wave pattern and subjective experience of hypnosis are quite different from those of true sleep. Nevertheless, a state of profound muscular relaxation can be suggested and achieved through the focused attention of hypnosis.

Hypnosis has two stages. *Presuggestion*, the first stage, is the same physiological state as the relaxation response. The second stage, *suggestion*, is characterized by an action or image that is intended to be evoked.

Many individuals are capable of learning to induce a hypnotic state in themselves, a process known as *self-hypnosis*. Self-hypnosis can be learned from reading about the subject or after experiencing a hypnotic trance through induction by a skilled hypnotist, usually a psychiatrist, clinical psychologist, or other trained therapist.

A review of the literature on hypnosis suggests that it can enhance longevity and reduce premature mortality through positive effects on the aging process (Morse, 1989). The review suggests that the benefits of hypnosis occur through its influence on the stress process and immune system functioning. Specifically, hypnosis can modulate the immune response to stress in healthy volunteers (Walker, Johnson, & Eremin, 1993).

Hypnosis can be applied to a wide variety of common problems, including pain control, smoking cessation, weight control, phobias, and other stress-related, psychosomatic problems. Hypnosis is of little lasting value when the individual has no firm urge to change; however, when there is a sufficient commitment to change, conscious or unconscious, the technique can be quite useful (Crasilneck & Hall, 1975).

Susceptibility to hypnosis seems to be related to a stable trait from childhood involving imaginative involvements. People who are susceptible have the ability to ignore distractions and become totally immersed in an activity. Responsive hypnotic subjects have been able to stop bleeding; control asthma, migraines, and pain; alter blood flow; and heal skin and other diseases (Justice, 1988). In one classic study, individuals were hypnotized and asked to visualize their lymphocytes as sharks attacking germs. They were then trained to use self-hypnosis and continue the imaging for a week. Results showed a significant increase in immune system functioning (Hall, 1982–1983).

How hypnosis works is somewhat unclear; it may enhance believability. Through images focused on, the mind communicates an expectation to the body. Research evidence strongly suggests that when people form images of their body doing something, internal changes occur accordingly (Achterberg, 1985).

Autogenic training is a method of self-hypnosis developed from experiments with medical hypnosis in the early 1920s by the German psychiatrist J. H. Schultz, whose work is available in English in a rather forbidding six-volume medical text (Luthe, 1969). A more readable manual for self-instruction was prepared by Jencks (1979) and is available from the American Society of Clinical Hypnosis. Like hypnosis, autogenic training is best learned from an experienced clinical psychologist or other qualified therapist. It is a relaxation method that may be best suited to the control of individual reactivity or responses to specific stressors.

Autogenic training emphasizes the development of individual control over physiological processes through organ- and symptom-specific exercises. Once a person has mastered the basic method of autohypnosis and the six standard autogenic training exercises (a process that Schultz said should take 2–3 months in a healthy trainee), he or she is ready to use a variety of special formulas. *Intentional formulas* are used to achieve behavioral change by reinforcing mental resolve to omit undesirable behav-

Exhibit 12.1. Sample Formula for Autogenic Training

Intentional (behavior change) formulas

Reducing mental tension
- "I meet my troubles calm, collected, and cheerful."
- "Don't think, don't do, don't want anything."
- "Calm, content, comfortable."

Coping with present stress
- "I am free from frustration and fright."
- "Detach! . . . do not mind."
- "Calm, careful, courageous."

Coping with memories of past stress
- "Past pains perish; pleasant peace prevails."
- "The past has passed; the present prevails."

Decision making
- "Correct decisions come quickly [inhalation]."
- "I decide what I want."
- "I decide what seems best."

Reduction of smoking and drug or alcohol abuse
- "Less pills, less poison!"
- "Skip smelly smoking."
- "Alcohol at no time, at no place, on no occasion."

Slimming
- "Break bread briefly."
- "Less bread, less spread."
- "Calm, content, satisfied, and satiated."

Organ-specific formulas

Respiration
- "My breath flows calm and free [exhalation]."
- "Breathe easy [exhalation]."

Eyes
- "Eyes cool [inhalation] and relaxed [exhalation]."
- "Blood circulates in the retina."

Blushing
- "Face is cool and pale [inhalation]—warmth and redness flow to trunk and legs [exhalation]."

Intestines
- "Intestines work warmly, smoothly [exhalation], and strongly [inhalation]."

Hemorrhoids
- "Anus is relaxed and wide [exhalation]—cool water irrigates it [inhalation]."

Itching
- "My . . . is cool [inhalation], relaxed, and soft [exhalation]."

Rheumatic pains
- "Shoulders and elbows stay warm and relaxed [exhalation]."

Note. Reprinted from *Exercise Manual for J. H. Schultz's Standard Autogenic Training and Special Formulas* by B. Jencks, 1979, Des Plaines, IL; American Society of Clinical Hypnosis, pp. 38–39.

iors or to perform new behaviors. *Organ-specific formulas* are used to modify specific physiological processes. Examples of these formulas are given in Exhibit 12.1.

Biofeedback Training

In chapter 3, the stress response was defined as a well-organized pattern of autonomic nervous system and endocrine system responses. Figure 3.2 listed many of the physiological actions of the sympathetic part of the autonomic nervous system. Because physiological responses such as changes in blood pressure, heart rate, and sweating occur without conscious effort, they were originally thought to be involuntary responses. However, some striking examples of voluntary control of "autonomic" function stimulated medical researchers to explore the extent to which control of visceral functions could be learned. The tool as well as the product of this exploration has been biofeedback.

Like autogenic training, biofeedback may be especially suitable to the control of individual reactivity or responses to specific stressors. For example, biofeedback may be an appropriate prevention and treatment method for irritable bowel syndrome, which is among the most common presenting problems for gastroenterologists (M. S. Schwartz, 1995). Lehrer, Carr, Sargunaraj, and Woolfolk (1994) reviewed the variety of specific methods of biofeedback, such as electromyographic biofeedback and thermal biofeedback, that may be used independently or in conjunction with one of the cognitive methods of primary prevention discussed in chapter 11. Phillips (1991) outlined the principles of biofeedback training in the context of health psychology, considered some of the more popular applications, and assessed the clinical effectiveness of biofeedback.

Biofeedback has received limited use in the workplace. An early application by the Equitable Life Assurance Society's Emotional Health Program found significant net savings could be achieved through the control of work-related stress symptoms, even factoring in the cost of equipment. These savings are calculated by comparing the cost of biofeedback training with the savings in employee and physician time from reduced illness-related visits to the medical department (Manuso, 1979a).

The term *feedback* was coined at about the beginning of this century by the pioneers in radio. Mayr (1970) quoted Norbert Wiener, a mathematician who was instrumental in feedback research, describing feedback quite simply as "a method of controlling a system by reinserting into it the results of its past performance." Biofeedback is possible whenever a physiological function can be recorded and amplified by electronic instruments and its characteristics reported back to a person through any of the five senses. The equipment reflects the individual's response much the way a mirror reflects his appearance. Figure 12.1 illustrates the basic feedback loop in biofeedback. Although any of the five basic senses can be used,

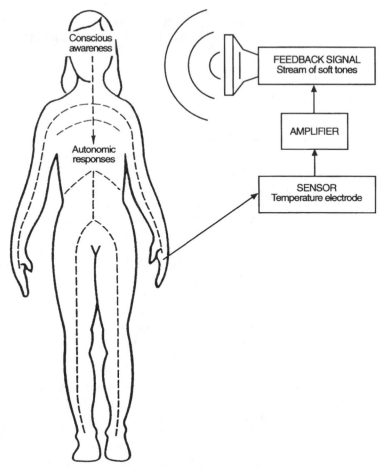

Figure 12.1.   Example of the feedback loop in biofeedback.

feedback is generally auditory (tones of varying pitch or rhythm) or visual (blinking lights, colors, graphs).

In clinical biofeedback, the focus is usually on one physiological measurement—skin temperature, for example. A temperature-sensitive electrode is attached to the skin, and an amplifier converts the skin temperature reading to a stream of soft tones. The colder the skin, the faster the tones. The person is not instructed to make his skin warmer but to slow the tones. By imagining warm places, like a beach, the desert, or the sun, individuals can increase blood flow and the warmth of the hands or other parts of the body (Schwartz, 1984). Although medical researchers have demonstrated many of the anatomical and functional nervous system connections that are involved in the feedback loop, the exact way in which an individual "learns" from the feedback remains somewhat of a mystery.

Biofeedback can be applied to any physiological function that can be easily measured. For example, sweating is measured by the galvanic skin response (GSR), muscle tension by electromyography (EMG), brain waves by electroencephalography (EEG), heart rate and heart rhythm by electrocardiography (ECG), blood flow by plethysmography, blood pressure by sphygmomanometry, intestinal movement by amplification of the stethoscope sounds, and stomach acid by a pH meter.

Although any of these measurements can be used, the three most commonly used for relaxation therapy are muscle tension, brain waves, and sweating. To achieve relaxation through control of muscle tension, the EMG sensors are connected to either the forehead (frontalis muscle) or the back of the neck (trapezius muscle). By learning to relax these muscles, many people experience a generalized sense of relaxation. Alternatively, brain waves can be monitored with sensors attached to the scalp and hooked to an EEG machine. One type of brain wave, the slow alpha wave, is associated with feelings of relaxation and well-being. The biofeedback EEG machine is programmed to recognize this waveform and to provide visual or auditory information corresponding to its presence. Using an "alpha trainer," which is a specialized EEG device, can increase relaxation by teaching the person how to increase alpha brain waves and reduce other brain waves. Biofeedback has a distinct advantage over other methods in that it provides individuals with precise data about their state of relaxation. However, the cost and convenience are significant limiting factors in the use of biofeedback. A skilled instructor is required as is specialized equipment. The accuracy and reliability of available equipment vary greatly, and quality and price are not always highly correlated. Recognizing a good buy requires an experienced operator of biofeedback equipment.

Girdano and Everly (1979) divided biofeedback equipment into three categories: *home trainers*, which usually cost less than $200 but are "virtually worthless"; *clinical trainers*, which range in price from $250 to $1,000 and are usually dependable, although limited in their capabilities; and research units, which can cost over $10,000, are generally accurate, and provide a great deal of versatility.

Successful clinical applications of biofeedback have included beneficial effects on such conditions as tension headaches, potentially serious heartbeat irregularities, and chronic pain (Fuller, 1978; Gentry, 1975; Miller & Dworkin, 1977). Repeated blood pressure monitoring has a modest hypotensive effect on hypertensive patients. Monitoring is thus a form of high blood pressure biofeedback (Chesney, 1987). In a study of 44 patients with chronic low back pain, electromyographic biofeedback was associated with lower pain intensity, lower perceived levels of disability, and lower levels of depression (Newton-John, Spence, & Schotte, 1995). The National Aeronautics and Space Administration uses biofeedback to help astronauts control motion sickness. Approximately 85% of those trained learn to control motion sickness within 6 hours (Bartholomew, 1994). A National Institutes of Health technology assessment panel recommended that behavior therapies like biofeedback for chronic cancer pain be accepted and reimbursed in the same manner as surgery and chemotherapy (Eastman, 1995).

Momentary Relaxation

Many relaxation methods require a place free from interruption and a period of at least 10–20 minutes. For the typical manager or employee, it may be possible to practice relaxation at most once each working day. Yet the average workday is usually filled with a number of small stresses, which can accumulate bit by bit, and one or two major stressors, such as a report deadline or a public presentation. For such situations, momentary relaxation (Albrecht, 1979; Roskies, 1978) or the 6-second quieting response (Manuso, 1982) can be useful. Once an individual has mastered a deep relaxation technique such as the relaxation response or progressive relaxation, the skill of momentary relaxation should come easily. Albrecht (1979) described momentary relaxation with the following examples:

> The next time you find yourself about to deal with a challenging, stressful situation, simply pause for a few seconds, turn your attention to your body, and allow your whole body to relax as much as you can, keeping the situation in mind. You can easily learn to do this "quickie" relaxation technique in a few seconds and without the slightest outward sign of what you are doing. Anyone looking at you would notice, at most, that you had become silent and that you seemed to be thinking about something for a few seconds. You need not even close your eyes to do this.
>
> If you happen to have a few moments alone before entering the challenging situation, you can relax yourself somewhat more thoroughly. Sit down, if possible, get comfortable, and close your eyes. Use your built-in muscle memory to bring back the feeling of deep relaxation and hold it for about a full minute. Then open your eyes and, as you go about the task at hand, try to retain the feeling of calmness that came with the relaxation. (pp. 198–199)

Momentary relaxation draws on an individual's mental and physical "memory" of deep relaxation to achieve partial relaxation rapidly. Taking a few deep, slow breaths usually helps bring on relaxation. The effectiveness of deep breathing depends not only on its usual associations with relaxation practices but also on neurological reflexes that result in lowered muscle tone and heart rate following a few deep breaths. In fact, it is theorized that the relaxation that some people derive from smoking a cigarette results in part from the first few slow, deep breaths at the time the smoker lights the cigarette and not from the process of smoking.

Like autogenic training and biofeedback, brief relaxation may be highly suitable for the control of individual reactivity or responses to specific stressors. For example, one study of 102 patients with mixed migraine–muscle contraction headaches who received biofeedback and cognitive–behavioral treatment found in 3-month to 4-year follow-ups that 69% of the improved patients reported the continued daily use of brief relaxation, compared to only 39% of those with less improvement (Lake & Pingel, 1988). In another study of 80 men's responses to acute pain, brief relaxation was found to result in greater blood pressure recovery, although it did not appear to affect the experience of pain or emotion (Bruehl, Carlson, & McCubbin, 1993).

Whatever the form, relaxation training can be an effective method of preventive stress management. Studies have shown that levels of the stress hormones cortisol and the catecholamines decrease following relaxation (Jemmott & Locke, 1984). Relaxation also has beneficial effects on the immune system, as previously noted. Early research with medical students by Kiecolt-Glaser and her colleagues (1986) found that on examination days, the students had significant decreases in their level of helper T cells. When half of the students practiced relaxation exercises, their T-cell levels increased, with the percentage of increase related to the frequency with which the students practiced relaxation.

Spirituality and Faith

A number of relaxation practices are rooted in the spiritual or religious traditions, such as the Eastern practice of TM previously discussed or the Judeo–Christian tradition of prayer noted by Benson and Stark (1996). Hence relaxation practices may intertwine and overlap with one's spiritual and faith practices. Organ (1970) described the long history of systematic efforts to achieve mental and physical relaxation dating at least to the sixth century BC, when the Indian scripture the Upanishad suggested that individuals could reach a state of spiritual unity "by means of restraint of breath, withdrawal of sense, meditation, concentration, contemplation, and absorption" (p. 303). Since that time, various means for achieving mental or physical relaxation have been described largely within religious contexts. Chinese Taoism, Japanese Shintoism, Zen Buddhism, Judaism, and various Christian leaders and sects have described practices for achieving individual relaxation.

The power of spirituality and faith in maintaining and restoring health has been increasingly recognized by mainstream medical research over the past 2 decades. For example, a central element in Ornish's (1990) plan for reducing heart disease is "opening your heart to a higher self" (p. 229). Because mind, body, and spirit are all interconnected, practices that focus on the physical heart alone are insufficient and lead to recurrent disease. By addressing the spiritual and emotional dimensions, comprehensive healing may begin.

Impressive empirical evidence has emerged for what many individuals have long known to be true: that spirituality and faith are important in health and well-being. People who attend church regularly have less cardiovascular disease, emphysema, and cirrhosis of the liver, and lower blood pressure (Comstock & Partridge, 1972). In a classic study performed in Alameda County, California, the researchers asked whether individuals regularly attended a church or synagogue. It was found that individuals with weak attendance had a mortality rate 2–3 times higher than those with strong attendance (Berkman & Syme, 1979).

Patients over age 55 undergoing open heart surgery who received comfort from their religious beliefs had a survival rate 3 times higher than those who did not have such beliefs (Oxman, Freeman, & Manheimer, 1995). In a review of existing research on the connection between spirituality and physical health, a strong positive relationship emerged (Matthews, Larson, & Barry, 1994). Among patients with cancer and heart disease, religious involvements were related to increased survival and quality of life and decreased anxiety, depression, anger, and substance abuse. In an impressive review of epidemiological studies, Levin (1994) concluded that a belief in God lowered mortality rates and increased health and well-being.

The reasons for the connection between belief and health are not fully understood. Levin (1994) suggested that religious involvements produce a sense of belonging and fellowship that buffers the negative effects of stress by triggering biological processes that lead to improved health. Eliot (1995) suggested that religious support offers a sense of optimism about the future and that the forgiveness, hope, and understanding provided by religious involvements are powerful stress reducers. Benson and Stark (1996) argued for a biological predisposition to believe in a higher power and to practice those beliefs. He suggested that the health benefits of belief are rooted in the ability to short-circuit the nonproductive worries and doubts that elicit the fight-or-flight response. These nonproductive thoughts lead to stress-related illnesses and hinder healing capacities. Justice (1988) said that a sense of inner control is easier to obtain for those who have strong faith and that this sense of control reduces the risk of disorders and enhances psychological well-being.

We suggest that faith and spirituality constitute the highest form of secure attachment, one that transcends human relationships (J. D. Quick, Nelson, Matuszek, Whittington, & Quick, 1996). We agree with Benson and Stark (1996) that it is instinctual to form secure attachments with God. Opening one's heart to a higher power, as Ornish (1990) calls the process, means knowing that there is a higher power to help and that one simply needs to ask. This applies to all spiritual teachings, whether Protestant, Catholic, Jewish, Moslem, Hindu, Buddhist, or from any other religion. A person of faith always has a secure attachment figure and thus a sense of felt security.

This security is the basis for transformational coping. Empirical support for this position can be found in the work of Sethi and Seligman (1993), who explored studies dating back 100 years to find an association between religious beliefs and well-being. They looked at optimistic versus pessimistic thinking in three faiths, Orthodox Judaism, Calvinism, and Islam, and found that the optimism stemmed from the hope that these religions engendered.

Spirituality and faith provide powerful ways of managing one's response to stress. When used for preventive stress management, they provide optimism, inner control, and a secure attachment that transcends human relationships. Their connection with health and well-being is impressive.

Emotional Outlets

Use of emotional outlets is excellent for ventilating the effects of stressful events such as job loss (Spera, Buhrfeind, & Pennebaker, 1994) and accelerating the process of coping with such events (Pennebaker, Colder, & Sharp, 1990). Unfortunately, there are often social barriers to use of emotional outlets. People learn to keep their feelings to themselves. Some individuals learn not to cry to avoid appearing weak. However, there is a price to be paid for inhibition—emotional outlets provide an important means of dissipating stress-induced energy that may otherwise become counterproductive (Pennebaker, 1990). Talking with coworkers, friends, and other people; writing out one's feelings in one form or another; and acting out the feelings in a controlled way are all viable means to release tension arising from organizational demands. In a review of the evidence concerning the cancer-prone personality, Eysenck (1996) noted that the occurrence of cancer is substantially correlated with the suppression and inhibition of emotion. Cancer-prone individuals tend to suppress emotions like fear and anger and appear to other people to operate on an even keel.

Talking It Out

The simple, age-old method of "talking it over" is an effective means of emotional expression. Social support from others, whether they are colleagues at work or trusted friends, provides catharsis, or emotional ventilation; this may be the primary mechanism through which social support affects health (Gottlieb, 1996). Groups can provide this catharsis if they are safe, supportive environments in which individuals feel secure. Kahn (1966) argued that catharsis initiates the recovery of the autonomic nervous system after stress arousal.

Sometimes managers are uncomfortable with the expression of emotion at work. They fear that stirring things up may disrupt productivity. However, discussion of feelings in a controlled atmosphere can relieve tension and allow employees to return to productive work. Discussing stressful situations allows individuals to work through their feelings and get beyond the unwanted intrusions on their concentration (Braverman, 1992).

The value of talking it out is not only in the expression of feelings but also in the opportunity to reconstruct and integrate the experience through verbal expression. Talking about a stressful experience allows some people to put the experience behind them and move on. Talking it out is associated with reduced stress, reduced strain on the restorative mechanisms of the body, a reduced tendency to ruminate and obsess about events, and an increased likelihood of making sense of the stressful experience (Everly & Mitchell, 1995).

Writing It Out

Writing letters and keeping journals or diaries are age-old, socially accepted methods for expressing emotions that do not find adequate expression elsewhere. For example, Abigail Adams used letter writing as a method of coping with the stressful 10-year period surrounding the Revolutionary War (Gelles, 1994). The use of writing as a means of emotional release at the workplace is most visible in office or interdepartmental memos. Corporate executives, secretaries of state, and humble managers have been embarrassed, demoted, or expelled as a result of angry and intolerably candid memos. At the same time, a well-tempered and carefully composed letter or memorandum can be an effective tool for ventilating tension as well as communicating information that may be useful in moderating future demands.

For a written communication to be emotionally cathartic without jeopardizing one's good standing, the first draft should be written while the frustration or anger is fresh, but it should be saved for a day or two to be revised under calmer circumstances. Often the process of writing the draft is an end in itself; many hostile memos and letters of resignation have landed in the wastebasket, with the writer much relieved and no one the wiser. Written expressions of emotion, whether kept to oneself or shared with others, should be viewed as a legitimate form of stress control and not, as sometimes happens, a childish self-indulgence. Provided the writing process serves to ventilate the feelings, it is useful.

Writing about emotional trauma can be beneficial for the immune system. Pennebaker and his colleagues demonstrated this by asking a group of undergraduate students to write for 20 minutes on 4 consecutive days (Pennebaker, Kiecolt-Glaser, & Glaser, 1988; Pennebaker & Susman, 1988). Half of the students were asked to write about a trauma in their lives, and the other half were asked to write about trivial events. Blood samples were taken before, after, and throughout the exercise, and visits to the health center were monitored for 4 weeks before and 6 weeks after the experiment. The students who wrote about their traumas showed an increase in immune system activity, whereas those who wrote about trivial events showed no change. The study was conducted during midterm examinations and peak cold and flu season. The self-disclosing group made fewer visits to the health clinic, and the visits of the group writing about trivial events increased. Writing about emotional trauma, therefore, can improve immune system functioning and reduce the need to seek health care.

Acting It Out

There are many ways of releasing tension by "acting it out." Crying, shouting, screaming, and especially laughing are all legitimate forms of expression. They need not happen in public to be effective. Anger can be talked out, cried out, or yelled out. Other, more creative avenues can also be explored. The manager of a small retail shop, for example, found that beating a pillow with a plastic baseball bat for 15 or 20 minutes after particularly stressful days during peak season gave him his appetite back and made his evenings at home much more enjoyable. Other ways of acting it out include throwing darts at a dartboard or punching a punching bag.

The two guidelines for acting out emotions are (a) that no one is harmed, including the person who is expressing his or her feelings, and (b) that the action is truly effective in releasing tension. Within these guidelines, pillow fights, punching bags, dartboards, pulling weeds, and a variety of other creative solutions are all permissible.

The role of humor in managing stress bears special mention. Tension often is released through laughing. One Type A individual expressed the value of her cadre of Type B friends by remarking that they poked fun at her and made her laugh at herself. Talking with trusted colleagues can often help one see the funny side of stressful situations.

Physical Fitness

Employee wellness and corporate fitness programs have proliferated over the past 3 decades, making physical exercise much more available to employees (Gebhardt & Crump, 1990). The enthusiasm for exercise and physical fitness as a means of health promotion may seem relatively recent, yet the concept and practice of physical fitness has a long history. The first printed work recommending exercise as a health-promoting and disease-preventing activity was published in Seville in 1553 by Christobal Mendez (Kilgour, 1960). The first company-supported recreation and fitness program in the United States may have been the one started by the National Cash Register Company in 1904 (Duggar & Swengios, 1968). The United States military services have long and distinguished histories of physical fitness regulations and standards for their personnel (Nelson, Quick, & Quick, 1989).

There are three core elements of physical fitness, as reflected in Exhibit 11.1: aerobic fitness, muscle flexibility, and muscle strength training. These aspects of physical fitness may be achieved in various ways other than through employee wellness programs. For example, recreational sports and activities such as bowling, softball, horseback riding, racket games, gardening, and chopping wood all contribute to physical fitness and may also serve as physical outlets for stress-induced energy, frustration, and aggression. There are specific benefits in these various forms of physical activity, such as increased energy, strength, and flexibility.

Aerobic Fitness

Aerobic fitness refers primarily to the cardiovascular fitness achieved through aerobic exercise, which is any form of repetitive physical activity that produces sustained heart rate, respirations, and metabolic rate for a period of at least 20–30 minutes. Jogging, swimming, aerobic dance, brisk walking, rowing, continuous bicycling, vigorous tennis or other racket games, and cross-country skiing are examples of such exercise. The key is that the exercise must involve the large muscle groups and be rhythmic and continuous. Aerobic exercise is the only form of exercise that can predictably produce cardiovascular fitness. An 8-week aerobic training program experiment with 30 college students found enhanced parasympathetic nervous system activity and decreased central nervous system laterality to be mechanisms underlying particular aerobic training effects (Kubitz & Landers, 1993).

A recent review of the literature found that physical exercise leads to a variety of emotional, psychological, and physiological benefits (Salmon, 1993). One study of 11 male athletes aged 17–25 years found that aerobic power and body size influenced exercise-induced stress hormone responses in different environmental conditions (McMurray, Kocher, & Horvath, 1994). Hence, environmental conditions should be considered in one's exercise program. The effects of physical exercise on one's response to mental stress are mixed: One study found few reliable differences between experimental groups in the patterns of physiological responsivity to mental stress after training (Steptoe, Moses, Edwards, & Mathews, 1993), and a longitudinal study in the Netherlands found that regular exercise did not increase the resistance to stress-related disorders in 62 untrained men (de Geus, Van Doornen, & Orlebeke, 1993). However, in a study of 48 women, aerobic exercise was found to dampen physiological reactivity while reducing the frequency and intensity of anxiety-related thoughts (Rejeski, Thompson, Brubaker, & Miller, 1992). These findings are consistent with research showing that jogging and the relaxation response were consistently more effective for women than men (Berger, Friedmann, & Eaton, 1988). Berger, Friedmann, and Eaton also found no long-term benefits from jogging, suggesting the importance of maintaining a discipline of that activity to achieve benefits.

Muscle Flexibility

There are milder forms of physical fitness training that may also be important to individual preventive stress management. Because of the redirection of blood flow to the brain and large muscle groups in stressful circumstances, there is a need for a countereffect aimed at achieving flexibility and muscular relaxation through regular, rhythmic routines that are not necessarily intense enough to produce cardiovascular conditioning. Examples include simple calisthenics and "muscle-toning" exercises, modern dance, the recently popular traditional Chinese system of symbolic movements known as Tai Chi Chuan, and other systems of Eastern origin such as hatha yoga and aikido.

Muscle stretching and flexibility training may be used in the context of relaxation training because the practice lowers subjective and objective states of arousal (Carlson, Collins, Nitz, & Sturgis, 1990). Tai Chi, a moving meditation, is characterized as a moderate physical activity that may have superior effects in recovery from stressful events (Jin, 1992). During a 6-week study of employees in an electronics assembly plant, modest improvements in mood and flexibility were found as the result of a daily 10-minute strength and flexibility program (Pronk, Pronk, Sisco, & Ingalls, 1995). Muscle flexibility and strength are related; it is difficult to develop full strength in tense muscles that lack flexibility.

Muscle Strength Training

Muscle strength training is a third component of overall physical fitness, and it may be central to the successful management of specific demands or stressors. Some occupations and work tasks require muscle strength for successful performance. For example, U.S. Air Force pilots who were put on a weight-training program for increasing muscle strength were able to tolerate higher gravitational (G)-forces caused by high linear accelerations in fighter aircraft such as the F-15 Strike Eagle than pilots in an aerobic training program or control group. Muscle strength training by itself does not usually achieve cardiopulmonary conditioning, but it can be effective in venting hostilities, relaxing tense muscles, and improving self-image. Furthermore, such strength training increases muscle mass, which can boost the rate at which the body burns calories. At least one study found that muscle strength training (i.e., anaerobic exercise) did not produce as positive a set of outcomes as did aerobic training (Norris, Carroll, & Cochrane, 1990).

Physical Fitness: Overall Evidence

The physiological and psychological benefits that have been claimed for regular physical exercise are legion. Decreased muscle tension, heightened mental energy, improved feelings of self-worth, greater sense of well-being, improved memory, greater self-awareness, and realization of "peak experience" have been claimed, as have the workplace benefits of decreased absenteeism, improved performance, and lower attrition. Although some of the evidence is anecdotal, consisting largely of individual testimonials, the consistency and fervor of these reports are striking. Well-designed, controlled studies confirm many of the results.

The psychological benefits of exercise have been demonstrated among both the mentally well and those with psychological and psychiatric disorders (Baun, Bernacki, & Herd, 1987). Aerobic exercise has been associated with an increased sense of control, lower levels of depression and anxiety, fewer sick days, and increased work satisfaction (Justice, 1988; Pauley, Palmer, Wright, & Pfeiffer, 1982).

There is even greater support for some of the physiological benefits of exercise. Regular programs of vigorous conditioning have fairly consistently been found to increase bone density, lower resting heart rate and blood pressure, decrease the formation of blood clots, improve oxygen utilization, and create a more favorable cholesterol and triglyceride profile (Ornish, 1990). Clinical studies have demonstrated a salutary effect on such stress-related problems as high blood pressure, back and other muscle aches, chronic lung disease, diabetes, and mobility difficulties in the elderly (Fentem & Bassey, 1979; Yarvote, McDonheh, Goldman, & Zuckerman, 1974). Epidemiological studies have confirmed that a sedentary lifestyle increases the likelihood of heart attack in comparison with a lifelong pattern of regular physical activity (Leon, Connett, Jacobs, & Rauramaa, 1987; Paffenbarger & Hyde, 1980).

Evidence indicates that even moderate exercise leads to health benefits. In one study of 10,000 men and 3,000 women, the participants were given treadmill tests and divided into five groups ranging from least to most fit (Blair, Kohl, & Paffenberger, 1989). Researchers followed the participants for 8 years to determine the relationship between their level of physical fitness and death rates. The results showed that the death rate of the least fit group was more than 3 times higher than that of the most fit group. In addition, walking 30 minutes per day (or the equivalent) was as effective in preventing early death as running 30 miles per week.

Similarly, in a 7-year study of over 12,000 middle-aged men, those who engaged in moderate exercise had one third fewer deaths from all causes than those who did not exercise (Leon et al., 1987), and those who engaged in high levels of exercise reaped no more health benefits than those who exercised moderately.

The physiological pathways by which exercise achieves its beneficial cardiovascular effects are already partly known, and each year more information is available. The relationship between exercise and the stress response is also becoming more clearly understood. Both stress and exercise stimulate an increase in the catecholamines adrenaline and noradrenaline, the effects of which were described in chapter 3. However, the Institute for Aerobics Research in Dallas, Texas, has found that under resting conditions, aerobically fit individuals have a lower level of catecholamines in their bloodstream. In addition, the institute has found aerobically fit individuals to have a better interplay between their activating, stress-responding sympathetic nervous system and their relaxing, restorative parasympathetic nervous system. This finding suggests that fit individuals may be less physiologically reactive in stressful situations. Eliot (1995) suggested that exercise flushes out the body through the cleansing action of the lymphatic system.

The mechanisms by which exercise achieves its psychological effects are much less clear. Part of the answer may be the improved self-image that comes with a trimmer, well-conditioned body. Regular exercise also results in more restful sleep. Some researchers have suggested that the primary effect of any form of exercise is diversion—a mental break (Morgan, Horstman, Cymerman, & Stokes, 1980). Exercise allows an individual to divert attention from a stressor and receive emotional relief through an alternative. Most intriguing is the recent evidence that vigorous exercise can lead to a transient quadrupling of the blood levels of *endorphins,* which are naturally occurring morphinelike hormones associated with pain relief and feelings of well-being (Gambert, Hagen, Garthwaite, Duthie, & McCarty, 1981). The mood-elevating effect of exercise may in fact be a naturally produced biochemical "high."

Whatever the mechanism, there is general agreement that regular physical exercise is an effective stress reduction technique for many individuals. Management support for exercise programs is reflected in the multimillion dollar health and fitness programs initiated by Kimberly-Clark, Xerox, Exxon, Tenneco, and numerous other corporations. Rather than focusing on only one or two modes of exercise, most programs offer a variety of activities. Fitness programs at many large companies are endowed with a range of sophisticated conditioning equipment and extensive facilities, but managers interested in exercise programs should recognize that a large capital investment is not a prerequisite for an effective program. Classrooms, rooftops, large multipurpose indoor rooms, and parking lots have all been used successfully. More important than facilities is the availability of a small number of well-trained fitness instructors and the scheduling of time.

As a final caution, individuals interested in starting a personal or company exercise program should be aware of safety guidelines. First, people who have not exercised regularly should begin gradually. Walking and easy bicycling are generally safe and easy ways to start. When able to walk briskly or bicycle for 30 minutes a day, most people can begin a program of jogging, more vigorous bicycle riding, swimming, or other activity. Anyone with diabetes, heart disease, lung disease, or a history of other serious medical illness should see a physician before beginning an exercise program. In addition, many medical organizations and practicing physicians recommend that those over the age of 35 check with their physician before starting a program of regular exercise. Although this is certainly the cautious approach, it can be costly and is probably unnecessary for individuals who have been in good health and who use good judgment in choosing their exercise. If a person chooses to see a physician, it should be a physician who is in good physical condition and is attuned to the monitoring of exercising individuals.

A second caution is that there should be an *exercise plan* that includes gradual conditioning and sufficient warm-up and cool-down periods. Individuals who suffer adverse consequences of exercise programs usually have attempted to progress too rapidly or have failed to recognize their own limits.

Finally, exercise is for enjoyment and relaxation. Some individuals, particularly those with the Type A behavior pattern, turn exercise into another form of competition and, as a result, create more tension and distress for themselves. Individuals should be careful to choose a form of exercise that is stress relieving rather than stress inducing.

Nutrition

An effective program of self-care that helps individuals manage their response to stress must include nutrition. Too often, stressed individuals eat too much, eat too little, or eat the wrong foods. When one is overwhelmed with life's responsibilities, it seems much easier to drop by a fast-food restaurant than to plan a more nutritious meal. A long-term high-fat junk food diet can impair the immune system (Justice, 1988), and what one eats is even more important when one is under stress. The production of cortisol is enhanced during stressful times, which causes the body both to retain salt and to crave more salt. Stress also alters the body's ability to metabolize carbohydrates, and catecholamines can cause an increased appetite for sweets (Eliot, 1995).

What one eats can have an impact on attention span, memory, and mood, similar to the effects of drugs. Studies have shown that a high-carbohydrate, low-protein meal induces a relaxed mood and reduced mental acuity, whereas a low-carbohydrate, high-protein meal does the opposite (Spring, Maller, Wurtman, Digman, & Cozolino, 1982–1983). When one eats is also of importance. A stable flow of blood sugar is essential for responding to stressors effectively. The brain needs a steady flow of glucose to function properly. The body uses nutrients more efficiently with four or five small meals a day. Individuals who ingest the bulk of their caloric intake in one large evening meal risk weight gain and increased cholesterol levels.

Chronic stress is associated with increased blood cholesterol levels, a risk factor for heart disease and other maladies. Research by Ornish (1990) has shown that managing stress helps lower blood cholesterol levels and reverses obstructions in blood vessels. Along with stress management, Ornish prescribes a diet that is very low in fat for reversing heart disease. His studies have indicated that a diet in which fat is limited to less than 10% of total calories, combined with the use of stress management activities for 1 hour per day, can reverse the progression of heart disease. Ornish's reversal diet consists of 10% fat, 70–75% carbohydrate, 15–20% protein, and 5 mg of cholesterol per day. His prevention diet is similar, with fats no more than double the amount in the reversal diet. Ornish recommends that total cholesterol levels be kept lower than 150 mg, and that the ratio of total cholesterol to high-density lipoprotein (HDL) cholesterol be less than 3.0 (HDL is the healthy form of cholesterol).

As new findings are published about nutrition and diet, recommendations can become complex and daunting. The following 10 steps compose a comprehensive but simple prescription for a healthy diet that enhances the ability to cope with stress (M. Davis, Eshelman, & McKay, 1995).

1.   Eat a variety of foods.
2.   Maintain an ideal weight. Excess weight is associated with a plethora of health risks, including diabetes, heart attack, and

stroke. Even a few extra pounds can affect self-esteem and the ability to respond to stress.

3. Avoid fats. The typical American diet is 37% fat, which is too high and puts many people at risk.

4. Eat more whole foods. By eating raw or steamed vegetables, fruits, and grains such as rice and cereals, one increases the consumption of fiber, which is important for weight control and disease prevention.

5. Avoid sugar. Providing nothing but calories, sugar produces a quick "high," after which the blood sugar drops to a level lower than before the sugar was ingested. This rollercoaster effect is energy depleting. Complex carbohydrates, in contrast, provide a more stable source of energy.

6. Use salt in moderation. Sodium is particularly hazardous to those with high blood pressure.

7. Use alcohol in moderation. High in calories, alcohol depletes the body of B vitamins, which are important in coping with stress.

8. Use caffeine in moderation. Caffeine induces the fight-or-flight response and inhibits the ability to cope with stress. It also depletes the body of vitamin B.

9. Use vitamin and mineral supplements. There is considerable controversy about such supplementation of the diet. However, stressed individuals require more of all vitamins and minerals, especially the B vitamins. Ornish recommends a multivitamin without iron.

10. Eat frequent meals and eat calmly. Frequent meals avoid the stresses of being overly hungry and maintain more constant blood sugar levels. Natural relaxation can be derived from nutritious foods eaten in a peaceful setting.

Summary

This chapter has reviewed five categories of secondary, or response-directed, methods of preventive stress management for individuals. Whereas the primary prevention methods of chapter 11 are aimed at helping individuals alter the demands to which they are subject, the secondary prevention methods of chapter 12 are aimed at helping individuals alter their reactivity and responsiveness to inevitable demands. The two chapters therefore present complementary sets of skills for preventive stress management. This chapter presented in detail a variety of methods for eliciting the relaxation response, from progressive relaxation and meditation through hypnosis and biofeedback. The chapter also discussed spirituality and the faith factor, and the importance of emotional outlets, physical fitness, and nutrition in achieving a healthy responsiveness to stressful events. A third set of preventive stress management methods focuses on the symptoms of distress. These tertiary techniques are described in chapter 13. The three levels of prevention methods form a comprehensive set of tools that individuals can use to manage the stress of their lives.

13

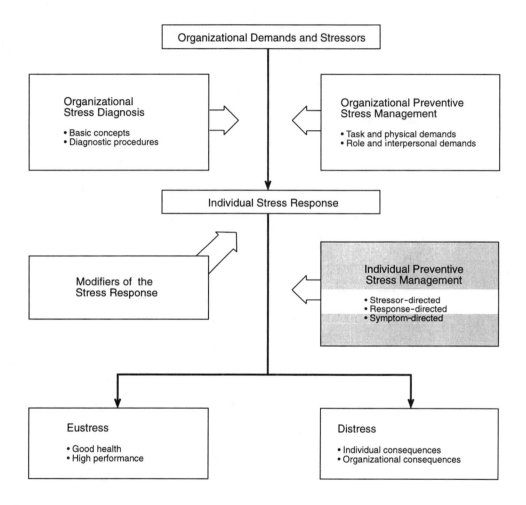

Tertiary Prevention for Individuals: Healing the Wounds

This is the third of three chapters concerning preventive stress management for individuals. In the best of all organizations, primary and secondary prevention would be enough to manage the demands of work life; organizational change and individual adaptation would allow employees to achieve good health and high performance. Yet despite the best efforts of individuals and organizations, distress does occur; people suffer, organizations break down, and healing the resulting wounds becomes necessary. Tertiary prevention concerns therapeutic treatment for those who suffer; it is symptom-directed. Tertiary prevention and treatment of casualties may, in some cases, be a first-order priority, as in the ICI-Zeneca stress management strategy presented in chapter 14. The present chapter discusses tertiary prevention and therapy from psychological, medical, and behavioral perspectives, giving consideration to both self-help and professional help. The chapter is organized around the three categories of tertiary prevention noted in Exhibit 11.1. The final section of the chapter presents an approach for a preventive stress management plan.

This chapter presents an overview of action options, rather than a comprehensive or in-depth treatment guide, for the many forms of individual and organizational distress, disorders, problems, and diseases discussed in chapters 4 and 5. Most of the forms of individual and organizational distress discussed in those chapters have multiple causes or contributing factors beyond stress. Some tertiary treatment interventions may be multifaceted and complex, therefore, requiring multidisciplinary efforts for successful healing within an organization. We refer the reader to books that provide a more in-depth discussion of individual health problems such as cardiovascular disease, cancer, mental illness, and personality problems (Cooper, 1996) or of the organizational problems of layoffs, downsizing, and major restructuring (Noer, 1993).

A word about our philosophy of treatment and healing is in order. Our presumption is that healing is a natural process and that individuals, groups, and organizations have a great capacity to heal themselves. In addition, individuals, groups, and organizations may at some point in time, or for specific forms of distress, benefit substantially from the help of trained and licensed professionals. A balance of self-help and professional help may be most suitable for those in distress. Although professionals differ in their philosophies of treatment, there are more important differences in the efficacy and evidence of effectiveness of the treatments they use or propose. The choices are more than differences of opinion; they are matters of evidence. Western medicine, including surgery and drug treatment, is basically suited for acute infection and chronic, life-threatening diseases such as hypertension, diabetes, and cancer. Osteopathic medicine addresses some of the same problems as Western medicine, but with a more preventive orientation. Traditional Chinese Medicine and Ayurveda (the ancient tradition in Indian medicine) are effective for a variety of musculoskeletal problems, digestive disorders, and other self-limited conditions, as opposed to life-threatening conditions; these approaches facilitate a person's natural healing energy. Traditional Chinese Medicine, Ayurveda, psychotherapeutic approaches, and other forms of alternative medicine may also be used to support and complement the effects of Western medical treatment of more serious health problems. Understanding treatment efficacy and evidence of effectiveness is important to the acceptance of responsibility for one's health.

Many professionals use more than one philosophy or orientation in their treatment of disorders. For example, Siegel (1990) is a traditionally trained cancer surgeon who, after 15 years of performing traditional cancer surgery, began to address some of the psychological and spiritual concerns of his patients in individual and group settings. He found that love and medicine both contributed to the healing process for some cancer patients (whom he called "exceptional"), sometimes yielding miraculous cures. Miraculous cures, or miracles, are so labeled because the healing that occurs is unexplainable on the basis of the medical and psychological evidence; that is, there is a quantum improvement in health. Chopra (1989) used the principles of quantum physics in a medical context to help explain unanticipated, miraculous cures that appear to be very much out of the ordinary to mainstream doctors. He suggested that releasing the full force of a person's natural capacity to heal lies at the root of all healing. Related to miraculous cures and quantum healing is the placebo effect in medicine. Benson (1985) suggested that the placebo effect in medicine hinges on (a) the patient's beliefs and expectations, (b) the physician's beliefs and expectations, and (c) the relationship between the patient and the physician. If one generalizes to the psychological healing process, the same three factors may well influence therapeutic success, that is, the patient's beliefs and expectations, the therapist's beliefs and expectations, and the relationship between the patient and the therapist.

Psychological Counseling and Therapy

Psychological counseling and therapy are forms of tertiary prevention and treatment appropriate for individuals, groups, and organizations. This section of the chapter reviews five categories of psychological counseling and therapy and provides illustrative examples of their application in the workplace: symptom-specific programs, individual psychotherapy, behavior therapy, group therapy, and career counseling. With the exception of some of the symptom-specific programs such as alcohol counseling, most employee programs aim to provide short-term and supportive therapy. Individuals requiring long-term or intensive therapy are almost invariably referred to outside professionals or community facilities. A wide variety of psychological counseling and therapies are available (Gurman & Messer, 1995; McKay & Paleg, 1992). Wagenaar and La Forge (1994) have provided some guidelines and cautionary notes for the theory and practice of stress counseling. In one study of 250 English post office employees and 100 controls, stress counseling led to significant declines in sickness absence days and events, clinical anxiety, somatic anxiety, and depression, although job satisfaction and commitment were unaffected (Cooper & Sadri, 1991).

In November of 1995, *Consumer Reports* magazine concluded that patients benefited substantially from psychological counseling and therapy, that long-term treatment was considerably better than short-term treatment, and that psychotherapy alone did not differ in effectiveness from medication plus psychotherapy (Seligman, 1995). The *Consumer Reports* data suggested that psychologists, psychiatrists, and social workers are equally effective treaters and are better than marriage counselors and family doctors. Finally, Seligman (1995) concluded that patients whose length of therapy or choice of therapist was limited by insurance availability or managed care had worse outcomes. Hence insurance coverage limitations and managed health care may have an adverse impact on mental health, so that important clinical and administrative issues need to be addressed in this context (Feldman & Fitzpatrick, 1992).

Symptom-Specific Programs

Alcoholism, drug abuse, cigarette smoking, and obesity were among the most common stress-related symptoms discussed in chapter 4. Many of the earliest ventures of business and industry into the field of counseling were in the area of alcoholism. Eastman Kodak, Dupont, Equitable Life, and Consolidated Edison of New York are among the companies that, decades ago, pioneered the development of employee alcoholism programs. The Association of Labor-Management Administrators and Consultants on Alcoholism (ALMACA) helps manage and staff alcohol abuse programs, and occupational alcoholism programs commonly exist in the United States. The extent of alcoholism and need for corporate involvement were recognized nearly 2 decades ago by Warshaw (1979), who wrote the following:

> In my view, any organization that does not have an alcoholism program, or which has not recently examined an established program to make sure that it is up to date and working well, is needlessly dissipating its human and financial resources and failing its responsibilities as a corporate citizen. (pp. 104–105)

Of the various reasons for establishing workplace alcoholism programs, the two most compelling are that they are capable of achieving high success rates, which many freestanding programs are not, and that they are cost-effective. The National Council on Alcoholism cites recovery rates of 33, 40, 50, 70, and 80% for occupational programs. An important element in successful programs is a "job jeopardy" or "performance approach," in which specific penalties, including dismissal, are part of a therapeutic contract with the employee (Warshaw, 1979).

The loss of productive time and additional expense from alcohol-associated accidents, absenteeism, and interpersonal troubles is considerable, and therefore it is not surprising that a review of occupational alcoholism programs concluded that these programs are generally cost-effective when well managed (Levens, 1979).

Although drug abuse, smoking cessation, and weight-control programs have not been as thoroughly studied, they nevertheless have an important role in preventive management programs. The U.S. military, for example, has been particularly concerned with weight-control programs. Similar programs aimed at smoking cessation have been slow in developing, but they are now gaining wider support.

Individual Psychotherapy

Whereas fitness and relaxation training have been popular and well-supported by industry, personal counseling may be the weakest part of employer-initiated preventive stress management programs. Although we list counseling under tertiary prevention, like other tertiary techniques it also can have an important impact as a primary or secondary prevention measure, depending on the availability and emphasis of counseling services. For example, psychological counseling may be tertiary prevention for a senior executive but constitute primary prevention for the tens, hundreds, or thousands of employees working under that executive.

In the context of stress management, most counseling is aimed at reducing or controlling the stress response by providing information and insight about the stressor or the individual's reasons for perceiving a certain condition as a stressor. Psychological counseling may be helpful to an individual in achieving a better fit with aspects of the organization. Programs vary considerably in their emphasis. Some are concerned primarily with providing psychological first aid, or support, for individuals during a time of crisis. Other programs provide short-term individual or family counseling to help resolve a specific problem or evaluate the need for ongoing therapy. Counseling also can be directed at developing specific personal skills, such as greater comfort with common stressful situations like public speaking or meeting new clients. Long-term in-depth psychotherapy to deal with major life issues is generally provided through outside services, with referrals made through the organization's employee assistance program (EAP), although some large companies include comprehensive in-house counseling programs.

For some, a stigma continues to be associated with psychological counseling and therapy, which reflects a lack of appreciation for the wide range of services provided by the discipline of psychology. Too often those receiving psychological counseling and therapy are classified as "mentally ill." There is an important distinction between stress-related adjustment problems or affective disorders and serious, major mental illness, the latter often requiring long-term in-depth psychotherapy, pharmacological intervention, or both. Psychological triage services, in an organization, such as provided by an EAP, should be able to help distinguish between people in these significantly different categories.

Another fear that sometimes inhibits the development of an effective counseling program is concern about the maintenance of confidentiality. Counseling programs must ensure the confidentiality of the managers, employees, and other organizational members who use the services including the security of any records related to those services. Accomplishing this may be somewhat more problematic in a small company, and the issue of confidentiality may turn out to be difficult enough to necessitate that counseling be handled by outside services.

Who is doing the counseling is also an important issue. Seligman (1995) suggested that psychologists, psychiatrists, and social workers seem to achieve equally positive results, whereas results by other counseling professionals do not appear to be as positive. A psychological consultant to Mobil Corporation, Moss (1981) suggested that senior management, as well as the organization's medical personnel and outside professional counselors, may play important roles in individual counseling and triage. For example, senior managers can help young managers and executives on the basis of their understanding of peer competition, problems with authority, career development, internal corporate relationships, and related issues, while referring young men and women to professional counselors when issues beyond their scope arise.

Psychotherapy offered by companies may include in-depth psychoanalysis, client-centered therapy, existential therapy, gestalt therapy, or other types of treatment. In the context of stress management, psychological counseling and therapy are primarily aimed at cognitive and behavioral interventions that provide individuals with insights into the psychodynamics of their perceptions and responses to stress and the use of these insights to cope more effectively with job stress. Benson's (1985) comments about the important role of the physician in the therapeutic relationship are relevent to psychotherapy, too. The beliefs of the particular therapist may be as important as, if not more important than, the particular school of therapy with which the counselor is affiliated in influencing therapeutic success.

Limited cost-effectiveness evaluations of individual counseling programs exist. For example, Jones and Vischi (1979) reviewed 22 counseling programs and found that significant reductions in the use of general health care services usually followed treatment for stress-related problems (Jones & Vischi, 1979). More recently, a study at McDonnell Douglas found reduced health claims, financial savings, and lower absentee rates for its EAP counseling "graduates" (Landy et al., 1994).

Behavior Therapy

Behavior therapy is a form of psychological counseling and intervention that places less emphasis on insight and psychological understanding and greater emphasis on achieving demonstrable changes in behavior. Whereas psychodynamic therapies may look to historical causes of current behavior, behavior therapy and behavior change strategies influence behavior by managing its consequences (i.e., reinforcers) (Luthans & Kreitner, 1985). The goal is to substitute new, socially effective responses for old, inappropriate, or distressing responses. Specific types of behavior therapy include systematic desensitization, modeling, assertiveness training, token economies, and aversion training.

An important principle of behavior therapy is that of *counterconditioning*. Counterconditioning is the process of unlearning an old reaction pattern by practicing a more desirable pattern—one that is incompatible with the old pattern. This is commonly done through a procedure known as *systematic desensitization*. The client is first taught to achieve a relaxed state, usually through one of the methods mentioned earlier in this chapter. He is then told to imagine a common situation that he finds stressful. The mental image usually undoes some of the relaxation and the client is reminded of the necessity of maintaining good relaxation. Eventually, the therapist presents a hierarchy of events or situations that the client finds increasingly stressful. Each time the client begins to respond with tension, she is reminded to substitute relaxation. Systematic desensitization involves substituting relaxation for tension in increasingly difficult situations.

Some therapists suggest that individuals prepare their own hierarchy of stressors related to a particular area of difficulty. Table 13.1 presents such a hierarchy for someone who finds public speaking difficult. The individual is asked to use an arbitrary scale (e.g., from 1 to 100) to rank the stressors according to the degree of disturbance or stress they create. When applied to a specific stressor, such as public speaking, behavior therapies serve a dual role as both stressor-directed and response-directed interventions.

Successive approximations to the desired behavior are applicable beyond the therapeutic encounter. Consider, for example, a manager with angina pectoris (i.e., chest pains from a heart condition) who has severe attacks whenever he speaks to large groups. These episodes might be prevented with larger doses of heart medication, but behavior therapy may be even more effective. The patient is first taught how to achieve relaxation. Then, in the therapeutic setting, he imagines himself in front of a small group and, as tension begins to develop, reestablishes a feeling of calm. Once this can be done during a therapy session, the individual proceeds to talking in front of a small, informal group. When he is able to remain calm and pain-free in a small group, he begins to speak to even larger groups; eventually, he can lecture to a large audience and respond to questions and criticisms without pain (Eliot, 1979).

A system of *self-reinforcement* is frequently encouraged by behavior

Table 13.1. Sample Hierarchy for Systematic Desensitization for Public Speaking

Rank	Degree of stress	Event
1	100	Presenting a serious managerial problem to an unsympathetic meeting of the company board—interruptions frequently made
2	95	Presenting as above, but to a more understanding audience
3	90	Presenting as in 1, but to a small, special committee instead of the full board
4	85	Giving a talk to a large gathering of the Rotary Club at a local hall
5	80	Being interviewed live for a TV news item
6	75	Receiving a telephone call from the managing director to attend a special board meeting as in 2 above
7	70	Briefly introducing a speaker to a large audience at a women's institute
8	65	Driving to the meeting described in 1 above
9	60	Receiving a letter requesting attendance next week at the meeting described in 3 above
10	55	Making a brief, recorded TV appearance
11	50	Giving a speech at a prize-giving ceremony at your old school
12	45	Standing up and heckling a speaker in a crowded hall at a political meeting
13	40	Making a prepared statement to a small workers' delegation about altered conditions of employment
14	35	Receiving a telephone call and invitation from the headmaster with reference to 11 above
15	30	Giving a "pep" talk to the members of your department at work
16	25	Acting as chairperson in a lighthearted debate at the workers' social club
17	20	"Officiating" for an hour at the youth club disco patronized by your daughter
18	15	Giving directions to a group of tourists you meet in an art gallery
19	10	Being telephoned by the producer with respect to 10 above
20	5	Telling six of your colleagues in the staff dining room about some news items you have read

Note. From *A Behavioral Approach to the Management of Stress* (pp. 69–70), by H. R. Beech, L. E. Burns, and B. F. Sheffield, 1982, New York: Wiley. Reprinted with permission.

therapists. The individual sets certain behavioral objectives and identifies rewards that are freely available but that she reserves for reinforcing her successes. The manager with angina pectoris, for example, might reward himself for a major presentation with a 3-day weekend or lunch at a special restaurant.

Controlled research on systematic desensitization has demonstrated significant positive results. In a 2-year follow-up study of 57 college students with severe public speaking anxiety, 85% of those treated by systematic desensitization showed lasting improvement, compared with 50% improvement among those treated by dynamic psychotherapy and 22% improvement among those who received no treatment (Paul, 1967). In another randomized study of 35 individuals with three common phobias, 72% recovered completely through systematic desensitization versus 12% recovery in the control group (A. Lazarus, 1961).

Although some psychodynamic therapists have expressed the concern that treating symptoms without providing the patient with insights into their origin and meaning may result in the expression of the presumed underlying conflict in some other way, experienced behavior therapists frequently perform a functional analysis of behavior as part of their therapy and do help the patient gain some insight into the behavior. Moreover, maladaptive behaviors often become self-perpetuating; simply substituting a more rewarding response pattern may provide sufficient reinforcement and improvement in an individual's self-image to make insight irrelevant. Milton Erickson placed emphasis on achieving therapeutic change, rather than insight, holding that insight can be distinctly untherapeutic. Haley (1973) wrote that Erickson's "emphasis is upon bringing about change and expanding a person's world, not upon educating [the patient] about his inadequacies" (p. 67). Although it is effective for changing specific behaviors, behavior therapy may be less effective for global anxieties, for people with major maladaptive problems, and for individuals with marked personality disturbances.

Group Therapy

Individual counseling offers many potential benefits to employees, and behavior therapy may change specific behaviors. Group approaches may complement these methods with some distinct advantages. Group therapy makes efficient use of the therapist's time and skills, allowing limited resources to benefit more people. Group therapy may provide or strengthen social support in an organization while taking advantage of the influence of peer feedback. Peer pressure can serve as a powerful motivating mechanism for participation as well as for constructive personal change and growth. Group therapy and support are often used in conjunction with medical care of cardiovascular problems and cancer (e.g., Siegel, 1990).

There are many types of group therapy. It may be used for adapting to the stress of loss or for chronic mental illness and either on a short-term or a long-term basis (McKay & Paleg, 1992; Piper, McCallum, & Azim, 1992; Stone, 1996). Self-help or support groups formed of individuals sharing common stressful experiences may be quite helpful. For example, basic trainees adjusting to the stress and rigors of military life took part in support groups, through which most developed adequate self-reliance to complete the training program successfully (J. C. Quick, Joplin, Nelson, Mangelsdorff, & Fiedler, 1996). The common stressors for such a group may be organizational ones, which affect both home and work life, or outside stressors, which are relevant to the workplace because of the global impact they may be having on the individuals involved. Examples of issues considered by existing groups of managers (or their spouses) are living abroad, parenting without partners, two-career couples, and heavy travel schedules (Moss, 1981).

Group therapy may occur formally or informally in the context of the organization, or it may be obtained on outside time and paid for with the participant's own funds. When the therapy is provided by the workplace, the organization has a responsibility for the quality and potential ill effects. It is important to review the qualifications and experience of the group leader to ensure that they meet professional standards.

Career Counseling

Counseling for career development may be a proactive strategy of primary prevention, as discussed in chapter 9, or a therapeutic strategy of tertiary prevention for those who have experienced organizational restructuring, job loss, or organizational dead-ending (McDaniel & Gysbers, 1992; Spera, Buhrfiend, & Pennebaker, 1994). In other words, systematic attention to career development should help individuals progress along career paths in which the demands are suited to their skills and interests. If the demands are optimum, there should be little stress and even less distress. Unfortunately, this is not always the situation.

Sometimes individuals find themselves in jobs to which they are not suited. The person–job mismatch may result from the individual's personality, temperament, ability, or training; from the nature of the work environment and peer group; from promotions that were too rapid or too slow; or from a transitional crisis such as frequently occurs during midlife. Once any of these circumstances has occurred, career counseling of a remedial nature is warranted. Universities as well as professional organizations provide a wide variety of resources as a basis for sound career counseling (Gray, Gault, Meyers, & Walther, 1990). The Minnesota Multiphasic Personality Inventory (MMPI) may be used as a measure of personal adjustment in career counseling (Peterson & Clark, 1990), although a wide variety of other psychological tests may be useful to the career counselor working with an individual.

Traumatic Event Debriefing

Traumatic events such as job loss, aggression, harassment, discrimination, and violence may create levels of extreme stress for individuals in organizations and require therapeutic intervention aimed at preventing posttraumatic stress experiences (J. A. Miller, 1995; Murphy, Hurrell, Sauter, & Keita, 1995). Stressful life events may influence the subsequent course of psychotic illness (van Os et al., 1994). In military organizations, combat and war traumas may lead to personality change and the "heart-of-darkness" syndrome, which is characterized by a feeling of vulnerability, lack of empathy for the enemy, and a positive attitude toward killing (Bradshaw, Ohlde, & Horne, 1993). Whereas surveillance and public health planning may help avert some traumatic events such as workplace violence (Mack, Shannon, Quick, & Quick, in press), traumatic event debriefing may be useful to prevent posttraumatic stress disorder (PTSD) and the heart-of-darkness syndrome once a traumatic event has occurred. Milgram and Toubiana (1988) provided recommendations for identifying high-risk client groups who may be subjected to political or ideological bias for receiving psychological services in response to traumatic events. Marsella, Friedman, Gerrity, and Scurfield (1996) discuss ethnocultural issues in research and clinical application related to PTSD. Traumatic event debriefing is a psychological intervention and may be done individually or in a group (Busuttil & Busuttil, 1995). For individuals exposed to the same trauma, a structured group format may be helpful as an opportunity to piece together what happened (Busuttil & Busuttil, 1995). The theory of traumatic event debriefing suggests that ventilation and normalization of reactions afford protection against psychological sequelae; however, Bisson and Deahl (1994) have suggested that more research is needed to address empirically the efficacy of debriefing.

Professional caregivers may be exposed to secondary traumatic stress, or "compassion stress," as they help those working through traumatic events (Yassen, 1995). In this context, individual debriefing may be useful. For example, individual debriefing was helpful to some of the emergency service personnel who worked with victims of the Oklahoma City bombing of a federal office building because it promoted emotional processing and provided psychological support for the professionals. Short-term psychotherapy may also be useful as an intervention for the acute onset of posttraumatic stress at some time after the event has passed (Everly, 1994). However, crises and disasters are only the most extreme of traumatic events that create high stress for individuals. Job loss, relationship loss, death of a colleague or mentor, and a business failure such as bankruptcy are traumatic events appropriate for psychological debriefing or other forms of psychological intervention.

Traumatic event debriefing is a form of confessional process in which one confides in another; as such, it has healing and therapeutic power. Expressive writing as in diaries, as discussed in chapter 12, is a complementary way of promoting the emotional processing of a traumatic event to prevent PTSD (Pennebaker, 1990). Busuttil and Busuttil (1995) suggested that debriefing may not be appropriate as an "end of trauma" session for events that are ongoing over a period of weeks because the presentation of traumatic material without allowing sufficient time for the habituation of anxiety may serve as a retraumatization experience for some.

The changing economics and circumstances of industrial work life, as reflected in the range of organizational downsizing, restructuring, reengineering, and revitalization activities occurring (Gowing et al., in press), is a key traumatic event for many people at work. Sera, Morin, Buhrfeind, and Pennebaker (1994) found that people who wrote to express their feelings about the trauma of losing their jobs were significantly more likely to find employment in a short amount of time than controls. Hence, whereas traumatic event debriefing appears to be a useful psychological intervention for extremely stressful events, expressive writing about traumatic events such as job loss may also contribute to the prevention of posttraumatic stress experiences and subsequent psychological disorders and distress.

Medical Care

Standard medical care is another form of tertiary prevention for suffering, discomfort, distress, disability, and death from stress-induced conditions. When organizational change and individual adaptation have been pushed to the limit, individuals may present themselves to physicians with any of the range of stress-related conditions described in chapter 4. Until recently, physicians usually responded to stress-related illness with some ad hoc advice and, in many cases, a drug prescription. Through advances in behavioral medicine and occupational health, family physicians are increasingly recommending exercise, relaxation breaks, and other forms of primary and secondary prevention for individuals in need of additional stress skills. Growing public awareness of preventive medicine and health promotion leads people to seek help earlier and has thereby given physicians the opportunity to use more preventive approaches. Nevertheless, much of the care provided by physicians is still aimed at treating major manifestations of stress-related illness with medications, surgery, and sometimes physical therapy. We would prefer to see primary and secondary preventive measures used more frequently and more effectively; nevertheless, it is useful to review the range of benefits that can be derived from standard medical therapies.

Medications

Anxiety or nervousness is probably the most common symptom of distress treated by the family physician and general practitioner. Diazepam (e.g., Valium) is a widely known and commonly prescribed antianxiety drug. Its popularity with both physicians and patients is a testament to its perceived efficacy. For short-term use to help individuals through periods of crisis or unusually severe stress, diazepam and other antianxiety drugs are quite effective and reasonably safe (Rosenbaum, 1982). Antianxiety drugs may also be useful for the short-term treatment of insomnia. Continued use of such agents, however, is fraught with potentially serious problems. First, although it was not initially appreciated, diazepam and related drugs can be addictive and have a rather complex withdrawal pattern. Second, use of these drugs may be hazardous while performing activities requiring mental alertness. If poor work performance is one of the sources of stress, drugs can make the problem worse by dulling mental and physical capabilities. Finally, by blunting distressful feelings and making the individual feel better, antianxiety drugs may eliminate the motivating force for the individual to make effective, permanent life changes.

Although diazepam and related drugs are often prescribed as muscle relaxants, they may not be as effective as muscle relaxation training (e.g., progressive relaxation), massage, or the application of moist heat. Antianxiety drugs are sometimes used in low doses to treat alcohol abuse. Although this may represent the substitution of one addiction for another, diazepam probably allows for better work and social performance and is certainly less toxic to the body.

Depression, manifested by sleep disturbance, increased alcohol consumption, fatigue, muscle aches, and a variety of other symptoms, is another common stress-induced condition. Although they are not recommended as a long-term solution, antidepressant medications may be clinically effective for alleviation of depressive symptoms, providing enough of an improvement in a person's mental outlook to allow the person to make the necessary changes in coping style associated with long-term recovery (Ravindran, Griffiths, Waddell, & Anisman, 1995). When people feel better, they can make constructive life changes as part of a more permanent solution to the problems that precipitated the depression. It is unfortunate that many people shun the use of antidepressant medications, because these drugs are often highly effective as short-term therapy to facilitate the resolution of a major depression.

Other types of pharmacotherapy are also relevant to stress reduction. For example, medication for peptic ulcer disease, one of the classic stress-related illnesses, has undergone several advances in the recent past. Optimum healing of ulcers and prevention of ulcer complications require regular medical care and adherence to medication, diet, and other special advice. In addition, mild-to-moderate high blood pressure may respond well to pharmacotherapy. Angina pectoris, heart failure, and some of the other cardiovascular conditions may also benefit from pharmacological interventions. The drug buspirone is considered a treatment for coronary-prone behavior including hostility, anxiety, impatience, and stress (Littman, Fava, McKool, & Lamon-Fava, 1993). When an individual has any of these potentially serious problems, it is important to continue regular medical care; if relaxation, diet, and exercise are not sufficient, drug therapy is appropriate. Similarly, even though diet and exercise are the first-line treatment for adult diabetes, regular office visits and, if necessary, oral medications or insulin injections should not be avoided simply because an individual is being conscientious with diet and exercise regimens.

Surgery

Surgery is a tertiary preventive measure for serious medical distress, such as cardiovascular disease or cancer, but at the same time it is a psychological stressor that requires psychological intervention (Salmon, 1992). Coronary artery bypass surgery has become a popular treatment for arteriosclerosis of the coronary arteries and the resulting chest pains (angina pectoris). Bypass surgery is effective only for certain types of heart blockage, however, and despite the pain and expense involved, the procedure adds an average of only about 1 year of life beyond that offered by standard medical therapy. Relief of anginal pains following surgery makes the procedure worthwhile for most people in whom the surgery is indicated, but primary and secondary prevention are preferable. A related procedure, endarterectomy, is available to correct the blood flow in the arteries to the head in individuals having transient ischemic attacks (TIAs), or "little strokes."

Surgery is also available for the treatment of cigarette-induced cancers (such as lung or esophagus cancers), severe ulcer disease, certain types of arthritic deformities, some alcoholism-induced conditions, and the intractable foot infections to which persons with diabetes are prone. Surgical treatment of these conditions is sometimes effective, but it is invariably more costly, more painful, and less satisfactory than primary and secondary prevention.

A final caveat is in order regarding surgery for abdominal pain. There are many causes for recurrent abdominal pain, one of which is chronic and recurrent stress. Individuals suffering from such pains are constantly looking for a cure, and surgery is sometimes seen as the simple, definitive solution. Unfortunately, unless there is a specific diseased organ, surgery may be fruitless. Individuals suffering from recurrent abdominal pain— particularly women, in whom the potential causes of such pain are more varied—should insist on a careful evaluation and explanation of the likely problem before agreeing to surgery.

Physical Therapy

In the military and in some large companies, the physical therapist is an integral part of the medical care team. Often, however, the potential contribution of physical therapists to the treatment of stress-related illness is neglected. The human body is designed for a wide variety of functions (Jones & Barker, 1996), and physical therapy is intended to help individuals achieve or return to full function. It is particularly useful for individuals suffering from muscle tension in the back, neck, or elsewhere. People with arthritis, whose mobility or functioning is limited, can benefit from evaluation and treatment by a physical therapist. Special exercises, ultrasound treatments, whirlpool treatments for specific muscles and joints, and several other therapeutic methods are available.

Physical therapy in the form of massage treatment is available as Swedish massage and is an integral part of Traditional Chinese Medicine and osteopathy but not of Western medicine. Massage is a highly appropriate form of physical therapy for pain due to tension or soreness, in contrast to pain due to torn or ruptured tissue, in the large muscle groups.

For example, a professional massage or osteopathic treatment may help combat backache, neck ache, and other stress-related symptoms arising from tense muscles. It is preferred to muscle-relaxant drugs by many people and is less likely to have side effects than drug therapy. Massage may also reinforce the role of social support in a relationship.

Creating a Personal Preventive Stress Management Plan

Whether stress management is handled by the medical, psychology, social work, human resource, personnel, or occupational health department in an organization or left as an individual matter, each employee should be encouraged to develop his or her own preventive stress management plan. An appropriate plan may be simple and brief or more complex and elaborate. The planning process itself may be as important and valuable as the final product.

Many early stress management programs took a narrow, almost tunnel-vision approach to stress control, recommending exercise or relaxation alone as the solution. We have presented a wide range of methods of preventive stress management for individuals that vary in focus, complexity, cost, accessibility, and effectiveness. We recommend a systematic approach to creating a preventive stress management plan that consists of the following five steps: (a) identify demands and stressors, (b) identify stress responses, (c) identify action options, (d) make a plan, and (e) modify the plan.

Creating a preventive stress management plan is as much art as science. The process is time consuming at first, insight-oriented, individualized, and in the end, one of trial and error. Most people can formulate a basic plan without professional guidance. Information available in the text, text references, and the appendix of this volume should provide managers and other employees with sufficient background. There is always the option of professional guidance.

1. Identify Demands and Stressors

Self-observation is the first step in preventive stress management. Demands and stressors may be identified by an individual through an informal process of personal reflection or a more structured approach using one of the methods described in chapter 7. Cooper's Management Audit provides a conceptual framework for identifying stressors, but the Life Events Scale, Stress Diagnostic Survey, and Stressors Checklist are examples of more specific measurement tools (see chapter 7 for descriptions and citations). In using any standardized assessment method, it is important for the individual to bear in mind that it is merely a tool, not an end in itself. Individuals should come away from the diagnostic process not with a score or checklist pattern but with a knowledge of the specific stressors that exist in their life and the relative impact of these stressors.

2.   Identify Stress Responses

The signs of the stress response and resulting distress were listed and described in chapters 3 and 4. Individuals can learn to monitor their own stress responses and to note when, for example, their cigarette consumption is rising. Simply becoming aware of one's own stress and distress is the first step, including recognition of one's patterns of self-talk and worry. Responses can manifest themselves as subtle physiological changes such as a rise in heart rate, as behavioral changes such as increased smoking or alcohol consumption, as psychological changes such as depression or sexual dysfunction, or as frank medical symptoms such as headaches or chest pain. It is important for individuals to develop an internal barometer that monitors these responses and tells them when stress responses and distress are increasing. With some symptoms, it is not easy to determine the relationship to stress. Even the individual's personal physician may have difficulty separating stress from other causes of disease. Therefore, individuals should be cautious in attributing major symptoms to stress, particularly new or persistent ones, without medical confirmation. Behavioral measures, a daily log of stress-related symptoms, the Maslach Burnout Inventory, the Cornell Medical Index, and other diagnostic procedures described in chapter 7 are useful devices for structuring the identification of responses.

3.   Identify Action Options

Most people develop coping habits on their own. Identifying these habits, deciding which ones seem to work best, and learning to apply these methods when tension begins to develop is an important first step. In addition, as Exhibit 11.1 indicates, there is a broad set of action options for individual preventive stress management. An effective stress management plan depends on narrowing the action options to those that seem to be *acceptable*, *feasible*, and *appropriate* to the individual's particular demands, stressors, stress responses, and strain. First, acceptability of a specific method is a prerequisite for including it in a stress management plan. For example, a traditional activity such as knitting or a mystical relaxation technique such as Zen meditation may be wholly unacceptable to a Chase Manhattan Bank vice president; on the other hand, his life might be greatly improved by daily exercise, involvement in a men's prayer group, or use of progressive relaxation. Action options must be selected and adapted to fit one's lifestyle. Second, feasibility is important in identifying action options. Although most individual methods of preventive stress management require little in the way of equipment, a number require trained instructors, psychologists, physicians, or other professionals. If these individuals are unavailable or their cost is prohibitive, the action options are limited to those that involve minimal expense. However, one should balance the cost of prevention with the the cost of inaction with regard to the particular distress, which may be considerable to oneself, one's family, and one's organization. In contrast, some individuals value only what they have spent a significant amount of money on.

Finally, the action options should be appropriate to the person's particular demands, stressors, stress responses, and symptoms of distress. One reason for classifying preventive stress management methods as stressor-directed, response-directed, and symptom-directed is the help it provides in selecting specific methods for individual use. For example, the manager who deals with all aspects of her job except public presentations may benefit from using a stressor-directed technique. One of the illustrations of constructive self-talk given in Table 11.2 was of anticipation of a public address. Earlier in this chapter we demonstrated how systematic desensitization, a behavior therapy technique, can be used as a stressor-directed method for this problem. Other individuals are troubled more by specific responses than by specific stressors. Low backache is a common symptom that people may experience in response to a variety of demands. Relaxation training, physical exercise, and massage are response- and symptom-directed techniques that can be useful in countering the discomfort of low back pain. In considering organizational stressors, the individual may find it useful to classify demands and stressors as *changeable*, *avoidable*, or *inevitable*. While pursuing preventive stress management to moderate organizational demands, individuals can best use their energy in areas where the demands are avoidable or changeable.

4. Make a Plan

After an individual has identified the range of action options available, he or she should select the action options that seem most acceptable, feasible, and appropriate to formulate into a preventive stress management plan. Figure 13.1 provides an example of one individual's plan and can be used as a template. Although many people deal with daily stress without a written plan, a plan helps one think concretely about stress and accept responsibility for managing it preventively. A plan also serves as a contract with oneself and as a reminder of one's action options for managing stress. A plan provides for action options in the full range of individual prevention methods; however, many people rely on a limited subset of methods. In the example in Figure 13.1, the individual has no plan to seek professional help at this time. A plan that considers demands, stressors, stress responses, and work for the individual is sufficient.

5. Modify the Plan

Preventive stress management is as much art as science, and it is impossible to know in advance what methods work best for a particular individual. Therefore, the personal stress management plan should always be viewed as tentative, and the process of developing a plan should be seen as one of "trial and success." The bottom line is whether or not the individual feels a sense of relief and achieves the feeling we described earlier

PREVENTIVE STRESS MANAGEMENT PLAN

Name: Jon Dickinson   Date: 2-14-97

Personal Perceptions of Stress	1)Practice constructive self-talk
	2)Learn to recognize the inevitable
	3)_____
Personal Work Environment	1) Learn to say No! (nicely)
	2)Each day make a to do list and daily plan
	3)_____
Lifestyle Choices	1)Take an out-of-town 3-day weekend every 2 months
Leisure time use:	
Other:	2)Don't forget vacations
Relaxation Method(s)	1) Practice progressive relaxation each evening
	2) Use momentary relaxation at work
	3)_____
Physical Fitness	1)Jog 30 minutes every other day
	2)Tennis or golf each weekend
	3)_____
Emotional Fitness	1)Take time to talk-out work frustrations with the wife
	2) Practice controlled expression of anger at supervisors
Professional Help	1) None now
	2)_____

Figure 13.1. Personal preventive stress management plan.

as eustress. The basic question is, "When you use the action options outlined, how do you feel at the end of the day?"

If a particular activity in the stress management plan does not seem to make an individual feel any better or provide other benefits, an alternative activity might be considered. For example, some executives find video games to be quite relaxing, whereas others find them annoying and frustrating. Options that do not work can be replaced. One should avoid the trap of making an action option into a stressor. Even the most basic relaxation method can become a stressor if people worry about whether or not they are "relaxing correctly." Leisure activities such as vacations can become stressful if tight travel deadlines are set and one is overly concerned with achieving a "successful vacation." Finally, personal stress management is an evolutionary process. As new or more demanding situations arise or one's work environment changes, different methods may be needed to achieve the healthy, positive, constructive outcome defined earlier as eustress.

Summary

Chapters 11, 12, and 13 reviewed a diverse range of preventive stress management methods for individuals. Many of these methods are easily available to the individual with or without the help of management or the organization. Others, such as counseling or medical care, are available only if management provides them or if the individual makes an effort to seek them outside the organization. This chapter reviewed a range of psychological and medical treatment methods for which the individual may require professional help. In addition, the chapter discussed appropriate self-help methods for individuals. Management plays a central role in determining what supports are available, what activities are encouraged, and what facilities are provided. Some of the activities, such as comprehensive health promotion programs, can be extremely costly. Chapter 14 examines some of the programs that organizations are currently using to manage stress and provide healthy workplaces. The chapter also presents a model for formulating an overall preventive stress management strategy and some questions to consider in implementing such a program.

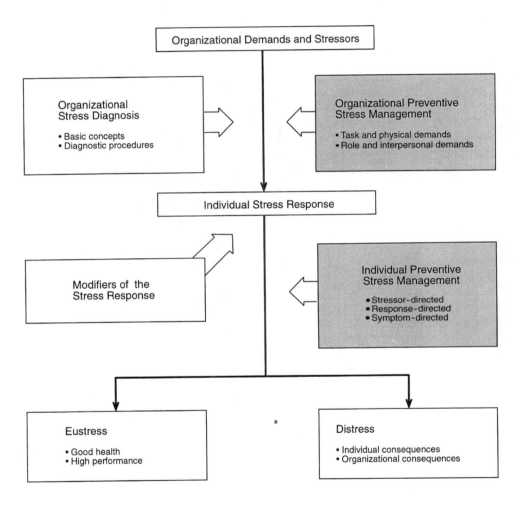

14

Preventive Stress Management for Healthy Organizations

The previous five chapters presented details of preventive stress management methods for organizations and individuals. These methods and practices are aimed at reducing distress at work while enhancing eustress, performance, and productivity. The purpose of this chapter is twofold. First, the chapter reviews programs with an organizational focus and programs with an individual focus, each falling under the rubric of "preventive stress management for designing healthy organizations." Second, the chapter presents a framework for implementing preventive stress management programs in organizations.

Prevention programs aimed at improving the health of companies benefit the organizations and the people in them because they reflect a value placed on people, human activities, and human relationships (Rosen, 1986; Schein, 1990). Healthy organizations are created through the sciences of design, rather than the natural sciences (Simon, 1969/1996). Implementing preventive stress management is an idiographic process accomplished on a case-by-case basis using a creative process of design. Cooper and Williams (1994) offered a design framework for healthy organizations based on the World Health Organization (WHO) and International Labour Office (ILO) definition of the aims of occupational health. Within the framework, the practitioner should know the organization well and design selectively to maximize health and optimize the person–environment fit and therefore the performance of each (Edwards, 1996; Edwards & Cooper, 1990).

Designing Healthy Organizations

The design and implementation of preventive stress management programs may begin with a focus on the organization or on the individual. The emphasis in programs with an organizational focus is on the overall social system, with the aim to design, change, or modify elements of the organization. The emphasis in programs with an individual focus is on the care, treatment, and development of the individual employee.

Programs With an Organizational Focus

Programs with an organizational focus take the organization as a whole as the level of concern, rather than the individual. The emphasis in these programs in on designing structures, establishing goals, implementing technologies, and developing organizational cultures as a healthy context in which individuals may produce, serve, grow, and be valued. The intention is the creation of healthy, productive work environments, as opposed to stress-free work environments at one extreme or sweatshops at the other. Programs with a focus on the organization include those concerning organizational culture and leadership, organizational structures for preventive stress management, organizational development, legal protection, and management consultation.

Organizational culture and leadership. Organizational culture is the connective tissue knitting the people, structures, technology, and goals of the organization together into one, cohesive whole (see Figure 5.3; also see Cummings, 1996; J. C. Quick, 1992; Schein, 1990). Healthy organizational cultures enhance the experience of eustress and performance by members of the organization, and unhealthy ones inhibit, frustrate, and distress people at work. Founders and other key organizational leaders are central to the creation and embedding of organizational culture (Schein, 1985). Herb Kelleher of Southwest Airlines and Gordon Forward of Chaparral Steel Company are two founders and organizational leaders who designed healthy organizational cultures in the context of industrial challenges in the service and manufacturing sectors of American industry.

Healthy organizational cultures are characterized by the values promoted by organizational leaders. Vaillant (1977) suggested that humor and altruism are among the attributes of individuals who adapt effectively to the stress of life. Metcalf and Felible (1992) characterized humor as the capacity to access joy in times of adversity. In fact, an American tax court, in a ruling 75 years ago, said that "success in business is largely obtained by pleasurable interest therein" (Wilson v. Eisner, 1922). Leaders who are able to help people through the culture of the organization meet difficult and stressful circumstances with good humor contribute to empowering them to overcome adversity. Another value of a healthy organizational culture, and one that Kelleher and Forward appear to share, is its emphasis on people, human activity, and human relationships. In business, people and profits are both important; they are not mutually exclusive nor necessarily in conflict.

SOUTHWEST AIRLINES. Herb Kelleher's leadership has enabled the workers at Southwest Airlines to accept challenges, overcome difficulties, and work through adversities with a sense of goodwill and humor (J. C. Quick, 1992). The early history of Southwest Airlines was characterized by challenge, difficulty, stress, struggle, and adversity. Grounded by legal battles from its founding in 1967 until its legal victory in 1971, Southwest was unable to fly an airplane commercially during its first 4 years. As a lawyer, Kelleher was professionally prepared to lead the organization through this time of adversity and stress. The people of Southwest Airlines emerged from this difficult period with a sense of humor and perspective rather than bitterness. This difficult liftoff period was followed by a mature period of success and achievement within the airline industry, as indicated by the company's recognition by the Department of Transportation for its high quality service and on-time performance.

In addition to the sense of goodwill and humor that characterize the organizational culture, there is an altruistic element in the culture of Southwest Airlines. The most concrete illustration of this charitable spirit is the personal and corporate generosity of the airline to the Ronald McDonald Houses within the network of cities served. In addition to the money given corporately and personally, Southwesterners including Chairman and CEO Herb Kelleher personally prepare and serve meals for families in the Ronald McDonald Houses. Humor and altruism are only two attributes of the airline's organizational culture; another is a seriousness about work and service performance. A careful review of internal company communication suggests that Herb Kelleher is a straightforward and direct communicator when it comes to the business and financial performance of the airline. Rather than creating a stress-free work environment, Kelleher has designed a challenging organizational culture that values both people and profits.

CHAPARRAL STEEL COMPANY. Gordon Forward is an engineer and metallurgist by education who worked to design an organizational culture with humanistic values similar to those expressed by Douglas McGregor in *The Human Side of Enterprise* (Forward et al., 1991). The five core values within the Chaparral culture are humor, trust, risk taking, challenge, and learning. Forward and his leadership team built an organizational culture that values people and involves them in a healthy, dynamic manner. Viewing Chaparral through the lens of a learning laboratory, Leonard-Barton (1992) described the organization as a complex ecosystem that integrates problem solving, internal knowledge, innovation and experimentation, and external information. Forward's concept of "mentofacturing" emphasizes engaging the mind (*mento*) in the production process, rather than treating the individual as an expendable tool. The steel industry in the United States has continued to be stressful and challenging during Chaparral's 25-year history, and the company has restructured in a way that ensures that people and profits are not tradeoffs. This has been done by building a team-oriented work environment and relying primarily on natural attrition if it is necessary to reduce personnel.

Organizational structures. There are at least two possible structures through which preventive stress management may be integrated and implemented in an organization: the preventive stress management task force and the organizational health center.

PREVENTIVE STRESS MANAGEMENT TASK FORCE. Preventive stress management programs may be integrated and implemented through the use of the task force concept. Large organizations need to integrate individual and organizational health programs and professional specialties concerned with different aspects of health. For example, physical fitness programs, counseling services, dietary functions, and alcoholism programs are scattered throughout various parts of an organization. Each program relates in one way or another to the healthy (e.g., fitness programs) and unhealthy (e.g., alcoholism services) ways individuals and organizations respond to stress. Preventive stress management task forces accomplish two primary purposes. First, the task force coordinates and integrates the related programs, with possible resource savings through reduced duplication of services or equipment. Second, the task force provides interdisciplinary blending of medical, physiological, psychological, and administrative specialties by ensuring each discipline is represented. The knowledge exchange and skill blending are both essential to the comprehensive response to organizational stress. A preventive stress management task force is best set up by an organization's top management and structured to involve at minimum representatives from departments of finance, human resources, medicine, psychology, and social work as well as line managers from the organization's primary businesses and operations.

ORGANIZATIONAL HEALTH CENTER. The idea of an organizational health center has been pioneered by Dr. Joyce Adkins, a lieutenant colonel in the U.S. Air Force Biomedical Science Corps (Adkins, 1995, 1996; Adkins & Schwartz, 1996). The mission of an organizational health center is to maximize human potential and productivity through optimum health—physical, behavioral, and organizational. Because organizational health is the responsibility of the executives, an organizational health center is best positioned at the executive level rather than in the medical, psychological, or human resources department. The organizational health center staff should be an integrated, multidisciplinary team of professionals including psychological, medical, and organizational development specialists. An organizational health center monitors occupational stress hazards and risks, personal strain and distress, and coping resources using interviews, observations, archival data, and self-report questionnaires. Figure 14.1 shows Occupational Stress Inventory (see chapter 7, page 129) results for five U.S. Air Force organizations: two air logistics and depot maintenance centers (AFMC-1, AFMC-2), two pilot training organizations (AETC-1, AETC-2), and one air combat unit (ACC). Although these data show little difference across the five organizations on the four measures of coping resources, Figure 14.1 suggests two stress and strain differences. First, members of the two AFMC organizations, compared with the other three organizations, report higher levels of role stress (i.e., insufficiency, ambiguity, and boundary) coupled with higher levels of strain (i.e., vocational, psychological, and interpersonal). Second, the ACC unit members, compared with the other four organizations, report higher levels of responsibility and physical stress without notably higher personal strain and distress. These and other data may be used to structure organizational development interventions for improving work conditions; to design education and training programs; to share information with leaders and employees throughout an organization; and to enrich the psychological health services for everyone in the organization. Preliminary studies suggest an organizational health center may help decrease mortality rates and productive years lost, medical visits and health care utilization rates for job-related illness and injury, and workers' compensation claims.

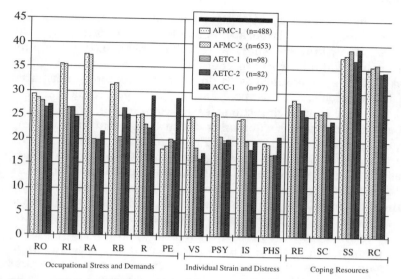

Figure 14.1. Occupational stress in five U.S. Air Force organizations. Courtesy of the United States Air Force. RO = Role overload, RI = Role insufficiency, RA = Role ambiguity, RB = Role boundary, R = Responsibility, PE = Physical environment, VS = Vocational strain, PSY = Psychological strain, IS = Interpersonal strain, PHS = Physical strain, RE = Recreation, SC = Self-care, SS = Social support, RC = Rational–cognitive skills.

Organizational development. Organizational development is aimed primarily at group processes and structures such as decision-making patterns, communication channels and styles, conflict management, structure of lines of authority, and the organization as a system. The goal of organizational development work is organizational health in terms of both productivity and adaptability. Whereas organizational development in the 1970s and 1980s focused on the growth and well-being of the organization, organizational development in the 1990s has an important mission to address the traumas of layoffs and to revitalize downsized organizations (Noer, 1993).

Organizational development activities may be initiated at the level of the organization's structure, technology, people, goal, or culture, as noted in Figure 5.3 (p. 95). For example, structural changes were the touchstone for development for Tenneco during the 1970s in dealing with the stress of traffic congestion in Houston during that city's boom era. Tenneco made two structural changes. First, the company wrote a corporate policy specifying a number of alternative 8-hour flexible work schedules around a core period of 8 a.m. to 4:45 p.m. and including the purpose and operation of this program. A Tenneco employee could apply for a daily schedule that began between 7 a.m. and 9 a.m. (in 30-minute increments) and ended between 3:45 p.m. and 5:45 p.m. As long as the department was adequately staffed during the core period and the department head approved, the individual was able to work during the chosen hours. This structural change in the organization had the intended positive effects on employees. Second, Tenneco established a program of corporate vanpools that operated from the suburbs of Houston to downtown. There were 130 vanpools in the company, each composed of individuals working the same flextime schedule. More than one third of Tenneco's employees in downtown Houston participated voluntarily in the vanpools. The vanpool and flextime programs were designed to work together in relieving the stress of commuting.

The economic and competitive demands of the 1990s that are affecting organizations, as described by Martin and Freeman (in press) and others, are creating a new set of challenges for organizational development. Noer (1993) reported distressful outcomes of these demands in layoff survivors who succumbed to "survivor sickness." To address this organizational problem, he advanced a four-level process for handling layoffs to enhance healthy survival. Level 1 concerned the layoff process itself; he suggested that attention to feelings, compassion, and the human side of the organization in layoff planning may serve a useful primary prevention function. Level 2 encouraged expression of the necessary grieving process so that people could move through the inevitable emotions of a layoff. Level 3 focused on breaking any chains of codependency within the organization by encouraging responsible, autonomous behavior on the part of the individual and the organization. Finally, Level 4 aimed to revitalize the organization by building new employment relationships in which people were empowered to accept responsibility for themselves and their behavior. Organizational development can help heal the wounds of organizational traumas such as layoffs and downsizing when it is systematically applied.

Legal protection programs. As the risk of legal liability for distress on the job has risen, there is an increased need for organizations to develop programs in preventive stress management that afford the organization legal protection while advancing the health of the organization and individuals within it. Ivancevich et al. (1985) set forth a five-point program to help organizations address this area of risk.

1. *Formulate a preventive law strategy.* Preventive law integrates traditional legal research with quantitative methods of analysis and forecasting to minimize the exposure of the organization to legal liability. Successful preventive law is future-oriented and anticipates legal, legislative, and regulatory changes that may affect the organization. This task can be difficult when one relies on retrospective case precedents and legal statutes. Legal audits are an integrative element of preventive law practice.

2. *Develop a stress diagnostic system.* Chapters 6 and 7 set forth a systematic framework for organizational stress diagnosis. Organizations such as Johnson & Johnson Health Management are increasingly making organizational stress diagnosis a feasible and practical task within organizations.

3. *Involve top-level management.* Active involvement from top-level management is an essential element for preventive stress management in organizations. There are several ways in which this may occur, such as

the highly visible participation in physical fitness programs at Hospital Corporation of America by Chairman Tom Frist and at Xerox Corporation by David Kearns during their tenures.

4. *Evaluate current programs.* Program evaluation is an essential ingredient in an organizational change program, especially in the case of preventive stress management. The foundation for the program evaluation is the stress diagnostic system described earlier. If the organization's preventive stress management programs are effective, improvements should be noticed in the stress diagnostic system.

5. *Document what's done.* Finally, the organization should be able to demonstrate what it has in fact done to act responsibly in the area of individual and organizational preventive stress management. Courts require proof, and the failure to provide it, no matter what good work has been done, may leave the organization with an indefensible liability.

Management consultation. Frequently, changes in job design, organizational roles, physical environment, support systems, career development opportunities, or decision-making patterns occur as a result of the analysis and recommendations of a consultant charged with improving the work environment and reducing stress or conflict in an organization. The work often is done by an internal consultant: a corporate vice president, a new personnel manager, the medical director, a staff industrial psychologist, or someone else from management who is adept in the methods of organizational behavior. The internal consultant may be charged with a one-time evaluation, with periodic stress assessment, or with an ongoing role in monitoring the organization's stress patterns. Preventive stress management activities can also be initiated as a result of the work of an outside consultant. Psychologists, psychiatrists, and other mental health professionals from universities or private practice are often hired to analyze company stress patterns and to suggest changes. Management consultants from universities and private consulting groups are also becoming active in the area of stress management. Like internal consultants, their preventive stress management tools are essentially those described in chapters 9 and 10 and variations thereof.

Outside consultants may offer the advantage of greater objectivity and lack of vested interest in existing management practices and behavior patterns. At the same time, however, without a thorough knowledge of the organization and the subtleties of its operation, an outside consultant may be less able to discern which intervention techniques have the greatest likelihood of success.

Selection of an outside consultant should be made with great care. Management consulting firms may lack expertise in the psychodynamics and complex social psychology of organizational stress, whereas consultants drawn from mental health fields sometimes lack experience and insight with regard to business and industry. One organization, for example, contracted with the department of psychiatry at a local university to study work-related stress among its employees and to evaluate the medical department's stress management program. After more than a year of diligent probing and careful analysis by the team, the chairperson of the department presented the team's findings. The report unfortunately contained nothing of practical value that had not already been known by the medical director and management (Warshaw, 1979).

When carefully selected, external consultants can play an invaluable role as resources for managerial decision making about preventive stress management programs. This point is illustrated by the case of a pharmaceutical laboratory that hired two consultants to investigate the production manager's conviction that the turnover and absenteeism rates were unacceptable and required action. An examination of the work areas, physical layout of the plant, employee comments and complaints, and actual absenteeism and turnover rates suggested a healthy organization. The consultants recommended that no training program be undertaken at that juncture, given the cost and lack of projected benefit. An independent consultation, therefore, may play a key role in preventive stress management, even when no specific action is required.

An important caution with regard to the use of outside consultants is that they too may have vested interests. Consultants hired by management and dependent on this relationship for their livelihood may cater to the interests and desires of management rather than make suggestions that benefit the whole organization. This potential conflict may be most apparent in the balance that is struck between organizational-level interventions aimed at changing the demands that the organization puts on the individual and interventions aimed at helping the individual deal more effectively with those demands.

Programs With an Individual Focus

Chapters 11, 12, and 13 described a wide range of methods for personal stress management. Most of these methods are accessible to the average employee outside the workplace. Specific methods may be available through self-study, the employee's personal physician, local counseling and human service agencies, or organizations such as the local church or synagogue. Increasingly, however, training in personal stress management is available at the workplace through the medical, psychology, or health department; employee assistance programs; stress management programs; physical fitness programs; or comprehensive health promotion programs. These programs are often viewed as part of the employee benefit package, although they could easily be justified as preventive maintenance costs for the company's human resources. Programs with a focus on the individual include medical, psychology, and health departments; stress management programs; physical fitness programs; and comprehensive health promotion programs.

Medical, psychology, and health departments. Many of the activities that are now considered part of preventive stress management traditionally fell to the medical, psychology, or occupational health departments.

These departments may be staffed by occupational physicians, occupational nurses, family physicians, psychiatrists, psychoanalysts, psychologists, and social workers. Union counselors, industrial chaplains, and pastoral counselors may work separately or through the medical department to provide additional services. The skills and potential contributions of each of these professional groups are well described in Warshaw's *Managing Stress* (1979).

Routine medical care, relaxation training, exercise prescription, and a host of different types of counseling programs are among the services that may be offered by medical departments. In many companies, the medical or health department offers the best point of entry for introducing new programs aimed at individual stress reduction. Basic medical department services are usually offered without charge, but optional stress management activities sometimes must be funded by charging employees for the service.

Introducing stress management activities through the medical department has its potential difficulties and limitations. As long as the medical staff is on management's payroll, the physicians are company doctors, meaning that the needs of management come first. Occupational physicians have become so sensitive to this criticism that in 1976 the American Occupational Medical Association adopted a new code of ethical conduct for physicians providing occupational medical services. Among other things, the code specifies that physicians should "practice on a scientific basis with objectivity and integrity" and "avoid allowing their medical judgment to be influenced by any conflict of interest." To the extent that medical departments follow this code, there should be no difficulty in introducing stress management activities through the medical department.

Another concern is that the medical staff may lack background in organizational and administrative sciences and therefore may not fully appreciate the context of organizational stress and available nonmedical interventions. This concern has led some organizations to initiate stress management programs through employee relations or personnel departments or through newer divisions such as human resources management.

Warshaw (1979) suggested eight elements of clinical stress management programs at the workplace. These include first aid, case finding, evaluation, treatment, referral, rehabilitation, screening, and prevention. Even small organizations may provide valuable counseling services with a limited financial investment by the company, as illustrated in the case of Southern Connecticut Gas Company, an employer of fewer than 600 persons in both white and blue collar occupations (see Reardon, 1976). The company began a program in 1975 through agreements with the two local family service agencies that operated in the area of the company's headquarters. The contract with the social service agencies called for the company to pay $35 for each initial intake interview, and additional costs were borne directly by the employee or by his major medical and other health insurance coverage. The company's two local unions endorsed the program and were represented at the training sessions. It cost Southern Connecticut Gas $4,620 in worker hours to train 90 supervisors and union officials. In terms of time required to design the program, the effort was well worth making.

Employee assistance programs. Employee Assistance Programs (EAPs) have their historical roots in efforts to help employees with alcohol, drug, and substance abuse problems. They have evolved into more elaborate programs aimed at helping employees address a variety of personal problems that intrude on their job performance and organizational involvement. EAPs appear to have been more systematically implemented in the United States during the 1980s than in some other parts of the world, such as the United Kingdom (Cooper & Williams, 1994). Many companies offer extensive on-site counseling programs aimed at specific problem areas such as poor coworker relations, alcohol or drug abuse, marital troubles, and personal finances. Ford Motor Company, 3M, B. F. Goodrich Company, General Mills, and The Equitable Life Assurance Society of the United States are among the larger companies offering EAPs. EAPs may be found in any number of organizational locations, including medical, psychology, health, human resource management, personnel, employee relations, and social work departments.

Stress management programs. Personal stress management programs and periodic stress management seminars at the workplace began to develop during the late 1970s and 1980s in the United States. They were organized through personnel or medical departments or as a joint effort between the two departments. The content of these programs varies; commonly, the seminars include training in one or more relaxation methods, discussion of the role of physical exercise, and a description of some of the personal coping techniques and lifestyle management issues discussed in chapters 11 and 12. Company stress management programs that restrict themselves to teaching one relaxation method are using a limited approach that should be viewed only as a starting point for a more comprehensive stress management program. Brief examples include the following:

- Metropolitan Life Insurance Company's Center for Health Help offers a program in work-site stress management to employees and markets the program to other corporations. The program emphasizes reduction of distress through behavior modification techniques such as reducing time urgency pressure, developing interpersonal communication skills, and relaxing voluntary muscles.
- Illinois Bell's Training and Development Department periodically offers a stress management course at the request of employees.
- Equitable Life Insurance Company's Emotional Health Program uses biofeedback to help employees learn to ease their tensions. The company informally estimates that each $15 that it spends on a treatment session relieves symptoms that would have cost 3 times that much in lost productivity.
- New York Telephone Company piloted the use of clinically stan-

dardized meditation for stress management and, on the basis of its success, has made the training regularly available to employees.

- B. F. Goodrich Tire's Group Learning Center has prepared a training program entitled Manage Your Stress, a 9-hour program presented in three sessions designed to teach employees to identify their own stress responses and to assume responsibility for altering their responses.

An international example of a stress management program comes from the chief medical officer of Zeneca Pharmaceuticals and a psychiatric consultant to Imperial Chemical Industries (ICI) Pharmaceuticals in the United Kingdom (Teasdale & McKeown, 1994). ICI Pharmaceuticals' experience with stress in the workplace dates to the mid-1980s, when the the number of cases of stress-related illness reported to the occupational health department indicated a disturbing upward trend. ICI-Zeneca had begun a growth period during that time that led to manufacturing operations in 17 countries, sales in 130 countries, and major operations in the United Kingdom, United States, Western Europe, and Japan by 1992. Research in the mid-1980s identified 12 likely reasons for the increase, including organizational change, the rapid growth in the business, increasing complexity in the business, an "international" thrust, profit and production pressure, new work overload, and high quality work expectations. ICI-Zeneca developed a stress management strategy in response to the increase in stress-related disorders. The company used as its conceptual backdrop the stress and performance relationship shown in Figure 14.2.

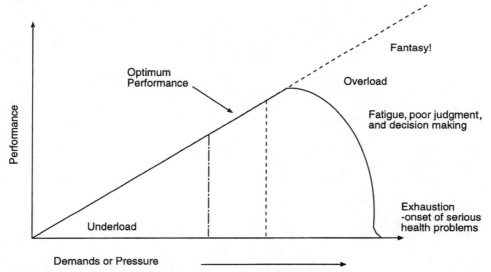

Figure 14.2. The stress and performance relationship. From Managing Stress at Work: The ICI-Zeneca Pharmaceuticals Experience 1986–1993, by E. L. Teasdale and S. McKeown, in *Creating Healthy Work Organizations* (p. 140), by C. L. Cooper and S. Williams (Eds.), 1994, Chichester, England: Wiley. Reprinted with permission.

ICI-ZENECA'S STRESS MANAGEMENT STRATEGY. The company developed a six-level stress management strategy, which is summarized in Table 14.1. Because the disturbing upward trend in stress-related illnesses and disorders was the impetus for the development of the program, the first level of intervention was the treatment of the stress-induced casualties. The second level in the strategy was to engage public health surveillance activities to detect other casualties in order to define the extent of the problem within the company. The third level of the strategy legitimized stress-related disorders through senior management. Levels 4 and 5 of the strategy increased awareness of stress and stress-related disorders throughout the company, with an accompanying program to teach behavioral, emotional, and cognitive skills for effective stress management. Level 6 in the strategy aimed to improve the organizational culture (see the earlier section in this chapter on organizational culture and leadership).

THE CHIEF EXECUTIVE OFFICER'S LETTER. Stress management programs are most effective when implemented through senior management, and that is what occurred at ICI-Zeneca, where all department heads received the following letter:

> I know that in recent months a number of managers and employees have been concerned about the increasing demands of the business on employees and have seen this exemplified in a small but significant number of employees with serious problems.
>
> The business will continue to expand and it is important that appropriate pressure is placed on staff. Some stress is good for both individuals and the business leading to job satisfaction, motivation and good performance. Too much or inappropriate pressure on people who are unable to cope with it is bad for them and bad for the business.
>
> It is important for Managers to keep under surveillance the total workload on individuals and groups making sure that priorities and reasonable timescales are set. For example, I see it as important that staff have enough free time for outside pursuits. If work takes up more than a reasonable proportion of an individual's time, over too long a period, the business is unlikely to benefit in the long term. In this context an individual's holiday arrangements should only rarely be dis-

Table 14.1.   ICI-Zeneca Stress Management Strategy

Level	Aim	Facilitator
1	Treat casualties	Occupational health professionals
2	Detect other cases	Occupational health professionals and managers
3	Legitimize stress	Senior management
4	Increase awareness	Managers, training programs, and occupational health professionals
5	Teach skills	Training and occupational health professionals
6	Improve culture	Total organization

Note. From Managing Stress at Work: The ICI-Zeneca Pharmaceuticals Experience 1986–1993, by E. L. Teasdale and S. McKeown, in *Creating Healthy Work Organizations* (p. 145), by C. L. Cooper and S. Williams (Eds.), 1994, Chichester, England: Wiley. Reprinted with permission.

rupted. The sensible planning and allocation of work within your departments is a vital factor in maximizing efficiency. I would ask you to pay particular attention to staff whose duties oblige them to do a lot of traveling, and ensure that they plan their schedules in a sensible way.

I have asked the Personnel and Occupational Health departments to pursue with you a number of detailed proposals designed to ensure a fuller appreciation of these issues and to minimize the incidence of stress-related problems in the organization. (Teasdale & McKeown, 1994, p. 147)

MEASURABLE BENEFITS OF A STRESS MANAGEMENT STRATEGY. ICI-Zeneca tracked a number of measurable as well as less tangible benefits of the stress management strategy. Two of the measures used to evaluate the stress management strategy were the General Health Questionnaire (GHQ; see chapter 7 for a description) and medical, psychological, or referral visits. The GHQ was administered to employees both before and after they attended stress workshops over a period of 3–4 months. A 15–20% improvement in scores on this individual measure of distress was found. In addition, a 10-year history of the number of individuals who needed to be referred to psychiatrists or psychologists or who had attended the ICI medical centers or their own family doctors' clinics was tracked. The increase in referrals before the development of the stress management strategy and the decrease following the stress management workshops are evident in Figure 14.3.

Physical fitness programs. Of the preventive stress management methods described in chapters 11, 12, and 13, physical fitness training has

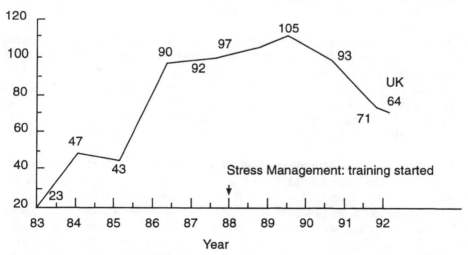

Figure 14.3. Ten years of referrals within ICI-Zeneca. From Managing Stress at Work: The ICI-Zeneca Pharmaceuticals Experience 1986–1993, by E. L. Teasdale and S. McKeown, in *Creating Healthy Work Organizations* (p. 162), by C. L. Cooper and S. Williams (Eds.), 1994, Chichester, England: Wiley. Reprinted with permission.

probably received the greatest financial commitment from business and industry. Historically, the military services have been among the strongest advocates of physical fitness programs owing to the physical demands placed on ground soldiers and marines, seagoing sailors, and airmen (Nelson, Quick, & Quick, 1989). Following are some examples of the resources committed to early corporate programs of physical fitness:

- Weyerhaeuser Company in 1972 invested $73,000 to construct and equip a colorful gymnasium at the company's headquarters in Tacoma, Washington. The facility, which includes indoor courts, a well-equipped exercise room, saunas, and a locker room, is open daily to employees and their families.
- Johns-Manville spent $17,000 to equip a small company gym at its Denver headquarters. Like many corporate fitness programs, participants must have a medical examination before beginning and are given specific exercise guidelines.
- When Exxon Corporation planned its Manhattan headquarters building, which opened in 1972, it set aside a 2,900-square-foot area for its physical fitness laboratory. Under the supervision of the medical department, over 300 executives have participated regularly in prescribed exercise programs, achieving significant improvements in several health parameters.
- The Life Insurance Company of Georgia set up the Tower Health Club atop its building in Atlanta. Its executives, over 200 of whom are members, pay a subsidized membership fee, which is about one third of the fee for other tenants in the building. Facilities, which include handball and squash courts, massage and exercise rooms, and a rooftop track, are open 12 hours daily on weekdays.

Although corporate fitness programs seem to attract larger management investments in facilities and staffing than other techniques with stress-reduction potential, the fitness program frequently serves as the focal point from which a variety of other programs, including relaxation training, develop. Often the elaborate facilities constructed for fitness programs also serve as meeting places for broader stress management seminars and training programs.

Comprehensive health promotion programs. In an effort to stem the tide of rising employee health care costs and health insurance premiums and to reduce the high cost of premature death and disability among executives, managers, and skilled employees, an increasing number of companies use comprehensive health promotion and disease prevention programs. Thorough health examinations to detect asymptomatic disease and disease risk factors, fitness programs, behavioral change efforts aimed primarily at smoking and weight control, and stress management are key components of most programs.

Comprehensive health promotion programs offer a tremendous potential for managing the individual and organizational costs of distress

(Landy et al., 1994; Weiss, Fielding, & Baum, 1991). Comprehensive health promotion programs are increasingly being set up as skill-based programs that teach individuals how to enhance their lifestyle including the use of cognitive and behavioral health management skills—not just how to avoid negative health behaviors such as smoking, excessive alcohol consumption, and overeating. The intent is to teach people to manage health risk factors while reducing vulnerability.

KIMBERLY-CLARK CORPORATION. One of the earliest comprehensive health promotion programs is the Health Management Program initiated by Kimberly-Clark (Dedmon, 1979, 1980; Dedmon, Gander, O'Connor, & Paschke, 1979). The Health Management Program reflects Kimberly-Clark's overall care and concern for its employees; the corporation believes that well-informed, healthy employees tend to be happier, safer, and more productive; to have better attendance records; and to incur lower health care costs. The staff believes that an individual's level of health can be improved through accessible and cost-effective health screening, limited primary care, exercise programs, nursing services, and employee assistance programs.

Kimberly-Clark was a forerunner in work-site health promotion with the implementation of its Health Management Program in April of 1977 and continues to assist employees in meeting their objectives in the areas of health promotion, health protection, and preventive services. At the corporation's locations in Neenah, Wisconsin, Roswell, Georgia, and Coosa Pines, Alabama, the Kimberly-Clark Health Management Program consists of four integrated teams that work together in a multidisciplinary approach to provide quality health promotion, protection, and preventive services.

The Health Promotion Center in Neenah includes an 8,000-square-foot clinical and occupational health nursing area and a 38,000-square-foot exercise facility with an indoor running track, outside running–walking trail, 25-meter Olympic pool, weight and aerobic equipment room, sauna, whirlpool, and locker facilities. It is available to 5,000 employees (2,900 salaried and 2,100 hourly), retirees, and spouses. A staff of 30, including 19 health professionals, is responsible for the screening, evaluation, fitness training, counseling, and lifestyle modification program.

The Roswell, Georgia, program began in 1981 and includes a 3,000-square-foot health screening unit and a 21,000-square-foot exercise facility with outside running trail, 25-meter Olympic pool, weight and exercise room, sauna, whirlpool, and locker facilities. Over 1,900 employees, retirees, and spouses have access to health promotion services at the facility. The multidisciplinary team in Roswell includes a professional staff of 10.

The Coosa Pines, Alabama, program began in 1989 with a health screening program housed in a 3,500-square-foot area. In 1990, a 35,000-square-foot exercise facility was opened that includes an indoor banked track and an outdoor track and nature trail for walking, biking, and jogging and serves over 4,000 employees. The professional team in Coosa consists of eight people.

Participants enter the program through a series of five steps. Kimberly-Clark requires a health screening prior to participating in its exercise program. The first step is a health history and risk appraisal. The second step is a series of laboratory tests to assess liver, heart, kidney, and lung functions as well as hearing and vision. The third step is a complete physical examination, a monitored exercise test, and a fitness assessment. Follow-up examinations are offered every 3 years with annual health status reviews. The fourth step is the exit interview (making use of the "teachable moment"); a health professional reviews the screening results and assists the client in identifying and implementing lifestyle changes. An exercise prescription outlines individual exercise recommendations following American College of Sports Medicine guidelines. Referrals may be made to any member of the health management team or a personal physician for further evaluation, education, or treatment. The fifth step is admission to the fitness facility for orientation.

In Neenah, which has the largest health services center, approximately 80% of employees take advantage of the voluntary and confidential health screening. More than 46,500 initial and follow-up health screenings have been completed at the Neenah Health Center. An additional 21,541 screenings have been completed for employees at 22 other company locations in the United States by the Worksite Screening Program. Retesting of employees showed reductions in systolic and diastolic blood pressure and serum triglyceride levels. Changes in weight, percentage of body fat, cholesterol level including HDL cholesterol, and fasting blood glucose were also evident. Testing also showed an increase in fitness levels. Over 100,000 visits were made to the Neenah exercise facility in 1995, with 20% of eligible members participating on a regular basis (twice weekly or more). Participants average 9.6 visits per month, with 57% of visits from salaried employees, 14% from hourly employees, 15% from retirees, and 14% from spouses.

The Neenah center's customer orientation has evolved into a variety of preventive and educational services including stress management, international travel, family wellness, health and fitness fairs, personal training, nutrition education, sports injury prevention, cardiopulmonary resuscitation and first aid, ergonomics and back safety, sport-specific workshops, OSHA surveillance, DOT testing, testing for AIDS and other bloodborne pathogens, and drug–alcohol education and awareness.

JOHNSON & JOHNSON. This company initiated a comprehensive health promotion program called Live for Life. Presently, Johnson & Johnson Health Care Systems offers an even more comprehensive health program that includes health management consulting, a fitness center, health assessments, wellness programs, ergonomics training, and educational and promotional products. Early evaluations of the Johnson & Johnson program in numerous of its companies suggested that exercise and health behaviors (Blair, Piserchia, Wilbur, & Crowder, 1986) and employee work attitudes (Holzbach, Piserchia, McFadden, Hartwell, Herrmann, & Fielding, 1990) were affected. There even appeared to be a positive benefit in health status for nonparticipants that accrued from their association with health program participants. Hence, the health status of an entire working population can be enhanced even though only a percentage of that population is actively involved in a program. Three key elements of the program include health risk assessment, creative educational units, and physical fitness training.

1. *Health risk assessment.* Health risk assessments and health profiles are an integral part of the Johnson & Johnson approach. The approach to health risk assessment involves an in-depth look at lifestyle practices that affect health status for the individual. The health profile can include an analysis of stress, fitness, nutrition, blood pressure, time management, home safety, and personal ergonomics. Health profiles are a form of feedback to the individual that identify the person's areas of strength and potential vulnerability.

2. *Creative educational units.* The J&J program has a diverse and well-formed educational component in the Live for Life Program, consisting of a wide range of creative educational units organized into the following 10 major topical areas: (a) general health program management, (b) stress management, (c) weight management, (d) nutrition education and cholesterol management, (e) smoking cessation, (f) blood pressure management, (g) medical topics such as cancer and women's health issues, (h) exercise education, (i) safety, and (j) ergonomics. A variety of media, such as written, audio, and audiovisual, are used to deliver the messages.

3. *Physical fitness training.* The Live for Life Program has a physical fitness component as well. Although elements such as target heart-rate guidelines are standardized, exercise routines are tailored to fit the particular work site and population of employees. For example, the use of upper arm motions in aerobics classes is often a key element in elevating the heart rate during exercising. However, at Johnson & Johnson Medical, a major manufacturer of surgical gloves, the employees on the production lines used these upper arm motions all day long to pull gloves off the production belts. Hence, the director of the program had her aerobics instructors observe these production lines and design aerobic activities that would complement the employees' daily routine.

In addition to Kimberly-Clark and Johnson & Johnson, a growing number of other major corporations are initiating comprehensive health promotion programs that include a variety of stress management activities. The Xerox Health Management Program, Control Data Corporation's Stay Well Self–Health Management Program, the General Dynamics Health Fitness Center, and Citicorp's Manage Your Health Program are examples. Although many of the major corporate health promotion programs are based in large physical fitness facilities, such facilities are not necessary to the implementation of a comprehensive health promotion program.

Implementing Preventive Stress Management Programs

Knowing the range of organizational and individual stress management techniques and potential mechanisms for their implementation accom-

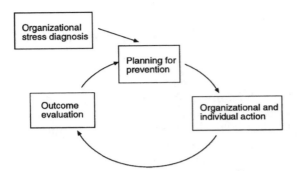

Figure 14.4. Implementation cycle for preventive stress management.

plishes little without a specific implementation strategy. Formulating and implementing a program of preventive stress management involves four basic steps: (a) organizational stress diagnosis, (b) planning for prevention, (c) organizational and individual action, and (d) outcome evaluation. These steps form the implementation cycle for preventive stress management, shown in Figure 14.4, and are fundamental to systematic organizational growth and development.

Organizational Stress Diagnosis

The initial diagnostic process is a comprehensive effort to discover the major sources of stress and unique demands to which the organization and the individuals within it are subjected. The diagnostic effort can draw heavily on the measures described in chapter 7. An assessment involves a listening orientation: Management should proceed with a sense of curiosity, investigation, and sensitivity to the total organization, its components, and the individual employees. A complete assessment includes a survey of conditions and relationships that employees find stressful, a survey of employees to determine the incidence of stress reactions, a general health survey, a review of worker–management or union–management relationships, and a review of absentee rates, productivity, and other objective measures listed in chapter 6.

As we noted in chapter 6, selection of the diagnostician is an important consideration. A knowledgeable occupational physician should be involved in the selection and interpretation of health surveys, and a trained clinical or industrial psychologist or organizational behavior specialist should be involved in the use of psychological surveys. The most accurate and useful assessment probably results from the interaction of a multidisciplinary assessment group of professionals and management, as illustrated in the cases of ICI-Zeneca and Kimberly-Clark.

In the process of conducting this diagnosis of organizational stress, management should consider a variety of key questions. These questions should guide the diagnostic process, but they should not limit it. As other questions arise, they should also be pursued to completion.

- What are the unique characteristics of the industry in which the organization operates?
- What are the unique demands placed on employees by the nature of the work and the technology used by the organization?
- What changes are likely to occur in the industry? How soon?
- What key events may affect suppliers, competitors, and customers?

Prevention Planning

The objective of prevention planning is to establish organizational goals for preventive stress management programs in the organization and to identify the means by which these goals can be achieved with available resources. The planning process itself lays the groundwork for implementation; therefore, it is important to involve key decision makers and the individuals who implement the plans. Support building for any organizational change begins with the planning process.

The assessment identifies the major areas for improvement. Often it is necessary to address the most symptomatic area first, before attempting a broad, long-term program. Drawing on the interventions described in chapters 9 through 13, the planners should identify the most attractive potential solutions and estimate the cost, expected benefits, time for implementation, and feasibility for each. Two or three of the most promising interventions, aimed at the high priority problems, should be selected for implementation. These and the most attractive interventions that were not selected for immediate implementation should be used to create a longer term 3- to 5-year preventive stress management plan.

As in the diagnostic stage, there are several key questions to ask in this stage of implementing preventive stress management in an organization. These key questions should stimulate the planning process, not constrain it. As additional questions arise, they should be addressed by the planning group. The key questions are as follows:

- What is the burden of suffering (human and organizational costs) attributable to stress in the organization?
- What has been previously attempted to reduce this burden of suffering? What were the results?
- What outside community resources are available to prevent distress?
- What are the priorities of identified problems and possible preventive interventions?
- What resource people (inside and outside the organization) are available?
- What are other companies in the industry doing?

The planning group may also refer to the tables in chapter 6 as a source of ideas about measures to consider and as a basis for developing strategies for preventive managerial interventions.

When one is addressing these questions and selecting among proposed interventions, the balance between organizational and individual approaches should be kept in mind. For stresses that are unavoidable, programs aimed at teaching individual employees how to minimize distress are reasonable. However, individual stress management programs should not be used to buffer the consequences of correctable and sometimes inexcusable organizational demands. Organizational techniques generally involve different people and different resources than do techniques aimed at the individual. These differences may influence the perceived feasibility and cost of alternative interventions.

Organizational and Individual Action

Any change is itself a potential stressor. When possible, preventive stress management proposals should be presented in a positive way: The support and participation of those affected should be solicited; the actions should be introduced on a voluntary basis; and the changes should be supported by key individuals in the organization. If the planning process has adequately involved these key individuals, much of the support will exist even before the program is initiated. Although unnecessary delays should be avoided, false starts can be costly, frustrating, and harmful to the credibility of preventive stress management efforts. A program that starts and fails may be worse than no program at all.

The scope of the program should be realistic. Setting expectations can be a useful motivating force, but if they are too ambitious, the implementation of the program may only increase distress. Once a program has been introduced, consistent follow-through is necessary to ensure its continuation. Commitment of time and resources on the part of management should be sufficient to support the program.

The need for program balance. A major emphasis in industry programs for stress management is on the more active approaches to coping with stress-induced energy, such as physical fitness training. Although physical fitness is an important part of stress management for individuals, it may be overdone. A young dietitian trained for and ran a marathon while also participating in a soccer league and some other sports. She was overdoing her exercise, was constantly keyed up and stressed, and became unable to meditate, relax, or pray. The active approaches to managing stress need to be balanced with the more passive approaches of meditation and relaxation. The origins of these more passive approaches are found in both the Judeo–Christian tradition and Eastern philosophy. It must be remembered, however, that these passive approaches clash with some 20th-century values. A Southwestern stress management clinic had difficulty selling its services to local businesses because the program was based largely on passive approaches. After 2 years of operation and much red ink, the operation was terminated. There is value in the balance of active and passive strategies for prevention.

Organizational politics. Organizational politics is one of the more powerful influences in work life, and the best ideas or programs are of little value unless they have the support of key organizational participants. Teasdale and McKeown (1994) emphasized the importance of politics in the informal organization to the implementation and success of the ICI-Zeneca stress management strategy. There are various strategies and tactics that people employ to exert influence, and managers may benefit from inevitable political influence and behavior in organizations by being proactive (Kumar & Thibodeaux, 1990). Although some political tactics, such as ingratiation (Ferris & Judge, 1991), lead to effective influence attempts, other tactics, such as threatening and pressure (Keys & Case, 1990), lead to failed influence attempts. The implementation of preventive stress management succeeds only with the support and encouragement of the key organizational participants and coalitions. If one is insensitive to these individuals and groups or does not gain their backing, the implementation of the intended program is difficult at best and fails at worst. Because the political processes in an organization do not always operate rationally or logically, one cannot necessarily rely on reason as a basis for countering political opposition in the implementation process. More likely, one must rely on internal political proponents.

Outcome Evaluation

Any major organizational change needs to be followed up with a systematic evaluation. Initially, informal feedback may be useful for making minor modifications in the program and for responding to significant misperceptions of the program. A more structured evaluation should be conducted 3, 6, or 12 months after the changes have been put into effect. The evaluation should focus on the various individual and organizational health indicators that have been previously discussed, because health is the ultimate objective of preventive stress management. The results of this evaluation can be used to determine whether the change was worthwhile and, if so, what modifications might be made to make the changes even more effective. As Figure 14.4 indicates, the evaluation feeds back into the planning process.

The evaluation process may use many of the same diagnostic instruments that are used in the initial assessment. Comparison of before and after scores provides an excellent method of determining the impact of the intervention. Clearly, *any* single intervention can be expected to influence only a subset of the organizational and individual markers of distress. The results of a formal evaluation can also be useful in modifying the 3- or 5-year plans for preventive stress management.

Cost–Benefit Ratio of Preventive Stress Management

Management has a responsibility for the well-being of its employees and to others in the organization, such as stockholders. Therefore, the relative costs and benefits of preventive interventions are of considerable importance. Most preventive interventions are investments with long-term payback periods; hence, the cost–benefit and return-on-investment analyses should be seen in terms of years rather than weeks or months. For example, in the ICI-Zeneca case, one of the company's analyses covered a 10-year period (Teasdale & McKeown, 1994).

Alcohol treatment programs, which are among the oldest of the symptom-directed interventions, have generated the most cost–benefit information. Pritchett and Finley (1971), for example, found that the annual cost of providing an alcoholism control program for a corporation of 1,700 employees amounted to $11,400. The price of not providing the program— measured by the costs of lateness and absenteeism, poor decisions, terminations, early retirement, and so on—was over $100,000 annually. Similarly, Hilker, Asthma, and Eggert (1972) estimated that the Illinois Bell Telephone–sponsored alcohol rehabilitation program resulted in annual corporate savings of over $90,000 for extended illnesses alone. Taking into consideration their documented reductions in off-duty and on-the-job accidents, improved job efficiency, and reductions in hospitalization expenses would make the savings even higher. Evidence from General Motors (Stessin, 1977) has also demonstrated substantial benefits from alcoholism treatment programs.

There is some evidence that short-term psychotherapy is associated with financial benefits. Follette and Cummings (1967) found that both outpatient and inpatient medical services decreased significantly for a group of individuals receiving short-term psychotherapy. In another study of people seeking outpatient psychotherapy, Reiss (1967) found that patients increased their earnings by an amount 4 times that of a control group of individuals in comparable occupations. Jameson, Shuman, and Young (1978) reported that average hospitalization costs were decreased by 50% among a Blue Cross population using the program's outpatient psychiatric benefits. Employee counseling programs have received less attention. In a study at Kennecott Copper Company in Salt Lake City, Engdahl and Walsh (1980) found that the employee assistance program was associated with a 50% decrease in absenteeism and a 55% reduction in hospital medical and surgical costs. Finally, Cooper and Sadri (1991) found significant declines in absence days for 250 post office workers in the United Kingdom who obtained stress counseling. Using the cost calculations outlined in chapter 5, organizations can project the financial benefits of such behavioral change.

One reliable set of cost–benefit data on organizational stress management comes from a study by Manuso (1979a) in which biofeedback formed a central part of an in-house corporate stress management training program. Experience with 15 employees suffering from headaches and 15 with anxiety suggested a return on investment of over 5 dollars for every dollar invested. This return is based on a comparison of pretreatment costs of employing an individual with chronic headache or anxiety with posttreatment costs. The costs of headaches and anxiety were found to result not from lateness and absenteeism but from visits to the health center, interference with capacity to work, and the effect of these symptoms on coworkers, bosses, and subordinates. With regard to comprehensive health intervention programs, Bly, Jones, and Richardson (1986) found lower mean in-patient health care cost increases, lower rates of increase in hospital days, but no differences in outpatient and other health care costs for two Johnson & Johnson health promotion groups compared to one control group.

Manuso (1982) concluded in his review of cost–benefit ratios of stress management programs that interventions enjoy a return on investment on the order of 200 to 800%, depending on the type of program, the setting, and the variable examined. Although each organization should conduct its own cost–benefit and return-on-investment analysis (C. L. Cooper & Williams, 1994), it is also important to be mindful of the indirect, even intangible, costs of distress noted in chapter 5. Continued research into the cost–benefit ratios of alternative preventive stress management strategies is important, but it is equally important to recognize that a favorable cost–benefit ratio is not always necessary to stimulate corporate action. For example, large sums of money have been spent on corporate exercise facilities simply because they were felt to be worth having. There is great popular support for fitness programs, but there are virtually no cost–benefit data to justify such expenses. Considerations of quality of life alone may justify effective preventive stress management programs. A favorable cost–benefit analysis may be sufficient to obtain approval for a new program, but it should not always be considered necessary.

Summary

Simply knowing the range of possible preventive stress management methods described in chapters 9 through 13 does not necessarily lead to effective prevention of distress. At the organizational level, management training programs for all levels of management, organizational development activities, internal or external consultants, and ad hoc task forces can be useful in introducing preventive stress management activities. At the individual level, medical or health departments, stress management programs, fitness programs, and comprehensive health promotion programs can each be vehicles for bringing individual stress management techniques into the organization. Implementing preventive stress management in an organization requires (a) organizational stress diagnosis, (b) planning for prevention, (c) organizational and individual action, and (d) outcome evaluation. These functions form an iterative model for implementing preventive stress management that is intended to foster continuing growth and development of the organization and the individuals within it.

Integration of organizational change and individual adaptation can lead to optimum use of humans and materials. Individual interventions should not be used to pacify employees in the face of unnecessarily distressful organizational practices. At the same time, individuals should learn how to minimize the distress caused by inevitable and unchangeable stressors.

15 _____

Preventive Stress Management:
From Threat to Opportunity

The thesis of this book is that stress is an inevitable and integral ingredient to the growth, development, and performance of individuals, groups, and organizations. The distress and strain that all too often result from stressful or traumatic events are not inevitable. Stress does not kill us; the successful adaptation to stress is what enables us to live—and to live fully and well (Vaillant, 1977). This book sets forth a public health, psychological, and preventive medicine framework for understanding the stress process and the responsible actions or interventions individuals, groups, and organizations may employ in successfully adapting to stress and stressful events. Stress-induced energy is one of our best God-given assets for managing legitimate emergencies and achieving peak performance. The wide array of medical, psychological, and behavioral stress skills set out in the chapters of the book are useful weapons in the war against distress, strain, and suffering; however, they may not be quite enough.

Each person has limitations of time, energy, money, and other resources. The final question we are left with is, What happens when these methods are not quite adequate, when we have done all we can do that is humanly possible and it does not seem to be enough to manage the stress or relieve the distress? At those times, one may take a leap of faith. The truly self-reliant person has a secure attachment to a higher power and turns to that power, to God, or to the place of his or her ultimate faith when all that is humanly possible has been done (Ornish, 1990; J. D. Quick et al., 1996). In the final analysis, that is the source of grace, peace, and salvation. For example, the sacred ballad *Amazing Grace, How Sweet the Sound* communicates powerfully to Christians about the stressful and distressing times in life, as reflected in the third stanza:

> Through many dangers, toils, and snares, I have already come;
> 'Tis grace has brought me safe thus far, and grace will lead me home.

Those of other faiths may well have other sources that lead them to the same place. Hence, a spiritually secure attachment to the source of life is the answer to the question about what to do when everything humanly possible is not enough for stress and distress at work.

Each person is powerful and blessed with talents and strengths yet at the same time limited in power. Knowing that, one may be a source of strength and power for others in their time of distress, strain, and suffering. This book is intended to be other-centered as opposed to self-centered. Although the book discusses ways of managing one's stress, that is not the end in itself. Rather, the purpose of self-care through preventive stress management is to become more competent in managing stress, to become healthier, and as a result of that competence and health, to be a stronger asset for the groups and organizations in which one participates.

The purposes of this chapter are twofold: first, to summarize briefly the preventive stress management model elaborated throughout the book and, second, to set forth an agenda for scientists and researchers, executives and leaders, educators and trainers, physicians, psychologists, employees, and public health officials working in the domain of stress in organizations. These agendas are important for designing, building, and maintaining healthy organizational work environments as the 21st century approaches. In the long run, healthy organizations will survive and thrive.

The Preventive Stress Management Model

The preventive stress management model is based on a three-stage process approach to stress in organizations (see Figure 1.4). The stress process begins with organizational demands and stressors that trigger the stress response, whose intensity, duration, and frequency are influenced by a number of individual and interpersonal modifiers. The process ends in either healthy (eustress) or unhealthy (distress) individual and organizational outcomes. The model has a diagnostic component as well as individual and organizational intervention strategies.

The Stress Process

Organizational demands and stressors. Chapter 2 presents a detailed discussion of the physical, task, role, and interpersonal demands that trigger the stress response in organizational life. Organizations vary in the dominant demands they place on their members, and in each organization everyone is not equally subject to the same demands and stressors. The chapter finishes with a discussion of extraorganizational demands (e.g., marital discord) and transitional demands (e.g., preparing for retirement) that must be considered in one's total stress load.

The stress response and its modifiers. Chapter 3 explains the stereotypical psychophysiological reaction of the stress response, resulting from the combined action of the sympathetic nervous system and the endocrine system, which mobilizes and energizes a person to meet the demands of a situation successfully. The chapter also discusses modifiers of the response to stress that influence the intensity, duration, and frequency of an individual's stress response and specific vulnerability for distress and strain.

Consequences of stress. Two chapters address the consequences of stress. Chapter 4 discusses individual consequences, and chapter 5 discusses organizational consequences. These consequences may be either healthy and eustressful or unhealthy and distressful.

INDIVIDUAL CONSEQUENCES. The eustressful consequences of stress for individuals include health, vitality, productivity, and well-being. The distressful consequences fall into three categories: *behavioral*, such as substance abuse (e.g., alcohol and tobacco), accidents, violence, and appetite disorders; *psychological*, such as burnout, depression, family and sexual dysfunctions, and psychogenic disorders; and *medical*, such as cardiovascular disease, headaches and backaches, peptic ulcer disease, and some forms of cancer.

ORGANIZATIONAL CONSEQUENCES. The eustressful consequences of stress for organizations include organizational health, vitality, productivity, and well-being. The distressful consequences fall into two categories: *direct costs*, such as participation and membership problems, job performance problems, health care costs, and compensation awards, and *indirect costs*, such as communication problems, faulty decision making, and violence.

Organizational Stress Diagnosis

Two chapters address organizational stress diagnosis. Chapter 6 contains a diagnostic model, whereas chapter 7 presents individual and organizational diagnostic instruments. These fall into three major categories: measures of organizational demands and stressors, measures of individual and organizational distress, and measures of the modifiers of the stress response.

Preventive Stress Management

Chapter 8 sets forth a philosophy and framework of preventive stress management for healthy, productive organizations by translating the public health concepts of primary, secondary, and tertiary prevention from preventive medicine into an organizational context. The chapter frames organizational and individual prevention strategies in this framework.

Organizational prevention. Chapters 9 and 10 discuss a set of nine organizational strategies for preventive stress management. These strategies include job redesign methods, participative management, career development, flexible work schedules, physical settings redesign, role analysis, goal setting programs, social support, and team building. These are not intended to be a delimiting set of organizational prevention strategies, yet they may serve as a starter list for executives and organizations interested in enhancing organizational and individual health.

Individual prevention. Chapters 11, 12, and 13, respectively, address primary, secondary, and tertiary prevention for individuals. Primary prevention concerns managing the demands and source of stress in organizations; secondary prevention concerns strategies for altering how a person responds to inevitable and necessary demands and stressors; and tertiary prevention is intended to help heal individuals in distress. Traumatic events do happen in organizations, and distress does occur. Healing the wounds may not be easy, but it is possible.

An Agenda for the Future

Stress in organizations is alive and well, and that is not all bad. Eustress is good; distress is bad. Preventive stress management helps one convert stress from a threat into an opportunity for health and achievement. In the 80 years since Walter B. Cannon first identified the complex of physiological processes he labeled the emergency response, the knowledge and understanding of the physiological and psychological elements of stress have been advanced dramatically. However, the field of stress is still an active and fertile one, and the concerns centered on stress in organizations are also active. Therefore, the questions for those in the field in the late 1990s are as follows: Where do we go from here? How do we turn a potential threat into an opportunity? We believe there is an active agenda for at least seven constituencies concerned with stress in organizations. These constituencies include: scientists and researchers, executives and leaders, educators and trainers, physicians, psychologists, employees, and public health officials.

Scientists and Researchers

A key arena for further research concerns effectiveness and efficacy evaluation research. Much core medical and psychological knowledge has been established through the decades of basic research. The next frontier is applied research in organizational settings, aimed at specifying the physical and psychosocial attributes of healthy work environments and healthy personalities for specific work environments. A dual emphasis on the work environment and the person is essential because of the differential impact that stress has on individuals. Organizational designers may come up with great concepts for healthy organizations (C. L. Cooper & Williams, 1994), and those design concepts must be rigorously evaluated (Teasdale & McKeown, 1994). Therefore, efficacy and effectiveness research is able to tell what works, what is useful, and under what conditions. Scientists and researchers play a critical, pivotal role in establishing a basis for preventive action.

Executives and Leaders

Occupational stress and organizational health are leadership challenges. Stress management skills are important for executives and leaders for at least two reasons. First, stress management skills are critical to business success in the face of contemporary economic and competitive challenges (Whetton & Cameron, 1995). Second, work-related psychological disorders and distress are among the 10 leading occupational health risks in the United States (Sauter et al., 1990). There is reason for optimism and hope in meeting these challenges because people management is more important than all other factors in predicting profitability, and stress management is people management (T. Cox, 1995). Interviews with 402 highly effective managers, as identified by peers and superiors in a sample of business, health care, educational, and state government organizations, identified managing stress as one of 10 key skills of effective managers (Whetton & Cameron, 1995).

Managing time and stress was second on this list. Mastering the skills of time and stress management benefits the executive or leader personally, and it benefits the organization and its employees. First, the organization benefits from an executive's health, along with the personal benefit to the executive, because of the reduced health care costs for that executive. Second, the organization benefits from the function executives and leaders serve as role models for employees, thus advancing organizational health and preventive stress management at work. The famous physician and educator William Osler responded to a medical student commenting on a "typical neurotic" during grand rounds one day by saying, "Funny, isn't it, how they run the world?" In the framework of preventive stress management, healthy executives, not neurotics, are sought as the role models of healthy stress management for others in the organization.

Educators and Trainers

Educators and trainers have available to them sufficient objective and cognitive-skill knowledge to design courses and educational modules in preventive stress management. Courses in stress management, preventive stress management, and combat stress are found in colleges of business administration, departments of psychology, schools of public health, departments of behavioral sciences, and military service academies (Cameron et al., 1995; Raymond et al., 1990). The Whetton and Cameron (1995) educational module on managing stress is sufficiently substantive to build a university course around it. Organizational courses in hardiness training, preventive stress management, humor, and speaking skills for people under pressure are also offered to executives and employees under the rubric of executive education and human resources management development (Maddi, 1987, 1994; Metcalf, 1990).

In addition to developing curricula and teaching, educators and trainers may help identify high-risk populations or work sites for which information can make a difference. Although it would be ideal to begin the educational process early in the life cycle—in kindergarten and elementary school preferably—reality suggests that educational intervention occurs later in the life cycle. Hence, concentrating educational resources on high-risk populations and work sites may yield the highest returns.

Physicians

Physicians, especially occupational medicine physicians, can advance the practice of preventive stress management by overcoming specialty boundaries and developing a deeper appreciation for the person as a whole. The development of specialties throughout Western medicine has led to a reductionistic focus on specialized knowledge. Although it is valuable at one level, the risk of overspecialization is the loss of the general practitioner's perspective. This is especially problematic in the domain of stress because stress is a generalized response; Selye called it the general adaptation syndrome. The emergence of psychoneuroimmuniology and other mind–body disciplines has helped in this regard. If the physician does not have an appreciation for the whole person and the systemic interrelationships, he or she may respond only to a specific symptom and miss a much bigger problem. Furthermore, the contribution of stress to various disorders calls for the generalist perspective, which considers the work and life context factors that may play contributory roles to specific disorders.

Psychologists

A key emerging specialty within psychology that is compatible with preventive stress management is occupational health psychology. At the crossroads of health psychology and public health, it is concerned with healthy people in healthy work environments and with healthy interactions between work and family–home environments. A key question in occupational health psychology is, How do we take the distress out of work without taking out the inevitable risk, challenge, and difficulty?

Employees

Like executives, employees have a responsibility to learn the skills of preventive stress management. Self-reliance is a key tenet of our work, and self-reliance calls for taking responsibility to learn the skills and knowledge necessary for successful work achievement. This applies no less to time and stress management skills than it does to job content skills. Hence, the acceptance of responsibility for one's work and one's work environment demands learning the necessary cognitive and behavioral skills to manage successfully the demands that accompany the work environment. This task entails a proactive stance in learning about the demands of a job and organization before accepting a position and being assertive about acquiring the additional knowledge and skills to be successful once there.

Public Health Officials

A key role for public health officials in preventive stress management concerns surveillance of physical and psychosocial health risks in organizations and work environments. As Kasl and colleagues pointed out, epidemiological surveys of hazards and outcomes can be instrumental to successful surveillance activities (Landy, Quick, & Kasl, 1994). They proposed a process of environmental monitoring, surveillance of disorders, and examination of hazard–disorder linkages. At present, effective environmental monitoring and surveillance systems for psychosocial work-related disorders and psychological distress do not exist. The development of such epidemiological systems in organizations may be helpful in establishing environmental risk factors as well as identifying target executive and employee populations who may be especially vulnerable to distress at work.

Conclusion

Is stress a threat or an opportunity? The question was asked in chapter 1. The answer is, "It is both." Stress may become a threat to a person's health and well-being when (a) the stress response is elicited too intensely, for too long a period of time, or too frequently; (b) early warning signs of problems, disorders, and distress are ignored; or (c) the person does not have the skills and repertoire of behaviors that meet the challenges and demands an organization presents. Stress may become a threat to a person who works in an unhealthy, high strain position in which it is difficult or impossible to achieve success and fulfillment.

Stress is an opportunity when it challenges people to be all they can be. Stress is an opportunity when it enables people to display the talents, skills, knowledge, and gifts with which they are endowed. Stress is an opportunity when one grows, learns, changes, and develops through the experience. It is a challenge when it leads people to transform themselves, adapt to changing circumstances, and live well.

What makes the difference in whether stress is a threat or an opportunity may be found in the framework of preventive stress management. Preventive stress management is a flexible framework that enables a person to develop the necessary skills, tools, and information for transforming a threat into an opportunity. When people become divided within themselves and enter the stage of resistance with its inevitable conflict and struggle, stress becomes a threat. When a person becomes unified and focused through the experience of stress and chooses action options for using the stress-induced energy, stress becomes an opportunity for success and achievement.

Appendix A _____

Sources of Diagnostic Instruments

Organizational Stressors

1. *Quality of Employment Survey*
   Source: Dr. Richard Price, Survey Research Center, Institute for Social Research, The University of Michigan, Ann Arbor, MI 48106
   Approximate completion time: 30 minutes
2. *Occupational Stress Indicator*
   Source: Dr. Cary Cooper, Windsor, U.K., NFER-Nelson
   Approximate completion time: 20 minutes
3. *Occupational Stress Inventory*
   Source: S. J. Osipow and A. R. Spokane, Psychological Assessment Resources, Odessa, FL 33556
   Approximate completion time: 25 minutes
4. *Job Stress Survey*
   Source: Dr. Charles Spielberger, Psychological Assessment Resources, Odessa, FL 33556
   Approximate completion time: 20 minutes
5. *Job Content Questionnaire*
   Source: Dr. Robert Karasek, University of Massachusetts, Lowell, MA 01850
   Approximate completion time: 30 minutes
6. *NIOSH Generic Job Stress Questionnaire*
   Source: Dr. Joseph Hurrell, NIOSH, 4676 Columbia Parkway, Cincinnati, OH 45226
   Approximate completion time: Varies from 15 minutes to 45 minutes, depending on the number of modules used
7. *Stress Audit*
   Source: L. H. Miller and A. D. Smith, Biobehavioral Associates, 1101 Beacon St., Brookline, MA 02146
   Approximate completion time: 1 hour
8. *Stressors Checklist*
   Source: Dr. Alan McLean, *Work Stress*, 1979, Addison-Wesley Publishing Company, Reading, MA
   Approximate completion time: 10 minutes
9. *Stress Diagnostic Survey* (work and nonwork versions)
   Source: Dr. John M. Ivancevich, University of Houston, Houston, TX 77004
   Approximate completion time: 40 minutes for both

10. *Organizational Diagnosis*
    Source: Dr. Harry Levinson, *Organizational Diagnosis*, 1972, Harvard University Press, Cambridge, MA
    Approximate completion time: Varies from hours to days
11. *The Management Audit*
    Source: Dr. Cary L. Cooper and Dr. Judi Marshall, "An Audit of Managerial (Di)Stress," *Journal of Enterprise Management*, Vol. 1, 1978, pp. 185–196
    Approximate completion time: Varies by individual and organization
12. *Life Events Scale*
    Source: T. H. Holmes and R. H. Rahe, "The Social Readjustment Rating Scale," *Journal of Psychosomatic Research*, Vol. 11, 1967, pp. 213–218
    Approximate completion time: 15 minutes
13. *The Hassles and Uplifts Scales*
    Source: A. D. Kanner, J. C. Koyne, C. Schaefer, and R. S. Lazarus, "Comparison of Two Modes of Stress Measurement: Daily Hassles and Uplifts Versus Major Life Events," *Journal of Behavioral Medicine*, Vol. 4, 1982, pp. 25–36
    Approximate completion time: 15 minutes each

Individual Distress Measures

1. *Cornell Medical Index*
   Source: Cornell University Medical College, 1300 York Avenue, Box 88, New York, NY 10021
   Approximate completion time: 30 minutes
2. *General Health Questionnaire*
   Source: Institute of Psychiatry, DeCrespigny Park, Denmark Hill, London, S.E.5, England
   Approximate completion time: 10 minutes for long form, 5 minutes for short form
3. *Daily Log of Stress-Related Symptoms (in Managing Your Stress)*
   Source: CRM McGraw-Hill, 110 15th Street, Del Mar, CA 92014
   Approximate completion time: 20 minutes each time
4. *SCL-90-R*
   Source: Leonard R. Derogatis, 1228 Wine Spring Lane, Baltimore, MD 21204
   Approximate completion time: 30 minutes
5. *Maslach Burnout Inventory*
   Source: Consulting Psychologists Press, 577 College Avenue, Palo Alto, CA 94306
   Approximate completion time: 20–30 minutes
6. *State–Trait Anxiety Inventory*
   Source: Consulting Psychologists Press, 577 College Avenue, Palo Alto, CA 94306
   Approximate completion time: 10 minutes

7. *Profile of Mood States*
   Source: Educational and Industrial Testing Service, San Diego, CA 92107
      Approximate completion time: 5 minutes

Modifiers of the Response to Stress

1. *Hardiness* (third-generation measure)
   Source: Hardiness Institute, 5 Revere Drive, Suite 200, Northbrook, IL 60062
      Approximate completion time: 30 minutes
2. *Jenkins Activity Survey* (Type A behavior)
   Source: Psychological Corporation, 575 3rd Avenue, New York, NY 10017
      Approximate completion time: 15 minutes
3. *Workaholic Questionnaire and Coping Mechanisms Assessment*
   Source: Addison-Wesley Publishing Company, Reading, MA, 1979
      Approximate completion time: 15 minutes each
4. *Locus of Control*
   Source: Julian B. Rotter, "Generalized Expectancies for Internal Versus External Control of Reinforcement." *Psychological Monographs*, Vol. 80, no. 1 (Whole No. 609), 1966
      Approximate completion time: 15 minutes

Appendix B _____

Resource Groups

General

American Association of Occupational Health Nurses, 50 Lenox Pointe, Atlanta, GA 30324, 404-262-1162.

American College of Occupational and Environmental Medicine, 55 W. Seegers Road, Arlington Heights, IL 60005, 708-228-6850.

American Health Foundation, 320 E. 43rd Street, New York, NY 10017, 212-953-1900.

American Heart Association, 7320 Greenville Avenue, Dallas, TX 75231, 800-242-8721.

American Hospital Association, Center for Health Promotion, 840 North Lake Shore Drive, Chicago, IL 60611.

American Institute of Stress, 124 Parks Avenue, Yonkers, NY 10703, 914-963-1200.

American Occupational Health Nurses Association, 79 Madison Avenue, New York, NY 10016.

American Occupational Medical Association, 150 N. Wacker Drive, Chicago, IL 60606.

Boston University, Center for Industry and Health Care, 53 Bay State Road, Boston, MA 02215.

Department of Health, Education and Welfare, Office of Health Information and Promotion, 721B Hubert Humphrey Building, 200 Independence Avenue, S.W., Washington, DC 20201.

Human Economy Center and Society for Human Economy, P.O. Box 28, West Swanzey, NH 03469, 603-355-1250.

National Institute for Occupational Safety and Health, 4676 Columbia Parkway, C-22, Cincinnati, OH 45226, 202-401-6997.

U.S. Department of Health and Human Services, Public Health Service, Centers for Disease Control and Prevention, National Center for Health Statistics, 6525 Belcrest Road, Room 1064, Hyattsville, MD 20782.

Relaxation Training

Association for Applied Psychophysiology and Biofeedback, 10200 W. 44th Avenue, Wheat Ridge, CO 80033, 800-477-8892.

Maharishi International University, International Center for Scientific Research, Fairfield, IA 52556.

Physical Fitness

American College of Sports Medicine, P.O. Box 1440, Indianapolis, IN 46206, 317-637-9200.

American Medical Joggers Association, 28240 Agoura Road, Agoura Hills, CA 91301, 818-706-2049.

American Running and Fitness Association, 4405 East-West Highway, Suite 405, Bethesda, MD 20814, 800-776-ARFA.

Association for Worksite Health Promotion, 60 Revere Drive, Suite 500, Northbrook, IL 60063, 847-480-9574.

President's Council on Physical Fitness and Sports, 450 5th Street, N.W., Washington, DC 20001, 202-272-3430.

Psychological Counseling and Therapy

American Academy of Psychoanalysis, 47 E. 19th Street, New York, NY 10003, 212-475-7980.

American Association for Marriage and Family Therapy, 1133 15th Street, N.W., Suite 300, Washington, DC 20005, 202-452-0109.

American Psychiatric Association, 1400 K Street, N.W., Washington, DC 20005, 202-682-6000.

American Psychological Association, Office of Professional Affairs, 750 First Street, Washington, DC 20002, 202-336-6170.

National Institute of Mental Health, National Clearinghouse for Mental Health Information, 5600 Fishers Lane, Rockville, MD 20857.

National Mental Health Association, 1021 Prince Street, Alexandria, VA 22314, 703-684-7722.

Alcoholism and Drug Abuse Treatment

Al-Anon Information Center, 200 Park Avenue, New York, NY 10166, 212-254-7230.

Alcoholics Anonymous, 475 Riverside Drive, New York, NY 10115, 212-870-3400.

Employee Assistance Professionals Association, 2101 Wilson Boulevard, No. 500, Arlington, VA 22201, 703-522-6272.

National Association on Drug Abuse, Provide Addict Care Today, 355 Lexington Avenue, New York, NY 10017, 212-986-1170.

National Clearinghouse for Alcoholism and Drug Abuse, 11426 Rockville Pike, Bethesda, MD 20815, 301-468-2600.

National Council on Alcoholism and Drug Dependence, 12 W. 21st Street, New York, NY 10010, 800-NCA-CALL.

Other Resource Groups

American Society of Clinical Hypnosis, 2200 East Devon Avenue, Des Plaines, IL 60019, 847-297-3317.

Association for Advancement of Behavior Therapy, 305 7th Avenue, New York, NY 10001, 212-647-1890.

Y's Way to a Healthy Back Program, Pacific Region YMCA, 3080 La Selva, San Mateo, CA 94400.

References

Abercrombie, M. L. J. (1976). Architecture: Psychological aspects. In S. Krauss (Ed.), *Encyclopaedic handbook of medical psychology*. London: Butterworths.

Abramson, J. H. (1966). The Cornell Medical Index as an epidemiological tool. *American Journal of Public Health, 56,* 287–298.

Achterberg, J. (1985). *Imagery in healing: Shamanism and modern medicine*. Boston: New Science Library.

Adams, G. T. (1987). Preventive law trends and compensation payments for stress-disabled workers. In J. C. Quick, R. S. Bhagat, J. E. Dalton, & J. D. Quick (Eds.), *Workstress: Health care systems in the workplace* (pp. 235–245). New York: Praeger.

Adams, J. D. (1978). Improving stress management: An action-research-based OD intervention. In W. W. Burke (Ed.), *The cutting edge*. San Diego, CA: University Associates.

Adams, J. D. (1980). *Understanding and managing stress: A workbook in changing life styles*. San Diego, CA: University Associates.

Adams, L., & Lenz, E. (1979). *Effectiveness training for women*. New York: Wyden.

Adams, P. F., & Benson, V. (1992). Current estimates from the National Health Interview Survey. *Vital Health Statistics, 10*(194), 82–83.

Adkins, J. A. (1995, February). *Occupational stress: A leadership challenge*. Paper presented at the Air Force Material Command Horizons Conference, Albuquerque, NM.

Adkins, J. A. (1996, April). *Continuum of occupational violence prevention*. Paper presented at the 11th annual conference of the Society for Organizational and Industrial Psychology, San Diego, CA.

Adkins, J. A., & Schwartz, D. (1996, June). *Organizational health: An organizational systems perspective*. Paper presented at the third biennial International Conference on Advances in Management, Boston, MA.

Adler, N. E., Boyce, W. T., Chesney, M. A., Folkman, S., & Syme, S. L. (1993). Socioeconomic inequalities in health: No easy solution. *Journal of the American Medical Association, 269,* 3140–3145.

Affemann, R. (1979). Mental causes of social stress factors, spiritual causes of susceptibility to stress and educational approaches to stress relief. *Das Offentliche Gesundheitswesen, 41*(3), 117–123.

Aiello, J. R., & Kolb, K. J. (1995). Electronic performance monitoring: A risk factor for work stress in the Netherlands. In S. L. Sauter & L. R. Murphy (Eds.), *Organizational risk factors for job stress* (pp. 163–180). Washington, DC: American Psychological Association.

Alberti, R. E., & Emmons, M. (1974). *Your perfect right* (Rev. ed.). San Luis Obispo, CA: Impact Press.

Albrecht, K. (1979). *Stress and the manager.* Englewood Cliffs, NJ: Prentice-Hall.

Alderfer, C. P. (1972). *Existence, relatedness, and growth: Human needs in organizational settings*. New York: Free Press.

Alderfer, C. P. (1976). Change processes in organizations. In M. D. Dunnette (Ed.), *Handbook of industrial and organizational psychology* (pp. 1591–1638). Chicago: Rand McNally.

Alexander, C. N., Swanson, G. C., Rainforth, M. V., & Carlisle, T. W. (1993). Effects of the transcendental meditation program on stress reduction, health, and employee development: A prospective study in two occupational settings [Special issue: Stress and stress management at the workplace]. *Anxiety, Stress and Coping: An International Journal, 6,* 245–262.

Allen, R. W., & Madison, D. L. (1979). Organizational politics: Tactics and characteristics of its actors. *California Management Review, 22*(1), 77–82.

Allred, K. D., & Smith, T. W. (1989). The hardy personality: Cognitive and physiological responses to evaluative threat. *Journal of Personality and Social Psychology, 56,* 257–266.

American College of Sports Medicine. (1975). *Guidelines for graded exercise testing and exercise prescription*. Philadelphia: Lea & Febiger.

American Heart Association. (1980). *The cost of doing business*. Dallas, TX: Author

American Management Association. (1996). *Organizational staffing and disability claims*. Research report published exclusively for corporate members of AMA, New York.

American Psychiatric Association. (1994). *Diagnostic and statistical manual of mental disorders* (4th ed.). Washington, DC: Author.

Anderson, C. R. (1977). Locus of control, coping behaviors, and performance in a stress setting: A longitudinal study. *Journal of Applied Psychology, 62,* 446–451.

Anderson, H. (1981, August 24). Executives under stress. *Newsweek,* p. 53.

Anderson, J. L., & Cohen, M. (1977). *The West Point fitness and diet book*. New York: Avon Books.

Anderson, R. A. (1978). *Stress power.* New York: Human Sciences.

Anthony, W. A. (1979). *The principles of psychiatric rehabilitation*. Amherst, MA: Human Resource Development Press.

Antonovsky, A. (1987). *Unraveling the mystery of health: How people manage stress and stay well*. San Francisco: Jossey-Bass.

Argyris, C. (1952). *The impact of budgets on people*. Ithaca, NY: School of Business and Public Administration, Cornell University.

Armstrong-Stassen, M. (1994). Coping with transition: A study of layoff survivors. *Journal of Organizational Behavior, 15,* 597–621.

Asterita, M. F. (1985). *The physiology of stress*. New York: Human Sciences Press.

Astrand, N. E., Hanson, B. S., & Isacson, S. O. (1989). Job demands, job decision latitude, job support, and social network factors as predictors of mortality in a Swedish pulp and paper company. *British Journal of Industrial Medicine, 46,* 334–340.

Athos, A. G., & Gabarro, J. J. (1978). *Interpersonal behavior.* Englewood Cliffs, NJ: Prentice-Hall.

Bachler, C. J. (1995, January). Workers take leave of job stress. *Personnel Journal,* 38–48.

Back, K. W. (1973). Encounter groups and society. *Journal of Applied Behavioral Science, 9,* 7–20.

Bailey, D. S., & Foley, J. (1990, August). Pacific Bell works long distance. *HR Magazine,* pp. 50–52.

Bain, P., & Baldry, C. (1995). Sickness and control in the office: The sick building syndrome. *New Technology, Work, and Employment, 10,* 19–31.

Baker, D. G. (1977). Influence of a chronic environmental stress on the incidence of methycholanthrene-induced tumors. *Cancer Research, 37,* 3939–3944.

Bandura, A. (1969). *Principles of behavior modification*. New York: Holt, Rinehart & Winston.

Bandura, A. (1986). *Social foundations of thoughts and actions: A social cognitive theory*. Englewood Cliffs, NJ: Prentice-Hall.

Baratone, P. T., Ursano, R. T., Wright, K. M., & Ingraham, L. H. (1989). The impact of a military air disaster on the health of assistance workers: A prospective study. *Journal of Nervous and Mental Diseases, 177,* 317–328.

Barber, T. X. (Eds.). (1976). *Biofeedback and self-control,* Chicago: Aldine.

Bardwick, J. M. (1991). *Danger in the comfort zone*. New York: American Management Association.

Barefoot, J. C., Dahlstrom, W. G., & Williams, R. B. (1983). Hostility, CHD incidence, and total mortality: A 25-year follow-up study of 255 physicians. *Psychosomatic Medicine, 45,* 59–63.

Bar-Khama, A., Shoenfeld, Y., & Shuman, E. (1980). *The Israeli fitness strategy: A complete program of diet and exercise based on the training system of the Israeli defense forces.* New York: Morrow.

Barnes, L. B., & Hershon, S. A. (1976, July-August). Transferring power in the family business. *Harvard Business Review, 54,* 105–114.

Barnett, R. C., & Baruch, G. K. (1978). *The competent woman: Perspectives on development,* New York: Irvington.

Barnett, R. C., Biener, L., & Baruch, G. K. (Eds). (1987). *Gender and stress*. New York: Free Press.

Bartalos, M. K. (1993). Work, health, and recreation: Aspects of the total person. *Loss, Grief & Care, 6*(4), 7–14.

Bartholomew, A. (1994). *Biofeedback is back*. Omni, 17, 16.

Basil, D. C., & Cook, C. W. (1974). *The management of change*. London: McGraw-Hill.

Baughan, D. M. (1995). Barriers to diagnosing anxiety disorders in family practice. *American Family Physician, 52*, 447–450.

Baum, A. (1991). A psychophysiological perspective, with emphasis on relationships between leisure, stress, and well-being. In B. L. Driver, P. J. Brown, & G. L. Peterson (Eds.), *Benefits of leisure* (pp. 407–410). State College, PA: Venture Publishing.

Baumeister, R. F., Smart, L., & Boden, J. M. (1996). Relation of threatened egotism to violence and aggression: The dark side of high self-esteem. *Psychological Review, 103*, 5–33.

Baun, W. B., Bernacki, E. J., & Herd, J. A. (1987). Corporate health and fitness programs and the prevention of work stress. In J. C. Quick, R. S. Bhagat, J. E. Dalton, & J. D. Quick (Eds.), *Workstress: Health Care Systems in the Workplace* (pp. 217–234). New York: Praeger.

Beary, J. F., & Benson, H. (1974). A simple psychophysiologic technique which elicits the hypometabolic changes of the relaxation response. *Psychosomatic Medicine, 15*(2), 115–120.

Beatty, R. W. (1973). Blacks as supervisors: A study of training, job performance, and employers' expectations. *Academy of Management Journal, 16*, 196–206.

Becher, F. (1981). *Work space: Creating environments in organizations*. New York: Praeger.

Beech, H. R., Burns, L. E., & Sheffield, B. F. (1982). *A behavioral approach to the management of stress*. New York: Wiley.

Beehr, T. A., & Newman, J. E. (1978). Job stress, employee health, and organizational effectiveness: A facet analysis, model, and literature review. *Personnel Psychology, 31*, 665–696.

Beer, M. (1980). *Organization change and development: A systems view*. Santa Monica, CA: Goodyear.

Bell, J. L. (1995). Traumatic event debriefing: Service delivery designs and the role of social work. *Social Work, 40*(1), 36–43.

Bennett, A. E., & Ritchie, K. (1975). General health questionnaires. In A. E. Bennett & K. Ritchie (Eds.), *Questionnaires in medicine: A guide to their design and use* (pp. 68–83). New York: Oxford University Press.

Bennett, P., Wallace, L., Carroll, D., & Smith, N. (1991). Treating Type A behaviours and mild hypertension in middle-aged men. *Journal of Psychosomatic Research, 35*, 209–223.

Bennis, W. (1966). *The coming death of bureaucracy*. New York: International Business Machines Corporation.

Bennis, W. G., & Shepard, H. A. (1956). A theory of group development. *Human Relations, 9*, 415–457.

Bensahel, J. G. (1974). How to stay sane during a corporate crisis. *International Management, 29*, 17–18.

Bensahel, J. G. (1977). Taking heat out of a tense situation. *International Management, 32*, 31–32.

Benson, H. (1974, July-August). Your innate asset for combating stress. *Harvard Business Review*, 49–60.

Benson, H. (1975). *The relaxation response*, New York: Avon Books.

Benson, H. (1985, March 18–21). *Lectures in behavioral medicine*. Cambridge, MA: Harvard Medical School.

Benson, H., & Allen, R. (1980, September-October). How much stress is too much? *Harvard Business Review*, pp. 86–92.

Benson, H., Beary, J. F., & Carol, M. P. (1974). The relaxation response. *Psychiatry, 37*, 37–46.

Benson, H., Rosner, B. A., Marzetta, B. R., & Klemchuk, H. P. (1974). Decreased blood-pressure in borderline hypertensive subjects who practiced meditation. *Journal of Chronic Disease, 26*, 163–169.

Benson, H., Rosner, B. A., Marzetta, B. R., & Klemchuk, H. P. (1974, February 23). Decreased blood-pressure in pharmacologically treated hypertensive patients who regularly elicited the relaxation response. *Lancet*, 289–291.

Benson, H., & Stark, M. (1996). *Timeless healing: The power and biology of belief.* New York: Scribner.

Berger, B. G., Friedmann, E., & Eaton, M. (1988). Comparison of jogging, the relaxation response, and group interaction for stress reduction. *Journal of Sport & Exercise Psychology, 10,* 431–447.

Berger, B. G., & Owen, D. R. (1992). Preliminary analysis of a causal relationship between swimming and stress reduction: Intense exercise may negate the effects. *International Journal of Sport Psychology, 23*(1), 70–85.

Bergin, A. E., & Garfield, S. L. (1971). *Handbook of psychotherapy and behavior change.* New York: Wiley.

Berkman, L. F., & Syme, S. L. (1979). Social networks, host resistance, and mortality: A nine year follow-up study of Alameda County residents. *American Journal of Epidemiology, 109,* 186–204.

Bernstein, D. A., & Borkovec, T. D. (1973). *Progressive relaxation training: A manual for the helping professions.* Champaign, IL: Research Press.

Bettelheim, B. (1958). Individual and mass behavior in extreme situations. In E. E. Maccoby (Ed.), *Readings in social psychology* (3rd ed., pp. 300–310). New York: Holt, Rinehart & Winston.

Bhagat, R. S. (1983, October). Effects of stressful life events upon individual performance effectiveness and work adjustment processes within organizational settings: A research model. *Academy of Management Review,* pp. 660–671.

Bhagat, R. S., & Chassie, M. B. (1981). Determinants of organizational commitment in working women: Some implications for organizational integration. *Journal of Occupational Behavior, 2,* 17–30.

Bhagat, R. S., McQuaid, S. J., Lindholm, S., & Segovis, J. (1985). Total life stress: A multimethod validation of the construct and its effect on organizationally valued outcomes and withdrawal behaviors. *Journal of Applied Psychology, 70,* 202–214.

Biddle, B. J., & Thomas, E. J. (1966). *Role theory: concepts and research.* New York: Wiley.

Bigos, S. J., Battie, M. C., Spengler, D. M., Fisher, L. D., Fordyce, W. E., Hansson, T. H., Nachemson, A. L., & Wortley, M. D. (1991). A prospective study of work perceptions and psychosocial factors affecting the report of back injury. *Spine, 16*(1), 1–6.

Billings, A. G., & Moos, R. H. (1982). Work stress and the stress-suffering roles of work and family resources. *Journal of Occupational Behaviour, 3,* 215–232.

Binik, Y. M. (1985). Psychosocial predictor of sudden death: A review and critique. *Social Science and Medicine, 20,* 667–680.

Bisson, J. I., & Deahl, M. P. (1994). Psychological debriefing and prevention of post-traumatic stress: More research is needed. *British Journal of Psychiatry, 165,* 717–720.

Blackburn, H., & Leupker, R. (1992). Heart disease. In J. M. Last & R. B. Wallace (Eds.), *Public health and preventive medicine* (13th ed., pp. 827–847). Norwalk, CT: Appleton & Lange.

Blair, S. N., Kohl, H. W. III, & Paffenberger, R. S. (1989). Physical fitness and all cause mortality. *Journal of the American Medical Association, 262,* 2395–2401.

Blair, S. N., Piserchia, P. V., Wilbur, C. S., & Crowder, J. H. (1986). A public health intervention model for work-site health promotion. *Journal of the American Medical Association, 255,* 921–926.

Blanchard, E. G., & Epstein, L. H. (1978). *A biofeedback primer.* Reading, MA: Addison-Wesley.

Blau, P. M. (1964). *Exchange and power in social life.* New York: Wiley.

Bluedorn, A. C. (1982, March-April). Managing turnover strategically. *Business Horizons, 25*(2), 6–12.

Blumenthal, J. A., Fredrikson, M., Matthews, K. A., & Kuhn, C. M. (1991). Stress reactivity and exercise training in premenopausal and postmenopausal women. *Health Psychology, 10,* 384–391.

Bly, J. L., Jones, R. C., & Richardson, J. E. (1986). Impact of worksite health promotion on health care costs and utilization. *Journal of the American Medical Association, 256,* 3235–3240.

Bodensteiner, W. D., Gerloff, E. A., & Quick, J. C. (1989). Uncertainty and stress in an R & D project environment. *R & D Management, 19,* 309–323

Bolles, R. N. (1979). *What color is your parachute?* Berkeley, CA: Ten Speed Press.

Booth-Kewley, S., & Friedman, H. S. (1987). Psychological predictors of heart disease: A quantitative review. *Psychological Bulletin, 101,* 343–362.

Bortner, R. W. (1969). A short rating scale as a potential measure of Pattern A behavior. *Journal of Chronic Diseases, 22,* 87–91.

Bower, S. A., & Bower, G. H. (1976). *Asserting yourself.* Reading, MA: Addison-Wesley.

Bowlby, J. (1982). *Attachment* (2nd ed.). New York: Basic Books.

Bowman, G. W., Worthy, N. B., & Greyser, S. A. (1965). Problems in review: Are women executives people? *Harvard Business Review, 43,* 52–57.

Bracey, H., Sanford, A., & Quick, J. C. (1981). *Basic management* (Rev. ed.). Dallas, TX: Business Publications.

Bradshaw, S. L., Ohlde, C. D., & Horne, J. B. (1993). Combat and personality change. *Bulletin of the Menninger Clinic, 57,* 466–478.

Brady, L. S. (1994). Stress, antidepressant drugs, and the locus coeruleus. Second International Symposium on the Locus Coeruleus (1993, Orcas Island, Washington). *Brain Research Bulletin, 35,* 545–556.

Branch, C. L., Gates, R. L., Susman, J. L., & Berg, A. O. (1994). *Low back pain.* (Monograph, No. 185). Kansas City, MO: American Academy of Family Physicians.

Brandon, L. D. (1992). A dark side of productivity improvement techniques. *Work Study, 41,* 11–15.

Brandt, M., & Siegel, M. I. (1978). The effects of stress on cortical bone thickness of rodents. *American Journal of Physical Anthropology, 49*(1), 31–34.

Braverman, M. (1992). Posttrauma crisis intervention in the workplace. In J. C. Quick, L. R. Murphy, & J. J. Hurrell (Eds.), *Stress and well-being at work* (pp. 299–316). Washington, DC: American Psychological Association.

Brenner, B., & Selzer, M. L. (1969). Risk of causing a fatal accident associated with alcoholism, psychopathology, and stress: Further analysis of previous data. *Behavioral Science, 14,* 490–495.

Bridges, P. K. (1974). Recent physiological studies of stress and anxiety in man. *Biological Psychiatry, 8*(1), 95–111.

Brief, A. P., Burke, M. J., George, J. M., Robinson, B. S., & Webster, J. (1988). Should negative affectivity remain an unmeasured variable in the study of job stress? *Journal of Applied Psychology, 73,* 193–198.

Brief, A. P., Schuler, R. S., & Van Sell, M. (1981). *Managing job stress.* Boston: Little, Brown.

Brodman, K., Erdmann, A. J., Jr., Lorge, I., & Wolff, H. G. (1949). The Cornell Medical Index. *Journal of the American Medical Association, 140,* 530–534.

Brodman, K., Erdmann, A. J., Jr., Lorge, I., & Wolff, H. G. (1951). The Cornell Medical Index-Health Questionnaire: II. As a diagnostic instrument. *Journal of the American Medical Association, 145,* 152–157.

Brody, S. (1994). Traditional ideology, stress, and psychotherapy use. *Journal of Psychology, 128,* 5–13.

Bronfenbrenner, U., & Mahoney, M. A. (1975). *Influences on human development* (2nd ed.). Hinsdale, IL: Dryden Press.

Brooks, W. T., & Mullins, T. W. (1989). *High impact time management.* Englewood Cliffs, NJ: Prentice-Hall.

Brousseau, K. R., & Mallinger, M. A. (1981). Internal-external locus of control, perceived occupational stress, & cardiovascular health. *Journal of Occupational Behaviour, 2,* 65–71.

Brown, B. (1977). The implications for concepts of healing: Biofeedback. *Journal of Holistic Health, 2,* 29–32.

Brown, B. (1977). *Stress and the art of biofeedback.* New York: Harper & Row.

Bruehl, S., Carlson, C. R., & McCubbin, J. A. (1993). Two brief interventions for acute pain. *Pain, 54*(1), 29–36.

Bruhn, J. G. (1996). Social support and heart disease. In C. L. Cooper (Ed.), *Handbook of stress, medicine, and health* (pp. 253–268). Boca Raton, FL: CRC Press.

Buchanan, D. (1987). Job Enrichment is Dead: Long Live High Performance Work Design! *Personnel Management, 19*(5), 40–43.

Buck, V. E. (1972). *Working under pressure.* New York: Crane, Russak.

Budd, J. W., Arvey, R. D., & Lawless, P. (1996). Correlates and consequences of workplace violence. *Journal of Occupational Health Psychology, 1,* 197–210.

Buell, J. C., & Eliot, R. S. (1979). The role of emotional stress in the development of heart disease. *Journal of the American Medical Association, 242,* 365–368.

Burack, E. H., Staszak, F. J., & Pati, G. C. (1972). An organizational analysis of manpower issues in employing the disadvantaged. *Academy of Management Journal, 15,* 255–271.

Bureau of Labor Statistics. (1995). *National Census of Fatal Occupational Injuries* (Publication No. USDL-96-315). Washington, DC: Author.

Burke, R. J. (1971). Are you fed up with work? *Personnel Administration, 34,* 27–31.

Burke, R. J. (1987). Issues and implications for health care delivery systems. In J. C. Quick, R. S. Bhagat, J. E. Dalton, & J. D. Quick (Eds.), *Work stress: Health care systems in the workplace* (pp. 27–49). New York: Praeger.

Burke, R. J. (1994). Stressful events, work-family conflict, coping, psychological burnout, and well-being among police officers. *Pyschological Reports, 75*(2), 787–800.

Burke, R. J., & Belcourt, M. L. (1974). Managerial role stress and coping responses. *Journal of Business Administration, 5,* 55–68.

Burke, R. J., & Greenglass, E. R. (1995). A longitudinal examination of the Cherniss model of psychological burnout. *Social Science and Medicine, 40,* 1357–1363.

Burke, R. J., & Richardsen, A. M. (1996). Stress, burnout, and health. In C. Cooper (Ed.), *Handbook of stress, medicine, and health* (pp. 101–117). Boca Raton, FL: CRC Press.

Burke, R. J., & Weir, T. (1980). Coping with the stress of managerial occupations. In C. L. Cooper & R. Payne (Eds.), *Current concerns in occupational stress* (pp. 229–335). New York: Wiley.

Burke, R. J., Weir, T., & DuWors, R. E., Jr. (1979). Type A behavior of administrators and wives' reports of marital satisfaction and well-being. *Journal of Applied Psychology, 64,* 57–65.

Burke, R. J., Weir, T., & DuWors, R. E., Jr. (1980). Work demands on administrators and spouse well-being. *Human Relations, 33,* 253–278.

Burns, L. E. (1981). Relaxation in the management of stress. In J. Marshall & C. L. Cooper (Eds.), *Coping with stress.* London: Gower.

Burns, M. O., & Seligman, E. P. (1989). Explanatory style across the life span: Evidence for stability over 52 years. *Journal of Personality and Social Psychology, 56,* 471–477.

Burns, T., & Stalker, G. M. (1961). *The management of innovation.* London: Tavistock.

Buros, O. (1995). *Twelfth mental measurements yearbook.* Highland Park, NJ: Gryphon Press.

Busuttil, A., & Busuttil, W. (1995). Psychological debriefing. *British Journal of Psychiatry, 166,* 676–677.

Buunk, B. P., Doosje, B. J., Jans, L. G. J. M., & Hopstaken, L. E. M. (1993). Perceived reciprocity, social support, and stress at work: The role of exchange and communal orientation. *Journal of Personality and Social Psychology, 65,* 801–811.

Cameron, K., Hurrell, J. J., Maddi, S., Nelson, D. L., Dilla, B. L., & Quick, J. C. (1995, August). Paper presented at the Academy of Management meetings, Vancouver, Canada.

Campbell, D. T., & Stanley, J. C. (1973). *Experimental and quasi-experimental designs for research.* Chicago: Rand McNally.

Cannon, B. (1994). Walter Bradford Cannon: Reflections on the man and his contributions. *International Journal of Stress Management, 1*(2), 145–158.

Cannon, W. B. (1929a). *Alternative satisfactions for the fighting emotions. Bodily changes in pain, hunger, fear and rage: An account of recent researches into the function of emotional excitement* (pp. 377–392). New York: Appleton. (Original work published 1915)

Cannon, W. B. (1929b). *Bodily changes in pain, hunger, fear and rage.* New York: Appleton-Century.

Cannon, W. B. (1932). *The wisdom of the body.* New York: Norton.

Caplan, G., & Killilea, M. (Eds.). (1976). *Support systems and mutual help: Multidisciplinary explorations.* New York: Grune & Stratton.

Caplan, R. (1971). *Organizational stress and individual strain: A social-psychological study of risk factors.* Unpublished doctoral dissertation, University of Michigan, Ann Arbor.

Caplan, R. D., Cobb, S., French, J. R. P., Jr., Harrison, R. V., & Pinneau, S. R. (1975). *Job demands and worker health* (DHHS [NIOSH] Publication No. 75-160). Washington, DC: U.S. Government Printing Office.

Caplan, R. D., Cobb, S., French, J. R. P., Harrison, R. V., & Pinneau, S. R., Jr. (1980). *Job demands and worker health: Main effects and occupational differences*, Research Report Series, Institute for Social Research, University of Michigan, Ann Arbor.

Carayon, P. (1994). Stressful jobs and non-stressful jobs: A cluster analysis of office jobs. *Ergonomics, 37*, 311–323.

Carlson, C. R., Collins, F. L., Nitz, A. J., & Sturgis, E. T. (1990). Muscle stretching as an alternative relaxation training procedure. *Journal of Behavior Therapy and Experimental Psychiatry, 21*(1), 29–38.

Carlson, C. R., & Hoyle, R. H. (1993). Efficacy of abbreviated progressive muscle relaxation training: A quantitative review of behavioral medicine research. *Journal of Consulting and Clinical Psychology, 61*, 1059–1067.

Carrington, P. (1978). *Freedom in meditation*. New York: Anchor Press/Doubleday.

Carrington, P., Collings, G. H., Benson, H., Robinson, H., Wood, L. W., Lehrer, P. M., Woodfolk, R. L., & Cole, J. W. (1980). The use of meditation-relaxation techniques for the management of stress in a working population. *Journal of Occupational Medicine, 22*, 221–231.

Carroll, S. J., & Tosi, J. L. (1970). Goal characteristics and personality factors in a management-by-objectives program. *Administrative Science Quarterly, 15*, 295–305.

Carroll, S. J., & Tosi, J. L. (1973). *Management by objectives: Applications and research*. New York: Macmillan.

Carver, C. S., Scheier, M. F., & Weintraub, J. K. (1989). Assessing coping strategies: A theoretically based approach. *Journal of Personality and Social Psychology, 56*, 267–283.

Cascio, W. F. (in press). Learning from outcomes: Financial experiences of 300 firms that have downsized. In M. Gowihg, J. Kraft, & J. C. Quick, *The New Organizational Reality: Downsizing, Restructuring, and Revitalization*. Washington, DC: American Psychological Association.

Caudron, S. (1990, November). Monsanto responds to diversity. *Personnel Journal*, pp. 72–80.

Chan, K. B. (1977). Individual differences in reactions to stress and their personality and situational determinants. *Social Science and Medicine, 11*, 89–103.

Chesney, M. A. (1987). Behavioral factors in hypertension: Lessons from the work setting. In J. C. Quick, R. S. Bhagat, J. E. Dalton, & J. D. Quick (Eds.), *Work stress: Health care systems in the workplace* (pp. 111–129). New York: Praeger.

Chesney, M. A., & Rosenman, R. (1980). Type A behavior in the work setting. In C. L. Cooper & R. Payne (Eds.), *Current concerns in occupational stress* (pp. 187–212). New York: Wiley.

Chopra, D. (1989). *Quantum healing: Exploring the frontiers of mind/body medicine*. New York: Bantam Books.

Clark, L. K., & Miller, S. M. (1990). Self-reliance and desire for control in the Type A behavior pattern [Special issue: Type A behavior]. *Journal of Social Behavior and Personality, 5*, 405–418.

Cobb, S. (1976). Social support as a moderator of life stress. *Psychosomatic Medicine, 38*, 300–314.

Coburn, D. (1978). Work and general psychological and physical well-being. *International Journal of Health Services, 8*, 415–435.

Coffey, R. E., Athos, A. G., & Raynolds, P. A. (1975). *Behavior in organizations: A multidimensional view*. Englewood Cliffs, NJ: Prentice-Hall.

Cohen, A. R., & Gadon, H. (1978). *Alternative work schedules: Integrating individual and organizational needs*. Reading, MA: Addison-Wesley.

Cohen, J. (1979). Stress and wound-healing. *Acta Anatomica, 103*(2), 134–141.

Cohen, S. (1992). Stress, social support, and the buffering hypothesis. *Psychological Bulletin, 98*, 310–357.

Cohen, S., & Edwards, J. R. (1989). Personality characteristics as moderators of the relationship between stress and disorder. In W. J. Neufeld (Ed.), *Advances in the investigation of psychological stress* (pp. 235–283). New York: Wiley.

Cohen, S., & Wills, T. A. (1985). Stress, social support, and the buffering hypothesis. *Psychological Bulletin, 98,* 310–357.

Cohen, W. S. (1985). Health promotion in the workplace: A prescription for good health. *American Psychologist, 40*(2), 213–216.

Cohn, R. M. (1978). The effect of employment status change on self-attitudes. *Social Psychology, 41*(2), 81–93.

Cole, P. A., Pomerleau, C. S., & Harris, J. K. (1992). The effects of noncurrent and concurrent relaxation training on cardiovascular reactivity to a psychological stressor. *Journal of Behavioral Medicine, 15,* 407–414.

Coleman, J. C. (1973, May-June). Life stress and maladaptive behavior. *American Journal of Occupational Therapy, 27,* 169–180.

Colligan, M. J., Smith, M. J., & Hurrell, J. J. (1977). Occupational incidence rates of mental health disorders. *Journal of Human Stress, 3*(3), 34–39.

Colligan, M. J., & Stockton, W. (1978). The mystery of assembly-line hysteria. *Psychology Today, 12*(1).

Collins, M. L. (1977). *Employee fitness.* Ottawa, Canada: Minister of Supply and Services.

Comstock, G. W., & Partridge, K. B. (1972). Church attendance and health. *Journal of Chronic Diseases, 25,* 665–672.

Conger, J., & Kanungo, R. (1988). Charismatic leadership: The elusive factor in organizational effectiveness. New York: Jossey-Bass.

Connelly, J. (1995, March 6). Let's hear it for the office. *Fortune,* pp. 221–222.

Conway, T. L., Vickers, R. R., Jr., Ward, H. W., & Rahe, R. H. (1981). Occupational stress and variation in cigarette, coffee and alcohol consumption. *Journal of Health and Social Behavior, 22*(2), 155–165.

Cooper, C. L. (1982). *The stress check.* Englewood Cliffs, NJ: Prentice-Hall.

Cooper, C. L. (Ed.). (1996). *Handbook of stress, medicine, and health.* Boca Raton, FL: CRC Press.

Cooper, C. L., & Cartwright, S. (1994). Healthy mind: Healthy organizations. *Human Relations, 47,* 455–471.

Cooper, C. L., & Crump, J. (1978). Prevention and coping with occupational stress. *Journal of Occupational Medicine, 20,* 420–426.

Cooper, C. L., & Davidson, M. J. (1982, Spring). The high cost of stress on woman managers. *Organizational Dynamics,* pp. 44–53.

Cooper, C. L., & Faragher, E. B. (1993). Psychosocial stress and breast cancer: The interrelationship between stress events, coping strategies and personality. *Psychologic Medicine, 23,* 653.

Cooper, C. L., & Marshall, J. (1976). Occupational sources of stress: A review of the literature relating to coronary heart disease and mental ill health. *Journal of Occupational Psychology, 48,* 11–28.

Cooper, C. L., & Marshall, J. (1977). *Understanding executive stress.* New York: PBI.

Cooper C. L., & Marshall, J. (1978). An audit of managerial (Di) stress. *Journal of Enterprise Management, 1,* 185–196.

Cooper, C. L., & Melhuish, A. (1980). Occupational stress and managers. *Journal of Occupational Medicine, 22,* 588–592.

Cooper, C. L., & Payne, R. (Eds.). (1978). *Stress at work.* New York: Wiley.

Cooper, C. L., & Payne, R. (Eds.). (1980). *Current concerns in occupational stress.* New York: Wiley.

Cooper, C. L., & Roden, J. (1985). Mental health and satisfaction amongst tax officers. *Social Science & Medicine, 221,* 474–481.

Cooper, C. L., & Sadri, G. (1991). The impact of stress counselling at work [Special issue: Handbook on job stress]. *Journal of Social Behavior and Personality, 6,* 411–423.

Cooper, C. L., Sloan, S. J., & Williams, S. (1988). *Occupational stress indicator management guide.* Oxford, England: NFER-Nelson.

Cooper, C. L., & Watson, M. (1991). Cancer and stress: Psychological, biological, and coping studies. Chichester, England: Wiley.

Cooper, C. L., & Williams, S. (1994). *Creating healthy work organizations.* Chichester, England: Wiley.

Cooper, K. (1970). *The new aerobics.* New York: Bantam Books.

Cooper, K. (1982a). *The aerobics program for total well-being.* New York: Evans.

Cooper, K. (1982b). *The aerobics way.* New York: Evans.

Cooper, M., & Cooper, K. (1978). *Aerobics for women.* New York: Bantam Books.

Corcoran, K. (1995). Measuring burnout: An updated reliability and convergent validity study. In R. Crandell & P. Perrewe (Eds.), *Occupational stress: A handbook* (pp. 263–268). Washington, DC: Taylor & Francis.

Cordes, C. L., & Dougherty, T. W. (1993). A review and integration of research on job burnout. *Academy of Management Review, 18,* 621–656.

Coronary-Prone Behavior Review Panel. (1981). Coronary-prone behavior and coronary heart disease: A critical review. *Circulation, 63,* 1199–1215.

Cosper, R. (1979). Drinking as conformity: A critique of sociological literature on occupational differences in drinking. *Journal of Studies on Alcohol, 40,* 868–891.

Cox, T. (1980). Repetitive work. In C. L. Cooper & R. Payne (Eds.), *Current Concerns in Occupational Stress* (pp. 23–41). New York: Wiley.

Cox, T. (1995, April). *European legislation and the management of work-related stress.* Paper presented at the Fifth International Conference on Stress Management, Leeuwenhorst Congress Center, Noordwijkerhout, The Netherlands.

Cox, V. C., Paulus, P. B., McCain, G., & Karlovac, M. (1982). The relationship between crowding and health. In A. Baum & J. Singer (Eds.), *Advances in environmental psychology* (Vol. 4). Hillsdale, NJ: Erlbaum.

Crandall, R., & Perrewe, P. L. (1995). *Occupational stress: A handbook.* Washington, DC: Taylor & Francis.

Crasilneck, H. B., & Hall, J. A. (1975). *Clinical hypnosis.* New York: Grune & Stratton.

Cui, X. J., & Vaillant, G. E. (1996). Antecedents and consequences of negative life events in adulthood: A longitudinal study. *American Journal of Psychiatry, 153,* 21–26.

Cummings, T. (1996, April 12). *How organizations create new forms of organizing.* Paper presented at the 11th annual Texas Conference on Organizations, Austin, TX.

Cummings, T. G., & Cooper, C. L. (1979). A cybernetic framework for studying occupational stress. *Human Relations, 32,* 395–418.

Cushway, D. (1992). Stress in clinical psychology trainees. *British Journal of Clinical Psychology, 31*(2), 169–179.

Dalton, D. R., Krackhardt, D. M., & Porter, L. W. (1981). Functional turnover: An empirical assessment. *Journal of Applied Psychology, 66,* 716–721.

Dalton, D. R., Tudor, W. D., & Krackhardt, D. M. (1982). Turnover overstated: The functional taxonomy. *Academy of Management Review, 7*(1), 117–123.

Davidow, W. H., & Malone, M. S. (1992). The virtual corporation. New York: Harper Collins.

Davidson, M. J., & Cooper, C. L. (1983). *Stress and the woman manager.* Oxford, England: Martin Robertson.

Davis, E. (1995). Have modem, won't travel. *Management Review, 84,* 7.

Davis, L., & Taylor, J. (Eds.). (1979). *Design of jobs.* Santa Monica, CA.

Davis, M., Eshelman, E. R., & McKay, M. (1995). *The relaxation and stress reduction workbook* (4th ed.). Oakland, CA: New Harbinger.

Davis, S., & Lawrence, P. (May-June 1980). Problems of matrix organizations. *Harvard Business Review,* pp. 131–142.

Dayal, I., & Thomas, J. M. (1968). Operation KPE: Developing a new organization. *Journal of Applied Behavioral Science, 4,* 473–506.

Decade of the executive woman. (1993). Los Angeles: Korn/Ferry International.

Decker, P. J., & Borgen, F. (1993). Dimensions of work appraisal: Stress, strain, coping, job satisfaction, and negative affectivity. *Journal of Counseling Psychology, 40,* 470–478.

Dedmon, R. E. (1979). Kimberly-Clark's health management program: Results and prospects (mimeographed). Neenah, WI: Kimberly-Clark.

Dedmon, R. E. (1980, April). Employees as health educators: A reality at Kimberly-Clark. *Occupational Health and Safety,* pp. 18–24.

Dedmon, R. E., Gander, J. W., O'Connor, M. P., & Paschke, A. C. (1979, November). An industry health management program. *The Physician and Sports Medicine, 7,*(11), 56–67.

de Geus, E. J., Van Doornen, L. J., & Orlebeke, J. F. (1993). Regular exercise and aerobic fitness in relation to psychological make-up and physiological stress reactivity. *Psychosomatic Medicine, 55,* 347–363.

Delistraty, D. A., Greene, W. A., Carlberg, K. A., & Raver, K. K. (1992). Cardiovascular reactivity in Type A and B males to mental arithmetic and aerobic exercise at an equivalent oxygen uptake. *Psychophysiology, 29,* 264–271.

DeLongis, A., Folkman, S., & Lazarus, R. S. (1988). The impact of daily stress on health and mood: Psychological and social resources as mediators. *Journal of Personality and Social Psychology, 54,* 486–495.

DeMarco, A. (1995). The dawning of the telecommuter age. *Facilities Design & Management, 14,* 48–51.

Dembroski, T. M. (Ed.). (1978). *Coronary-prone behavior.* New York: Springer-Verlag.

Department of Health and Human Services. Centers for Disease Control. (1986). *The health consequences of involuntary smoking: A report of the Surgeon General* (DHHS Publication No. CDC 87-8398). Washington, DC: Author.

Department of Health and Human Services. Centers for Disease Control. (1987a). *Smoking and health: A national status report* (2nd ed.) (DHHS Publication No. CDC 89-8411. Washington, DC: Author.

Department of Health and Human Services. (1987b). *Sixth special report to the U.S. Congress on alcohol and health from the secretary of health and human services* (DHHS Publication No. ADM 87-1519). Rockville, MD: Author.

Department of Health and Human Services. (1989). *Reducing the health consequences of smoking: 25 years of progress. A report of the surgeon general* (DHHS Publication No. [CDC] 89-8411). Washington, DC: U.S. DHHS, Centers for Disease Control.

Depue, R. L. (1979). Turning inward: The police officer counselor. *FBI Law Enforcement Bulletin, 48*(2), 8–12.

Derogatis, L. R. (1981). *Description and bibliography for the SCL-90-R* (mimeographed). Baltimore: Johns Hopkins University School of Medicine.

Derogatis, L. R., Lipman, R. S., Covi, L., & Rickels, K. (1972, November). Factorial invariance of symptom dimensions in anxious and depressive neuroses. *Archives of General Psychiatry, 27,* 659–665.

Deus v. Allstate Insurance Company, Civil Action Case No. 88-2099 (U.S. District Court, Western District of Louisiana, 1990–1992).

Dewe, P. (1992). The appraisal process: Exploring the role of meaning, importance, control and coping in work stress. [Special issue: Occupational stress, psychological burnout and anxiety]. *Anxiety, Stress and Coping: an International Journal, 5*(1), 95–109.

Dimsdale, J. E., & Moss, J. (1980, January 25). Plasma catecholamines in stress and exercise. *Journal of the American Medical Association, 243,* 340–342.

Dobrzanski, T., & Rychta, R. (1977). Cattel 16 personality factors and biochemical responses to occupational noise exposure. *Polskie Archiwum Weterynaryjne, 58,* 427–435.

Dohrenwend, B. S., & Dohrenwend, B. P. (Eds.). (1974). *Successful life events: Their nature and effects.* New York: Wiley.

Dohrenwend, P. P., Raphael, K. G., Schwartz, S., Stueve, A., & Skodol, A. (1993). The structured event probe and narrative rating method for measuring stressful life events. In L. Goldberger & S. Breznitz (Eds.), *Handbook of stress: Theoretical and clinical aspects* (2nd ed., pp. 174–199). New York: Free Press.

Dorian, D., & Taylor, C. B. (1984). Stress factors in the development of coronary artery disease. *Journal of Occupational Medicine, 26,* 747–756.

Drennen, W. T., Vidic, J. J., & Nay, R. (1988). Biofeedback and effects of set and sex with Type A and Type B college students: An exploratory study. *Psychological Reports, 63,* 787–790.

Drucker, P. F. (1954). *The practice of management.* New York: Harper & Row.

Duffy, C. A., & McGoldrick, A. (1990). Stress and the bus driver in the UK transport industry. *Work and Stress, 4,* 17–27.

Duggar, B. C., & Swengios, G. V. (1968). The design of physical activity programs for industry. *Journal of Medicine, 11,* 322–329.

Dunham, R. B., & Smith, F. J. (1979). *Organizational surveys: An internal assessment of organizational health.* Glenview, IL: Scott, Foresman.

Eastman, P. (1995). Panel endorses behavioral therapy for cancer pain. *Journal of the National Cancer Institute, 87,* 1666–1667.

Eden, D. (1990). Acute and chronic job stress, strain, and vacation relief. *Organizational Behavior and Human Decision Processes, 45*(2), 175–193.

Edwards, J. A. (1991). The measurement of Type A behavior pattern: An assessment of criterion-oriented validity, content validity, and construct validity. In C. L. Cooper & R. Payne (Eds.), *Personality and stress: Individual differences in the stress process* (pp. 151–180). New York: Wiley.

Edwards, J. R. (1996). An examination of competing versions of the person-environment fit approach to stress. *Academy of Management Journal, 39*(2), 292–339.

Edwards, J. R., & Cooper, C. L. (1990). The person-environment fit approach to stress: Recurring problems and some suggested solutions. *Journal of Organizational Behavior, 11*(4), 293–307.

El-Batavi-Mostafa. (1978, June). Work related diseases. *World Health Magazine,* pp. 10–13.

Eliot, R. S. (1979). *Stress and the major cardiovascular disorders.* Mt. Kisco, NY: Futura.

Eliot, R. S. (1982, February). Stress reduction: Techniques that can help you and your Patients. *Consultant,* pp. 91–112.

Eliot, R. S. (1995). *From stress to strength: How to lighten your load and save your life.* New York: Bantam Books.

Eliot, R. S., & Breo, D. L. (1984). *Is it worth dying for?* New York: Bantam Books.

Ellis, A. (1955). *How to live with a neurotic.* New York: Crown.

Ellis, A. (1978). What people can do for themselves to cope with stress. In C. L. Cooper & R. Payne (Eds.), *Stress at work* (pp. 209–222). New York: Wiley.

Engdahl, R., & Walsh, D. (1980). *Mental wellness programs for employees.* New York: Springer-Verlag.

Engel, G. L. (1978). Psychologic stress, vasodepressor (vasovagal) syncope and sudden death. *Annals of Internal Medicine, 89,* 403–412.

Etzion, D., & Westman, M. (1994). Social support and sense of control as moderators of the stress-burnout relationship in military careers. *Journal of Social Behavior and Personality, 9,* 639–656.

Evans, G. W. (1979). Behavioral and physiological consequences of crowding in humans. *Journal of Applied Social Psychology, 9*(1), 27–46.

Everly, G. S., Jr. (1989). *A clinical guide to the treatment of the human stress response.* The Plenum series on stress and coping. New York: Plenum Press.

Everly, G. S. (1994). Short-term psychotherapy of acute adult onset of post-traumatic stress: The role of weltanschauung. Fifth International Montreux Congress on Stress (1993, Montreux, Switzerland). *Stress Medicine, 10*(3), 191–196.

Everly, G. S., & Benson, H. (1989). Disorders of arousal and the relaxation response: Speculations on the nature and treatment of stress-related diseases. [Special issue: Biofeedback and diagnostic techniques]. *International Journal of Psychosomatics, 36*(1–4), 15–21.

Everly, G. S., & Mitchell, J. T. (1995). Prevention of work-related posttraumatic stress: The critical incident stress debriefing process. In L. R. Murphy, J. J. Hurrall, S. L. Sauter, & G. P. Keita (Eds.), *Job stress interventions* (pp. 173–184). Washington, DC: American Psychological Association.

Ewart, C. K. (1991). Social action theory for a public health psychology. *American Psychologist, 46,* 931–946.

Eysenck, H. J. (1996). Personality and cancer. In C. L. Cooper (Ed.), *Handbook of stress, medicine, and health* (pp. 193–215). Boca Raton, FL: CRC Press.

Eysenck, H. J., & Wilson, G. D. (1976). *A texbook of human psychology.* Lancaster, England: MTP Press.

Faragher, E. B. (1996). Life events, coping, and cancer. In C. L. Cooper (Ed.), *Handbook of stress, medicine, and health* (pp. 159–175). Boca Raton, FL: CRC Press.

Fayol, H. (1929). *General and industrial management.* Geneva, Switzerland: International Management Institute.

Feinstein, A. R. (1977). *Clinical biostatistics.* Saint Louis, MO: Mosby.

Feinstein, A. R. (1967). *Clinical judgment.* Baltimore: Williams & Wilkins.

Feldman, J. L., & Fitzpatrick, R. J. (1992). *Managed mental health care: Administrative and clinical issues*. Washington, DC: American Psychiatric Press.

Fentem, P. H., & Bassey, E. J. (1979). The case for exercise. *Sports Council Research Working Papers* (Vol. 8). London: Sports Council.

Ferguson, M., & Gowan, J. (1976, Summer). TM: Some preliminary findings. *Journal of Humanistic Psychology, 16*(3), 51–60.

Fernberg, P. M. (1990). Why "white collar" doesn't mean "danger-free." *Modern Office Technology, 35*, 49–52.

Ferris, G. R., & Judge, T. A. (1991). Personnel/human resources management: A political influence perspective. *Journal of Management, 17*, 447–488.

Fiedler, F. E., Potter, E. H., Zais, M. M., & Knowlton, W. A. (1979). Organizational stress and the use and misuse of managerial intelligence and experience. *Journal of Applied Psychology, 64*, 635–647.

Fielding, J. E. (1992). Smoking: Health effects and control. In J. M. Last & R. B. Wallace (Eds.), *Public health and preventive medicine* (13th ed., pp. 715–740). Norwalk, CT: Appleton & Lange.

Fineman, S. (1979). A psychosocial model of stress and its application to managerial unemployment. *Human Relations, 32*, 323–345.

Fisher, C. D., & Gitelson, R. (1983). A meta-analysis of the correlates of role conflict and ambiguity. *Journal of Applied Psychology, 68*, 320–333.

Fletcher, B. (1991). *Work, stress, disease and life expectancy*. Chichester, England: Wiley.

Folkman, S., & Lazarus, R. J. (1980, September). An analysis of coping in a middle-aged community sample. *Journal of Health and Social Behavior, 21*, 219–239.

Folkman, S., & Lazarus, R. (1988). *Manual for the Ways of Coping Questionnaire*. Palo Alto, CA: Consulting Psychologists Press.

Folkman, S., Schaefer, C., & Lazarus, R. S. (1979). Cognitive processes as mediators of stress and coping. In V. Hamilton & D. M. Warburton (Eds.), *Human stress and cognition* (pp. 265–298). Chilchester, England: Wiley.

Follette, W., & Cummings, N. (1967). Psychiatric services and medical utilization in a prepaid health plan setting. *Medical Care, 5*, 25–35. San Francisco: Kaiser Foundation Hospital.

Ford, D. L., Jr. (Ed.). (1976). *Readings in minority-group relations*. La Jolla, CA: University Associates.

Forrest, W. R. (1978). Stress and self-destructive behaviors of dentists. *Dental Clinics of North America, 22*, 361–371.

Forward, G. E., Beach, D. E., Gray, D. A., & Quick, J. C. (1991). Mentofacturing: A vision for American industrial excellence. *Academy of Management Executive, 5*, 32–44.

Foss, L., & Rothenberg, K. (1987). *The second medical revolution: From biomedical to infomedical*. Boston, MA: New Science Library.

Frankenhaeuser, M. (1991). The psychophysiology of workload, stress, and health: Comparison between the sexes. *Annals of Behavioral Medicine, 13*, 197–204.

Frankenhaeuser, M., Lundberg, U., & Chesney, M. (Eds.). (1991). *Women, work, and health: Stress and opportunities*. New York: Plenum Press.

Frasure-Smith, N., & Prince, R. (1985). The ischemic heart disease life stress monitoring program: Impact on mortality. *Psychosomatic Medicine, 4*, 432–445.

French, J. R. P., Jr., & Caplan, R. D. (1972). Organizational stress and individual strain. In A. J. Marrow (Ed.), *The failure of success* (pp. 30–66). New York: AMACOM.

French, J. R. P., Jr., Caplan, R. D., & Harrison, R. V. (1982). *Mechanisms of job stress and strain*. New York: Wiley.

French, J. R. P., Jr., & Kahn, R. L. (1962). A programmatic approach to studying the industrial environment and mental health. *Journal of Social Issues, 18*, 1–47.

French, W. L., & Bell, C. H., Jr. (1978). *Organization development: Behavioral science interventions for organization improvement* (2nd ed.). Englewood Cliffs, NJ: Prentice-Hall.

French, W. L., & Bell, C. H. (1990). *Organization development* (4th ed.). Englewood Cliffs, NJ: Prentice Hall.

Freud, S. (1956a). *Collected papers* (Vols. I–V). London: Hogarth Press and The Institute of Psycho-Analysis.

Freud, S. (1956b). *The interpretation of dreams*. New York: Basic Books.

Freud, S. (1961). *Civilization and its discontents*. New York: Norton.

Frew, D. R. (1974). Transcendental meditation and productivity. *Academy of Management Journal, 17*, 362–368.

Friedman, M. (1984). Alteration of Type A behavior and reduction in cardiac recurrences in postmyocardial infarction patients. *American Heart Journal, 108*, 237–248.

Friedman, M. D., & Rosenman, R. H. (1974). *Type A behavior and your heart*. New York: Knopf.

Friedman, M., Rosenman, R. H., & Carroll, V. (1958). Changes in serum cholesterol and blood clotting time in men subjected to cyclic variations of occupational stress. *Circulation, 17*, 852–861.

Froelicher, V., Battler, A., & McKirnam, M. D. (1980). Physical activity and coronary heart disease. *Cardiology, 65*, 153–190.

Fromm, E. (1973). *The anatomy of human destructiveness*. New York: Holt, Rinehart & Winston.

Frone, M. R., Russell, M., & Barnes, G. M. (1996). Work-family conflict, gender, health-related outcomes: A study of employed parents in two commmunity samples. *Journal of Occupational Health Psychology, 1*, 57–69.

Fuller, G. D. (1978). Current status of biofeedback in clinical practice. *American Psychologist, 33*, 39–48.

Funch, D. P., & Marshall, J. (1983). The role of stress, social support, and age in survival from breast cancer. *Journal of Psychosomatic Research, 27*(1), 77–83.

Gallup, G. H. (1978). *The Gallup Poll: Public opinion 1971–1977* (Vol. 2). Wilmington, DE: Scholarly Resources.

Gambert, S. R., Hagen, T. C., Garthwaite, T. L., Duthie, E. H., Jr., & McCarty, D. J. (1981). Exercise and the endogenous opioids. *New England Journal of Medicine, 305*, 1590–1591.

Ganster, D. (1995). Interventions for building healthy organizations: Suggestions from the stress research literature. In L. R. Murphy, J. J. Hurrell, S. L. Sauter, & G. P. Keita (Eds.), *Job stress interventions* (pp. 323–336). Washington, DC: American Psychological Association.

Ganster, D. C., & Schaubroeck, J. (1991). Work stress and employee health. *Journal of Management, 17*, 235–271.

Gardell, B. (1987). Efficiency and health hazards in mechanized work. In J. C. Quick, R. S. Bhagat, J. E. Dalton, & J. D. Quick (Eds.), *Work stress: Health care systems in the workplace* (pp. 50–71). New York: Praeger.

Garland C., & Garland F. (1986). Digestive diseases. In J. Last (Ed.), *Public health and preventive medicine* (12th ed.). Norwalk, CT: Appleton-Century-Crofts.

Gearing, S. (1994). *Female executive stress syndrome: The working woman's guide to a balanced, successful life*. Fort Worth, TX: The Summit Group.

Gebhardt, D. L., & Crump, C. E. (1990). Employee fitness and wellness programs in the workplace [Special issue: Organizational psychology]. *American Psychologist, 45*(2), 262–272.

Gelles, E. B. (1994). Letter writing as a coping strategy: The case of Abigail Adams. *Psychohistory Review, 22*, 193–209.

Gentry, W. D. (1975). Behavioral treatment of somatic disorders. *University Programs Modular Studies*, 1–16.

Gentry, W. D., Chesney, A. P., Gary, H. E., Jr., Hall, R. P., & Harburg, E. (1982, May). Habitual anger-coping styles: I. Effect on mean blood pressure and risk for essential hypertension. *Psychosomatic Medicine, 4*, 195–202.

Gerloff, E., & Quick, J. C. (1978). A study of hierarchical communication and consensus within the context of a goal-setting program. *Academy of Management Proceedings*, 324–328.

Gice, J. (1993, June). Taking the emotion out of workers compensation stress claims. *CPCU Journal, 46*(2), 98–106.

Gill, J. J. (1985). Reduction in Type A behavior in healthy middle-aged American military officers. *American Heart Journal, 108*, 503–514.

Gillingham, K. K. (1988). High G-stress and orientational stress: Physiologic effects of aerial maneuvering. *Aviation, Space, and Environmental Medicine, 59*, A10–A20.

Girdano, D. A., & Everly, G. S., Jr. (1979). *Controlling stress and tension: A holistic approach.* Englewood Cliffs, NJ: Prentice-Hall.

Goldberg, D. P., Rickels, K., Downing, R., & Hesbacher, P. (1976, July). A comparison of two psychiatric screening tests. *British Journal of Psychiatry, 129,* 61–67.

Goldberg, R. J. (1982). Anxiety reduction by self-regulation: Theory, practice, and evaluation. *Annals of Internal Medicine, 96,* 483–487.

Goldstein, M. G., & Niaura, R. (1992). Psychological factors affecting physical condition. Cardiovascular disease literature review: Part 1. Coronary artery disease and sudden death. *Psychosomatics, 33,* 134–145.

Goldston, E. (1973, September-October). Executive sabbaticals: About to take off? *Harvard Business Review,* pp. 57–68.

Gottlieb, B. H. (1987). Using social support to protect and promote health. *Journal of Primary Prevention, 8*(1–2), 49–70.

Gottlieb, B. H. (1996). Theories and practices of mobilizing support in stressful circumstances. In C. L. Cooper (Ed.), *Handbook of stress, medicine, and health* (pp. 339–356). Boca Raton, FL: CRC Press.

Gowing, M., Kraft, J., & Quick, J. C. (in press). *The new organizational reality: Downsizing, restructuring, and revitalization.* Washington, DC: American Psychological Association.

Grant, I., Kyle, G. C., Teichman, A., & Mendels, J. (1974). Recent life events and diabetes in adults. *Psychosomatic Medicine, 36,* 121.

Grant, J. M. (1996). *The great Texas banking crash: An insider's account.* Austin, TX: University of Texas Press.

Gray, D. A., Gault, F. M., Meyers, H. H., & Walther, J. E. (1990). Career planning. *Prevention in Human Services, 8*(1), 43–59.

Greenberger, R. S. (1981, April 23). How burnout affects corporate managers and their performance. *Wall Street Journal, 67*(79), 1, 18.

Greenhaus, J. H., & Beutell, N. J. (1985). Sources of conflict between work and family role. *Academy of Management Review, 10,* 76–88.

Greller, M. M., Parsons, C. K., & Mitchell, D. R. D. (1992). Additive effects and beyond: Occupational stressors and social buffers in a police organization. In J. C. Quick, L. R. Murphy, & J. J. Hurrell (Eds.), *Stress and well-being at work* (pp. 33–47). Washington, DC: American Psychological Association.

Griest, H. H., Klein, M. H., Eischens, R. R., & Faris, J. W. (1978). Antidepressant running. *Behavioral Medicine, 5*(6), 19–24.

Griffin, R. W. (1982). *Task design and integrative approach.* Glenview, IL: Scott, Foresman.

Griffin, R. W., O'Leary-Kelly, A. M., & Collins, J. (Eds.). (in press). *Dysfunctional behavior in organizations. Violent behaviors in organizations* (Vol. 1) and *Nonviolent behaviors in organizations* (Vol. 2). Greenwich, CT: JAI Press.

Guinn, S. L. (1989). The changing workforce. *Training and Development Journal, 43,* 36–39.

Gunderson, E. K. (1978). Organizational and environmental influences on health and performance. In B. T. King, S. Streufert, & F. E. Fiedler (Eds.), *Managerial control and organizational democracy* (pp. 43–60). New York: Halsted Press.

Gurman, A. S., & Messer, S. B. (Eds.). (1995). *Essential psychotherapies: Theory and practice.* New York: Guilford Press.

Hackman, J. R. (1977). Work design. In J. R. Hackman & J. L. Suttle (Eds.), *Improving life at work* (pp. 96–162). Santa Monica, CA: Goodyear.

Hackman, J. R., & Oldham, G. R. (1976). Motivation through the design of work: Test of a theory. *Organizational Behavior and Human Performance, 16,* 250–279.

Hackman, J. R., & Oldham, G. R. (1980). *Work redesign.* Reading, MA: Addison-Wesley.

Haley, J. (1973). *Uncommon therapy: The psychiatric techniques of Milton H. Erickson, M.D.* New York: Norton.

Hall, D. T. (1976). *Careers in organizations.* Santa Monica, CA: Goodyear.

Hall, D. T., & Hall, F. S. (1980). Stress and the two-career couple. In C. L. Cooper & R. Payne (Eds.), *Current concerns in occupational stress* (pp. 243–266). New York: Wiley.

Hall, D. T., & Mansfield, R. (1971). Organizational and individual response to external stress. *Administrative Science Quarterly, 16,* 533–547.

Hall, D. T., & Rabinowitz, S. (1981). Changing correlates of job involvement in three career stages. *Journal of Vocational Behavior, 18,* 138–144.

Hall, H. R. (1982–1983). Hypnosis and the immune system: A review with implications for cancer and the psychology of healing. *Journal of Clinical Hypnosis, 25,* 92–103.

Hammar, N., Alfredsson, L., & Theorell, T. (1994). Job characteristics and incidence of myocardial infarction. *International Journal of Epidemiology, 28,* 277–284.

Hammarstrom, A. (1994). Health consequences of youth unemployment: Review from a gender perspective. *Social Science Medicine, 38,* 699–709.

Handy, C. (1978). The family: Help or hindrance. In C. L. Cooper & R. Payne (Eds.), *Stress at work* (pp. 107–123). New York: Wiley.

Hansen, J. C., & Campbell, D. P. (1985). *Manual for the SVIB-SCII* (4th ed.). Stanford, CA: Stanford University Press.

Harrison, R. V. (1978). Person-environment fit and job stress. In C. L. Cooper & R. Payne (Eds.), *Stress at work* (pp. 175–205). New York: Wiley.

Hartley, D., Roback, H. B., & Abramowitz, S. I. (1976). Deterioration effects in encounter groups. *American Psychologist, 31,* 247–255.

Harvey, M. G., & Cosier, R. A. (1995). Homicides in the workplace: Crisis or false alarm? *Business Horizons, 38,* 11–20.

Hawkins, N. G., Davis, R., & Holmes, T. H. (1957). Evidence of psychosomatic factors in the development of pulmonary tuberculosis. *American Review of Tubercular Pulmonary Disease, 75,* 768–780.

Haynes, G. (1978). The problem of stress. *Nursing Times, 74,* 753–754.

Haynes, S., Levine, S., & Scotch, N. (1978). The relationship of psychosocial factors to coronary heart disease in the Framingham study: I. Methods and risk factors. *American Journal of Epidemiology, 107,* 362–393.

Haynes, S. G., Feinleib, M., & Kannel, W. B. (1978). The relationship of psychosocial factors to coronary heart disease in the Framingham study: II. Prevalence of coronary heart disease. *American Journal of Epidemiology, 107,* 384–402.

Hazan, C., & Shaver, P. (1990). Love and work: An attachment-theoretical perspective. *Journal of Personality and Social Psychology, 59,* 270–280.

Hedge, A., Erickson, W. A., & Rubin, G. (1992). Effects of personal and occupational factors on sick building syndrome reports in air-conditioned offices. In J. C. Quick, L. R. Murphy, & J. J. Hurrell, Jr. (Eds.), *Stress & well-being at work* (pp. 286–298). Washington, DC: American Psychological Association.

Hellman, C. J., Budd, M., Borysenko, J., McClelland, D. C., & Benson, H. (1990). A study of the effectiveness of two group behavioral medicine interventions for patients with psychosomatic complaints. *Behavioral Medicine, 16,* 165–173.

Henry, J. P. (1976). Understanding the early pathophysiology of essential hypertension. *Geriatrics, 31,* 59–72.

Herold, D. M., & Conlon, E. G. (1982). Alcohol consumption as a coping response to job induced stress. *Academy of Management Proceedings,* 292–296.

Herzberg, F., Mausner, B., & Snyderman, B. (1959). *The motivation to work.* New York: Wiley.

Hess, W. R. (1957). *The functional organization of the diencephalon.* New York: Grune & Stratton.

Hickox, K. (1994, January). Content and competitive. *Airman,* pp. 31–33.

Hilgard, E. R., Atkinson, R. L., & Atkinson, R. C. (1979). *Introductions to psychology* (7th ed.). London: Harcourt Brace Jovanovich.

Hilker, R. R., Asthma, F. E., & Eggert, R. L. (1972). A company-sponsored alcoholic rehabilitation program. *Journal of Occupational Medicine, 14,* 769–772.

Hillier, S. (1981, February 12). Stresses, strains and smoking. *Nursing Mirror,* pp. 26–30.

Hinkle, L. E., & Wolf, S. (1952). The effects of stressful life situations on the concentration of blood glucose in diabetic and nondiabetic humans. *Diabetes, 1,* 383.

Hirschfeld, A. H., & Behan, R. C. (1963). The accident process: I. Etiological considerations of industrial injuries. *Journal of the American Medical Association, 186,* 193–199.

Hirschfeld, A. H., & Behan, R. C. (1966). The accident process: III. Disability: Acceptable and unacceptable. *Journal of the American Medical Association, 197,* 125–129.

Hirschhorn, L. (1990). Leaders and followers in a postindustrial age: A psychodynamic view. *Journal of Applied Behavioral Science, 26,* 529–542.

Holden, E. W., & Wagner, M. K. (1990). Self-regulation and Type A behavior. *Journal of Research in Personality, 24*(1), 57–70.

Holmes, D. S., & Houston, B. K. (1974). Effectiveness of situation redefinition and affective isolation in coping with stress. *Journal of Personality and Social Psychology, 29,* 212–218.

Holmes, T. H., & David, E. M. (1989). *Life changes, life events, and illness: Selected papers.* New York: Praeger.

Holmes, T. H., Hawkins, N. G., Bowerman, C. E., Clark, E. R., Jr., & Joffee, J. R. (1957). Psychosocial and psychophysiological studies of tuberculosis. *Psychosomatic Medicine, 19,* 134–143.

Holmes, T. H., & Masuda, M. (1974). Life change and illness susceptibility. In B. S. Dohrenwend & B. P. Dohrenwend (Eds.), *Stressful life events: Their nature and effects* (pp. 45–72). New York: Wiley.

Holmes, T. H., & Rahe, R. H. (1967). The social readjustment rating scale. *Journal of Psychosomatic Research, 11,* 213–218.

The Holy Bible (Revised standard version).

Holzbach, R. L., Piserchia, P. V., McFadden, D. W., Hartwell, T. D., Herrmann, A., & Fielding, J. E. (1990). Effect of a comprehensive health promotion program on employee attitudes. *Journal of Occupational Medicine, 32,* 973–978.

Hoskisson, R. E., & Hitt, M. A. (1994). *Downscoping: How to tame the diversified firm.* New York: Oxford University Press.

Hosmer, L. T. (1995). Trust: The connecting link between organizational theory and philosophical ethics. *Academy of Management Review, 20,* 379–403.

House, J. S. (1972). *The relationshp of intrinsic and extrinsic work motivation to occupational stress and coronary heart disease risk.* Unpublished doctoral dissertation, University of Michigan, Ann Arbor.

House, J. S. (1981). *Work stress and social support.* Reading, MA: Addison-Wesley.

House, J. S., Landis, K. R., & Umberson, D. (1988). Social relationships and health. *Science, 241,* 540–545.

House, J. S., & Wells, J. A. (1978). Occupational stress, social support, and health. In A. McLean, G. Black, & M. Colligan (Eds.), *Reducing occupational stress: Proceedings of a conference* (pp. 8–19). DHEW (NIOSH) Publication No. 78-140.

House, R. J., & Rizzo, J. R. (1972). Role conflict and ambiguity as critical variables in a model of organizational behavior. *Organizational Behavior and Human Performance, 7,* 467–505.

Houtman, I. L. D., & Kompier, M. A. J. (1995). Risk factors and occupational risk groups for workplace stress. In S. L. Sauter & L. R. Murphy (Eds.), *Organizational risk factors for job stress* (163–180). Washington, DC: American Psychological Association.

Howard, J. H. (1978). Managing stress and job tension. *The Labour Gazette, 78,* 61–64.

Howard, J. H., Cunningham, D. A., & Rechnitzer, P. A. (1976). Health patterns associated with Type A behavior: A managerial population. *Journal of Human Stress, 2*(1), 24–31.

Howard, J. H., Cunningham, D. A., & Rechnitzer, P. A. (1977). Work patterns associated with Type A behavior: A managerial population. *Human Relations, 30,* 825–836.

Howard, J. H., Rechnitzer, P. A., & Cunningham, D. A. (1975). Coping with job tension: Effective and ineffective means. *Public Personnel Management, 4,* 317–326.

Hughes, C. L. (1965). *Goal setting: Key to individual and organizational effectiveness.* New York: American Management Association.

Hurrell, J. J., & McLaney, M. A. (1988). Exposure to job stress: A new psychometric instrument. *Scandinavian Journal of Work, Environment, and Health, 14,* 27–28.

Hurrell, J. J., & Murphy, L. R. (1991). Locus of control, job demands and health. In C. L. Cooper & R. Payne (Eds.), *Personality and stress: Individual differences in the stress process* (pp. 133–147). New York: Wiley.

Hurrell, J. J., & Murphy, L. R. (1992). An overview of occupational stress and health. In W. M. Rom (Ed.), *Environmental and occupational medicine* (2nd ed., pp. 675–684). Boston: Little, Brown.

Hurrell, J. J., Murphy, L. R., Sauter, S. L., & Cooper, C. L. (Eds.). (1988). *Occupational stress: Issues and developments in research*. New York: Taylor & Francis.

Huse, E. F. (1980). *Organizational development and change*. St. Paul, MN: West.

Israel, B. A., Baker, E. A., Goldenhar, L. M., & Heaney, C. A. (1996). Occupational stress, safety, and health: Conceptual framework and principles for effective prevention interventions. *Journal of Occupational Health Psychology, 1*, 261–286.

Ivancevich, J. M., & Matteson, M. T. (1980). *Stress at work*. Glenview, IL: Scott, Foresman.

Ivancevich, J. M., Matteson, M. T., & Richards, E. P. III. (1985). Who's liable for stress on the job? *Harvard Business Review, 64*, 60–72.

Jackson, S. E. (1992). *Diversity in the workplace: Human resource initiatives*. New York: Guilford Press.

Jacobson, B. (1981). *The ladykillers: Why smoking is a feminist issue*. New York: Pluto Press.

Jacobson, E. J. (1929). *Progressive relaxation*. Chicago: University of Chicago Press.

Jacobson, E. J. (1978). *You must relax*. New York: McGraw-Hill.

Jakubowski-Spector, P. (1973). Facilitating the growth of women through assertiveness training. *Counseling Psychologist, 4*, 75–86.

Jameson, J., Shuman, L., & Young, W. (1978). The effects of outpatient psychiatric utilization on the costs of providing third-party coverage. *Medical Care, 16*, 383–399.

Jamieson, A. O., & Becker, P. M. (1992). Management of the 10 most common sleep disorders. *American Family Physician, 45*, 1262–1268.

Janowiak, J. J., & Hackman, R. (1994). Meditation and college students' self-actualization and rated stress. *Psychological Reports, 75*, 1007–1010.

Jeffrey, N. A. (1996, October 28). Employers aggressively attack disability costs. *The Wall Street Journal*, p. B1.

Jemmott, J. B., & Locke, S. E. (1984). Psychosocial factors, immunologic meditation, and human susceptibility to infectious diseases: How much do we know? *Psychological Bulletin, 95*, 78–108.

Jencks, B. (1979). *Exercise manual for J. H. Schultz's standard autogenic training and special formulas*. Des Plaines, IL: American Society of Clinical Hypnosis.

Jenkins, C. D. (1982). Psychological risk factors for coronary heart disease. *Acta Medica Scandinavica* (Suppl, 660), 123–136.

Jenkins, C. D., Rosenman, R. H., & Friedman, M. (1966). Components of the coronary-prone behavior pattern: Their relation to silent myocardial infarction and blood lipids. *Journal of Chronic Diseases, 19*, 599–609.

Jenkins, C. D., Rosenman, R. H., & Friedman, M. (1967). Development of an objective psychological test for determination of the coronary-prone behavior pattern in employed man. *Journal of Chronic Diseases, 20*, 371–379.

Jenkins, C. D., Zyzanski, S. J., & Rosenman, R. H. (1971, May–June). Progress toward validation of a computer-scored test for the Type A coronary-prone behavior pattern. *Psychosomatic Medicine, 33*, 193–202.

Jenkins, C. D., Zyzanski, S. J., & Rosenman, R. H. (1979). *Jenkins Activity Survey (Form C)*. New York: Psychological Corporation.

Jewell, L. N., & Reitz, H. J. (1981). *Group effectiveness in organizations*. Glenview, IL: Scott, Foresman.

Jick, T. D. (1985). As the ax falls: Budget cuts and the experience of stress in organizations. In R. Bhagat & T. Beehr (Eds.), *Stress and cognition in organizations: An integrated perspective* (pp. 83–114). New York: Wiley.

Jick, T. D., & Mitz, L. F. (1985). Sex differences in work stress. *Academy of Management Review, 10*, 408–420.

Jin, P. (1992). Efficacy of tai chi, brisk walking, meditation, and reading in reducing mental and emotional stress. *Journal of Psychosomatic Research, 36*, 361–370.

Johansson, G., Aronsson, G., & Lindstrom, B. O. (1978). Social psychological and neuroendocrine stress reactions in highly mechanized work. *Ergonomics, 21*, 583–599.

Johnson, J. R., Hall, E. M., & Theorell, T. (1989). Combined effects of job strain and social isolation on cardiovascular disease morbidity and mortality in a random sample of the Swedish male working population. *Scandinavian Journal of Work, Environment and Health, 19*, 21–28.

Johnston, W. B., & Packer, E. A. (1987). *Workforce 2000: Work and workers for the 21st century.* Indianapolis, IN: Hudson Institute.

Jones, E. W., Jr. (1973, July-August). What it's like to be a black manager. *Harvard Business Review*, pp. 108–116.

Jones, J. W., & Boye, M. W. (1992). Job stress and employee counterproductivity. In J. C. Quick, L. R. Murphy, & J. J. Hurrell (Eds.), *Stress and well-being at work.* Washington, DC: American Psychological Association.

Jones, K., & Barker, K. (1996). *Human movement explained.* Boston: Oxford Press.

Jones, K. R., & Vischi, T. R. (1979). Impact of alcohol, drug abuse, and mental health treatment on medical care utilization: A review of the research literature. *Medical Care, 17*(12), Supplement.

Joplin, J. R., Quick, J. C., Nelson, D. L., & Turner, J. C. (1995). Interdependence and personal well-being in a training environment. In L. R. Murphy, J. J. Hurrell, Jr., S. L. Sauter, & G. P. Keita (Eds.), *Job stress interventions* (pp. 309–322). Washington, DC: American Psychological Association.

Justice, B. (1988). *Who gets sick: How beliefs, moods, and thoughts affect your health.* Los Angeles: Tarcher.

Kahn, M. (1966). The physiology of catharsis. *Journal of Personality and Social Psychology, 3,* 278–286.

Kahn, R. L. (1964). Role conflict and ambiguity in organizations. *Personnel Administrator, 9,* 8–13.

Kahn, R. L. (1987). Work stress in the 1980s: Research and practice. In J. C. Quick, R. S. Bhagat, J. E. Dalton, & J. D. Quick (Eds.), *Work stress: Health care systems in the workplace* (pp. 311–320). New York: Praeger.

Kahn, R. L., & Quinn, R. P. (1970). Strategies for management of role stress. In A. McLean (Ed.), *Occupational mental health.* New York: Rand McNally.

Kahn, R. L., Wolfe, R. P., Quinn, R. P., Snoek, J. D., & Rosenthal, R. A. (1964). *Organizational stress: Studies in role conflict and ambiguity.* New York: Wiley.

Kales, A., & Kales, J. D. (1974). Sleep disorders: Recent findings in the diagnosis and treatment of disturbed sleep. *New England Journal of Medicine, 290,* 487–499.

Kanner, A. D., Coyne, J. C., Schaefer, C., & Lazarus, R. S. (1981). Comparison of two modes of stress measurement: Daily hassles and uplifts versus major life events. *Journal of Behavioral Medicine, 4*(1), 1–39.

Kanter, R. M. (1977). *Work and family in the United States: A critical review and agenda for research and policy.* New York: Russell Sage Foundation.

Karasek, R. A. (1979, June). Job demands, job decision latitude, and mental strain: Implications for job redesign. *Administrative Science Quarterly, 24,* 285–308.

Karasek, R. A. (1985). *Job content questionnaire and users guide.* Los Angeles: University of Southern California Department of Industrial and Systems Engineering.

Karasek, R. A., & Theorell, T. (1990). *Healthy work.* New York: Basic Books.

Karasek, R. A., Theorell, T., Schwartz, J. E., Schnall, P. L., Pieper, C. F., & Michela, J. L. (1988). Job characteristics in relation to the prevalence of myocardial infarction in the US health examination survey (HES) and the health and nutrition examination survey (HANES). *American Journal of Public Health, 78,* 910–918.

Karlsson, J., Sjostrom, L., & Sullivan, M. (1995). Swedish obese subjects (SOS)—An intervention study of obesity, measuring psychosocial factors and health by means of short-form questionnaires: Results from a method study. *Journal of Clinical Epidemiology, 48,* 817–823.

Kasl, S. V., & Cobb, S. (1970). Blood pressure changes in men undergoing job loss: A preliminary report. *Psychosomatic Medicine, 32,* 19–38.

Katz, C. A. (1978). Reducing interpersonal stress in dental practice. *Dental Clinics of North America, 22,* 347–359.

Keita, G. P., & Hurrell, J. J., Jr. (1994). *Job stress in a changing workforce: Investigating gender, diversity, and family issues.* Washington, DC: American Psychological Association.

Kepos, P. (Ed.). (1994). Citicorp. In *International Directory of Company Histories* (Vol. 9, pp. 123–126). London: St. James Press.

Kessler, R. C., & Cleary, P. D. (1980). Social class and psychological distress. *American Sociological Review, 45,* 463–478.

Keys, B., & Case, T. (1990). How to become an influential manager. *Academy of Management Executive, 4,* 38–51.

Kiecolt-Glaser, J. K., & Glaser, R. (1992). Psychoneuroimmunology: Can psychological interventions modulate immunity? *Journal of Consulting and Clinical Psychology, 60,* 569–575.

Kiecolt-Glaser, J. K., & Glaser, R. (1995). Psychoneuroimmunology and health consequences: Data and shared mechanisms. *Psychosomatic Medicine, 57,* 269–274.

Kiecolt-Glaser, J. K., Glaser, R., Strain, E. C., Stout, J. C., Tarr, K. L., Holliday, J. E., & Speider, C. E. (1986). Modulation of cellular immunity in medical students. *Journal of Behavioral Medicine, 9,* 5–21.

Kiecolt-Glaser, J. K., Malarkey, W. B., Cacioppo, J. T., & Glaser, R. (1994). Stressful personal relationships: Immune and endocrine function. In R. Glaser and J. K. Kiecolt-Glaser (Eds.), *Handbook of human stress and immunity* (pp. 321–338). San Diego, CA: Academic Press.

Kiev, A. (1974). *A strategy for handling executive stress.* Chicago: Nelson-Hall.

Kiev, A., & Kohn, V. (1979). *Executive stress: An AMA survey report.* New York: American Management Association.

Kilgour, F. G. (Ed.). (1960). *Christobal Mendez book of bodily exercise.* New Haven, CT: Elisabeth Licht.

Kilgour, J. G. (1993, September). Workers' compensation reform in Oregon: A success story. *Employee Benefits Journal, 18*(3), 30–37.

Kimberly, J. R., & Miles, R. H. (1980). *The organizational life cycle.* San Francisco: Jossey-Bass.

Kinzer, N. S. (1979). *Stress and the American woman.* New York: Anchor Press/Doubleday.

Kirkcaldy, B. D., & Cooper, C. L. (1993). The relationship between work stress and leisure style: British and German managers. *Human Relations, 46,* 669–680.

Kirkcaldy, B. D., Cooper, C. L., Shephard, R. J., & Brown, J. S. (1994). Exercise, job satisfaction and well-being among superintendent police officers [Special issue: Stress research in Europe]. *European Review of Applied Psychology, 44*(2), 117–123.

Kirn, A. G., & Kirn, M. O. (1978). *Life work planning* (4th ed.). New York: McGraw-Hill.

Kobasa, S. C. (1979). Stressful life events and health: An inquiry into hardiness. *Journal of Personality and Social Psychology, 37,* 1–11.

Kobasa, S. C. (1982). The hardy personality: Toward a social psychology of stress and health. In J. Suls & G. Sanders (Eds.), *The social psychology of health and illness* (pp. 3–32). Hillsdale, NJ: Erlbaum.

Kobasa, S. C. (1988). Conceptualization and measurement of personality in job stress research. In J. J. Hurrell, Jr., L. R. Murray, S. L. Sauter, & C. L. Cooper (Eds.), *Occupational stress: Issues and developments in research* (pp. 100–109). New York: Taylor & Francis.

Kobasa, S. C., Maddi, S. R., & Courington, S. (1981). Personality and constitution as mediators in the stress-illness relationship. *Journal of Health and Social Behaviour, 22,* 368–378.

Kobasa, S. C., Maddi, S. R., & Kahn, S. (1982). Hardiness and health: A prospective study. *Journal of Personality and Social Psychology, 42,* 168–177.

Kofodimos, J. R. (1990). Why executives lose their balance. *Organizational Dynamics, 19*(1), 58–73.

Konkov, F. E. (1991). Primary psychological intervention with families of earthquake survivors in Armenia. *American Journal of Family Therapy, 19*(1), 54–59.

Korff, E. (1975). Leisure-free time: The way to creative organization of free time activities. *Praktische Psychologie, 29*(5), 152–157.

Kostrubala, T. (1976). *The joy of running.* Philadelphia: Lippincott.

Kotter, J. P., Faux, V. A., & McArthur, C. C. (1978). *Self-assessment and career development,* Englewood Cliffs, NJ: Prentice-Hall.

Krackhardt, D. M. (1981). Supervisory behavior and employee turnover. *Academy of Management Journal, 24,* 249–259.

Kraus, H. (1970). *Clinical treatment of back and neck pain.* New York: McGraw-Hill.

Kraus, H., Melleby, A., & Graston, R. R. (1977). Back pain correction and prevention. *New York State Journal of Medicine, 77,* 1335–1338.

Kraus, H., & Raab, W. (1961). *Hypokinetic Disease.* Springfield, IL: Charles C Thomas.

Krause, C. (1994). *How healthy is your family tree?* New York: Macmillan.

Kreisberg, L. *The sociology of social conflict.* Englewood Cliffs, NJ: Prentice-Hall.

Kreitner, R., Woods, S. D., & Friedman, G. M. (1979, August). Just how fit are your employees? *Business Horizons,* pp. 39–45.

Kroes, W. H., Margolis, B. L., & Hurrell, J. J., Jr. (1974). Job stress in policemen. *Journal of Police Science and Administration, 2*(2), 145–155.

Kubitz, K. A., & Landers, D. M. (1993). The effects of aerobic training on cardiovascular responses to mental stress: An examination of underlying mechanisms. *Journal of Sport & Exercise Psychology, 15,* 326–337.

Kuder, F., & Diamond, E. (1979). *Kuder Occupational Interest Survey.* Worthington, OH: Science Research Associates.

Kumar, K., & Thibodeaux, M. S. (1990). Organizational politics and planned organizational change. *Group and Organizational Studies, 15,* 354–365.

Kuna, D. J. (1975, June). Meditation and work. *Vocational Guidance Quarterly, 23,* 342–346.

Kushnir, T., & Kasan, R. (1992). Major sources of stress among women managers, clerical workers, and working single mothers: Demands vs. resources. *Public Health Review, 20,* 215–219.

Kushnir, T., & Melamed, S. (1991). Work-load, perceived control, and psychological distress in Type A/B industrial workers. *Journal of Organizational Behavior, 12,* 155–168.

Laing, R. D. (1971). *The politics of the family and other essays.* New York: Pantheon Books.

Laing, R. D., & Esterson, A. (1964). *Sanity, madness, and the family: Families of schizophrenics* (Vol. 1). London: Tavistock.

Lake, A. E., & Pingel, J. D. (1988). Brief versus extended relaxation: Relationship to improvement at follow-up in mixed headache patients. *Medical Psychotherapy: An International Journal, 1,* 119–129.

Lakein, A. (1973). *How to get control of your time and your life.* New York: Wyden.

Lakey, B., & Ross, L. T. (1994). Dependency and self-criticism as moderators of interpersonal and achievement stress: The role of initial dysphoria. *Cognitive Therapy and Research, 18,* 581–599.

Landsbergis, P. A., Schnall, P. L., Deitz, D., & Friedman, R. (1992). The patterning of psychological attributes and distress by "job strain" and social support in a sample of working men. *Journal of Behavioral Medicine, 15,* 379–405.

Landy, F., Quick, J. C., & Kasl, S. (1994). Work, stress, and well-being. *International Journal of Stress Management, 1*(1), 33–73.

Last, J. M. (1988). *A dictionary of epidemiology* (2nd ed.). New York: International Epidemiological Association.

Last, J. M., & Wallace, R. B. (Eds.). (1992). *Public health and preventive medicine* (13th ed.). Norwalk, CT: Appleton & Lange.

Latham, G. P., & Yukl, G. A. (1975). A review of research on the application of goal setting in organizations. *Academy of Management Journal, 18,* 824–845.

Lawler, E. E. III (1994). From job-based to competency-based organizations. *Journal of Organizational Behavior, 15,* 3–16.

Lazarus, A. A. (1961). Group therapy of phobic disorders by systematic desensitization. *Journal of Abnormal Social Psychology, 63,* 504–510.

Lazarus, R. S. (1967). *Psychological stress and the coping process.* New York: McGraw-Hill.

Lazarus, R. S. (1981, July). Little hassles can be hazardous to health. *Psychology Today,* pp. 58–62.

Lazarus, R. S. (1991). Progress on a cognitive-motivational-relational theory of emotion. *American Psychologist, 46,* 819–834.

Lazarus, R. S., DeLongis, A., Folkman, S., & Gruen, R. (1985). Stress and adaptational outcomes: The problem of confounded measures. *American Psychologist, 40,* 770–779.

Lazarus, R. S., & Folkman, S. (1984). *Stress, appraisal and coping.* New York: Springer.

Leavitt, H. (1965). Applied organizational change in industry: Structural, technological and humanistic approaches. In J. G. March (Ed.), *Handbook of organizations* (p. 1145). Chicago: Rand McNally.

Lehmann, P. (1974). Job stress: Hidden hazard. *Job Safety and Health, 2,* 4–10.

Lehrer, P. M., Carr, R., Sargunaraj, D., & Woolfolk, R. L. (1994). Stress management techniques: Are they all equivalent, or do they have specific effects? *Biofeedback and Self Regulation, 19,* 353–401.

Leon, A. S., Connett, J., Jacobs, D. R., & Rauramaa, R. (1987). Leisure time physical activity levels and risk of coronary heart disease and death. *Journal of the American Medical Association, 258,* 1483–1489.

Leonard-Barton, D. (1992). *Modes of internal technology transfer and the growth of capabilities.* Boston, MA: Division of Research, Graduate School of Business Administration, Harvard University.

LeShan, L. (1966). An emotional life-history pattern associated with neoplastic disease. *Annals of New York Academy of Science, 125,* 780–793.

Levens, E. (1979). The cost-benefit and cost-effectiveness of occupational alcoholism program. *Professional Safety, 21*(21), 36–41.

Levi, L. (1967). *Stress: Sources, management, and prevention.* New York: Liveright.

Levi, L. (1971). *Stress and disease: The psychosocial environment and psychosomatic diseases.* London: Oxford University Press.

Levi, L. (1977). Social structures and processes as producers of stress and illness. *Scheizer Archiv für Neurologie, Neurochirurgie und Psychiatrie, 121*(1), 21–31.

Levi, L. (1979). *Occupational stress: Sources, management, and prevention.* Reading, MA: Addison-Wesley.

Levi, L. (1981). *Preventing work stress.* Reading, MA: Addison-Wesley.

Levi, L. (1995, April). Global review and state of the art approaches in stress management and prevention. Paper presented at *The Fifth International Conference on Stress Management.* Leeuwenhorst Congress Center, Noordwijkerhout, The Netherlands.

Levin, J. S. (1994). Religion and health: Is there an association, and is it causal? *Social Science and Medicine, 38,* 1475–1482.

Levinson, D. J. (1978). *The seasons of a man's life.* New York: Knopf.

Levinson, H. (1971). Conflicts that plague family businesses. *Harvard Business Review, 44,* 90–98.

Levinson, H. (1975). *Executive stress.* New York: New American Library.

Levinson, H. (1978, May-June). The abrasive personality. *Harvard Business Review, 56,* 86–94.

Levinson, H. (1978). A psychoanalytic view of occupational stress. *Occupational Mental Health, 3*(2), 2–13.

Levinson, H. (1981a). *Executive.* Cambridge, MA: Harvard University Press.

Levinson, H. (1981b, May-June). When executives burn out. *Harvard Business Review, 59,* 73–81.

Levinson, H., Molinari, J., & Spohn, A. G. (1972). *Organizational diagnosis.* Cambridge, MA: Harvard University Press.

Levitt, H. (1965). Applied organizational change in industry: Structural, technological, and humanistic approaches. In J. G. March (Ed.), *Handbook of organizations* (pp. 1144–1170). Chicago: Rand McNally.

Lewin, K. (1974). Group decision and social change. In J. Newcomb & E. Hartley (Eds.), *Readings in social psychology* (pp. 197–211). New York: Holt, Rinehart & Winston.

Lewin, K., Lippitt, R., & White, R. K. (1939). Social climates. *Journal of Social Psychology, 10,* 271–299.

Lewis, S. (1996). Personality, stress, and chronic fatigue syndrome. In C. L. Cooper (Ed.), *Handbook of stress, medicine, and health* (pp. 233–249). Boca Raton, FL: CRC Press.

Likert, R. (1961). *New patterns of management.* New York: McGraw-Hill.

Lindemann, H. (1973). *Relieve tension the autogenic way.* New York: Wyden.

Lindenthal, J. J., Myers, J. K., & Pepper, M. P. (1972). Smoking, psychological status, and stress. *Social Science Medicine, 6,* 583–591.

Lindsey, K. (1977, November). Sexual harassment on the job and how to stop it. *Ms.*, pp. 48–51, 76–78.

Lindstrom, K. (1995). Finnish research in organizational development and job redesign. In

L. R. Murphy, J. J. Hurrell, Jr., S. L. Sauter, & G. P. Keita (Eds.), *Job stress interventions* (pp. 283–293). Washington, DC: American Psychological Association.

Littman, A. B., Fava, M., McKool, K., & Lamon-Fava, S. (1993). Buspirone therapy for Type A behavior, hostility, and perceived stress in cardiac patients. *Psychotherapy and Psychosomatics, 59*(2), 107–110.

Locke, E. A. (1968). Toward a theory of task motivation and incentives. *Organizational Behavior and Human Performance, 3,* 157–189.

Locke, E. A., & Latham, G. P. (1990). *A theory of goal setting and task performance.* Englewood Cliffs, NJ: Prentice-Hall.

Long, B. C., & Kahn, S. E. (Eds.). (1993). *Women, work, and coping: A multidisciplinary approach to workplace stress.* Montreal, Canada: McGill–Queens University Press.

Lublin, J. S. (1980, September 17). On-the-job stress leads many workers to file—and win —compensation awards. *Wall Street Journal,* p. 33.

Lundberg, U. (1996). Influence of paid and unpaid work on psychophysiological stress responses of men and women. *Journal of Occupational Health Psychology, 1*(2), 117–130.

Lundberg, U., Mardberg, B., & Frankenhaeuser, M. (1994). The total workload of male and female white collar workers as related to age, occupational level, and number of children. *Scandinavian Journal of Psychology, 35,* 315–327.

Luthans, F., & Kreitner, R. (1985). *Organizational behavior modification and beyond.* Glenview, IL: Scott, Foresman.

Luthe, W. (Ed.). (1969). *Autogenic therapy* (Vols. I–IV). New York: Grune & Stratton.

Lynch, J. J. (1977). *The broken heart: The medical consequences of loneliness.* New York: Basic Books.

Lyons, T. (1971). Role clarity, need for clarity, satisfaction, tension, and withdrawal. *Organizational Behavior and Human Performance, 6,* 99–110.

Macan, T. H. (1994). Time management: Test of a process model. *Journal of Applied Psychology, 79,* 381–391.

MacCrimmon, K. R., & Taylor, R. N. (1976). Decision making and problem solving. In M. D. Dunnette (Ed.), *Handbook of industrial and organizational psychology* (pp. 1397–1453). Chicago: Rand McNally.

Mack, D. A., Nelson, D. L., & Quick, J. C. (in press). The stress of organizational change: A dynamic process model [Special Issue]. *Applied Psychology: An International Review.*

Mack, D. A., Shannon, C., Quick, J. D., & Quick, J. C. (in press). Stress, prevention and workplace violence. In R. W. Griffin, A. O'Leary-Kelly, & J. Collins (Eds.), *Dysfunctional behavior in organizations: Vol. 1. Violent behavior in organizations.* Greenwich, CT: JAI Press.

MacKinnon, C. A. (1979). *Sexual harassment of working women.* New Haven, CT: Yale University Press.

Macy, B. A., & Mirvis, P. H. (1976). A methodology for assessment of quality of work life and organizational effectiveness in behavioral-economic terms. *Administrative Science Quarterly, 21,* 212–226.

Macy, B. A., & Mirvis, P. H. (1982, June). Organizational change efforts: Methodologies for assessing organizational effectiveness and program costs versus benefits. *Evaluation Review, 6,* 301–372.

Maddi, S. R. (1987). Hardiness training at Illinois Bell Telephone. In J. Opatz (Ed.), *Health Promotion Evaluation.* Stevens Point, WI: National Wellness Institute.

Maddi, S. R. (1990). Issues and interventions in stress mastery. In H. S. Friedman (Ed.), *Personality and disease* (pp. 121–154). New York: Wiley.

Maddi, S. R. (1994). The hardiness enhancing lifestyle program (HELP) for improving physical, mental and social wellness. *Wellness Lecture Series.* Oakland, CA: University of California/HealthNet.

Maddi, S. R. (1995, August). *Workplace hardiness for these turbulent times.* Paper presented at the annual meeting of the Academy of Management, Vancouver, Canada.

Maddi, S. R., & Kobasa, S. C. O. (1984). *The hardy executive: Health under stress.* Homewood, IL: Dow Jones–Irwin.

Maida, C. A., Gordon, N. S., & Farberow, N. L. (1989). The crisis of competence: Transitional stress and the displaced worker. *Brunner/Mazel psychosocial stress series,* (No. 16). New York: Brunner/Mazel, Inc.

Maier, N. R. F. (1967). Assets and liabilities in group problem solving: The need for an integrative function. *Psychological Review, 74,* 239–249.

Mannheim, B., & Schiffrin, M. (1984). Family structure, job characteristics, rewards and strains as related to work-role of employed and self-employed professional women with children. *Journal of Occupational Behaviour, 5,* 83–101.

Manning, M. R., Jackson, C. N., & Fusilier, M. R. (1996). Occupational stress and health care use. *Journal of Occupational Health Psychology, 1*(1), 100–109.

Manuso, J. S. J. (1979a, July 2). Biofeedback helps in dealing with stress. *Equinews, 8*(12), 1.

Manuso, J. S. J. (1979b). *Stress management training in a large corporation.* Unpublished manuscript.

Manuso, J. S. J. (1980). Manage your stress. *CRM multimedia module* (Facilitator's guide, film or videotape, audiocassette, exercise books). Del Mar, CA: McGraw-Hill Films.

Manuso, J. S. J. (1982). Stress management and behavioral medicine: A corporate model. In M. O'Donnel & T. Ainsworth (Eds.), *Health promotion in the work place.* New York: Wiley.

Manuso, J. S. J. (undated). *Preventive health care in the work setting: The relative efficacy of two intervention strategies in ameliorating Type A coronary prone behavior patterns.* New York: The Equitable Life Assurance Association of the United States.

March, J. G., & Simon, H. (1958). *Organizations.* New York: Wiley.

Marcus, J. B. (1977). *TM and business.* New York: McGraw-Hill.

Margolis, B. L., Kroes, W. H., & Quinn, R. R. (1974). Job stress: An unlisted occupational hazard. *Journal of Occupational Medicine, 16,* 659–661.

Markland, D., & Hardy, L. (1993). Anxiety, relaxation and anaesthesia for day-case surgery. *British Journal of Clinical Psychology, 32,* 493–504.

Marrow, A. J. (1960). *Making management human.* New York: McGraw-Hill.

Marsella, A. J. (1994). Work and well-being in an ethnoculturally pluralistic society: Conceptual and methodological issues. In G. B. Keita & J. J. Hurrell, Jr. (Eds.), *Job stress in a changing workforce* (pp. 147–160). Washington, DC: American Psychological Association.

Marsella, A. J., Friedman, M. J., Gerrity, E. T., & Scurfield, R. M. (Eds.). (1996). *Ethnocultural aspects of posttraumatic stress disorder: Issues, research, and clinical applications.* Washington, DC: American Psychological Association.

Marshall, G. N., & Lang, E. L. (1990). Optimism, self-mastery, and symptoms of depression in women professionals. *Journal of Personality and Social Psychology, 59,* 132–139.

Martin, R. E., & Freeman, S. J. (in press). Economic context of the new reality. In M. Gowing, J. Kraft, & J. C. Quick (Eds.), *The new organizational reality: Downsizing, restructuring, and revitalization.* Washington, DC: American Psychological Association.

Maslach, C. (1978). The client role in staff burnout. *Journal of Social Issues, 34,* 111–124.

Maslach, C. (1982). *Burnout: The cost of caring.* Englewood Cliffs, NJ: Prentice-Hall.

Maslach, C., & Jackson, S. E. (1981a). *Maslach burnout inventory: Research edition.* Palo Alto, CA: Consulting Psychologists Press.

Maslach, C., & Jackson, S. E. (1981b). The measurement of experiential burnout. *Journal of Occupational Behavior, 2,* 99–113.

Maslow, A. H. (1943). A theory of human motivation. *Psychological Review, 50,* 370–396.

Masuda, M., Perko, K. P., & Johnston, R. G. (1972, April). Physiological activity and illness history. *Journal of Psychosomatic Research, 16*(2), 129–136.

Matteson, M. (1987). Individual-organizational relationships: Implications for preventing job stress and burnout. In J. C. Quick, R. S. Bhagat, J. E. Dalton, & J. D. Quick (Eds.), *Work stress: Health care systems in the workplace* (pp. 156–170). New York: Praeger.

Matteson, M. T., & Ivancevich, J. M. (1979). Organizational stressors and heart disease: A research model. *Academy of Management Review, 4,* 347–358.

Matthews, D. A., Larson, D. B., & Barry, C. P. (1994). *The faith factor: An annotated bibliography of clinical research on spiritual subjects.* Rockville, MD: John Templeton Foundation, National Institute for Healthcare Research.

Matthews, D. B. (1990). A comparison of burnout in selected occupational fields. *Career Development Quarterly, 38,* 230–239.

Matthews, K. A. (1988). Coronary heart disease and Type A behaviors: Update on and alternative to the Booth-Kewley and Friedman (1987) quantitative review. *Psychological Bulletin, 104,* 373–380.

Matuszek, P. A. C., Nelson, D. L., & Quick, J. C. (1995). Gender differences in distress: Are we asking all the right questions? [Special issue on gender in the workplace, edited by N. J. Struthers]. *Journal of Social Behavior and Personality, 10,* 99–120.

Mayer, N. (1975). Leisure—or a coronary? *Psychology Today, 8,* 36–37.

Mayr, O. (1970, October). The origins of feedback control. *Scientific American, 223*(4), 111.

Mazzaferri, E. (Ed.). (1980). *Endocrinology: A review of clinical endocrinology* (2nd ed.). New Hyde Park, NY: Medical Examination Publishing.

McCann, J. (1972). The uptight executive. *Duns Review, 99,* 79–80.

McClelland, D. C. (1961). *The achieving society.* Princeton, NJ: Van Nostrand.

McDaniel, C., & Gysbers, N. C. (1992). *Counseling for career development: Theories, resources and practice.* San Francisco: Jossey-Bass.

McGrath, J. E. (1976). Stress and behavior in organizations. In M. D. Dunnette (Ed.), *Handbook of industrial and organizational psychology* (pp. 1351–1395). Chicago: Rand McNally.

McGregor, D. (1957, May-June). An uneasy look at performance appraisal. *Harvard Business Review,* pp. 89–94.

McKay, M., & Paleg, K. (1992). *Focal group psychotherapy.* Oakland, CA: New Harbinger Publications.

McLean, A. A. (1976). *Dealing with job stress* (cassettes and workbook). Darien, CT: Management Decision Systems.

McLean, A. A. (1979). *Work stress.* Reading, MA: Addison-Wesley.

McMorris, F. A. (1996, February 5). Can post-traumatic stress arise from office battles? *Wall Street Journal,* pp. B1, B10.

McMurray, R. G., Kocher, P. L., & Horvath, S. M. (1994). Aerobic power and body size affects the exercise-induced stress hormone responses to varying water temperature. *Aviation Space and Environmental Medicine, 65,* 809–814.

McNair, D. M., Lorr, M., & Droppleman, L. F. (1971). *Profiles of mood states.* San Diego, CA: Educational and Industrial Testing Service.

McQuade, W. (1972, January). What stress can do for you. *Fortune, 85*(1), 102–107, 134, 136, 141.

Melamed, S., Meir, E. I., & Samson, A. (1995). The benefits of personality-leisure congruence: Evidence and implications. *Journal of Leisure Research, 27*(1), 25–40.

Melton, C. E., Smith, R. C., McKenzie, J. M., Wicks, S. M., & Saldivar, J. T. (1978). Stress in air traffic personnel: Low-density towers and flight service stations. *Aviation Space and Environmental Medicine, 49,* 724–728.

Mendelson, W., Gillis, J., & Wyatt, R. (1977). *Human sleep and its disorders.* New York: Plenum Press.

Metcalf, C. W. (1990). *Humor, risk & change* [Manual and audiovisual]. Des Moines, IA: American Media.

Metcalf, C. W., & Felible, R. (1992). *Lighten up: Survival skills for people under pressure.* Reading, MA: Addison-Wesley.

Mettlin, C. (1976, July-August). Occupational careers and the prevention of coronary-prone behavior. *Social Science and Medicine, 10,* 367–372.

Meyer, H. H., Kay, E., & French, J. R. P. (1965). Split roles in performance appraisal. *Harvard Business Review, 43,* 123–129.

Michaels, R. R., Huber, M. J., & McCann, D. S. (1976). Evaluation of transcendental meditation as a method of reducing stress. *Science, 192,* 1242–1244.

Miles, R. H. (1976a). A comparison of the relative impacts of role perceptions of ambiguity and conflict by roles. *Academy of Management Journal, 19,* 25–35.

Miles, R. H. (1976b). Role requirements as sources of organizational stress. *Journal of Applied Psychology, 61,* 172–179.

Miles, R. H. (1979). *The Jim Heavner story (A), (B).* Boston: Harvard Case Clearing House, Harvard Business School.

Miles, R. H. (1980). Organizational boundary roles. In C. L. Cooper & R. Payne (Eds.), *Current concerns in occupational stress* (pp. 61–96). New York: Wiley.

Milgram, N. A., & Toubiana, Y. H. (1988). Bias in identifying and treating high-risk client groups. *Professional Psychology: Research and Practice, 19*(1), 21–25.

Miller, D., & Friesen, P. (1984). A longitudinal study of the corporate life cycle. *Management Science, 30,* 1161–1183.

Miller, J. A. (1995). "Traumatic event debriefing": Comment. *Social Work, 40,* 576.

Miller, L. H., & Smith, A. D. (1987). *Stress audit.* Brookline, MA: Biobehavioral Associates.

Miller, N. E, & Dworkin, B. R. (1977, June). Effects of learning on visceral functions: Biofeedback. *New England Journal of Medicine, 296,* 1274–1278.

Minicucci, R. (1988). Is your office hazardous to your health? *Today's Office, 22,* 38–45.

Mintzberg, H. (1973). *The nature of managerial work.* Englewood, Cliffs, NJ: Prentice-Hall.

Mira, J. J., Vitaller, J., Buil, J. A., Aranaz, J. M., & Herrero, J. F. (1992, December). Absenteeism as a symptom of occupational ill-health in hospitals and its repercussion on quality assurance. *Quality Assurance in Health Care, 4,* 273–287.

Mirvis, P. H., & Lawler, E. E. III. (1977). Measuring the financial impact of employee attitudes. *Journal of Applied Psychology, 62*(1), 1–8.

Mirvis, P., & Macy, B. A. (1974). *Guide to behavioral costing.* Ann Arbor, MI: Institute for Social Research, University of Michigan.

Mirvis, P. H., & Macy, B. A. (1982). Evaluating program costs and benefits. In S. E. Seashore, E. E. Lawler, P. H. Mirvis, & C. Cammann (Eds.), *Observing and measuring organizational change: A guide to field practice.* New York: Wiley Interscience.

Mitchell, A. (1969, Winter). Problems and pressures of rural life. *Mental Health,* pp. 2–4.

Mitchell, L. (1979). *Simple relaxation.* New York: Atheneum.

Mobley, W. H. (1982). *Employee turnover: Causes, consequences, and control.* Reading, MA: Addison-Wesley.

Modlin, H. C. (1977). Does job stress alone cause health problems? *Occupational Health and Safety, 47*(5), 38–39.

Monat, A., & Lazarus, R. S. (Eds.). (1977). *Stress and coping.* New York: Columbia University Press.

Monroe, S. M., Kupfer, D. J., & Frank, E. F. (1992). Life stress and treatment course of recurrent depression: I. Response during index episode. *Journal of Consulting and Clinical Psychology, 60,* 718–724.

Moorhead, G. (1982). *Organizational conditions as sources of stress.* Paper presented at the Southwestern Meeting of the Academy of Management, Dallas, TX.

Moos, R. H. (1981). *Work environment scale manual.* Palo Alto, CA: Consulting Psychologists Press.

Moos, R. H. (1992). *Coping responses inventory manual.* Palo Alto, CA: Cener for Health Care Evaluation, Department of Veterans Affairs and Stanford University Medical Center.

Moos, R. H., Fenn, C. B., Billings, A. G., & Moos, B. S. (1988). Assessing life stressors and social resources: Applications to alcoholic patients. *Journal of Substance Abuse, 1,* 135–152.

Morgan, W. P., Horstman, D. H., Cymerman, A., & Stokes, J. (1980, August). Exercise as a relaxation technique. *Hospital Physician,* pp. A22–A31.

Morris, J. N. (1955). The uses of epidemiology. *British Medical Journal, 2,* 395–401.

Morris, J. N. (1964). *The uses of epidemiology* (2nd ed.). Edinburgh, Scotland: E & S. Livingston.

Morrison, A. M., White, R. P., Van Velsor, E., & the Center for Creative Leadership. (1992). *Breaking the glass ceiling: Can women reach the top of America's largest corporations?* Reading, MA: Addison-Wesley.

Morse, D. R. (1989). The effects of hypnosis on reducing premature mortality and enhancing vigorous longevity. *Australian Journal of Clinical Hypnotherapy and Hypnosis, 10*(2), 55–63.

Morse, D. R., & Furst, M. L. (1979). *Stress for success: A holistic approach to stress and its management.* New York: Van Nostrand Reinhold.

Mortensen, J. T., Nygaard, B., & Johansen, J. P. (1993). The clientele at a clinic of occupational medicine—a medical statiscal review. *Ugeskr Laeger, 155,* 1765–1769.

Moss, L. (1981). *Management stress.* Reading, MA: Addison-Wesley.

Mott, P. E. (1972). *The characteristics of effective organizations.* New York: Harper & Row.

Mueller, E. F. (1965). *Psychological and physiological correlates of work overload among university professors*. Unpublished doctoral dissertation, University of Michigan, Ann Arbor.

Mulford, H. A. (1977). Stages in the alcoholic process: Toward a cumulative, nonsequential index. *Journal of Studies on Alcohol, 38*, 563–583.

Murphy, L. R., DuBois, D., & Hurrell, J. J. (1986). Accident reduction through stress management. *Journal of Business and Psychology, 1*, 5–18.

Murphy, L. R., Gershon, R. M., & Dejoy, D. (1996). Stress and occupational exposure to HIV/AIDS. In C. L. Cooper (Ed.), *Handbook of stress, medicine, and health* (pp. 178–190). Boca Raton, FL: CRC Press.

Murphy, L. R., Hurrell, J. J., Jr., Sauter, S. L., & Keita, G. P. (Eds.). (1995). *Job stress interventions*. Washington, DC: American Psychological Association.

Murray, C. J. L., & Lopez, A. D. (1994). Global and regional cause-of-death patterns in 1990. In C. J. L. Murray & A. D. Lopez (Eds.), *Global comparative assessments in the health sector* (pp. 21–54). Geneva, Switzerland: World Health Organization.

Murray, C. J. L., Lopez, A. D., & Jamison, D. T. (1994). The global burden of disease in 1990: Summary results, sensitivity analysis and future directions. In C. J. L. Murray & A. D. Lopez (Eds.), *Global comparative assessments in the health sector* (pp. 97–138). Geneva, Switzerland: World Health Organization.

Myers, D. C. (1978). A correlational causal analysis of the relationships between role stress and work attitudes and behavior. *Dissertation Abstracts International, 39-058*.

Nakano, K. (1990). Effects of two self-control procedures on modifying Type A behavior. *Journal of Clinical Psychology, 46*, 652–657.

Nason, R. W. (1976). The dilemma of black mobility in management. In D. L. Ford, Jr. (Ed.), *Readings in minority-group relations* (pp. 397–314). La Jolla, CA: University Associates.

National Center for Health Statistics. (1988). *Monthly Vital Statistics Report, 38*(5).

National Safety Council. (1990). *Accident facts*. Chicago: Author.

Nelson, D. L. (1985). Organizational socialization: A stress perspective. *Journal of Organizational Behavior, 8*, 311–324.

Nelson, D. L. (1990). Adjusting to a new organization: Easing the transition from outsider to insider. In J. C. Quick, R. E. Hess, J. Hermalin, & J. D. Quick (Eds.), *Career stress in changing times* (pp. 61–86). New York: Haworth Press.

Nelson, D. L., & Hitt, M. A. (1992). Employed women and stress: Implications for enhancing women's mental health in the workplace. In J. C. Quick, L. R. Murphy, & J. J. Hurrell (Eds.), *Stress and well-being at work: Assessments and interventions for occupational mental health* (pp. 162–177). Washington, DC: American Psychological Association.

Nelson, D. L., & Quick, J. C. (1985). Professional women: Are distress and disease inevitable? *Academy of Management Review, 10*, 206–218.

Nelson, D. L., & Quick, J. C. (1991). Social support and newcomer adjustment in organizations: Attachment theory at work? *Journal of Organizational Behavior, 12*, 543–554.

Nelson, P. L., & Quick, J. C. (1997). Socialization. In J. M. Stellman (Ed.), ILO Encyclopaedia of Occupational Health and Safety (Part I, pp. 34.38–34.39). Geneva, Switzerland: International Labor Office; and Chicago: Rand McNally.

Nelson, D. L., Hitt, M. A., & Quick, J. C. (1989). Men and women of the personnel profession: Some differences and similarities in their stress. *Stress Medicine, 5*, 145–152.

Nelson, D. L., Quick, J. C., Hitt, M. A., & Moesel, D. (1990). Politics, lack of career progress, and work/home conflict: Stress and strain for working women. *Sex Roles, 23*, 169–185.

Nelson, D. L., Quick, J. D., & Joplin, J. R. (1991). Psychological contracting and newcomer socialization: An attachment theory foundation. *Journal of Social Behavior and Personality, 6*, 55–72.

Nelson, D. L., Quick, J. C., & Quick, J. D. (1989). Corporate warfare: Preventing combat stress and battle fatigue. *Organizational Dynamics, 18*(1), 65–79.

Newbury, C. R. (1979). Tension and relaxation in the individual. *International Dental Journal, 29*, 173–182.

Newman, G. (1979). *Understanding violence*. New York: Lippincott.

Newman, J. E., & Beehr, T. A. (1979). Personal and organizational strategies for handling job stress: A review of research and opinion. *Personnel Psychology, 32*, 1–41.

Newton, D. A. (1979). *Think like a man. Act like a lady. Work like a dog*. Garden City, NY: Doubleday.

Newton-John, T. R. O., Spence, S. H., & Schotte, D. (1995). Cognitive-behavior therapy versus EMF biofeedback in the treatment of lower back pain. *Behavior Research and Therapy, 33*, 691–697.

Nicholson, N., Brown, C. A., & Chadwick-Jones, J. K. (1976). Absence from work and job satisfaction. *Journal of Applied Psychology, 61*, 728–737.

NIH Consensus Conference. (1994). *Helicobacter pylori* in peptic ulcer disease. *Journal of the American Medical Association, 272*, 66–71.

Nobel, E. P. (Ed.). (1978). *Third special report to the U.S. Congress on alcohol and health from the Secretary of Health, Education, and Welfare*. Rockville, MD: National Institute on Alcohol Abuse and Alcoholism.

Noer, D. M. (1993). *Healing the wounds*. San Francisco: Jossey-Bass.

Nollen, S. D. (1980, April). What is happening to flexitime, flexihour, gliding time, the variable day, and permanent part-time employment? And the four-day work week? *Across the Board*, pp. 6–21.

Norris, R., Carroll, D., & Cochrane, R. (1990). The effects of aerobic and anaerobic training on fitness, blood pressure, and psychological stress and well-being. *Journal of Psychosomatic Research, 34*, 367–375.

Numerof, R. E. (1987). Team-building interventions: An organizational stress moderator. In J. C. Quick, R. S. Bhagat, J. E. Dalton, & J. D. Quick (Eds.), *Work stress: Health care systems in the workplace* (pp. 171–194). New York: Praeger.

Nunnally, J. C. (1967). *Psychometric theory*. New York: McGraw-Hill.

Nunneley, S. A. (1978, Winter). Psychological responses of women to thermal stress: A review. *Medicine and Science in Sports, 10*, 250–255.

Oates, W. (1971). *Confessions of a workaholic*. New York: World.

Oh, S. H., Deagen, J. T., Whanger, P. D., & Weswig, P. H. (1978). Biological function of metallothionein versus its induction in rats by various stresses. *American Journal of Physiology, 234*, 282–285.

Ohlbaium, M. K. (1976). The visual stresses of the aerospace environment. *Journal of the American Optometric Association, 47*, 1176–1186.

Ohlott, P. J., Ruderman, M. N., & McCauley, C. D. (1994). Gender differences in managers' developmental job experiences. *Academy of Management Journal, 37*, 46–67.

Ojesjo, L. (1980, October). The relationship to alcoholism of occupation, class, and employment. *Journal of Occupational Medicine, 22*, 657–666.

Olbrisch, M. E. (1981). Evaluation of a stress management program for high utilizers of a prepaid university health service. *Medical Care, 19*(2), 153–159.

O'Leary-Kelly, A. M., Griffin, R. W., & Glew, D. J. (1996). Organization-motivated aggression: A research framework. *Academy of Management Review, 21*(1), 225–253.

O'Leary-Kelly, A. M., Paetzold, R. L., & Griffin, R. W. (1995). *Sexual harassment as aggressive action: A framework for understanding sexual harassment*. Best Paper Proceedings of the annual meeting of the Academy of Management, Vancouver, BC, Canada.

Oliver, T. R. (1993). Analysis, advice, and congressional leadership: The Physician Payment Review Commission and the politics of Medicare. *Journal of Health, Politics, Policy, and Law, 18*, 113–174.

Organ, T. W. (1970). *The Hindu quest for the perfection of man*. Athens, OH: Ohio University Press.

Ornish, D. (1990). *Dr. Dean Ornish's program for reversing heart disease*. New York: Ivy Books.

Orpen, C. (1979). The effects of job enrichment on employee satisfaction, motivation, involvement, and performance: A field experiment. *Human Relations, 32*, 189–217.

Orth-Gomer, K., Eriksson, I., Moser, V., Theorell, T., & Fredlund, P. (1994). Lipid lowering through work stress reduction. *International Journal of Behavioural Medicine, 1*, 204–214.

Osipow, S. H., & Davis, A. S. (1988). The relationship of coping resources to occupational stress and strain. *Journal of Vocational Behavior, 32*, 1–15.

Osler, W. (1910). The Lumleian lectures on angina pectoris. *Lancet, 1*, 839–844.

Osterhaus, J. T., Gutterman, D. L., & Plachetka, J. R. (1992). Healthcare resource and lost labor costs of migraine headache in the U.S. *PharmacoEconomics, 2*(1), 67–76.

Ouchi, W. (1981). *Theory z.* Reading, MA: Addison-Wesley.

Overbeke, J. E. (1975). Pressures build on today's manager. *Industrial Week, 187,* 21–24.

Owasoyo, J. O., Neri, D. F., & Lamberth, J. G. (1992). Tyrosine and its potential use as a countermeasure to performance decrement in military sustained operations. *Aviation Space and Environmental Medicine, 63,* 364–369.

Oxman, A. D., Muir, D. C., Shannon, H. S., Stock, S. R., Hnizdo, E., & Lange, H. J. (1993). Occupational dust exposure and chronic obstructive pulmonary disease: A systematic overview of the evidence. *American Review of Respiratory Disease, 148,* 38–48.

Oxman, T. E., Freeman, D. H., Jr., & Manheimer, E. D. (1995). Lack of social participation or religious strength and comfort as risk factors for death after cardiac surgery in the elderly. *Psychosomatic Medicine, 57,* 5–15.

Paffenbarger, R. S., & Hyde, R. T. (1980). Exercise as protection against heart attack. *New England Journal of Medicine, 302*(18), 1026–1027.

Paoline, A. M., Wells, C. L., & Kelly, G. T. (1978). Sexual variations in thermoregulation during heat stress. *Aviation Space and Environmental Medicine, 49,* 715–719.

Parikh, D. J., Ghodasara, M. B., & Raumanathan, N. L. (1978). A special thermal stress problem in ceramic industry. *European Journal of Applied Physiology, 40*(1), 63–72.

Parkes, C. M., Benjamin, B., & Fitzgerald, R. G. (1969). Broken heart: A statistical study of increased mortality among widowers. *British Medical Journal, 1,* 740–742.

Parkes, K. R., Mendham, C. A., & von Rabenau, C. (1994). Social support and the demand-discretion model of job stress: Tests of additive and interactive effects in two samples. *Journal of Vocational Behavior, 44*(1), 91–113.

Parrott, A. C. (1995). Stress modulation over the day in cigarette smokers. *Addiction, 90,* 233–244.

Pastor, L. H. (1995). Initial assessment and intervention strategies to reduce workplace violence. *American Family Physician, 52*(4), 38–48.

Paul, G. L. (1967). Insight versus desensitization in psychotherapy two years after termination. *Journal of Consulting Psychology, 31,* 333–348.

Pauley, J. T., Palmer, J. A., Wright, C. C., & Pfeiffer, H. (1982). The effect of a 14-week employee fitness program on selected physiological and psychological parameters. *Journal of Occupational Medicine, 24,* 457–463.

Paykel, E. S. (1976, September). Life stress, depression, and attempted suicide. *Journal of Human Stress,* pp. 3–12.

Payne, R. (Ed.). (1978). *Stress at work* (pp. 259–283). New York: Wiley.

Payne, R. (1980). Organizational stress and social support. In C. L. Cooper & R. Payne (Eds.), *Current concerns in occupational stress* (pp. 269–298). New York: Wiley.

Payne, R., Jick, T. D., & Burke, R. J. (1982, January). Whither stress research: An agenda for the 1980's. *Journal of Occupational Behaviour, 3*(1), 131–145.

Peale, N. V. (1952). *The power of positive thinking.* New York: Prentice Hall.

Pearlin, L. I., & Schooler, C. (1978). The structure of coping. *Journal of Health and Social Behavior, 19,* 2–21.

Peck, M. S. (1978). *The road less traveled: A new psychology of love, traditional values and spiritual growth.* New York: Simon & Schuster.

Pelletier, K. R. (1977). *Mind as healer, mind as slayer.* New York: Dell.

Pelletier, K. R. (1984). *Healthy people in unhealthy places: Stress and fitness at work.* New York: Delacorte Press/Seymour Lawrence.

Pelletier, K. R. (1992). *Mind as healer, mind as slayer: A holistic approach to preventing stress disorders.* New York: Delta/Seymour Lawrence.

Pelletier, K. R. (1995). *Sound mind, sound body: A new model for lifelong health.* New York: Fireside.

Pennebaker, J. W. (1990). *Opening up: The healing power of confiding in others.* New York: Avon Books.

Pennebaker, J. W., Colder, M., & Sharp, L. K. (1990). Accelerating the coping process. *Journal of Personality and Social Psychology, 58,* 528–537.

Pennebaker, J. W., Kiecolt-Glaser, J. K., & Glaser, R. (1988). Disclosures of traumas and immune function: Health implications for psychotherapy. *Journal of Consulting and Clinical Psychology, 56,* 239–245.

Pennebaker, J. W., & Susman, J. R. (1988). Disclosure of traumas and psychosomatic processes. *Social Science and Medicine, 26,* 327–332.

Perrewe, P. L., & Ganster, D. C. (1989). The impact of job demands and behavioral control on experienced job stress. *Journal of Organizational Behavior, 10,* 213–229.

Peters, L. H., Youngblood, S. A., & Greer, C. R. (Eds.). (1997). *The Blackwell dictionary of human resource management.* Oxford, England: Blackwell.

Peters, R. K. (1980). *Daily relaxation response breaks.* Cincinnati, OH: National Institute for Occupational Safety and Health, Division of Biomedical and Behavioral Science.

Peters, R. K., & Benson, H. (1978, January-February). Time out from tension. *Harvard Business Review, 56,* 120–124.

Peters, R. K., Benson, H., & Porter, D. (1977). Daily relaxation response breaks in a working population: I. Effects on self-reported measures of health, performance, and well-being. *American Journal of Public Health, 67,* 954–959.

Peterson, G. W., & Clark, D. A. (1990). The use of the MMPI as a measure of personal adjustment in career counseling. *Journal of Career Development, 16,* 297–307.

Peterson, C., Seligman, M. E. P., & Vaillant, G. E. (1988). Pessimistic explanatory style is a risk factor for physical illness: A thirty-five-year longitudinal study. *Journal of Personality and Social Psychology, 55,* 23–27.

Phillips, K. (1991). Biofeedback. In M. Pitts & K. Phillips (Eds.), *The psychology of health: An introduction* (pp. 106–120). London: Routledge.

Piltch, C. A., Walsh, D. C., Mangione, T. W., & Jennings, S. E. (1994). Gender, work, and mental distress in an industrial labor force: An expansion of Karasek's job strain model. In S. L. Sauter & L. R. Murphy (Eds.), *Organizational risk factors for job stress* (pp. 39–54). Washington, DC: American Psychological Association.

Piper, W. E., McCallum, M., & Azim, H. F. A. (1992). *Adaptation to loss through short-term group psychotherapy.* New York: Guilford Press.

Plant, M. A. (1979a). *Drinking careers.* London: Tavistock.

Plant, M. A. (1979b, September). Occupations, drinking patterns and alcohol-related problems: Conclusions from a follow-up study. *British Journal of Addiction, 74,* 267–273.

Polatin, P. S., Kinney, R. K., & Gatchel, R. J. (1993). Psychiatric illness and chronic low-back pain: The mind and the spine—which goes first? *Spine, 18*(1), 66–71.

Pondy, L. R. (1967). Organizational conflict: Concepts and models. *Administrative Science Quarterly, 12,* 297–320.

Porter, G. (1996). Organizational impact of workaholism: Suggestions for researching the negative outcomes of excessive work. *Journal of Occupational Health Psychology, 1,* 70–84.

Porter, L. W., Lawler, E. E. III, & Hackman, J. R. (1975). *Behavior in organizations.* New York: McGraw-Hill.

President's Council on Physical Fitness and Sports. (undated). *Fitness in the workplace: A handbook on employee programs.* Washington, DC: Author.

Pritchard, R. D., Roth, P. L., Jones, S. D., Galgay, P. J., & Watson, M. D. (1988). Designing a goal setting system to enhance performance: A practical guide. *Organizational Dynamics, 17,* 69–78.

Pritchett, S., & Finley, L. (1971). Problem drinking and the risk management function. *Risk Management, 18,* 16–23.

Pronk, S. J., Pronk, N. P., Sisco, A., & Ingalls, D. S. (1995). Impact of a daily 10-minute strength and flexibility program in a manufacturing plant. *American Journal of Health Promotion, 9,* 175–178.

Quick, J. C. (1979a). Dyadic goal setting and role stress: A field study. *Academy of Management Journal, 22,* 241–252.

Quick, J. C. (1979b). Dyadic goal setting within organizations: Role making and motivational considerations. *Academy of Management Review, 4,* 369–380.

Quick, J. C. (1989). An ounce of prevention is worth a pound of cure. *Stress Medicine, 5,* 207–210.

Quick, J. C. (1992). Crafting an organizational culture: Herb's hand at Southwest Airlines. *Organizational Dynamics, 21,* 45–56.

Quick, J. C., Barab, J., Fielding, J., Hurrell, J. J., Jr., Ivancevich, J. M., Mangelsdorff, A. D., Pelletier, K. R., Raymond, J., Smith, D. C., Vaccaaro, V., & Weiss, S. (1992, September-October). Occupational mental health promotion: A prevention agenda based on education and treatment. *American Journal of Health Promotion, 7*(1), 37–44.

Quick, J. C., Bhagat, R. S., Dalton, J. D., Jr., & Quick, J. D. (1987). *Work stress: Health care systems in the workplace.* New York: Praeger.

Quick, J. C., & Gray, D. A. (1979). Dyadic goal setting as a developmental technique: Training through role planning. *Proceedings of the 1979 Academy of Management meeting, Southwest division*, pp. 147–151.

Quick, J. C., & Gray, D. A. (1989–1990). Chaparral: Bringing "world class manufacturing" to steel. *National Productivity Review, 9*(1), 51–58.

Quick, J. C., & Griffin, R. W. (1980). *Situational determinants of goal-setting behaviors and evaluation: Task variability.* Paper presented at the meeting of the Southwestern Academy of Management, San Antonio, TX.

Quick, J. C., Hess, R. E., Hermalin, J., & Quick, J. D. (Eds.). (1990). *Career stress in changing times.* New York: Haworth Press.

Quick, J. C., Joplin, J. R., Nelson, D. L., Mangelsdorff, A. D., & Fiedler, E. (1996). Self-reliance and military service training outcomes. *Military Psychology, 8*, 279–293.

Quick, J. C., Joplin, J. R., Nelson, D. L., & Quick, J. D. (1991, September). *Self-reliance for stress and combat.* Proceedings of the eighth Combat Stress Conference (pp. 1–5), U.S. Army Health Services Command, Fort Sam Houston, TX.

Quick, J. C., Kulisch, A., Jones, N. D., O'Connor, E. J., & Peters, L. (1981, May). *The goals and objectives program: 1981 evaluation report* (Technical Report No. 1). University of Texas at Arlington, Department of Management.

Quick, J. C., Murphy, L. R., & Hurrell, J. J. (1992). *Stress and well-being at work.* Washington, DC: American Psychological Association.

Quick, J. C., & Nelson, D. L. (1997). Job stress. In L. H. Peters, S. A. Youngblood, & C. R. Greer (Eds.), *The Blackwell dictionary of human resource management* (pp. 193–194). Oxford, England: Basil Blackwell.

Quick, J. C., Nelson, D. L., & Quick, J. D. (1987). Successful executives: How independent? *Academy of Management Executives, 1*(2), 139–146.

Quick, J. C., Nelson, D. L., & Quick, J. D. (1990). *Stress and challenge at the top: The paradox of the successful executive.* New York: Wiley.

Quick, J. C., Nelson, D. L., & Quick, J. D. (1991). The self-reliance inventory. In J. W. Pfeiffer (Ed.), *The 1991 annual: Developing human resources* (pp. 149–161). San Diego, CA: Pfeiffer.

Quick, J. C., & Quick, J. D. (1979). Reducing stress through preventive management. *Human Resource Management, 18*(3), 15–22.

Quick, J. C., & Quick, J. D. (1984a). *Organizational stress and preventive management.* New York: McGraw-Hill.

Quick, J. C., & Quick, J. D. (1984b). How good working relationships can help relieve pressures on the job. *Management Review, 73*, 43–45.

Quick, J. C., & Quick, J. D. (1990). The changing times of life: Career in context. *Prevention in Human Services, 8*(1), 1–23.

Quick, J. C., & Quick, J. D. (1997b). Stress management programs. In L. H. Peters, S. A. Youngblood, & C. R. Greer (Eds.), *The Blackwell dictionary of human resource management* (pp. 338–339). Oxford, England: Blackwell.

Quick, J. C., Shannon, C., & Quick, J. D. (1983). Managing stress in the Air Force: An ounce of prevention! *Air University Review, 34*(4), 76–83.

Quick, J. D., Horn, R. S., & Quick, J. C. (1986). Health consequences of stress. *Journal of Organizational Behavior Management, 8*(2), 19–36.

Quick, J. D., Kertesz, J. W., Nelson, D. L., & Quick, J. C. (1985). Preventive management of stress. In D. W. Myers (Ed.), *Employee problem prevention and counseling* (pp. 125–157). Westport, CT: Greenwood Press.

Quick, J. D., Moorhead, G., Quick, J. C., Gerloff, E. A., Mattox, K. L., & Mullins, C. (1982, February). Decision-making among emergency room residents: Preliminary observations and a decision model. *Journal of Medical Education, 58*, 117–125.

Quick, J. D., Nelson, D. L., Matuszek, P. A. C., Whittington, J. L., & Quick, J. C. (1996).

Social support, secure attachments, and health. In C. L. Cooper (Ed.), *Handbook of stress, medicine, and health* (pp. 269–287). Boca Raton, FL: CRC Press.

Quick, J. D., & Quick, J. C. (1979). Organizational stress and preventive management. *Chronic Diseases and Therapeutics Research, 3*(13), 185–205.

Quick, J. F. (1990). Time to move on? In J. C. Quick, R. Hess, J. Hermaline, & J. D. Quick (Eds.), *Career stress in changing times* (pp. 239–250). New York: Haworth Press.

Quinn, R. P., & Shepard, L. J. (1974). *The 1972–1973 quality of employment survey.* Ann Arbor, MI: Survey Research Center.

Rabinowitz, S. (1981). Towards a developmental model of job involvement. *International Review of Applied Psychology, 30,* 31–50.

Rahe, R. H. (1972). Subjects' recent life changes and their near-future illness reports. *Annals of Clinical Research, 4,* 250–265.

Rahe, R. H. (1974). The pathway between subjects' recent life changes and their near-future illness reports: Representative results and methodological issues. In B. S. Dohrenwend & B. P. Dohrenwend (Eds.), *Stressful life events: Their nature and effects* (pp. 73–86). New York: Wiley.

Rahe, R. H., Gunderson, E. K. E., Pugh, W. M., Rubin, R. T., & Arthur, R. J. (1972, September). Illness prediction studies: Use of psychosocial and occupational characteristics as predictors. *Archives of Environmental Health, 25,* 192–197.

Rahe, R. H., Rubin, R. T., & Gunderson, E. K. E. (1972, April). Measures of subjects' motivation and affect correlated with their serum uric acid, cholesterol, and cortisol. *Archives of General Psychiatry, 26,* 357.

Ramey, E. (1990, May 3–5). *Gender differences in cardiac disease: The paradox of heart disease in women.* Keynote address at the Healing the Heart Conference, Boston.

Ramsey, J. D. (1978, June). Abbreviated guidelines for heat stress exposure. *American Industrial Hygiene Association Journal, 30,* 491–495.

Raskin, M., Bali, L. R., & Peeke, H. V. (1980). Muscle biofeedback and transcendental meditation. *Archives of General Psychiatry, 37,* 93–97.

Ravindran, A. V., Griffiths, J., Waddell, C., & Anisman, H. (1995). Stressful life events and coping styles in relation to dysthymia and major depressive disorder: Variations associated with alleviation of symptoms following pharmacotherapy. *Progress in Neuro-Psychopharmacology & Biological Psychiatry, 19,* 637–653.

Raymond, J. S., Wood, D. W., & Patrick, W. K. (1990). Psychology doctoral training in work and health. *American Psychologist, 45,* 1159–1161.

Reardon, R. W. (1976, January-February). Help for the troubled worker in a small company. *Personnel, 53,* 50–54.

Reed, P. (1994). *The medical disability advisor: Workplace guidelines for disability duration* (2nd Ed.). Horsham, PA: LRP Publications.

Reischl, V. (1977). Radiotelemetry-based study of occupational heat stress in a steel factory. *Biotelemetry, 4*(3), 115–130.

Reiss, B. (1967). Changes in patient income concomitant with psychotherapy. *International Mental Health Research Newsletter, 9,* 1–4.

Rejeski, W. J., Thompson, A., Brubaker, P. H., & Miller, H. S. (1992). Acute exercise: Buffering psychosocial stress responses in women. *Health Psychology, 11,* 355–362.

Rhodewalt, F., & Zone, J. B. (1989). Appraisal of life change, depression and illness in hardy and non-hardy women. *Journal of Personality and Social Psychology, 56,* 81–88.

Rhue, J. W., Lynn, S. J., & Kirsch, I. (Eds.). (1993). *Handbook of clinical hypnosis.* Washington, DC: American Psychological Association.

Riddle, S. C. (1979). *A life cycle analysis of a temporary project organization.* Unpublished master's thesis, University of Texas at Arlington.

Ritzer, G. (1977). *Working conflict and change.* Englewood Cliffs, NJ: Prentice-Hall.

Rizzo, J. R., House, R. J., & Litzman, S. J. (1970). Role conflict and ambiguity in complex organizations. *Administrative Science Quarterly, 15,* 150–163.

Rodahl, K., & Vokac, Z. (1977). Work stress in long-line bank fishing. *Scandinavian Journal of Work Environment and Health, 3*(3), 154–159.

Roethlisberger, F. J. (1941). *Management and morale.* Cambridge, MA: Harvard University Press.

Roethlisberger, F., & Dickson, W. J. (1939). *Management and the worker*. Cambridge, MA: Harvard University Press.

Roman, P. H., & Trice, H. M. (1972). Psychiatric impairment among "middle Americans": Surveys of work organizations. *Social Psychiatry, 7,* 157–166.

Romano, P. S., Bloom, J., & Syme, S. L. (1991). Smoking, social support, and hassles in an urban African-American community. *American Journal of Public Health, 81,* 1415–1421.

Rome, H. P. (1975). Emotional problems leading to cardiovascular accidents. *Psychiatric Annals, 5*(7), 6–9.

Ronen, S. (1981). *Flexible working hours: An innovation in the quality of work life*. New York: McGraw-Hill.

Rosch, P. J. (1983). Stress and cardiovascular disease. *Comprehensive Therapy, 9,* 6–13.

Rosch, P. J. (1991, May). Job stress: America's leading adult health problem. *USA Today*, pp. 42–44.

Rosch, P. J. (1996). Stress and cancer: Disorders of communication, control, and civilization. In C. L. Cooper (Ed.), *Handbook of stress, medicine, and health* (pp. 27–60). Boca Raton, FL: CRC Press.

Rosen, R. H. (1986). *The healthy company*. New York: G. P. Putnam.

Rosenbaum, J. F. (1982). The drug treatment of anxiety. *New England Journal of Medicine, 306,* 401–404.

Rosenberg, M. L., & Fenley, M. A. (Eds.). (1991). *Violence in America: A public health approach*. New York: Oxford University Press.

Rosengren, A., Orth-Gomer, K., Wedel, H., & Wilhelmsen, L. (1993). Stressful life events, social support, and mortality in men born in 1933. *British Medical Journal, 307,* 1102–1105.

Rosenman, R. H. (1996). Personality, behavior patterns, and heart disease. In C. L. Cooper (Ed.), *Handbook of stress, medicine, and health* (pp. 217–231). Boca Raton, FL: CRC Press.

Rosenman, R. H., & Friedman, M. (1977). Modifying Type A behavior patterns. *Journal of Psychosomatic Research, 21,* 323–331.

Rosenman, R. H., Friedman, M., & Strauss, R. (1966). CHD in the Western Collaborative Group Study. *Journal of the American Medical Association, 195,* 86–92.

Rosenman, R. H., Friedman, M., Strauss, R., Wurm, M., Kositchek, R., Hahn, W., & Werthessen, N. T. (1964). A predictive study of coronary heart disease. *Journal of the American Medical Association, 189,* 103–110.

Roskies, E. (1978). Changing the coronary-prone (Type A) behavior pattern. *Journal of Behavioral Medicine, 1,* 201–216.

Roskies, E. (1987). *Stress management for the healthy Type A: Theory and practice*. New York: Guilford Press.

Rotter, J. B. (1966). Generalized expectancies for internal versus external control of reinforcement. *Psychological Monographs, 80*(1).

Rotter, J. B. (1972). Generalized expectancies for internal versus external control of reinforcement. In J. B. Rotter, J. C. Chance, & E. J. Phares (Eds.), *Applications of a social learning theory of personality* (pp. 260–294). New York: Holt, Rinehart & Winston.

Rotter, J. B., Chance, J. E., & Phares, E. J. (1972). *Applications of social learning theory of personality*. New York: Holt, Rinehart & Winston.

Rountree, G. D. (1979, Fall). Renew your career: Take a sabbatical. *Hospital & Health Services Administration*, pp. 67–80.

Rousseau, D. M. (1990). New hire perceptions of their own and their employer's obligations: A study of psychological contracts. *Journal of Organizational Behavior, 11,* 389–400.

Roy, M., & Steptoe, (1991). The inhibition of cardiovascular responses to mental stress following aerobic exercise. *Psychophysiology, 28,* 689–700.

Royal Canadian Air Force. (1962). *Exercising plans for physical fitness*. New York: Pocket Books.

Russek, H. (1965). Stress, tobacco, and coronary heart disease in North American professional groups. *Journal of the American Medical Association, 192,* 189–194.

Russek, H. I., & Zohman, B. L. (1958). Relative significance of heredity, diet, and occupational stress in coronary heart disease of young adults. *American Journal of Medical Science, 235,* 266–275.

Sachs, B. C. (1982). Hypnosis in psychiatry and psychosomatic medicine. *Psychosomatics, 23,* 523–525.

Sales, S. M. (1969). Organizational role as a risk factor in coronary disease. *Administrative Science Quarterly, 14,* 325–336.

Salmon, P. (1992). Surgery as a psychological stressor: Paradoxical effects of preoperative emotional state on endocrine responses. Third International Society for the Investigation of Stress Conference: Psychoneuroendocrinology of stress (1990, Padua, Italy). *Stress Medicine, 8,* 193–198.

Salmon, P. (1993). Emotional effects of physical exercise. In S. C. Stanford & P. Salmon (Eds.), *Stress: From synapse to syndrome* (pp. 395–419). London: Academic Press.

Sauter, S., Hurrell, J. J., & Cooper, C. L. (1989). *Job control and worker health.* New York: Wiley.

Sauter, S. L., Murphy, L. R., & Hurrell, J. J. (1990). Prevention of work related psychological distress: A national strategy proposed by the National Institute of Occupational Safety and Health. *American Psychologist, 45,* 1146–1158.

Sbaih, L. (1993). Accident and emergency work: A review of some of the literature. *Journal of Advanced Nursing, 18,* 957–962.

Schaefer, J., & Moos, R. H. (1991). *Work stressors and coping among long term care staff.* Palo Alto, CA: Center for Health Care Evaluation, Department of Veterans Affairs Medical Centers.

Schaeffer, L., Donegan, P., Garry, M., & Mathews, R. (1995, April). Optimism takes hold [Special issue: 62nd Annual Report of the Grocery Industry]. *Progressive Grocer, 74*(4), 510–515.

Schaertel, T. (1976). Meditating housestaff. *Hospital Physician, 12*(7), 28–31.

Schaubroeck, J., Ganster, D., Sime, W., & Ditman, D. (1993). A field experiment testing supervisory role clarification. *Personnel Psychology, 46,* 1–25.

Schein, E. H. (1985). *Organizational culture and leadership.* San Francisco: Jossey-Bass.

Schein, E. H. (1990). Organizational culture. *American Psychologist, 45,* 109–119.

Schein, V. E. (1975). Relationship between sex roles, stereotypes, and requisite management characteristics among female managers. *Journal of Applied Psychology, 60,* 340–344.

Schindler, B. A., & Ramchandani, D. (1991). Psychological factors associated with peptic ulcer disease. *Medical Clinics of North America, 75,* 865–876.

Schneider, H. (1976). Frustration: A disruptive factor in cooperation and performance. *Personnel, 53*(1), 12–13.

Schuler, R. S. (1979). Time management: A stress management technique. *Personnel Journal, 58,* 851–854.

Schuster, C. R., & Kilbey, M. M. (1992). Prevention of drug abuse. In J. M. Last & R. B. Wallace (Eds.), *Public health and preventive medicine* (13th ed., pp. 769–786). Norwalk, CT: Appleton & Lange.

Schwartz, G. E. (1984). Psychophysiology of imagery and healing: A systems perspective. In A. A. Sheikh (Ed.), *Imagination and healing* (pp. 35–50). Farmingdale, NY: Baywood.

Schwartz, J. E., Pickering, T. G., & Landsbergis, P. A. (1996). Work-related stress and blood pressure: Current theoretical models and considerations from a behavioral medicine perspective. *Journal of Occupational Health Psychology, 1,* 287–310.

Schwartz, M. S. (1995). Irritable bowel syndrome. In M. S. Schwartz (Ed.), *Biofeedback: A practitioner's guide* (2nd ed.). New York: Guilford Press.

Schwarzer, R., Hahn, A., & Fuchs, R. (1994). Unemployment, social resources, and mental and physical health: A three-wave study on men and women in a stressful life transition. In G. P. Keita & J. J. Hurrell, Jr. (Eds.), *Job stress in a changing workforce* (pp. 75–88). Washington, DC: American Psychological Association.

Seashore, S. E. (1954). *Group cohesiveness in the industrial work group.* Ann Arbor, MI: Institute for Social Research, University of Michigan.

Seashore, S. E., Lawler, E. E., Mirvis, P. H., & Cammann, C. (1982). *Observing and measuring organizational change: A guide to field practice.* New York: Wiley Interscience.

Seigrist, J. (1996). Adverse health effects of high-effort/low-reward conditions. *Journal of Occupational Health Psychology, 1,* 27–41.

Seizer, M. L., & Vinokur, A. (1974). Life events, subjective stress, and traffic accidents. *American Journal of Psychiatry, 131,* 903–906.

Sekiguchi, C., Handa, Y., Gotoh, M., Kurihara, Y., Nagasawa, A., & Kuroda, I. (1978). Evaluation method of mental workload under flight conditions. *Aviation Space and Environmental Medicine, 49,* 920–925.

Seligman, M. E. P. (1975). *Helplessness: On depression, development and death.* San Francisco: Freeman.

Seligman, M. E. P. (1990). *Learned optimism.* New York: Knopf.

Seligman, M. E. P. (1995, December). The effectiveness of psychotherapy: The *Consumer Reports* study. *American Psychologist, 50,* 965–974.

Seligman, M. E. P., & Schulman, P. (1986). Explanatory style as a predictor of performance as a life insurance agent. *Journal of Personality and Social Psychology, 50,* 832–838.

Selkurt, E. E. (Ed.). (1975). *Basic physiology for the health sciences.* Boston: Little, Brown.

Selye, H. (1973). Evolution of the stress concept. *American Scientist, 61,* 692–699.

Selye, H. (1974). *Stress without distress.* Philadelphia: Lippincott.

Selye, H. (1976a). Forty years of stress research: Principal remaining problems and misconceptions. *Canadian Medical Association Journal, 115,* 53–56.

Selye, H. (1976b). *Stress in health and disease.* Boston: Butterworth.

Selye, H. (1976c). *The stress of life* (Rev. ed.). New York: McGraw-Hill. (Original work published 1956)

Selye, H. (1978, March). On the real benefits of eustress. *Psychology Today,* pp. 60–70.

Sethi, S., & Seligman, M. E. P. (1993). Optimism and fundamentalism. *Psychological Science, 4,* 256–269.

Sewil, C. (1969, November 10). Those patients with Wall Street sickness. *Medical Economics,* pp. 102–104.

Shapiro, A. P. (1961). An experimental study of comparative responses of blood pressure to different noxious stimuli. *Journal of Chronic Disorders, 13,* 293.

Sharpe, R. (1996, April 10). EEOC sues Mitsubishi unit for harassment. *Wall Street Journal,* pp. B1, B8.

Shaver, P., & Buhrmester, D. (1985). Loneliness, sex-role orientation, and group life: A social needs perspective. In P. Paulus (Ed.), *Basic group processes* (pp. 259–288). New York: Springer-Verlag.

Shaw, J. B., Fields, M. W., Thacker, J. W., & Fisher, C. D. (1993). The availability of personal and external coping resources: Their impact on job stress and employee attitudes during organizational restructuring. *Work and Stress, 7,* 229–246.

Sheehan, G. (1975). *Doctor Sheehan on running.* Mountain View, CA: Anderson World.

Shostak, A. B. (1980). *Blue-collar occupational stress.* Reading, MA: Addison-Wesley.

Shumaker, S. A., & Brownell, A. (1994). Toward a theory of social support: Closing conceptual gaps. *Journal of Social Issues, 40,* 11–16.

Siegel, B. S. (1990). *Love, medicine & miracles: Lessons learned about self-healing from a surgeon's experience with exceptional patients.* New York: Harper Perennial.

Siegrist, J. (1996). Adverse health effects of high-effort/low-strain reward conditions. *Journal of Occupational Health Psychology, 1,* 30.

Silver, B. J., & Blanchard, E. B. (1978). Biofeedback and relaxation training in the treatment of psychophysiological disorders: Or are the machines really necessary? *Journal of Behavioral Medicine, 1,* 217–239.

Sime, W. E. (1977). Comparison of exercise and meditation in reducing physiological response to stress. *Medicine and Science in Sports, 9,* 55.

Simon, H. A. (1996). *Sciences of the artificial* (3rd ed.). Cambridge, MA: MIT Press. (Original work published 1969).

Singh, J., Goolsby, J. R., & Rhoads, G. K. (1994). Behavioral and psychological consequences of boundary spanning burnout for customer service representatives. *Journal of Marketing Research, 31,* 558–569.

Sittig, D. F. (1993). Work-sampling: A statistical approach to evaluation of the effect of computers on work patterns in healthcare. *Methods of Information in Medicine, 32,* 167–174.

Smith, M. J., Colligan, M. J., & Hurrell, J. J., Jr. (1977, November). *A review of NIOSH psychological stress research—1977.* Los Angeles: The UCLA Conference on Job Stress.

Smith, P. C., Kendall, L. M., & Hulin, C. L. (1969). *The measurement of satisfaction in work and retirement*. Chicago: Rand McNally.

Sommer, R. (1974). *Tight spaces: Hart architecture and how to humanize It*. Englewood Cliffs, NJ: Prentice-Hall.

Sorensen, J. E., & Sorensen, T. L. (1974, March). The conflict of professionals in bureaucratic organizations. *Administrative Science Quarterly, 19,* 98–106.

Spector, P. L. (1988). Development of the work locus of control scale. *Journal of Occupational Psychology, 61,* 335–340.

Spera, S. P., Buhrfeind, E. D., & Pennebaker, J. W. (1994). Expressive writing and coping with job loss. *Academy of Management Journal, 37,* 722–733.

Spielberger, C. D. (1991). *State-trait anger expression inventory: Revised research edition*. Odessa, FL: Psychological Assessment Resources.

Spielberger, C. D. (1994). *Professional manual for the job stress survey (JSSS)*. Odessa, FL: Psychological Assessment Resources.

Spielberger, C. D., Gorsuch, R. L., & Lushene, R. E. (1970). *Manual for the State-Trait Anxiety Inventory (STAI)*. Palo Alto, CA: Consulting Psychologists Press.

Spielberger, C. D., Krasner, S. S., & Solomon, E. P. (1988). The experience, expression, and control of anger. In M. P. Janisse (Ed.), *Health psychology: Individual differences and stress* (pp. 89–108). New York: Springer-Verlag.

Spielberger, C. D., & Reheiser, E. C. (1994). The Job Stress Survey: Measuring gender differences in occupation stress. *Journal of Social Behavior and Personality, 9*(2), 199–218.

Spring, B., Maller, O., Wurtman, J., Digman, L., & Cozolino, L. (1982–1983). Effects of protein and carbohydrate meals on moods and performance: Interactions with sex and age. *Journal of Psychiatric Research, 17,* 155–167.

Spurgeon, C. F. E. (1970). *Mysticism in English literature*. Cambridge, England: The University Press.

Stallones, L., & Kraus, J. F. (1993). The occurrence and epidemiologic features of alcohol-related occupational injuries. *Addiction, 88,* 945–951.

Staw, B. M., Sandelands, L. E., & Dutton, J. E. (1981). Threat-rigidity effects in organizational behavior: A multilevel analysis. *Administrative Science Quarterly, 26,* 501–524.

Steele, F. I. (1973). *Physical settings and organizational development*. Reading, MA: Addison-Wesley.

Steers, R. M. (1975). Problems in the measurement of organizational effectiveness. *Administrative Science Quarterly, 20,* 546–548.

Steers, R. M. (1977). *Organizational effectiveness: A behavioral view*. Santa Monica, CA: Goodyear.

Steers, R. M., & Porter, L. N. (1974). The role of task-goal attributes in employee performance. *Psychological Bulletin, 81,* 434–452.

Steers, R. M., & Rhodes, S. R. (1978). Major influences on employee attendance: A process model. *Journal of Applied Psychology, 63,* 391–407.

Steffy, B. D., Jones, J. W., Murphy, L. R., & Kunz, L. (1986). A demonstration of the impact of stress abatement programs on reducing employees' accidents and their costs. *American Journal of Health Promotion, 1,* 25–32.

Steiner, J. (1972, March-April). What price success? *Harvard Business Review, 50,* 69–74.

Steptoe, A., Moses, J., Edwards, S., & Mathews, A. (1993). Exercise and responsivity to mental stress: Discrepancies between the subjective and physiological effects of aerobic training [Special issue: Exercise and psychological well being]. *International Journal of Sport Psychology, 24*(2), 110–129.

Sterling, T. D. (1978). Does smoking kill workers or working kill smokers? *International Journal of Health Services, 8,* 437–452.

Sterling, T. D., & Weinkam, J. J. (1976). Smoking characteristics by type of employment. *Journal of Occupational Medicine, 18,* 743–760.

Stessin, L. (1977, April 3). When an employer insists. *The New York Times*, Business and Financial Section, pp. 8–9.

Steumpf, S. A., & Rabinowitz, S. (1981). Career stage as a moderator of performance relationships with facets of job satisfaction and role perceptions. *Journal of Vocational Behavior, 18,* 202–218.

Stewart, N. (1978). *The effective woman manager.* New York: Wiley.

Stone, W. N. (1996). *Group psychotherapy for people with chronic mental illness.* New York: Guilford Press.

Storms, P. L., & Spector, P. E. (1987). Relationships of organizational frustration with reported behavioural reactions: The moderating effect of locus of control. *Journal of Occupational Psychology, 60,* 227–234.

Streidl, J. W. (1976). *Manager's guide to effective performance evaluation, coaching and counseling.* Houston, TX: Tenneco.

Strong, D., & Campbell, D. (1977). *Manual for the Strong Vocational Interest Blank*: Strong-Campbell Interest Inventory (2nd ed.). Stanford, CA: Stanford University Press.

Student, K. R. (1977). Changing values and management stress. *Personnel, 54,* 48–55.

Suinn, R. M., & Bloom, L. J. (1978). Anxiety management training for Pattern A behavior. *Journal of Behavioral Medicine, 1,* 25–35.

Suinn, R. M., Brock, L., & Edie, C. A. (1975). Behavior therapy for Type A patients [Letter to the editor]. *American Journal of Cardiology, 36,* 269.

Sullivan, H. S. (1953). *The interpersonal theory of psychiatry.* New York: Norton.

Suls, J., & Wan, C. K. (1989). The relations between Type A behavior and chronic emotional distress: A meta-analysis. *Journal of Personality and Social Psychology, 57,* 503–512.

Sutton, R. I., & Kahn, R. L. (1987). Prediction, understanding, and control as antidotes to organizational stress. In J. W. Lorsch (Ed.), *Handbook of organizational behavior* (pp. 272–285). Englewood Cliffs, NJ: Prentice-Hall.

Swezey, R., & Salas, E. (1991). *Teams: Their training and performance.* Norwood, NJ: Ablex.

Szilagyi, A. D., & Holland, W. E. (1980). Changes in social density: Relationships with functional interaction and perceptions of job characteristics, role stress, and work satisfaction. *Journal of Applied Psychology, 65,* 28–33.

Taché, J. (1979). Stress as a cause of disease. In J. Taché, H. Selye, & S. B. Day (Eds.), *Cancer, stress, and death* (pp. 1–9). New York: Plenum Medical.

Taché, J., Selye, H., & Day, S. B. (Eds.). (1979). *Cancer, stress, and death.* New York: Plenum Medical.

Taggart, P., Carruthers, M., & Somerville, W. (1973). Electrocardiogram, plasma catecholamines and lipids, and their modification by oxprenolol when speaking before an audience. *Lancet, 2,* 341–346.

Tannenbaum, R., & Massarik, F. (1950, August). Participation by subordinates in the managerial decision-making process. *Canadian Journal of Economics and Political Science, 16,* 408–418.

Taylor, J. W. (1911). *The principles of scientific management.* New York: Harper & Brothers.

Teasdale, E. L., & McKeown, S. (1994). Managing stress at work: The ICI-Zeneca Pharmaceuticals experience 1986–1993. In C. L. Cooper & S. Williams (Eds.), *Creating healthy work organizations* (pp. 133–165). Chichester, England: Wiley.

Temoshok, L., & Dreher, H. (1993). The Type C connection: The behavioral link to cancer and your health. New York: Penguin Books.

Tension in the public schools: Teachers under stress. (1979). *Behavioral Medicine, 6*(3), 28–31.

Terborg, J. R. (1977). Women in management: A research review. *Journal of Applied Psychology, 61,* 647–664.

Terra, N. (1995). The prevention of job stress by redesigning jobs and implementing self-regulating teams. In L. R. Murphy, J. J. Hurrell, Jr., S. L. Sauter, & G. P. Keita (Eds.), *Job stress interventions* (pp. 265–282). Washington, DC: American Psychological Association.

Tetrick, L. E. (1992). Mediating effect of perceived role stress: A confirmatory analysis. In J. C. Quick, L. R. Murphy, & J. J. Hurrell, Jr. (Eds.) *Stress and well-being at work,* 134–152. Washington, DC: American Psychological Association.

Tetrick, L. E., Miles, R. L., Marcil, L., & VanDosen, C. M. (1994). Child care difficulties and the impact on concentration, stress, and productivity among single and nonsingle mothers and fathers. In S. L. Sauter & L. R. Murphy (Eds.), *Organizational risk factors for job stress* (pp. 229–240). Washington, DC: American Psychological Association.

Thacher, F. J., Esmiol, P., Ives, H. R., & Mandelkour, B. (1977, December). Can onsite counselling programs aid workers, reduce health costs? *Occupational Health & Safety, 46,* 48–50.

Theorell, T., & Karasek, R. A. (1996). Current issues relating to psychosocial job strain and cardiovascular disease research. *Journal of Occupational Health Psychology, 1*(1), 9–26.

Theorell, J., Lind, E., & Floderus, B. (1976). The relationships of disturbing life changes and emotions to the early development of myocardial infarctions and other serious illnesses. *Revue D'epidemiologie et de Sante Publique, 24*(1), 41–59.

Thompson, J. D. (1967). *Organizations in action.* New York: McGraw-Hill.

Thurow, L. C. (1992). *Head to head: The coming economic battle among Japan, Europe, and America.* New York: Morrow.

Tichy, N., & Charan, R. (1989). Speed, simplicity, self-confidence: An interview with Jack Welch. *Harvard Business Review, 67*(5), 112–120.

Timio, M. (1977). Urinary excretion of adrenaline, noradrenaline and ilhydroxy-corticoids under job stress. *Giornale Italiano Di Cardiologia, 17,* 1080–1087.

Toivanen, H., Lansimies, E., Jokela, V., & Hanninen, O. (1993). Impact of regular relaxation training on the cardiac autonomic nervous system of hospital cleaners and bank employees. *Scandinavian Journal of Work, Environment and Health, 19,* 319–325.

Tolchinsky, P. D., & King, D. C. (1980). Do goals mediate the effects of incentives on performance? *Academy of Management Review, 5,* 455–467.

Tower of stress: The plight of air traffic controllers. (1979). *Behavioral Medicine, 6*(4), 38–41.

Tracy, L., & Johnson, T. W. (1981). What do the role conflict and role ambiguity scales measure? *Journal of Applied Psychology, 66,* 464–469.

Triandis, H. C., Feldman, J. M., Weldon, D. E., & Harvey, W. M. (1974). Designing pre-employment training for the hard to employ: A cross-cultural psychological approach. *Journal of Applied Psychology, 59,* 687–693.

Trice, H., & Roman, P. (1981). Perspectives on job-based programs for alcohol and drug problems. *Journal of Drug Issues, 11,* 167–169.

Tubbs, M. E., & Ekeberg, S. E. (1991). The role of intentions in work motivation: Implications for goal setting theory and research. *Academy of Management Review, 16,* 180–199.

Tuckman, B. W. (1965, June). Developmental sequence in small groups. *Psychological Bulletin, 63,* 384–399.

Umezawa, A. (1991). Changes of respiratory activity during laboratory stress. *Japanese Journal of Physiological Psychology and Psychophysiology, 9*(1), 43–55.

Uris, A. (1972). How managers ease job pressures. *International Management, 27,* 45–46.

Vaillant, G. E. (1977). *Adaptation to life.* Boston: Little, Brown.

VandenBos, G. R., & Bulatao, E. Q. (Eds.). (1996). *Violence on the job: Identifying risks and developing solutions.* Washington, DC: American Psychological Association.

Van Dosterom, A. (1975). Psychosocial problems of the working man. *Metamedical, 54*(7), 218–220.

Van Maanen, J. (Ed.). (1979, December). Qualitative methodology [Special issue]. *Administrative Science Quarterly, 24*(4).

Van Maanen, J., & Schein, E. J. (1977). Career development. In J. R. Hackman & J. L. Suttle (Eds.), *Improving life at work* (pp. 30–95). Santa Monica, CA: Goodyear.

van Os, J., Fahy, T. A., Bebbington, P. E., Jones, P., Sam, P., Russell, A., Giluarry, K., Lewis, S., & Toone, B. (1994). The influence of life events on the subsequent course of psychotic illness: A prospective follow-up of the Camberwell Collaborative Psychosis Study. *Psychological Medicine, 24,* 503–513.

Van Sell, M., Brief, A. P., & Schuler, R. S. (1981). Role conflict and role ambiguity: Integration of the literature and directions for future research. *Human Relations, 34*(1), 43–71.

Verbrugge, L. (1989a). Gender, aging, and health. In: K. S. Markides (Ed.), *Aging and health: Perspectives on gender, race, ethnicity, and class* (pp. 23–78). Newbury Park, CA: Sage.

Verbrugge, L. (1989b). Recent, present, and future health of American adults. *Annual Review of Public Health, 10,* 333–361.

Vital Statistics of the United States, 1985, Life tables, Vol. II, Section 6. (1985). (DHHS

Publication No. PHS 88-1104, January 1988). Washington, DC: U.S. Dept. of Health and Human Services, Public Health Service, National Center for Health Statistics.

Von, G., & Von, L. P. (1978). Stress. *Law and order, 26*(2), 54–55.

Von Dusch, T. (1868). *Lehrbuch der herzkrankheiten.* [Textbook of heart disease]. Leipzig: Verlag von Wilhelm Engelman.

Vroom, V. H. (1964). *Work and motivation.* New York: Wiley.

Wagenaar, J., & La Forge, J. (1994). Stress counseling theory and practice: A cautionary review. *Journal of Counseling and Development, 73*(1), 23–31.

Walcott-McQuigg, J. A., Sullivan, J., Dan, A., & Logan, B. (1995). Psychosocial factors influencing weight control behavior of African American women. *Western Journal of Nursing Research, 17,* 502–520.

Walker, C. R., & Guest, R. H. (1952). *The man on the assembly line.* Cambridge, MA: Harvard University Press.

Walker, L. G., Johnson, V. C., & Eremin, O. (1993). Modulation of the immune response to stress by hypnosis and relaxation training in healthy volunteers: A critical review. *Contemporary Hypnosis, 10*(1), 19–27.

Wall, R., & Nicholas, I. D. (1985). Health care costs: Getting to the heart of the problem. *Risk Management, 32*(7), 20–22.

Walsh, R. J. (1975). You can deal with stress. *Supervisory Management, 20,* 16–31.

Warshaw, L. J. (1979). *Managing stress.* Reading, MA: Addison-Wesley.

Watson, D., & Clark, L. A. (1984). Negative affectivity: The disposition to experience aversive emotional states. *Psychological Bulletin, 96,* 465–490.

Watson, D., & Slack, A. K. (1993). General factors of affective temperament and their relation to job satisfaction over time. *Organizational Behavior and Human Decision Processes, 54*(2), 181–202.

Weaver, R. L., Cotrell, H. W., & Churchman, E. C. (1988). Destructive dialogue: Negative self-talk and positive imaging. *College Student Journal, 22,* 230–240.

Webb, G. R., Redman, S., Hennrikus, D. J., Kelman, G. R., Gibberd, R. W., & Sanson, F. R. W. (1994). The relationships between high-risk and problem drinking and the occurrence of work injuries and related absences. *Journal of Studies on Alcohol, 55,* 434–446.

Weber, A., Jermini, C., & Grandjean, E. P. (1975). Relationship between objective and subjective assessment of experimentally induced fatigue. *Ergonomics, 18*(2), 151–156.

Weber, M. (1930). *The Protestant ethic and the spirit of capitalism* (T. Parsons, Trans.). London: Allen & Unwin.

Weick, K. E. (1984). Small wins: Redefining the scale of social problems. *American Psychologist, 39,* 40–49.

Weider, A., Wolff, H., Brodman, K., Mittlemann, B., & Wedsler, D. (1949). *Cornell Index Manual.* New York: Cornell Medical School.

Weiss, D. J., Davis, R. V., & England, G. W. (1967). *Manual for the Minnesota Satisfaction Questionnaire, XXII.* University of Minnesota Industrial Relations Center, Work Adjustment Project, Minnesota Studies in Vocational Rehabilitation, Minneapolis, MN.

Weiss, S. M. (Ed.). (1981). Coronary prone behavior and coronary heart disease: A critical review. *Circulation, 63,* 1199–1215.

Weiss, S. M., Fielding, J. E., & Baum, A. (1991). *Health at work.* Hillsdale, NJ: Erlbaum.

Wesley, E. (1953). Preservative behavior in a concept-formation task as a function of manifest anxiety and rigidity. *Journal of Abnormal and Social Psychology, 48,* 129–134.

Westcott, G., Svensson, P., & Zollner, H. F. K. (1985). *Health policy implications of unemployment.* Copenhagen: World Health Organization, Regional Office for Europe.

Whetton, D. A., & Cameron, K. S. (1993). *Developing management skills: Managing stress.* New York: HarperCollins.

White-Means, S. I., & Chang, C. F. (1994). Informal caregivers' leisure time and stress. *Journal of Family and Economic Issues, 15*(2), 117–136.

Whitlock, F. A., Stoll, J. R., & Rekhdahl, R. J. (1977). Crisis, life events and accidents. *Australian and New Zealand Journal of Psychiatry, 11,* 127.

Wilensky, H. L. (1964, September). The professionalization of everyone? *American Journal of Sociology, 69,* 137–158.

Williams, R. (1993). *Anger kills.* New York: Times Books.

Wilson, S. H., & Walker, G. M. (1993). Unemployment and health: A review. *Public Health, 107,* 153–162.

Wilson v. Eisner, #282f, 38, Second Circuit Court (1922).

Winett, R. A. (1995). A framework for health promotion and disease prevention programs. *American Psychologist, 50,* 341–350.

Wofford, J. C., & Daly, P. (in press). A cognitive process approach to understanding individual differences in stress response propensity. *Journal of Occupational Health Psychology.*

Wolberg, L. R. (1977). *The technique of psychotherapy* (3rd ed.). New York: Grune & Stratton.

Wolf, S. G. (1960). Stress and heart disease. *Modern Concepts of Cardiovascular Disease, 29*(7), 559–604.

Wolf, S. G., Jr. (1986). Common and grave disorders identified with occupational stress. In S. G. Wolf, Jr., & A. J. Finestone (Eds.), Occupational stress: Health and performance at work (pp. 47–53). Littleton, MA: PSG Publishing Co.

Wolf, S., & Wolff, H. G. (1943). *Gastric function: An experimental study of a man and his stomach.* New York: Oxford University Press.

Wolff, H. G. (1953). *Stress and disease.* Springfield, IL: Charles C Thomas.

Woodburn, L. T., & Simpson, S. (1994). Employee types: Who will be the next stress claimant? *Risk Management, 41,* 38–44.

Woolsey, C. (1995). Low-cost care need not be low quality. *Business Insurance, 29*(2), 22.

Wright, G., Iam, S., & Knecht, E. (1977). Resistance to heat stress in the spontaneously hypertensive rat. *Canadian Journal of Physiology and Pharmacology, 55,* 975–982.

Wright, L. (1988). The Type A behavior pattern and coronary artery disease. *American Psychologist, 43,* 2–14.

Wright, T. A., & Quick, J. C. (1997). Job burnout. In L. H. Peters, S. A. Youngblood, & C. R. Greer (Eds.), *The Blackwell dictionary of human resource management* (pp. 183–184). Oxford, England: Blackwell.

Yarvote, P. M., McDonheh, T. J., Goldman, M. J., & Zuckerman, J. (1974, September). Organization and evaluation of a fitness program in industry. *Journal of Occupational Medicine, 16,* 589–598.

Yassen, J. (1995). Preventing secondary traumatic stress disorder. In C. R. Figley (Ed.), *Compassion fatigue: Coping with secondary traumatic stress disorder in those who treat the traumatized* (Brunner/Mazel psychological stress series, No. 23, pp. 178–208). New York: Brunner/Mazel.

Yates, A. J. (1980). *Biofeedback and the modification of behavior.* New York: Plenum Press.

Yerkes, R. M., & Dodson, J. D. (1908). The relation of strength of stimulus to rapidity of habit-formation. *Journal of Comparative Neurology and Psychology, 18,* 459–482.

Zaleznik, A. M., Kets de Vries, F. R., & Howard, J. (1977). Stress reactions in organizations: Symptoms, causes, and consequences. *Behavioral Science, 22,* 151–162.

Zedeck, S. (1992). *Work, families, and organizations.* San Francisco: Jossey-Bass.

Zohman, L. (1979). *Exercise your way to fitness and heart health.* Coventry, CT: Mazola Corn Exercise Booklet.

Zweifler, J. (1993). Balancing service and education: Linking community health centers and family practice residency programs. *Family Medicine, 25,* 306–311.

Index

ABC priority system, 221
Abdominal pain, 269
Ability assessment, 178–179
Abrasive personalities, 35–36
Absenteeism, direct costs, 97–98
Accident proneness, 69
Accidents, direct costs, 100–102
"Achilles heel" phenomenon, 48–49
ACTH, 45–47
"Acting it out" method, 246–247
Acute stress disorder, 73
Adaptive energy, 105
Adkins, Joyce, 280
Administrators, 26–27. *See also* Managers
Adrenaline, 45–46
Adrenocorticotrophic hormone, 45–47
Aerobic fitness, 247
African Americans
  performance evaluation stress, 58
  workplace discrimination, 57–58
Age factors, stress response, 57
Aggression, 107–108
AIDS, 85–86
Air quality, indoor stressor, 22–23
Alcohol abuse, 67–68
  economic costs, 67
  occupational stress role, 67–68
  resource groups, 314
  treatment programs, 259–260
    cost-benefit ratio, 297
Alpha wave biofeedback, 241
Altruism, 278–279
Anger, hostility, 49–50
  interventions, 218
  Type A behavior lethal ingredient, 50, 78
Antianxiety drugs, 267–268
Antidepressant drugs, 268
Anxiety disorders, 73–74
  medications, 267–268
  occupational stress consequence, 73–74
Appraisal support, 197–198
Aptitude assessment, 178–179
Arthritis, 82–83
Assembly line jobs, 27–28
Asthma, 85
Attachment style, 60
Autogenic training, 237–239
Autonomic nervous system, 44–46
  biofeedback effects, 239
  and exercise, 250
  structure and function, 44–46

Autonomous functioning, 172–174

Back pain, 82–83
Back-to-work programs, 104
Behavior therapy, 262–264
Behavioral observations, 118
Beta-blockers, 218
B.F. Goodrich Tire's Group Learning Center, 286
Biofeedback training, 239–241, 298
Blood lipids, 77, 81
Blood pressure
  biofeedback effects, 241
  stress response, family history, 48
Blue collar workers, 26
Boredom, and routine job stress, 27–28
Bortner Scale, 144
Boundary-spanning activities, 29–30
Breast cancer, 82
Brief relaxation technique, 242–243
Buck Stop program, 175
Burnout
  in helping professions, 71
  inventory assessment, 141
  job performance decrements, 100
  phases of, 71
  time-off benefits, 226
Buspirone, 268

Cancer, 79, 81–82
Cancer-prone personality, 82
Cannon, Walter, 6–8
Cardiovascular disease, 77–81
  economic costs, 89–90
  and job strain, 79–80, 168
  sex differences, 54
  stress reduction effects, 81
  surgery, 269
  work stress relationship, 77–81
Career breaks, 226–227
Career counseling, 265
Career development, 177–180
  definition and purpose, 164
  and organizational socialization, 179–180
  and self-assessment, 178–179
Catecholamines, 45–46
Catharsis, 245–246
Challenge, 4

Chaparral Steel Company, 279
    mentofacturing value in, 15, 279
    organizational culture, 279
Cholesterol levels, 77
    and diet, 252
    stress reduction effect on, 81
    and work stress, 77, 79
Chronic fatigue syndrome, 86
Church attendance, 243
Cigarette smoking. *See* Tobacco use
Cirrhosis of the liver, 85
Clinically standardized meditation, 235
Cognitive appraisal, 9, 51
Cognitive distortion, 210–212
Cognitive restructuring, 210–211
Cognitive style, 209–212
Communication breakdowns, 106
Compensation payments, 103–105
Comprehensive health promotion pro-
    grams, 290–293
Computer facilities, 182–184
Computer workers, 27
Concurrent validity, stress measures, 119–
    120
Confidentiality
    counseling programs, 261
    and organization stress diagnosis, 122
Construct validity, stress measures, 119
Constructive self-talk, 212–213
Consultation, 282–283
Context Survey, 136
Control expectancies
    and high strain jobs, 169
    stress response moderator, 51–52
Conversion reaction, 76
Coping Responses Inventory, 145
Coping strategies
    cognitive appraisal relationship, 9
    in primary prevention, 156, 208–218
    questionnaire assessment, 144–145
    in secondary prevention, 156, 231–254
Cornell Medical Index, 139–140, 310
Coronary bypass surgery, 269
Coronary heart disease. *See* Cardiovascular
    disease
Coronary-prone behavior, 49–50, 78
    anger, hostility as lethal ingredient, 50,
    78
    assessment instruments, 143–144
    changing of, 215–218
    drug therapy, 268
Cortisol, 45–47
Cost-benefit ratio, 297–298
Counseling, 258–261
    confidentiality, 261
    cost-effectiveness evaluations, 261, 298
    goals of, 260
    resource groups, 314

Counterconditioning principle, 262
Counterdependence, 60–61
Crowding, 35
Customer service positions, 29–30

Daily Log of Stress-Related Symptoms,
    140–141, 310
Death rates
    and physical disease, 77–78
    sex differences, 54
Decentralized management, 173–174
Decision-making decrements, 106–107
Defense mechanisms, 106
Demand-control model. *See* Job strain
Dependent behavior. *See* Overdependence
Depression
    drug therapy, 268
    and work stress, 75–76
Deus v. Allstate case, 13, 104
Diabetes mellitus, 84–85
Diagnosis. *See* Stress diagnosis
Diazepam (Valium), 267–268
Diet, 61–62, 252–253
Direct costs, 96–105
Disability-adjusted life years, 77, 79
Disability awards, 103–105
Discriminant validity, stress measures, 119
Distress, 5–6. *See also* Job strain; Organi-
    zational distress
Diversity, workplace stressor, 37
Diversity programs, 188, 204–205
Downsizing
    current trends, 1
    and job future ambiguity, 28–29
Drug abuse, 68–69
    job stress role, 68–69
    resource groups, 314
Drug therapy, 267–268
Dual-career families, 34, 72–73

Eating disorders, 70
Ecological factors, 181–185
Economic costs. *See also* Cost-benefit ratio
    employee turnover, 98–99
    heart disease, 89–90
    organization distress, 96–105
Eczema, 85
Educational agenda, 305
EEG biofeedback, 241
Effort-reward imbalance
    adverse health effects, 91–93
    in job redesign, 170–171
Ego-ideal, 9–10
Electromagnetic radiation exposure, 23
Electromyographic biofeedback, 241

Electronic performance monitoring, 28
"Emergency reaction," 6–7
EMG biofeedback, 241
Emotion-focused coping, 156
Emotional outlets, 245–247, 265–267
Emotional support, 197–200
Employee assistance programs, 260, 285, 298
Employee participation, 194–195
Employee responsibilities, 306
Empowerment, 174
Enacted role, 190
Endarterectomy, 269
Endocrine system, 45–47
Endorphins, 251
Environmental stressors, 21–25
Equitable Life's emotional health program, 286
Ethnic groups, 57–59
    performance evaluation stress, 58
    workplace discrimination, 57–59
Ethnocentric attitudes, 37
Eustress
    definition, 4–5
    and job redesign, 165–166
    work and home life balance in, 224
    in Yerkes-Dodson curve, 156
Evaluation process, 296–297
Exchange relationships, 90–93
Executives
    leadership challenges, agenda, 304–305
    lifestyle balance importance, 225
    social support, 199
Exercise, 247–251
    health benefits, 250
    psychological benefits, 249–251
    safety guidelines, 251
Expected role, 189–190
Expressive writing, 266–267
External locus of control, 51–52, 145
Extraorganizational stressors, 37–38
Exxon's physical fitness program, 289

Faith practices, 243–244
Family businesses, 73
Family history factors, 48–49
Family relationships, 37–38, 71–73
    dual-career marriages, 72–73
    and life stage, 72
    lifestyle ingredient, 223–224
    work stressor interactions, 37–38, 71–73
Fathers, work-home demands, 34
Feedback channels, 167
Fight-or-flight response, 3, 43, 232
Flexible work schedules, 175–177
    goal of, 164

and home-job conflicts, 177
Flextime, 176–177
Forward, Gordon, 278–279
Four-day workweek, 176–177
Framingham Type A Scale, 144
Frank S. Deus v. Allstate case, 13, 104
Friedman, Milton, 49

Gastrointestinal conditions, 83–84
Gender differences, 54–56. See also Women
General adaptation syndrome, 8–9
General Health Questionnaire, 139–140, 310
Generic Job Stress Questionnaire, 130, 309
"Glass ceiling," 29, 55
Glucagon, 47
Goal setting, 188, 192–195
Grievances, 100–102
Group counseling, 218
Group sanctions, 36–37
Group therapy, 264–265

Hardiness
    rating-scale assessment, 143, 311
    stress response moderator, 52
    and transformational coping, 213–214
Hassles Scale, 135, 310
Headache, 84
Health care costs, 103
Health promotion programs, 290–292
Health risks, 12
Heart disease, 77–81
    economic costs, 89–90
    exercise benefits, 250
    stress reduction effects on, 81
    surgery, 269
    work stress relationship, 77–81
"Heart-of-darkness" syndrome, 265–266
Heart rate, and relaxation, 233
Helicobacter pylori, 83
Helper T cell levels, 243
Hispanics, workplace stress, 58
HIV-infection, 85–86
Home-job relationship
    demands, 34
    and flexible work schedule, 177
    maintaining balance in, 224–225
    women, 55
Home offices, 25
Hormones, 45–47
Hostility. See Anger, hostility
Humor, 247, 278–279
Hypertension
    biofeedback effects, 241

Hypertension (*Continued*)
  economic costs, 90
  stress response, family history, 48
  work stress relationship, 77
Hypnosis, 236–237
Hypochondriasis, 76

ICI-Zeneca's program, 286–288
Illinois Bell's programs, 286, 297
Illumination levels, 23
Immune function
  hypnosis effects, 237
  relaxation benefits, 243
  and social support, 59
Incentive compensation, 28
Indirect costs, 96, 105–108
Indoor climate, 22–23
Informal relationships, 187–189
Informational support, 197–198
Insomnia, 74–75
Instrumental support, 197–198
Intellectual ability, assessment, 178–179
Interest inventories, 178
Internal consistency, stress measures, 120
Internal locus of control, 51–52, 145
International competition, 1
Interpersonal leadership style, 36
Interpersonal stressors, 34–38
Interrater reliability, 120
Interview procedures
  advantages and limitations, 116
  organizational stress diagnosis, 115–116
Irritable bowel syndrome, 83

Jenkins Activity Survey, 143–144, 178
Job autonomy, 172–174
Job Content Questionnaire, 130, 309
Job Description Index, 136
Job enrichment, 171
"Job jeopardy" programs, 260
Job loading, 100–102
Job loss, trauma debriefing, 265–267
Job performance
  excessive stress effects, 100
  and organizational direct costs, 100–102
Job redesign, 164–172
  definition, 164
  effort-reward model, 170–171
  evaluation, 167
  job characteristics model, 165–167
  job enrichment strategy, 171–172
  job strain model, 168–170
  motivating potential score in, 165–166
  organizational contextual factors, 170
  principles of, 166–167

risks and opportunities, 167
Job security, 28–29
Job strain
  cardiovascular disease impact, 79–80, 168
  control latitude factor, 169
  definition, 5–6
  psychological demands, 168
Job Stress Survey, 129–130, 309
Jogging, 248, 250
Johns-Manville's fitness program, 289
Johnson & Johnson's health promotion program, 292–293

Kahn, Robert, 8–9
Kelleher, Herb, 278
Kimberly-Clark Corporation's health promotion program, 290–292
Kuder Occupational Interest Survey, 178

Layoff planning, 281
Lazarus, Richard, 9
Leadership challenges, 304–305
Leadership style, 36
Learned optimism, 209–212
Legal protection programs, 281–282
Leisure congruence, 225
Leisure time, 225–226
Levinson, Harry, 9–10
Life event stress
  measures, 133–135
  work stress interactions, 37–38
Life Events Scale, 133–135, 310
Life expectancy, 13–14
Life Insurance Company of Georgia, 289
Lifestyle, 223–227
  leisure time benefits, 225–226
  maintaining balance in, 224–225
  sabbaticals role, 226–227
Lighting levels, 23
Live for Life Program, 292–293
Liver cirrhosis, 85
Locus of control
  measures of, 145, 311
  stress response moderator, 51–52
Lung cancer, 81
Lung disease, 85

Management audit, 133, 310
Management by objectives programs
  goal setting in, 193–194
  and role ambiguity, 33
Management consultation, 282–283
Managers
  African Americans, 58

leadership challenges, 304–305
leadership style effects, 36
stress level, 26–27
Mantra meditation, 235
Marital problems, 71–73. *See also* Family relationships
Maslach Burnout Inventory, 141, 310
Mass production technology, 27–28
Massage, 269–270
Medical care, 267–270
Medical departments, 284–285
Medical hypnosis, 236–239
Medical problems, 76–86
    death and disability statistics, 77–79
    occupational stress relationship, 76–86
    tertiary prevention, 267–269
Medical tests, 137–138
Medications, 267–268
Meditation, 234–236
Mental disorders, 79
Mental diversion technique, 212–213
"Mental health" days, 225–226
Mental Measurements Yearbook, 178
Mentofacturing, 15, 279
Mentoring, 200–201
Metropolitan Life Insurance Company Center for Health Help, 286
Michigan Stress Assessment, 127–128
Midlife transition, 219–220
Migraine headache, 84
Military organizations
    career development, 180
    participative management, 175
    up-or-out policies, 99–100, 180
Minnesota Multiphasic Personality Inventory, 265
Minnesota Satisfaction Questionnaire, 136
Minority groups
    performance evaluation stress, 58
    workplace stress, 37, 57–59
Mobil Oil Corporation career development programs, 177
Modified-work programs, 104
"Monkey mind," 233
Morale problems, 105–106
Motivating potential score, 165–166
Motivation
    and indirect organizational costs, 105–106
    and job redesign, 165–166
Muscle flexibility training, 248–249
Muscle strength training, 249
Myocardial infarction, 79–80

Negative affectivity, 53
Negative thinking, 209–212

Network associations, 58
New York Telephone's stress management program, 286
Newcomer socialization, 201
NIOSH Generic Job Stress Questionnaire, 130, 309
Noise levels, 24
Nonresponse bias, questionnaires, 117
Noradrenaline, 45–46
Nutrition, 252–253

Obesity, 70
Observational techniques, 118–119
Occupational health psychology, 15, 306
Occupational physicians, 284, 306
Occupational stereotypes, 55–56
Occupational Stress Indicator, 128–129, 309
Occupational Stress Inventory, 129, 309
Office design
    basic functions of, 24–25
    and environmental stress, 24–25
Office workers, 27
Open office systems
    and social density, 35
    stressful aspects, 25
Opportunity analysis, 179
Opportunity costs, 108
Optimism-pessimism, 52–53
Organ inferiority hypothesis, 48
Organizational culture, 278–279
Organizational development, 280–281
Organizational diagnosis, 132–133, 310
Organizational distress
    definition, 5–6
    direct costs, 96–105
    indirect costs, 96, 105–108
Organizational health, 93–96
    definition, 94
    internal dimensions, 94–95
    and task environment adjustments, 95–96
Organizational health center, 280
Organizational politics, 296
Organizational science, 112–113
Organizational socialization
    and career development, 179–180
    support function, 201
Ornish diet, 252
Outcome evaluation, 296–297
Outdoor challenges, 202–203
Overdependence, 60–61
Overload avoidance, 221–222

Pacific Bell Telecommuting program, 176–177

Panic disorder, 74
Parenting, work-home demands, 34
Participative management, 172–175
    decentralization strategy, 173–174
    definition, 164, 172
    dynamic model, 172
    implementation, 174–175
    productivity benefits, 172–173
"Passive smoking," 66–67
Peer group, social support function, 60
Peptic ulcer disease, 83, 268
Perceived control, 51–52
Perceived stress, 208–218
Performance decrements. See Job
    performance
Performance evaluations
    minority group stress, 58
    support function of, 199–200
Person-environment fit, 8
Personal planning, 219
Personal preventive stress management
    plan, 270–274
Personal Views Survey, 143
Personality traits. See also Type A behavior
    pattern
    abrasiveness as stressor, 35–36
    stress response moderator, 51–54
Pessimistic cognitive style, 52–53, 209–
    210
Pets, 226
Pharmacotherapy, 267–268
Physical disease, 76–86; See also Cardio-
    vascular disease
    death and disability statistics, 77–79
    and occupational stress, 76–86
Physical fitness, 247–251, 288–290
    comprehensive health promotion pro-
        gram, 290–293
    core elements, 247
    health benefits, 250
    organization programs, 288–290
    psychological benefits, 249–251
    resource groups, 314
Physical setting
    design of, 181–185
    ecological analysis, 182
    as stressor, 21–25
Physical therapy, 269–270
Physicians, 284, 306
Physiological measures, 137–138
Piece-rate payments, 28
Placebo effect, 258
Planning strategies, 219–221
Political tactics, 296
Posttraumatic stress disorder, 265–267
    compensation awards, 105
    traumatic event debriefing, 265–267
    workplace events, 73–74

Predictive validity, stress measures, 120
Predisposing factors, 48–49
Preventive medicine model, 13–15
Preventive stress management task force,
    279–280
Primary prevention, 207–228
    definition, 154
    and problem-focused coping, 156
    strategies for individuals, 207–228
    in stress management model, 16, 154–
        156
Problem-focused coping, 156
Profile of Mood States, 142, 311
Progressive relaxation, 234
Psychoanalytic perspective, 9–10
Psychological contracts, 177–178
Psychological counseling. See Counseling
Psychological withdrawal strategy, 214–
    215
Psychometrics, 119–120
Psychophysiology, 3–4, 41–47
Psychotherapy, 258–261, 297–298, 314
Public health model, 10, 13–15, 154
Public health psychology, 15
Public speaking anxiety, 262–264

Qualitative procedures, 121
Qualitative work overload, 30
Quality circles, 173
Quality of Employment Survey, 128, 309
Quantitative procedures, 121
Questionnaires
    advantages and limitations, 117–118
    in organizational stress diagnosis, 117–
        118, 125–147
Quick recovery technique, 212

Racism. See Ethnic groups
Rational emotive therapy, 210
Recurrent abdominal pain, 269
Reflective interview technique, 116
Regressive coping, 214
Relaxation response, 232
    basic steps in, 232–233
    efficacy, 233
    fight-or-flight response comparison, 232
Relaxation training, 231–243, 313
Reliability, diagnostic procedures, 120
Religious involvements, 243–244
Repetitive work, 27–28
Research agenda, 304
Resource groups, 313–315
Response bias, questionnaires, 117
Rethinking technique, 213
Reticular activating system, 45

Retirement transition, 38, 220
Retreat formats, 202–203
Return-on-investment analysis, 297–298
Return-to-work programs, 104
Reversal diet, 252
Rigidity of response, 17
Role ambiguity
  causes of, 33
  goal-setting benefits, 195
Role analysis, 187–192
  definition, 188–189
  practical difficulties, 192
  procedure, 191–192
Role conflict
  and communication breakdowns, 106
  forms of, 32
  goal-setting benefits, 195
  work relationships deterioration, 107
Role senders, 31, 33, 190–192
Role set, 31
Role stress, 30–34, 189–192
  goal setting benefits, 195
  overview, 30–34
  and role analysis, 189–192
  theory of, 8–9
  in women, 55
Rosenman, Ray, 49
Routine jobs
  and piece-rate payments, 28
  stress levels, 27–28
Running, 250

Sabbaticals, 226–227
Schedule of Recent Experiences, 133–135
SCL-90-R, 141, 310
Secondary prevention, 231–254
  definition, 154
  and emotion-focused coping, 156
  strategies for individuals, 231–254
  in stress management model, 16, 154–156
Selective ignoring strategy, 215
Self-assessment, career planning, 178–179
Self-esteem, 53–54
Self-hypnosis, 237
Self-image, 9–10
Self-reinforcement method, 262–263
Self-reliance, 60–61
Self-talk, 212–213
Selye, Hans, 8
Sensitivity and specificity, tests, 137–138
Service-oriented occupations, 29–30
Sexual dysfunction, 75
Sexual harassment, 56
Short-term psychotherapy, 297–298
Sick building syndrome, 23

Sisyphus reaction, 50, 78
Skin disease, 85
Sleep disturbances, 74–75
Smoking. See tobacco use
Social contacts, and office design, 25
Social density, 35
Social Readjustment Rating Scale, 133–135
Social relationships, stressors, 34–38
Social status incongruity, 35
Social support, 59–60, 188, 195–201
  buffering effect, 59–60, 188, 196
  definitions, 195–196
  forms of, 59, 197
  and health, 196–197
  mortality link, 196
  organization peer group function, 60
  questionnaire assessment, 144
  sources of, 197–199
  and work stress reduction, 222–223
  in workplace setting, 199–200
Social support networks, 198
Social welfare workers, 26
Socialization. See Organizational socialization
Somatization, 76
Southern Connecticut Gas Company, 285
Southwest Airlines, organizational culture, 278–279
Spirituality, 243, 244, 301
State-Trait Anxiety Inventory, 141–142, 310
Status incongruity, 35
Stereotypes, occupational, 55–56
Strain. See Distress
Strategic Air Command Buck Stop program, 175
Strength training, 249
Stress Audit, 130–131, 309
Stress compensation claims
  organizational costs, 103–105
  typology, high-risk employees, 91–92
Stress diagnosis, 111–147
  basic concepts, 111–122
  interdisciplinary aspects, 112–113
  objective measures, 126–147, 309–312
  organizational science in, 112–113
  in organizations, 293–294
  procedures in, 115–119
    psychometrics, 119–120
  purposes, 111
Stress Diagnostic Survey, 131, 309
Stress management programs, 285–288
Stress response, 41–62
  "Achilles heel" phenomenon, 48–49
  age factors, 57
  anatomy, 44

Stress response (*Continued*)
  anger-hostility pattern, 49–50
  cognitive appraisal interactions, 51
  definition, 3
  dietary factors, 61–62
  ethnic groups, 57–59
  exercise relationship, 250
  gender differences, 54–56
  modifiers, 47–62
  personality factors, 51–54
  psychophysiological changes, 3–4, 41–47
  self-reliant pattern, 60–61
  social support role, 59–60
Stressful life events. *See* Life event stress
Stressor Checklist, 131–132, 309
Stressors, 21–39
  definition, 3
  interpersonal factors, 34–37
  physical environment, 21–25
  role demands effect, 30–34
  and task demands, 25–30
Strikes, direct costs, 98
Stroke
  economic costs, 90
  work stress impact, 81
Strong Interest Inventory, 178
Sudden cardiac death, 80
Suggestion, 236–237
Supervisors. *See also* Managers
  African Americans, 58
  leadership style effects, 36
  stress level, 26–27
Support groups, 264–265
Surgery, 268–269
Surveillance systems, 306–307
"Survivor sickness," 281
Sympathetic nervous system, 44–47
Symptom Check List-90-R, 141, 310
Systematic desensitization, 262–264

Tai Chi Chuan movements, 248–249
"Talking it out" method, 245–246
Tandem Computers, sabbatical program, 227
Tardiness, direct costs, 97–98
Task demands, 25–30
  and job future ambiguity, 28–29
  and occupational category, 26–27
  overview, 25–30
  routine job effects, 27–28
  service-oriented industries, 29–30
  and work overload, 30
Task force concept, 279–280
Team building, 201–203
  definition, 188, 201
  necessary conditions, 203

outcomes, 203
  process of, 202–203
  psychological benefits, 202
Teamwork, as stressor, 36–37
"Technostress," 30
Telecommuting, 25, 176–177
Tenneco's flextime program, 281
Tenure limit policies, 99–100
Tertiary prevention, 257–274
  definition, 154
  in stress management model, 16, 154–156
Thought stopping technique, 212
Threat-rigidity thesis
  key aspects of, 17, 108
  and opportunity costs, 108
Time management, 219–221
Time urgency, Type A behavior, 50
"To Do" list, 220–221
Tobacco use, 65–67
  excess mortality cause, 65–66
  and lung cancer, 81
  stress relationship, 67
Training agenda, 305
Transcendental Meditation, 234–236
Transformational coping, 213–214
Transient ischemic attacks, 269
Transitional factors, as stressor, 38
Traumatic event debriefing, 265–267
Turnover
  direct costs, 98–100
  functional aspects, 98
  optimum rate of, 99
Type A behavior pattern, 49–50, 215–218
  addiction model, 216–217
  anger, hostility as lethal ingredient, 50, 78, 217
  assessment instruments, 143–144
  changing of, 215–218
  definition, 49
  drug therapy, 268
  group counseling, 218
  "reengineering" procedures, 215–216
"Type C" personality, 82

Ulcer disease, 83–84, 268
Unconscious factors, 187–189
Up-or-out policies, 99–100, 180
Uplifts Scale, 135, 310

Vacations, 226
Validity, stress measures, 119–120
Valium, 267–268
Vertical loading, 167
Vibration exposure, 24

Video display terminals, 23
Violence. *See* Workplace violence
Virtual offices, 25

Walking, 250
Ways of Coping Questionnaire, 144–145
Weight training, 249
Welch, Jack, 172
Wells Fargo's sabbatical program, 227
Western Collaborative Group Study, 50
Weyerhaeuser Company, physical fitness
  program, 289
White collar occupations, 26
Wolf, Stewart, 49–50, 83
Wolff, Harold, 48
Women
  aerobic exercise benefits, 248
  family problems, 72–73
  job future ambiguity, 29
  occupational stereotypes, 55–56
  organizational politics access, 56
  role stress, 55
  sexual harassment, 56
  stress response differences, 54–56
  total workload, 222
  work-home demands, 34, 55, 72–73
Work environment

design of, 181–185
  stressors in, 21–25
Work Environment Scale, 136
Work-home demands. *See* Home-job
  relationship
Work overload
  coping strategies, 221–222
  forms of, 30
  qualitative aspects, 30
  women, 55
Work stoppages, direct costs, 98
Workaholic behavior, 224
Workaholic Questionnaire, 311
Workers' compensation. *See* Stress compen-
  sation claims
Working conditions. *See* Work environment
Working relationships, 107
Workplace violence, 69–70
  job stress role, 69–70, 107–108
  and office design, 24–25
"Writing it out" method, 246, 266–267

Yerkes-Dodson Law, 4–7, 156
Yogic relaxation, 235

Zen meditation, 235
Zeneca Pharmaceuticals, 286–288

About the Authors

James Campbell Quick, PhD, is professor of organizational behavior at The University of Texas at Arlington and Editor of *Journal of Occupational Health Psychology*. He was APA's stress expert to the National Academy of Sciences on National Health Objectives for the Year 2000. Recognized by the American Heart Association with the Texas Volunteer Recognition Award and listed in the 7th Edition of *Who's Who in the World*, he received The Maroon Citation from the Colgate University Alumni Corporation in 1993. Colonel Quick is in the U.S. Air Force Reserve and serves as Senior Individual Mobilization Augmentee to the Director of Financial Management, San Antonio Air Logistics Center (AFMC), Kelly AFB, Texas. His military awards and decorations include the Meritorious Service Medal and National Defense Service Medal with Bronze Star. He is married to the former Sheri Grimes Schember.

Jonathan D. Quick, MD, MPH, is a Program Director for the World Health Organization in Geneva, Switzerland, and adjunct associate professor of public health at Boston University. He has authored or edited six books and over 30 articles in stress management, preventive medicine, and public health management. He was an officer in the U.S. Public Health Service and has spent the last twelve years in international public health. He served as health services development advisor for the Afghan mujahedin in Peshawar, Pakistan and helped design a health financing system in East Africa while based in Nairobi, Kenya. A Fellow of the American College of Preventive Medicine, a Fellow of the Royal Society of Medicine (UK) and listed in the *1995/1996 International Who's Who in Medicine*, he led the way with his brother in transferring the public health concepts of prevention from preventive medicine to organizational stress. He has three daughters with his wife Tina, who is an author, nurse, and amateur athlete.

Debra L. Nelson, PhD, is CBA associates professor of business administration and professor of management at Oklahoma State University. She received her PhD from the University of Texas at Arlington, where she was the recipient of the R. D. Irwin Dissertation Fellowship Award. Her research interests include organizational stress management, newcomer socialization, and management of technology. Dr. Nelson's research has been published in the *Academy of Management Executive, Academy of Management Journal, Academy of Management Review, MIS Quarterly, Organizational Dynamics, Journal of Organizational Behavior*, and other journals. In addition, she is coauthor of two additional books: *Stress and Challenge at the Top: The Paradox of the Successful Executive* (John Wiley & Sons, 1990) and *Organizational Behavior: Foundations, Realities, and Challenges, Second Edition* (West Publishing, 1997). She was the recipient of the Regents' Distinguished Teaching Award in 1994 and the Burlington

Northern Faculty Achievement Award at OSU in 1991. Dr. Nelson also serves on the editorial review boards of the *Journal of Occupational Health Psychology* and the *Journal of Organizational Behavior.*

Joseph J. Hurrell, Jr., PhD, is an adjunct professor of psychology at Xavier University in Cincinnati, Ohio, and Associate Editor of *Journal of Occupational Health Psychology*. He received his PhD in psychology from Miami University. Dr. Hurrell has had a long standing research interest in the relationship between occupational stress and health, and he has published numerous articles and edited five books on the topic.